Charles Wright

Charles Wright

A Companion to the Late Poetry, 1988–2007

Robert D. Denham

McFarland & Company, Inc., Publishers
Jefferson, North Carolina, and London

Excerpts from *Buffalo Yoga* by Charles Wright. Copyright © 2004 by Charles Wright. Reprinted by permission of Farrar, Straus and Giroux, LLC. Excerpts from *Littlefoot* by Charles Wright. Copyright © 2007 by Charles Wright. Reprinted by permission of Farrar, Straus and Giroux, LLC. Excerpts from *Negative Blue: Selected Later Poems* by Charles Wright. Copyright © 2000 by Charles Wright. Reprinted by permission of Farrar, Straus and Giroux, LLC. Excerpts from *Scar Tissue* by Charles Wright. Copyright © 2006 by Charles Wright. Reprinted by permission of Farrar, Straus and Giroux, LLC. Excerpts from *A Short History of the Shadow* by Charles Wright. Copyright © 2002 by Charles Wright. Reprinted by permission of Farrar, Straus and Giroux, LLC. Quotations from Charles Wright, "Miseducation of the Poet," "Narrative of the Image," and "ET & WNC Express Lines" in *Quarter Notes: Improvisations and Interviews* (Ann Arbor: University of Michigan Press, 1995) reproduced by permission. Copyright © 1995 by the University of Michigan Press. Quotations from "Halflife: A Commonplace Notebook," "With Sharod Santos (1981)," "With Antonella Francini," "With Carol Ellis," and "With Sharod Santos (1987)" in *Halflife: Improvisations and Interviews, 1977–1987* (Ann Arbor: University of Michigan Press, 1988) reproduced by permission. Copyright © 1988 by the University of Michigan Press. Wave Books/Verse Press for permission to quote from Andrew Zawacki's interview with Charles Wright in *The Verse Book of Interviews*, ed. Brian Henry and Andrew Zawacki (Amherst, MA: Verse Press, 2005), 18–29. Steerforth Press for permission to quote from Aldo Buzzi, "Notes on Life," in *A Weakness for Almost Everything*, translated from the Italian by Ann Goldstein (South Royalton, VT: Steerforth Press, 1999). Exact Change for permission to quote from Franz Kafka's *The Blue Octavo Notebooks*, The Third Notebook, 11 December 1917, ed. Max Brod, trans. by Ernst Kaiser and Eithne Wilkins (Cambridge, MA: Exact Change, 1991), 31. ICS Publications for permission to quote from *The Dark Night*, in *The Collected Works of St. John of the Cross*, trans. Kieran Kavanaugh, OCD, and Otilio Rodriguez, OCD, rev. ed. (Washington, D.C.: ICS Publications, 1991). David Hinton for permission to quote from his translations: *The Selected Poems of T'ao Ch'ien* (Port Townsend, WA: Copper Canyon Press, 1993); *Selected Poems of Tu Fu* (New York: New Directions, 1989); and *Mountain Home: The Wilderness Poetry of Ancient China* (Washington, D.C.: Counterpoint, 2002). The Balkin Agency for permission to quote from Martin Buber's *Ecstatic Confessions* (New York: Harper & Row, 1985). Excerpts from *The Nag Hammadi Library in English*, 3rd, completely revised edition by James M. Robinson, general editor. Copyright © 1978, 1988 by E.J. Brill, The Netherlands. Reprinted by permission of HarperCollins Publishers. The Overlook Press for permission to quote from Osip Mandelstam, "Conversation About Dante," in Mandelstam's *The Complete Critical Prose and Letters*, trans. Jane Gary Harris and Constance Link (Ann Arbor, MI: Ardis, 1979).

LIBRARY OF CONGRESS CATALOGUING-IN-PUBLICATION DATA

Denham, Robert D.
Charles Wright : a companion to the late poetry, 1988–2007 / Robert D. Denham.
p.   cm.
Includes bibliographical references and index.

ISBN-13: 978-0-7864-3242-4

softcover : 50# alkaline paper ∞

1. Wright, Charles, 1935–   —Critism and interpretation—
Handbooks, manuals, etc.   I. Title.
PS3573.R52Z63   2008   811'.54—dc22   2007030894

British Library cataloguing data are available

©2008 Robert D. Denham. All rights reserved

*No part of this book may be reproduced or transmitted in any form
or by any means, electronic or mechanical, including photocopying
or recording, or by any information storage and retrieval system,
without permission in writing from the publisher.*

Cover photograph: Titian (Tiziano Vecellio, c.1488–1576), *The Martyrdom of Saint Lawrence*, Chiesa dei Gesuiti (S. Maria Assunta), Venice, Italy. Cameraphoto Arte, Venice / Art Resource, NY

Manufactured in the United States of America

McFarland & Company, Inc., Publishers
Box 611, Jefferson, North Carolina 28640
www.mcfarlandpub.com

For Evelyn, Beatrice, Ella, Ivy, and Jack

Contents

Preface   1

List of Abbreviations and Shortened Forms   3

A Charles Wright Chronology   5

Introduction   9

Part I. The Third Trilogy: *Negative Blue*

Chapter 1. *Chickamauga*   23

Chapter 2. *Black Zodiac*   60

Chapter 3. *Appalachia* and *North American Bear*   97

Part II. The Fourth Trilogy and Its Coda

Chapter 4. *A Short History of the Shadow*   137

Chapter 5. *Buffalo Yoga*   165

Chapter 6. *Scar Tissue*   188

Chapter 7. *Littlefoot: A Poem*   214

Appendix: Reviews of Wright's Books
from *Chickamauga* through *Littlefoot: A Poem*   239

Index   245

Preface

This companion to the late poetry of Charles Wright is a reader's guide or handbook, intended to be used alongside his poems. It begins with the poems of *Chickamauga* (1995), the earliest of which were published in the late 1980s, and continues through the seven volumes that followed: *Black Zodiac* (1997), *Appalachia* (1998), *North American Bear* (1999), *A Short History of the Shadow* (2002), *Buffalo Yoga* (2004), *Scar Tissue* (2006), and *Littlefoot* (2007). The 265 poems in these books constitute slightly more than half of Wright's *oeuvre*.

There is widespread agreement that Wright's place in the pantheon of American poets is assured. His voice is important enough to deserve a close study, and his work is complex enough to require it. There have been more than 130 essays and articles about his work, some of which have been collected in *The Point Where All Things Meet: Essays on Charles Wright* (Oberlin College Press, 1995) and in the revised edition of this collection, *High Lonesome: On the Poetry of Charles Wright* (Oberlin College Press, 2006). His books have been widely reviewed: there are more than 170 reviews of the volumes that are the subject of the present study, and reviews of his most recent books continue, of course, to appear. He has received eighteen major awards for his work (see the Chronology). But for all this attention, no one has attempted a book-length study of his poetry. The focus of the present book is on Wright's late poetry—written over a nineteen-year period beginning in 1988: this large body of work represents the flowering of his long career. A companion to Wright's first eight volumes, collected in *Country Music* (1982) and *The World of the Ten Thousand Things* (1990), will follow in due course.

The commentaries follow the order of the poems as they appear in Wright's books. After the title of each poem I give its original place of publication, the page number in the book in which it was collected, the place or setting of the poem, the time (usually a month or season), and its "stanzaic pattern," a phrase explained in the introduction. Page numbers following the poem titles in Part I are first to the volume where they initially appeared (*Chickamauga*, *Black Zodiac*, and *Appalachia*) and then to *Negative Blue*; the notes refer to page and line numbers in *Negative Blue*.

Part I is devoted to *Negative Blue: Selected Later Poems*, "selected" meaning that Wright saw fit not to include six of the poems that appeared in the earlier collections. I have chosen to include these herein—five from *Chickamauga* and one from *Appalachia*. They are identified by an asterisk preceding their titles.

Wright often separates parts of his poems by a centered, short rule. I have referred to the parts so separated as "sections." Otherwise, those parts separated by a single blank space are referred to, conventionally, as "stanzas." I refer to the thirty-five numbered units of *Littlefoot: A Poem* as "parts," a designation that is somewhat arbitrary as each of these untitled lyrics is a discrete poem.

Notes that begin with "Cf." are intended to point to parallels, not borrowings, direct influences, or allusions. The double virgule is used to indicate the place where Wright drops down a line without returning it to the left margin, as in "Summer a holding pattern, // heat, haze, humidity." References to Wright's comments in interviews that are not included in *Halflife* and *Quarter Notes* are cited by the interviewer's last name, the full bibliographic record for which is in the list of abbreviations and shortened forms.

As I prepared the annotations for the poems, numerous questions arose about things I did not understand, could not identify, or only dimly perceived. Once I had completed the annotations for a volume, I would send them to Wright, highlighting questions I had. He replied to all my queries with good will and with great dispatch—within a day of so after receiving them—and I record my thanks to him here for filling in a number of blanks, as well as for his encouragement and support. I also thank the following people for responding to queries of one kind or another: Paula Closson Buck, Linda Cluxton, Wendy Flory, Vincent Gillespie, William Harmon, Philip Kuberski, Sebastian Matthews, Paul B. Roth, Richard Sieburth, Leon Surette, and Susan Tarrow.

List of Abbreviations and Shortened Forms

A	Charles Wright. *Appalachia*. New York: Farrar Straus Giroux, 1998.
Blackbird	*Blackbird Archive: An Online Journal of Literature and the Arts* 3, no. 1 (Spring 2004). http://www.blackbird.vcu.edu/v3n1/features/wright_c_051704/wright_c_text.htm
Bourgeois	Louis Bourgeois. "An Interview with Charles Wright." *VOX* 1, no. 2 (April 2006): 50-6.
BZ	Charles Wright. *Black Zodiac*. New York: Farrar, Straus and Giroux, 1997.
BY	Charles Wright. *Buffalo Yoga*. New York: Farrar, Straus and Giroux, 2004.
C	Charles Wright. *Chickamauga*. New York: Farrar, Straus and Giroux, 1995.
Caseley	Martin Caseley. "Through Purgatory to Appalachia: An Interview with Charles Wright." *PN Review* 27 (September–October 2000): 22-5.
CM	Charles Wright. *Country Music*. 2nd ed. Hanover, N.H.: Wesleyan/New England Press, 1991.
CT	Charles Wright. *China Trace*. Middletown, CT: Wesleyan University Press, 1977.
DA	Charles Wright. *The Dream Animal*. Toronto: House of Anansi, 1968.
Farnsworth	Interview with Elizabeth Farnsworth, National Public Radio, 15 April 1998.
GRH	Charles Wright. *The Grave of the Right Hand*. Middletown, CT: Wesleyan University Press, 1970.
Halflife	Charles Wright. *Halflife: Improvisations and Interviews, 1977-87*. Ann Arbor: University of Michigan Press, 1988.
HF	Charles Wright. *Hard Freight*. Middletown, CT: Wesleyan University Press, 1973.
HL	*High Lonesome: On the Poetry of Charles Wright*, ed. Adam Giannelli. Oberlin, OH: Oberlin College Press, 2006.
NB	Charles Wright. *Negative Blue: Selected Later Poems*. New York: Farrar, Straus and Giroux, 2000.
NHL	*The Nag Hammadi Library*, ed. James M. Robinson. Rev. ed. San Francisco: HarperCollins, 1988.
QN	Charles Wright. *Quarter Notes: Improvisations and Interviews*. Ann Arbor: University of Michigan Press, 1995.

Remnick	David Remnick. "An Interview with Charles Wright." *Partisan Review* 50, no. 4 (1983): 567–75.
Rubin	"'Metaphysics of the Quotidian': A Conversation with Charles Wright," an interview with Stan Sanvel Rubin and William Heyen, in *The Post-Confessionals: Conversations with American Poets of the Eighties*, ed. Earl Ingersoll, Judith Kitchen, and Stan Sanvel Rubin. Rutherford, NJ: Fairleigh Dickinson University Press, 1989. 25–38.
Schuldt	Morgan Schuldt. "An Interview with Charles Wright." *Sonora Review* 43 (2002): 74–80.
SHS	Charles Wright. *A Short History of the Shadow*. New York: Farrar, Straus Giroux, 2002.
Spiegelman	Willard Spiegelman. "Interview." *Literary Imagination: The Review of the Association of Literary Scholars and Critics* 2 (2000 Winter): 108–21.
ST	Charles Wright. *Scar Tissue*. New York: Farrar, Straus and Giroux, 2006.
Suarez	Ernest Suarez and Amy Verner. "Interview with Charles Wright," in *Southbound: Interviews with Southern Poets*, by Ernest Suarez with T.W. Stanford III and Amy Verner. Columbia: University of Missouri Press, 1999. 39–61.
Turner	David Cross Turner. "Oblivion's Glow: The (Post)Southern Sides of Charles Wright" [an interview]. *storySouth* (Summer 2005). http://www.storysouth.com/summer2005/wright_interview.html
UP	Charles Wright. *Uncollected Prose: Six Guys and a Supplement*. Salem, VA: Roanoke College, 2000.
Vadnie	Rebecca Swain Vadnie. "Interview with Poet Charles Wright: In Writing, I Just Follow the Pencil." *Orlando Sentinel* 11 October 2002: E3.
WER	Charles Wright. *The Wrong End of the Rainbow*. Louisville, KY: Sarabande Books, 2005.
WTTT	Charles Wright. *The World of the Ten Thousand Things*. New York: Farrar Strauss Giroux, 1990
Zawacki	Zawacki, Andrew. "Charles Wright." *The Verse Book of Interviews*, ed. Brian Henry and Andrew Zawacki. Amherst, MA: Verse Press, 2005. 18–29.

A Charles Wright Chronology

1935	Born on his father's birthday, 25 August, in Pickwick Dam, Hardin County, Tennessee
1936	Moves to Knoxville, Tennessee
1937	Moves to Corinth, Mississippi
1941	Moves to Hiwassee Village, North Carolina
1943	Moves to Oak Ridge, Tennessee
1945	Moves to Kingsport, Tennessee
1948–50	Attends summer camp at Sky Valley School, Hendersonville, North Carolina
1950–51	Attends Sky Valley School
1951–53	Attends Christ School, Arden, North Carolina
1953	Takes a summer job as police reporter for the *Kingsport [Tennessee] Times-News*
1953–57	Attends Davidson College; graduates with a degree in history
1957	Commissioned as a 2nd Lt. in the U.S. Army Intelligence Corps; reports for active duty to Ft. Holabird, Maryland, November 2
1958	Studies Italian at the Presidio's Army Language School, Monterey, California
1959–61	Works for the 430th CIC Detachment, U.S. Army, in Verona, Italy, January 1959 to autumn 1961. Discharged with rank of captain
1959	In March visits Catullus' villa on the peninsula of Sirmione, Lake Garda. Reads Pound's *Selected Poems*
1961	Turns down acceptance for study at the Columbia School of Journalism in order to study creative writing
1961	Begins study in the creative writing program at the University of Iowa
1961	Begins translating Montale's *Motets*
1963	Receives M.F.A. from the University of Iowa
1963	Publishes *The Voyage* (Iowa City: Patrician Press)
1963–65	Studies at the University of Rome as a Fulbright student; reads Dante with Maria Sampoli; completes translation of Montale
1964	Publishes *Six Poems* (London: David Freed)
1964	Death of mother, Mary Winter Wright, at age 54
1965–66	Returns to the University of Iowa for further study
1966	Begins teaching in the Creative Writing Center at the University of California, Irvine
1968	Publishes *The Dream Animal* (Toronto: House of Anansi)
1968–69	Serves as Fulbright lecturer at the University of Padua, Italy

1969	Publishes *Private Madrigals* (Madison, WI: Abraxas Press)
1969	Marries Holly McIntire, April 6
1969	Receives the Eunice Tietjens Award from *Poetry* magazine
1970	Publishes *The Grave of the Right Hand* (Middletown, CT: Wesleyan University Press)
1970	Birth of son, Luke Savin Herrick Wright
1971	Publishes *The Venice Notebook* (Boston: Barn Dream Press)
1972	Death of father, Charles Penzel Wright, at age 67
1973	Publishes *Backwater* (Santa Ana, CA: Golem Press)
1973	Publishes *Hard Freight* (Middletown, CT: Wesleyan University Press)
1974	Receives National Endowment for the Arts Award
1975	Publishes *Bloodlines* (Middletown, CT: Wesleyan University Press)
1975	Receives a Guggenheim Fellowship
1976	Receives the Melville Cane Award from the Poetry Society of America and the Edgar Allan Poe Award from the Academy of American Poets—both for *Bloodlines*
1977	Publishes *Colophons* (Iowa City: Windhover Press)
1977	Publishes *China Trace* (Middletown, CT: Wesleyan University Press)
1977	Writer in residence at Oberlin College
1977	Receives the Academy-Institute Award, American Academy and Institute of the Arts
1978	Oberlin College publishes Wright's translation of Eugenio Montale, *The Storm and Other Poems* (Field Translation Series 1)
1978	Begins systematic reading of Dante's *Commedia*
1979	Publication of *Wright: A Profile. New Poems by Charles Wright with an Interview and a Critical Essay by David St. John* (Iowa City: Grilled Flowers Press)
1979	Receives the PEN translation award for *The Storm and Other Poems*
1980	Publishes *Dead Color* (San Francisco: Meadow Press)
1980	Receives the Ingram Merrill Fellowship in Poetry
1981	Publishes *The Southern Cross* (New York: Random House)
1982	Publishes *Country Music: Selected Early Poems* (Middletown, CT: Wesleyan University Press)
1983	Publishes *Four Poems of Departure* (Portland, OR: Trace Editions)
1983	Receives the National Book Award for *Country Music*
1983	Visits London, September–December
1983	Begins teaching at the University of Virginia and settles permanently in Charlottesville
1983	Receives National Endowment for the Arts Award
1984	Publishes *The Other Side of the River* (New York: Vintage/Random House)
1984	Oberlin College publishes Wright's translation of Dino Campana, *Orphic Songs* (Field Translation Series 9)
1984	Nominated for the National Book Critics Circle Award for *The Other Side of the River*
1985	Publishes *Five Journals* (New York: Red Ozier Press)
1985	Spends part of the summer with Mark Strand at an Italian villa, Cà Paruta
1987	Receives the Brandeis Creative Arts Citation for poetry

A Charles Wright Chronology

1988	Publishes *A Journal of the Year of the Ox* (1988)
1988	Publishes *Zone Journals* (New York: Farrar Straus Giroux)
1988	Publishes *Halflife: Improvisations and Interviews, 1977-87* (Ann Arbor: University of Michigan Press)
1988	Is appointed Souter Family Professor of English at the University of Virginia
1988	Travels to China to attend meeting of American and Chinese writers at the 4th Sino-American Writer's Conference, 12 April
1990	Publishes *The World of the Ten Thousand Things: Poems 1980-1990* (New York: Farrar Straus Giroux)
1990	Publishes *Xionia* (Iowa City: Windhover Press)
1991	Becomes a member of the Fellowship of Southern Writers
1991	Is the subject of the annual Literary Festival at Emory & Henry College, Emory, VA
1992	Receives and Award of Merit Medal from the American Academy of Arts and Letters
1992	Serves as distinguished visiting professor, Universita Degli Studi, Florence, Italy
1993	Receives the Ruth Lilly Poetry Prize
1993	Receives Distinguished Contribution to Letters Award from the Ingram Merrill Foundation
1993	Reads at the Library of Congress, December 16
1995	Publishes *Chickamauga* (New York: Farrar, Straus and Giroux)
1995	Publishes *Quarter Notes: Improvisations and Interviews* (Ann Arbor: University of Michigan Press)
1995	Oberlin College publishes *The Point Where All Things Meet: Essays on Charles Wright*, ed. Tom Andrews
1995	Is elected to membership in the American Academy of Arts and Letters
1996	Receives the Lenore Marshall Poetry Prize from the Academy of American Poets
1997	Publishes *Black Zodiac* (New York: Farrar, Straus and Giroux)
1997	Receives the Book Prize, *Los Angeles Times*, and National Book Critics Circle Award for Poetry—both for *Black Zodiac*
1997	Receives an honorary Doctor of Letters degree from Davidson College
1998	Receives the Pulitzer Prize for Poetry and the Premio Antico Fattore Alla Poesia—both for *Black Zodiac*
1998	Receives the Ambassador Book Award from the English-Speaking Union for *Black Zodiac*
1998	Publishes *Appalachia* (New York: Farrar Straus Giroux)
1999	Publishes *North American Bear* (La Crosse, WI: Sutton Hoo Press)
1999	Begins two-year stint as poetry editor of the *New Republic*
2000	Publishes *Negative Blue: Selected Later Poems* (New York: Farrar, Straus and Giroux)
2001	Publishes *Night Music* (Exeter, Devon, England: Stride Publications)
2001	Italian translation of poems (*L'altra riva del fiume* [ExCogita Editore] and *Crepuscolo americano e altre poesie 1980-2000* [Jaca Book]) presented by Gaetano Pramapolini and Barbara Lanati at Salone del Libro, Turin (19 May)
2001	Attends a discussion of his work on May 25 at Fondazione Il Fiore, Florence
2002	Publishes *A Short History of the Shadow* (New York: Farrar Straus Giroux)
2002	Is elected as a fellow of the American Academy of Arts and Sciences

A Charles Wright Chronology

2004	Publishes *Buffalo Yoga* (New York: Farrar Straus Giroux)
2005	Publishes *The Wrong End of the Rainbow* (Louisville, Ky.: Sarabande Books)
2005	"Charles Wright at 70: A Celebration and Retrospective," Vancouver, BC, 31 March. Annual Meeting of the Associated Writing Programs
2006	Publishes *Scar Tissue* (New York: Farrar Straus Giroux)
2006	Oberlin College Press publishes *High Lonesome: On the Poetry of Charles Wright*, a revised and expanded edition of *The Point Where All Things Meet* (1995)
2007	Publishes *Littlefoot: A Poem* (New York: Farrar Straus Giroux)
2007	Receives the Griffin Prize for *Scar Tissue*

Introduction

This study contains commentaries and annotations. The commentaries reflect my own reading of Wright's poetry. Their intent is to tease out the meanings of the poems by attending closely to word and image, linear and spatial form, figure and theme. They combine paraphrase, explanation, and interpretation. They seek to trace the "argument" of the poems, as difficult as this sometimes is, and they play close attention to Wright's language. They frequently point to links among the poems, and they occasionally include brief thematic essays. When Wright has commented on an issue in his prose writings or interviews that seems to me apposite to the poem under consideration, I have reproduced the passage, ordinarily under the heading "Wright on Wright." Each of Wright's poems can be read as a discrete work, but each is also part of a larger quest begun in the early 1970s. Accordingly, the commentaries often provide the occasion to reflect on the contours of the whole—Wright's poetic pilgrimage. The scope of the present enterprise—to annotate and remark on each of the poems—has meant that the length of the commentaries has had to be restricted. As with any major poet, the poems naturally invite unlimited commentary.

The annotations, preceded by page and line number, include information that might not be immediately obvious to some readers. They are aids to becoming what Milton calls the "fit" reader, so they attempt to answer the question, what do we need to know to become more fully engaged readers? The annotations, then, are what one would expect in a critical edition of any poet's work. I have identified the sources that Wright draws on (for many of these his own notes point us to his sources) and the people, places, and events mentioned in the poems. The notes, which are sometimes incorporated into the commentaries, also record perceived influences, parallels to other poets, biographical details, historical explanation, and the like, and they translate the occasional foreign word and phrase.

The evocative powers of Wright's poems are practically boundless, but the principles that underlie the lyric poem are finite. One set of such principles can be adapted from what Aristotle says about drama. In the *Poetics* he remarks that there are six qualitative parts in dramatic tragedy: *mythos* (plot), *ethos* (character), *dianoia* (thought), *melos* (song), *lexis* (diction or word), and *opsis* (spectacle). Expanding the meaning of these terms from Aristotle's restricted and literal-minded definitions provide, by way of introduction, a convenient framework for reflecting briefly on the ends and means of Wright's considerable poetic achievement.

Mythos

If we define *mythos* not as plot in Aristotle's sense (characters engaging in some action defined by a tragic or comic plot that somehow resolves a conflict) but more broadly as a narrative movement from point A to B, then all works of literature have a linear movement, even Wright's one-line poem *Bygones*: "The rain has stopped falling asleep on its crystal stems" (CM,

128). Wright's individual poems have beginnings, middles, and ends in this sense. But more than this, his entire body of work, especially from the early 1970s, has a narrative shape.

In 1971, after he had written *Dog Creek Mainline* (CM, 36), Wright discovered that his subject matter would center on his own journey, starting from the place he grew up in Tennessee. The parenthetical conclusion of the last two stanzas of this poem is about the effect that a mystical journey back to a youthful time and place has on the poet's heart and ear and eye and finally on his poetic tongue. As Wright told J.D. McClatchy, he dates the beginning of his own style from the time of this poem (QN, 104). This finding of his métier had to do with moving from the writing of discrete poems to something larger—a pilgrimage rooted in his own experience of place (landscape) and the metaphysical quest that this entailed. Wright first referred to himself as a pilgrim in 1974—in *Skins* (CM, 101)—and uses the word as a self-reference on nine other occasions. The poet's pilgrimage is not a narrative in Dante's sense but a series of linked epiphanies forming their own larger structure.

Wright has always insisted that he is not a storyteller, saying repeatedly that he is the only Southerner he knows who can't tell a story (e.g., QN, 107). He, nevertheless, has a great deal to say about story in his poetry—that his story is circular, that it deals with circumference, that it functions as an under-narrative, and that his poems are concerned with a story line (QN, 106). He sometimes refers to his pilgrimage or autobiographical quest as a *sottonarrativa* or subnarrative. In an interview he remarks, "I realized that I wanted to tell my story. Everybody wants to tell his story. Some people have stories to tell; some don't. If you don't have a particularly fascinating one, then the work really begins, and you have to sort of make one up. And that's what I had to do. I had to go make one up. And since I couldn't tell it narratively, I was going to have to do it by accretion and by conjunctions of things with building blocks that made a kind of edifice" (Suarez, 45–6).

The undernarrative is "the story line that's underneath the imagistic line on the top. I discussed it once in terms of going through a series of tunnels on a train, then back out to the landscape again. You come out to the landscape and you see where you are and then you go back in the tunnel, then back out to the landscape again. And so on. The story line is what the poem is about, the journey you are reminded of each time you come back out to the landscape. And that's always running underneath the imagistic examples, rhetorical examples, or the narrative tidbits. What goes on in the tunnels is something else and often more exciting and mysterious" (ibid., 49–50). By the time he came to write *China Trace* Wright saw that "each individual poem was a chapter in an ongoing story about a character who went from childhood to his demise and inscription in the heaven of the fixed stars" (QN, 115).

Wright's pilgrimage is a variation on the quest romance. The hero starts out on a journey toward a discovery of some kind. He seeks to overcome numerous obstacles along the way. While the hope is for an "inscription in the heaven of the fixed stars"—an identification of the poet with the mysterious cycle of the cosmos—the end of the journey cannot yet be known: the pilgrim is still on his pilgrimage. And yet the goal of the quest is what is important. Wright's "improvisation" entitled "The Poem as Journey" (QN, 31–47), one of his most compelling prose pieces, will repay reading in its entirety. Here are a few extracts from the "improvisation" about the *mythos* of Wright's lifelong project, especially about the *anagnorisis*—the recognition or discovery.

> Most everyone thinks it's the road that counts, that the traveling is the point of the journey, both in life and in art. I disagree. It think it's what's at the road's end that is important, that where the road leads to is where the meaning is: it's not the telling of the story that's important, it's what the story has to tell. The telling is interesting, but the point is what's transcendent [QN, 31–2].

Poems are not just *about* journeys, of course, they *are* journeys. Like any organism, the good poem is a self-contained adventure, both physically and metaphysically.... without the interior journey, the exterior one is impossible [QN, 32].

At the heart of every poem is a journey of discovery. Something is being found out. Often the discovery is merely technical.... From time to time the discovery is spiritual, a way of looking at the world that affects the way we lead our lives, or how we think of them. Poems that cause us to say, after having read them, "Oh, that's nice," or "Ummm, not bad," do not participate in this voyage of discovery. No matter how new their paint job is, no matter how smart and crisp their sails, they never get out of the harbor. The journey belongs to others [QN, 32–3].

It's always been my contention that the shorter the distance, the harder the journey. By that I mean there is less time and less space to get said what has to be said. For that is the real journey after all—what you've got to say. We can metaphor and simile and weave intricate euphemisms till our pencils stub out of lead, but the fact remains that what you have to say is where you have to go [QN, 42].

Let's consider the structure of the pilgrimage. After completing *China Trace* (1977) Wright became aware that with *Hard Freight* (1973) and *Bloodlines* (1975) he had a trilogy. He then projected the writing of another trilogy followed by still another. He describes the intended structure as "a series of pyramids that basically have the same structure but would be, instead of next to each other, superimposed, one on top of the other" (Suarez, 46). Thus began in the 1970s Wright's project to write a trilogy of trilogies, which he eventually completed with *Negative Blue*. The three-by-three structure is less neat than it might at first appear. With *China Trace* Wright had really completed his fourth book, so *The Grave of the Right Hand*, his first book, was abandoned as part of the large scheme, except for five prose poems that serve as a kind of prologue to *Country Music*. *The World of the Ten Thousand Things* also collects four rather than three books, though the last two, *Zone Journals* and *Xionia*, could be considered a single unit because they are of the same journal form. Similarly, *Negative Blue* has *North American Bear* placed at the end of the three major volumes as a coda. In several places Wright has talked about the analogy, *mutatis mutandis*, between his project, which he calls "a kind of quasi-spiritual autobiography" (Suarez, 43), and Dante's three-part *Commedia*. This structure might be represented by the following chart:

THE GRAVE OF THE RIGHT HAND: *Apprentice volume with interest in surface structure and technique*

COUNTRY MUSIC [1970s]

Condensed form; process of squeezing down; the pilgrimage moves upward; a book of separate poems

Hard Freight	Bloodlines	China Trace
• past • book of disparate individual lyrics • imagistic tone, narrative structure	• present • book of sequences • imagistic tone, narrative structure; imagistic structure, narrative tone	• future: movement toward a spiritual hope • a forty-six part poem beginning in childhood and ending in constellation of fixed stars • imagistic structure, narrative tone

THE WORLD OF THE TEN THOUSAND THINGS [1980s]

> Long lines and longer poems; process of stretching out; the development of the autobiographical *sottonarrativa* or submerged narrative; the pilgrimage moves horizontally; the beginning of poems that follow the seasonal cycle

The Southern Cross	The Other Side of the River	Zone Journals
• treatment of large concepts • focus on yesterday	• attention to narrative-based poems that are imagistically anecdotal • focus on today	• movement toward diaristic and quotidian reportage • focus on tomorrow

NEGATIVE BLUE [1990s]

> Combination of condensed form and long lines; a full book-length poem; Wright once thought of titling the book Tennessee Waltz

Chickamauga	Black Zodiac	Appalachia
inferno	*purgatorio*	*paradiso*
• movement downward; "an odd little inferno, really never getting past the anteroom of limbo, hellish enough for some people" (Caseley, 23)	• horizontal movement toward and into the things of this world; "suffers the purgatorial clear-out of all confessions—self-torture, self-mutation. Death-haunted, perhaps, but a way-station on the trail to a ghostlier X, a deadlier zone" (Caseley, 23); a cathartic process	• movement outward and upward; a secular *paradiso*, modeled on the Egyptian and Tibetan Books of the Dead • otherworldly concerns; thematically, a yearning for what is beyond

The publication of *Negative Blue* brought to completion a twenty-seven-year project, which was sufficient in scope and technical brilliance to have rounded off Wright's career. What followed, however, was an intensely productive period. In 2002 *A Short History of the Shadow* appeared; in 2004, *Buffalo Yoga*; in 2006, *Scar Tissue*; and in 2007, *Littlefoot*—four volumes within a five-year period, which was the amount of time it took to produce *Chickamauga* alone. The Dantean scheme has expanded into at least four trilogies, and there is no end in sight.

Ethos

The ethical focus of Wright's work—what Aristotle called *ethos*—is on the speaker of his poems and the relation of that speaker to us, his audience. Wright is fond of using the editorial "we," including his readers in his project or else casting himself in the role of poetic spokesman for us all. Very few characters contemporary with the poet enter into his poems. Wright does refer occasionally to his wife, son, parents, in-laws, and former friends, but these "characters" are in the service of something else. They are not people set in a rich social context who interact with the poet in the way we expect characters to do in narrative poems or literary fiction. There is essentially only one character, the poet. The dialogue he has with others is carried on in the community of Wright's saints (Dante, Pound, a large group of painters, Hopkins, Sappho, the Chinese poets of the T'ang dynasty, Gnostic visionaries, Stevens, Leopardi, Montale, Augustine, among a number of others)—artists and writers he admires and often borrows from.

The Romantic poets, breaking away from the historical and social fabric of the eighteenth-century lyric, taught us that the self could be a proper subject for the lyric (as in Coleridge's *Dejection: An Ode*) and even in the longer epic forms (as in Wordsworth's *The Prelude*). Wright is an heir to the Romantic tradition. Although he is obsessed with the tick-tock of time, there is no history here, outside of an occasional reference to an external event. Nor are these poems of community: they contain no social vision outside the Utopian desire for the transcendent light at the end of the journey. The movement is almost always centripetal: what we are asked to care about is the poet's interior life—his hopes and fears, his triumphs and tragedies, his observations and speculations, his prayers and testimonies. As we accompany him, we share his gallant effort to get to the other side of the river, to explore every leaf in his back yard, to project ineffable worlds from grains of sand, to ascend and descend the ladder of the *axis mundi*, to probe the blue skies and the black zodiac for some hint of the divine—forever keeping his eye on the landscape in front of him. The commentaries in the *Companion* focus a good deal of attention on the *ethos* of the poet.

Dianoia

Aristotle's *dianoia* is usually translated as "thought." In our expansion of the term it represents poetic meaning, or what our commentaries refer to as the themes, motifs, ideas, and subject matter in Wright's poetry. These are by no means synonymous terms, but they point to the formal cause of Wright's poems—*what* is represented or embodied or expressed, as well as his own judgments vis-à-vis the issue raised. He remarks in several places that the subject matter of his poems is three-fold—language, landscape, and the idea of God (*QN*, 81, 135; Vadnie). This means that his poems are often about metaphysical and religious questions, sometimes explicitly so and at other times only implied. But language, landscape, and the idea of God do not in any sense exhaust Wright's subject matter. His poetry, like Keats's letters, is filled with speculations on all manner of questions, such speculations forming the content of his work—"certain things in my mind I want to say" (*Halflife*, 87).

In three different interviews Wright quotes Philip Larkin's comment that form means nothing to him and that content is everything (*Halflife*, 86, 106, 153). One of the three includes the following gloss: "My comment would be that content means nothing to me. Form is everything.... I'm one of those people who thinks that content has nothing to do with subject matter. I think there's form, there's subject matter, and then there's content. Content is what it all 'means,' somehow. Subject matter is what it's 'about.' Form is how you organize it. Content in that case would be like a Greek chorus standing behind the point and informing it" (*Halflife*, 153-4). This means that subject matter is simply a topic without a predicate. An example would "the dead" as a subject matter in any number of Wright's poems, or "the idea of God." Content is the subject matter mediated through the poet's consciousness and about which something is asserted or suggested: subject matter, then, is how you get to the content. All content, Wright is saying, does have a predicate and does involve interpretation. When subject matter is given a meaning, it becomes content. Since content involves interpretation, the reader is involved as well. Wright's content is ultimately, he remarks in an interview, "the contemplation of the divine" (Ingersoll, 30).

All of these terms—meaning, content, subject matter, theme—are "essentially contested concepts," W.B. Gallie's phrase for ideas that are open to interpretation and so involve disagreements about their meaning and use. But they all fall under the heading of our expanded definition of *dianoia*. Thus, when in the commentaries that follow I speak of a poem's theme or what it is *about* or its meaning, those parts of the commentary should be taken as interpretations of the poem's *dianoia*. "What you have to say [*dianoia*]," says Wright, "is where you have to go [*mythos*]." In a poet as elliptical as Wright, the subjective response to his poems will of course contain a good measure of speculation and conjecture. The commentaries, as already suggested, are simply one reader's response to what Wright "has to say," *dianoia* or poetic thought being a primary center of interest in all lyric poetry.

Melos

We can expand Aristotle's *melopoiia* (the songs of Greek tragedy, especially the choral odes) to mean any appeal that poetry makes on the ear. The sounds of poetry derive from recurring features, the most obvious of which is meter. Poetry contains recurrent sounds, rhythms, and patterns. End rhyme, the principal sound-repetition of poetry, occurs only rarely in Wright's lyrics and then as if by accident. Half-rhymes and the repetition of words at the ends of lines occur occasionally. Anaphora and assonance appear with some regularity. Wright's poems contain many examples of syntactic and semantic repetition ("Drifting and rootless, rising and falling," "Never again never again," "Candor of marble, candor of bone," and so on), but the major form of sound repetition in his poetry is alliteration. None of these features of recurrence is regular. What is regular, as we shall see shortly, is the pattern of his stanzas.

From the early 1960s the meter of Wright's verse became syllabic rather than accentual (dependent on regular patterns of stress in each line). One can find numerous examples of the iambic foot in his poems, but this basic pattern of English poetry is never regular, and in fact Wright often intentionally upsets the pattern by the addition of another accent, as in "I think of the nightfall all the time" (*Night Music*), where the addition of the first "the" disrupts the basic iambic tetrameter. Wright's free verse depends rather on the number of syllables in each line. "The first time I ever had any 'sense' of a line as a line," he says, "was when I started writing syllables about thirty years ago, in 1963. It was the first time I had ever felt comfortable in lineation, and was doing something I felt was compatible to the way I thought, or felt I thought. I am still using a line that is syllabically based. It's true I try to manipulate the stress patterns within this syllabic framework, but the overriding urge and discipline is syllable count, almost always in odd numbers, anywhere from three to, say, twenty-one in a line" (*QN*, 171). Wright is very careful in counting the number of syllables per line, which, as he said, turns out almost always to be an odd number. For the shorter lines, seven syllables is something of a norm, for the longer ones, thirteen. This means that the sound patterns of the lines are unpredictable, and that they move in the direction of ordinary speech. In section 2 of *Meditation on Form and Measure* (*NB*, 90–2), for example, the syllable count per line varies from five to fifteen; six of the ten lines have thirteen syllables, two have nine, and one has five. In the poem as a whole twenty of the fifty lines have thirteen syllables, and Wright's syllable count, here as elsewhere, turns out to be an odd number. Only one line in the poem has an even number of syllables: "Everywhere under foot" (p. 92, l. 3). In *Appalachia* as a whole, the repetition of the number of syllables per line is regular only in one poem—*Paesaggio Notturno* (*NB*, 59), all twelve lines of which have seven syllables.

On several occasions Wright has referred to Eugenio Montale's remark that poetry arises from prose and longs to return to it (*QN*, 105, 136, 137; Bourgeois, 55; Zawacki, 24), and he says that "for the ten years of working on the books in *The World of the Ten Thousand Things* I was trying to take poetry and guide my poetic line in the direction of prose but keep it always from falling into prose. It goes in that direction, toward a conversational tone of voice, toward a prose kind of understanding of itself, but always stays just above, or just outside, and that tension, that keeping-it-apart is where the music in poetry lies, not in the completion. I like to think that the rhythms I'm using and the line I'm using keep it up enough from prose, and maybe that's why I'm so attracted to that particular statement by Montale" (*QN*, 138–9). Wright's increasingly long lines and his effort to produce lines that move in the direction of prose create the effect, not of recurrent rhythm, but of a rhythm of continuity.

"Measure" is the word we use in both music and poetry to refer to meter or metric units. "Without measure," Wright says in one poem, "there is no form" (*NB*, 91). That is, measure is the form we impose on time: otherwise we have only flux and chaos. But measure is also the form we impose on space—what Wright in the same poem calls "verbal architecture." This is a matter not of the ear but the eye: we will consider the spatial form of recurrence below. What almost always initiates a poem for Wright is not *dianoia* but *melos* and *opsis*: "it's always been rhythm and image for me, as opposed to, say, ideas, that get a poem going" (*QN*, 108).

Lexis

According to Wright, "When you say you write for the angels, for the dead, for that which is beyond you, you write for that part of yourself that is better than you are, for all of those things that are in this imaginary, mythical, still, brightly lit center of attention at the heart of the universe. Of course we suspect it's all talk. But it's the kind of talk that interests me and it's the kind of speculation and belief in a constructed reality that keeps me trying to work in language, because ultimately what we are doing is playing with words. Some people play with words in one way and some in another. I think there's a serious way and a nonserious way of playing with words. I think poetry is the most serious way in the world of playing with words; it certainly is for me" (*Halflife*, 128–9). The serious playing with words is the poetic *sine qua non*. Words propel the poem, affecting our ear and eye, to be sure, but words carry the semantic weight, whatever use they have for Wright's immediate purpose: to describe, to reflect, to meditate, to philosophize, to praise, to lament, to invoke, to remember, to register impressions, to exult, to enjoin, to capture emotional states, to borrow from others, and so on.

As already indicated, language is one of the three subjects of poetry for Wright—Aristotle's material cause turned into a formal cause. Wright's poems often speak of the impotence of language. He *tells* us repeatedly that language is an ineffectual tool, but then he turns around and with one of his pyrotechnic verbal displays *shows* us that it is not. Few have commented on Wright's poetry without praising his ingeniously creative use of words. The startling images and tropes are often used to capture some mystery in the landscape, but they are by no means restricted to the concrete details of what his eye takes in. As the commentaries will show, they attach themselves to abstractions as well. Wright's use of figurative language is everywhere creative, often startling in its originality, frequently witty, sometimes outrageous (in the Samuel Johnson yoked-by-violence-together mode).

When Wright finds the present lexicon insufficient, he adds to it by creating his own vocabulary, as in his not uncommon practice of changing one part of speech into another. In *Umbrian Dreams* (*NB*, 101), for example, he the changes nouns "horizon" and "tabula rasa" into verbs (past participles): "horizoned" and "tabula rasaed." He also uses "horizon" as a verb in *Black and Blue* (*C*, 44). One encounters such syntactic shifts frequently. In *Looking Around II* we have "Seurating," a proper noun used as a present participle (*SHS*, 7). A similar transformation is "Constabled" in *A Journal of English Days* (*WTTT*, 132). Other examples—there are scores of them—are "calicoed" in *Chickamauga* (*NB*, 33), "candescing" (present participle from the adjective "candescent" or the noun "candescence") in *Waiting for Tu Fu* (*NB*, 57), "Bibled" and "mottoed" in *Meditation on Song and Structure* (*NB*, 120), "appled," "arteried," and "membraned" in *Disjecta Membra* (*NB*, 132, 136), "dungeoned" in *Opus Posthumous* (*NB*, 159), "grunged" in *The Writing Life* (*NB*, 165), "sundowned" in *Remembering Spello, Sitting Outside in Prampolini's Garden* (*NB*, 184), and "dolce vitaed" in *A Journal of True Confessions* (*WTTT*, 143). These are all examples of the economy of condensation—the spare precision Wright always strives for. In all of these expressions, the simile is repressed. It would be easy to write "the light under the peach trees was like a brightly printed cloth" rather than "light calicoed under the peach trees." The former is tone-deaf and indifferent; the latter is concise and energetic; and its wit induces delight. What the syntactic shifts do is change a potential simile into a metaphor. Here is part of Wright's description of his Charlottesville back yard: "Now into June, cloverheads tight, Seurating the yard, / This land-washed *jatte* fireflied and Corgied." The underlying metaphor here is "cloverheads *are* painters: they paint the yard, which has become one of Georges Seurat's pointillist canvases, with dots of color rather than brushstrokes covering the surface. The back yard *is* a *jatte* (bowl), a pun triggered by the title of one of Seurat's paintings—*Sunday Afternoon on the Island of La Grande Jatte* or *The Seine at Le Grande Jatte*. La Grand Jatte is an island, washed by the sea; thus, the back yard *is* also an island, washed by land rather than water, and it *is* a large bowl, speckled with fireflies against its Welsh terrier black and tan (Wright owned a corgi at the time). The copula that joins the two different things does not of course have to be present for the identification of two different things to be affirmed. Witness Pound's textbook example: "The apparition of these faces in the crowd; / Petals on a wet, black bough" (*In a Station of the Metro*).

This is the metaphorical imagination at work. We all know that a back yard is not a canvas, yet metaphor identifies the two. It is easy enough to understand how a back yard is *like* a painter's canvas, for the logical mind can easily grasp analogies. And Wright is not averse to using similes: there are more than 1500 in his poems. But metaphor, which is counter-logical and paradoxical, throws the perceiving mind to another level of consciousness altogether, as in this metaphor about *lexis* itself: "Looming and phosphorescent against the dark, / Words, always words" (*WTTT*, 99). As Wright says in *Night Rider*: "Nothing prepares the soul for metaphor's sleight-of-hand" (*SHS*, 29). Nothing prepares the mind either, except an openness to the mysteries of identity. From the perspective of the *lexis* of Wright's poetry, metaphor is the most powerful use he makes of words. "I think in metaphor," says Wright (Remnick, 573).

Wright's metaphor-making is an aspect of that individual manner of expression we call style. "There is style," says Wright, "and there is Style. When everything clicks, style is Style, everything inextricably bound up in language and its ambitions, everything palpable in the isness, the radiance that language offers" (*QN*, 104–5). This radiance produces high style—discontinuous, epiphanic, visionary, intense, luminous—as in the opening lines of *Umbrian Dreams*:

> Nothing is flat-lit and tabula rasaed in Charlottesville,
> Umbrian sackcloth,
>   stigmata and *Stabat mater*
> A sleep and a death away,
> Night, and a sleep and a death away—
> Light's frost-fired and Byzantine here,
>   aureate, beehived,
> Falling in Heraclitean streams
> Through my neighbor's maple trees [*NB*, 101].

But Wright's style ranges widely from this hieratic mode to the demotic, what Wordsworth called the language really used by ordinary people—as in "Something will get you, the doctor said, // don't worry about that" (*NB*, 76) or "What's the body to do?" (*NB*, 153). Wright sometimes parodies the demotic, as in this droll reversal of a popular commonplace in *Body and Soul II*: "Don't just do something, sit there" (*SHS*, 79). Between the hieratic and the demotic is an array of stylistic registers and poetic voices—from the conversational to the meditative, the epigrammatic to the associative (stream-of-consciousness), the naive to the sentimental, the sententious to the sublime, the Parnassian to the transcendent.

Numerous occasions will present themselves in the commentaries that follow to reflect on Wright's use of metaphor and other tropes, key lexical features, which along with the *melos* and *opsis* of his verse define his personal manner of expression.

Opsis

As already suggested, the *lexis* of poetry exists halfway between the ear and the eye, between the linear pattern formed by sounds and the static pattern projected in space. The former yields at one extreme a poetry of pure sound, as in Swinburne and Poe; the latter, pure image as in concrete poetry. Poetry, therefore, has numerous analogues with music on the one hand, and with painting on the other. *Ekphrasis* in its limited sense—poems about paintings or poems in which paintings figure importantly—is relatively frequent in Wright's work. See, for example, *Portrait of the Poet in Abraham von Werdt's Dream* (*CM*, 20), de Chirico in *Self-Portrait* (*GRH*, 57), Piero della Francesca's *The Resurrection* in *Tattoos* no. 7 (*CM*, 62), Caravaggio's *The Beheading of St. John* in *Hard Dreams* (*SHS*, 75), William Blake's *Lucia* (Dante Illustrations, *Purgatorio* ix) in *Hard Dreams* (*SHS*, 75–6), Piet Mondrian's *Composition in Gray and Red* (1935) in *Summer Storm* (*NB*, 61), Titian's *The Martyrdom of St. Lawrence* in *Venetian Dog* (*NB*, 153), and Francesco del Cossa's *Salon of the Months* frescoes in the Schifanoia Palace in *A Journal of the Year of the Ox* (*WTTT*, 170–2). Moreover, artists are otherwise omnipresent. Some—Morandi, Cézanne, Mondrian, Rothko—come center stage. Others peep out from the wings—Leonardo, Lorrain, Titian, Carpaccio, Gyges of Lydia, Ryder, Avery, Kahn, Mantegna, Cosimo Tura, Munch, Giulio Romano, Poussin, Francesco del Cossa, Uccello, Seurat, Soutine, Tintoretto, and de Stael. A number of Wright's poems originate from photographs, and he has acknowledged in recent interviews that European film directors—Godard, Truffaut, Fellini, Antonioni, Monicelli—have doubtless had an effect on his work. All of these influences are a matter of the eye, illustrating that Wright is firmly in the tradition of *ut pictura poesis* in its several senses: the use of precise, concrete details in creating vibrant images; the framing, lighting, and foregrounding of scenes; and the moments of *ekphrasis* itself, when paintings enter poems as subjects. Wright's use of the image has a clear antecedent in the Neo-Platonic view of Pico della Mirandola, who thought that the image had a certain visionary power that could lure the viewer to meditate on metaphysical or religious realities. It often leads Wright in that direction. Regrettably, the economics of publishing has dictated that the reproductions of paintings that originally accompanied the commentaries be purged, but most of them that are not in standard art history texts are easily accessible on the worldwide web. The full effect of the ekphrastic poems cannot, of course, be felt without looking at the images.

As for the pattern or unit of recurrence in Wright's poetry from the point of view of *opsis*, it resides primarily in the stanza. This is not a feature that Wright wants us to be overly conscious of. In fact, the dropped-down lines (discussed on pages 18–19), which have become Wright's signature stylistic feature, tend to conceal the stanzaic patterns, and the larger the unit being repeated, the more difficult it is to see the repetition. At the same time it is clear that Wright is very self-conscious about the stanza as unit.

Consider, for example, the poems in *Appalachia*. At the macro level, this book has three numbered parts, each part having fifteen poems (45 poems altogether). Compare this arrangement with that of *Black Zodiac*, where number of *poems* in the five sections is palindromic: 1 + 5 + 8 + 5 + 1. "Reading" the pattern backwards is the same as reading it forwards. This is typical of the individual poems in *Appalachia* as well. In thirty of the poems (two-thirds of them) there is no variation on the number of lines per stanza, regardless of the number of stanzas (from two to six). The five-line stanza is Wright's preferred unit. Eight of the poems in *Appalachia* have the five-line stanza repeated four times (5 × 4); six, three times (5 × 3); and two, two times (5 × 2). Variations on this pentad are: 5–1–5–1–5–1 (twice), 5–1–5–1, and 5–4–5–4. Five-line stanzas dominate, then, in twenty poems. No poem in *Appalachia* exceeds twenty lines: they are single-page poems, with two exceptions.

Six is the next most frequent pattern: five poems have the 6 × 3 form; one is 6 × 2; one is 6–1–6–1–6; and one is 6–4–6. Six-line stanzas are in two other poems, though the form is not symmetrical (6–6–6–3 and 6–6–2). Six-line stanzas dominate, then, in ten poems.

As for four, we have 4 × 5, 4 × 4, and 4 × 3 (twice), with its variations: 4–2–4–2–4–2, 4–2–4–2–4, and 4–1–4–1. Four-line stanzas occur in seven poems. The three-line stanza, which is omnipresent in *Black Zodiac*, appears only twice in *Appalachia*: 3 × 6, and 3 × 5. Couplets appear three times, once regularly (2 × 6). Seven-line and eight-line stanzas appear once each (7 × 2 and 8 × 2). And we have one fourteen-line poem, the Wright sonnet, we might call it (*What Do You Write About*, not included in *Negative Blue*). Outside of the variations on six (above), that leaves only two poems where the mirror form (as in 4–2–4–2–4) is abandoned or where the stanza pattern is not regularly repeated. These are *Stray Paragraphs in April* (2–3–2–3–2–1–1–1) and *Remembering Spello* (2–3–2–3–2–3–3–2).

All of this is a matter of what Wright calls "measure," which typically describes a rhythmic unit, most often a meter in a phrase or a line. While Wright's lines, as we have seen, have their own syllabic measure, his chief unit of measure has been transferred from the phrase and the line to stanza. The rhythmic unit, in short, becomes the stanza.

In an interview Wright says about the visual pattern his lines form on the page, "As for organization of my poems, at least stanzaically, however the first group of lines arranges itself, however many the number of lines, that's my pattern for the rest of the poem. Unless the poem seems to call out for an arbitrary stanza base, *i.e.*, different numbered ones. This tends to happen if the thought patterns break down in smaller units, such as two- or three-line groups. I seem to have a lot of four-, five-, and six-line stanzas, for some reason. Perhaps that's as long as I can keep a stream of thought in my head. I *am* addicted to stanzas, however, and hardly ever, if ever, just have a block of lines down the page. That looks ugly to me, and rather suffocating, without breathing spaces or air vents" (Spiegelman, 188).

In Wright's longer poems the spatial organization is more complex. *Apologia Pro Vita Sua* (*NB*, 71–87), for example, has three parts, signified by Roman numerals. Each part has nine sections (separated from each other by a centered rule), each section has nine lines forming three stanzas, and each stanza has three lines. This yields a pattern of threes and nines: 3 × 3 = 9; 3 × 9 = 27; 3 × 27 = 81 (9 × 9). The *Envoi* (pp. 86–7) repeats the pattern: nine three-line stanzas, making for a total of 90 (9 × 10). The ninety tercets are not *terza rima*, but the systematic scheme is Dantesque.

Wright's long lines owe something to Whitman, though Wright came to feel that he could not keep the line afloat for as long as Whitman did. Thus, he began to break his lines, dropping part of the line down one step. He calls these lines variously the dropped line, the low rider, the downstep line, and the two-step line. The dropped line, however, does not always serve to break up the long line. Thus, we can have a seven-word, seven-syllable two-step:

> And so he did.
> Like John Keats.

On the other hand, Wright can have a seventeen-syllable line that is not dropped. These long lines are often too long for the page and have to be brought back to the left margin with no two-step. Wright first employed the dropped line in *Private Madrigal II*, published in 1968 (*DA*, 35). He thinks that his primarily influence here was Pound, though Pound's dropped line "almost always seems to be two individual lines, or more, while mine is always a continuation of the line it's dropped from, the line that precedes it, a giant caesura, if you will, a change in pitch, but the same tune—it's all the same long line" (Spiegelman, 112).

The dropped line is both a matter of *melos* and *opsis*. Wright says that he uses the two-step as a way of maintaining the integrity of the line musically—its sound pattern (*QN*, 79, 133), but it is also a function of his conception of space:

> There is a kind of spatial negation, a visual power in absence that painters understand and employ, and which I'm interested in poetically. It's a sort of white hole that has a kinetic draw to it that the lines of the poem float on and resist. Part of my interest in the dropped line for me is that it sets up a bit of this power field within the line itself; a rhythmic jolt sometimes might appear, small as it is, that kicks the line and the poem along, keeping it alive over the top of a force that would founder and sink it at any time. But everybody knows this. You keep the composition apart just a little to let this energy in and out, and to let the poem in and out of the energy generated by this emptiness. It's all about the same thing, the power and domination of what's not there, the energy of absence [*QN*, 173].

Where Wright will use the dropped line is not at all predictable. It appears to be a function of his intuitive sense of sound and sight.

For Aristotle *opsis* had reference to what the theater-goer would see on the stage. For us as readers, it refers both to what we see on the page (the lines and stanzas) and more importantly to the images the poet creates. Wright says, "I think in images and express myself in images. Any time I'm trying to explain something, I'm talking in images and metaphors.... My mind works in flashes and starts, visually, and, like a child, if I can see a picture, then I understand or at least I can start to think about what it means" (*Halflife*, 131–2). Images can be either literally descriptive ("Pool table. Zebra rug. // Three chairs in a half circle") or, as is most often the case with Wright, figurative (" ... dogwood, / Spring's sap-crippled, arthritic, winter-weathered, myth limb, / Whose roots are my mother's hair"). Wright's images come from direct observation or from a vision of his mind's eye resurrected from memory. Occasionally, they derive from what others, such as the T'ang poets, have reported seeing.

In *Quarter Notes* Wright reproduced nine letters that passed between him and Charles Simic, entitled "The Narrative of the Image." This suggests an unconventional way of thinking about imagery, as we usually conceive of the image in spatial rather than linear terms. A series of images can of course be linked, and we move through a poem from image to image, establishing connections between them. Images often connect associatively, and such connection is Wright's goal. He remarks that Pound's "luminous" image "is the sort of image I am interested in, and I'm interested in having strings of those images which then, somehow associatively, as I see them, make the poem. A string of those images like beads along a line and in a circle" (*Halflife*, 93). And he says in another context, "Narrative does not dictate the image; the image dictates the narrative" (*QN*, 110). But the image itself is something perceived by the (mind's) eye at a moment in time. It corresponds to a musical chord (sounds at a moment in time), rather than to the melody (a sequence of chords). In the correspondence with Simic, Wright wants to distinguish between Ezra Pound's notion of the image ("an intellectual and emotional complex in an instant of time") and Hart Crane's idea of the "logic of metaphor" as "constructed on a series of associational meanings and thought-extension" (*QN*, 57). But the whole discussion in the correspondence with Simic never quite clarifies the counterintuitive idea of the *mythos* of image. We will do better to examine what Wright has to say about the image in other places.

The image, first of all, often functions as Wright's muse. When asked whether he begins a poem with a cluster of images, he replied, "It does, actually. Perhaps not a cluster. One would do. Something I see, usually; something observed. The 'little dropped hearts' of the camellia blooms scattered under the huge camellia bush in my backyard in Laguna Beach fifteen years ago started the poem 'Tattoos.' And since 'Tattoos' begat 'Skins,' you could say that those fallen blossoms were the beginning of the entire book, *Bloodlines*, as the other eight poems went in to accentuate or ameliorate the two long central ones. Of course, each one had its own separate trigger, but the initial pull was off the dropped blossoms" (*QN*, 108). Wright also says that the layers of imagery in a poem form an iconostasis (literally, a standing image): an ecclesiastical screen, covered with images, that mediates between the nave (where we as readers are) and the altar (where the secrets of the poem lie) (Spiegelman, 111). The aim of what follows is to help reveal some of those secrets.

PART I

The Third Trilogy:
Negative Blue

CHAPTER 1

Chickamauga

Negative Blue: Selected Later Poems, published by Farrar, Straus, and Giroux in 2000, collects all but six of the poems that appeared in *Chickamauga* (1995), *Black Zodiac*, (1997), and *Appalachia* (1998). The British edition of *Negative Blue* was published by Stride Publications (Exeter, Devon, 2000). The cover art on the dust jacket of both editions is *The Creation and Expulsion of Adam and Eve from Paradise* by Giovanni di Paolo. The title contains echoes of Wallace Stevens's reference to the empyrean, "this dividing and indifferent blue" (*Sunday Morning*, st. 3, l. 15), and Kao Shih's *A Song of the Yen Country*: "In a place of death and blue void, with nothingness ahead" (*The Jade Mountain*, trans. Wittner Bynner [Garden City, NY: Anchor Books, 1964], 32). Paolo's painting, with God the Father descending from the blue empyrean and pointing to a concentric cosmic map, contains images that foreshadow several leitmotifs in the volume. The eleven circles of the cosmos represent the four elements, the seven planets, and the sign of the zodiac; and the garden with its four rivers is a mythical version of the Appalachian Eden of Wright's childhood.

Chickamauga won the Lenore Marshall Poetry Prize in 1996. The photograph on the dust jacket, by Holly Wright, is of Charles Wright's mouth.

The poems in *Chickamauga* were written over a five-year period, beginning in the fall of 1988, and although the poems themselves do not always follow a strictly chronological sequence, they do trace the course of the seasonal cycles from the fall of 1988 through the fall of 1993. *Negative Blue* omits the section headings of *Chickamauga*, the first of which is "Aftermath," twelve poems similar in form to the journals of *The World of the Ten Thousand Things*. The second, "Terra Cognita," contains three poems set in Italy (the "known land") in 1959. The third, "Broken English," has four poems, more discontinuous, as the section title suggests, than the others in this volume. "Mostly," Wright says about these four poems, "I open up a poem and stick something in the middle of it" (QN, 161). Section four, "Rosa Mistica" (the title of a poem by Hopkins) contains twenty poems in which the first-person pronoun appears only once. The fifth section contains two poems about China. And the last section, "Imaginary Endings," contains nine poems that relate in one way or another to conclusions, including death.

Sitting Outside at the End of Autumn

Orig. pub. *Gettysburg Review* 2, no. 2 (Spring 1989): 251.
C, 3; NB, 3
Pattern: 10 × 2
Time: Late autumn 1988
Place: Charlottesville

The poet had taken stock of his life three years earlier, pausing in his back yard to see if his writing had added up to anything. But the sums and quotients did not come out quite right, so he is back at it again, "looking to calculate, / Looking to see what adds up." In stanza 2 he at first abandons the mathematical metaphors in favor of the abstract contraries of the *Tao Te Ching*—something and nothing. "The myriad creatures in the world are born from / Something, and Something from Nothing," says Lao Tzu (*Tao Te Ching*, chap. 40, trans. D.C. Lau). The poet finds this form of Eastern metaphysical reasoning "Eminently sensible," and he offers as an example of something coming from nothing the empty snail shell that he rubs between his fingers. The "vocabulary or disguise" of the shell, he hopes, will yield some radiance. But in the end, relying on a Taoist mathematical metaphor, he finds with Lao Tzu that "one and one make nothing," and so he is left only with the infinite and omnipresent shadow cast by everything. "All things," says Lao Tzu, "bear the shade on their backs" (chap. 42, trans. R.B. Blakney). Or again, "As a thing the way is / Shadowy, indistinct. / Indistinct and shadowy. / Yet within it is an image; / Shadowy and indistinct, / Yet within it is a substance. / Dim and dark, / Yet within it is an essence. This essence is quite genuine" (chap. 21, trans D.C. Lau). Although light appears to be difficult to come by here—a theme that will reappear with some frequency in Wright's poems—the poem's conclusion is more complicated than this. In Taoism "Nothing" can be understood as "nonbeing" or "nothingness" (as it is in fact so rendered in at least five translations of the *Tao Te Ching*). The *Tao* or Way cannot be known by the kind of rational tallying up proposed in the first stanza, where one and one do make something. It is approached rather by resting in nothingness, and its essence is nonbeing. So in the final couplet the poet is actually returning to Lao Tzu's earlier pronouncement, "Everything comes from something, // only something comes from nothing," the unfathomable and invisible *Tao*—the unchanging One that is the source of the delicate shell. This, in the first poem of the "Aftermath" section, is what comes after math.

p. 3, ll. 11–12. *Everything comes ... more of less.* In addition to the lines from chap. 40 of the *Tao Te Ching*, cf. "The Tao that can be talked about is not the true Tao. / The name that can be named is not the eternal Name. / Everything in the universe comes out of Nothing. / Nothing—the nameless is the beginning" (*Tao Te Ching*, no. 1; trans. Man-Ho Kwok, Martin Palmer, and Jay Ramsay).

p. 3, l. 19. *one and one.* See chap. 1 of the *Tao Te Ching*, where the contraries are said to be the same, this sameness being a mystery.

*Lines After Rereading T.S. Eliot

Orig. pub. *Gettysburg Review* 2, no. 2 (Spring 1989): 250.
C, 4–5
Pattern: 4 × 8
Time: Late autumn 1988
Place: Charlottesville

The influence of Eliot here is primarily thematic—the pain suffered in the wasteland, the inability to forgive, the hell we feel in our bones, and the battle between ambition and anonymity—but there are *images* from Eliot's *The Waste Land* that make their way into the poem as well: cricket, wasteland, rocks, desert, and bones. In addition, "flesh," "abstraction," "blood," "time," and "forgive" echo the language of the *Four Quartets*. A poet of Eliot's stature naturally produces an anxiety of influence: what can one achieve in the face of all who have come before? One can understand, then, why the poem concludes with reflections on ambition. Ambition is like the small pear, illustrious because of the light shining on it but completely unknown and speechless. Such anonymity is what the poet wishes for himself, the fading away of his various selves into the darkening landscape. No, this Prufrock in Charlottesville is not Prince Hamlet, nor was meant to be.

Literature is made out of other literature, as Northrop Frye repeatedly reminded us, and the truism is everywhere apparent in Wright's poetry. The present poem, though not included in *Negative Blue*, is the first of his poems that call attention to this fact of literary production by having "reading" or "after reading" in their titles. The others are: *Reading Lao Tzu Again in the New Year* (NB, 4–5), *After Reading Wang Wei, I Go Outside to the Full Moon* (NB, 7), *Reading Rorty and Paul Celan One Morning in Early June* (NB, 10–11), *After Reading Tu Fu, I Go Outside to the Dwarf Orchard* (NB, 12), *After Reading T'ao Ch'ing, I Wander Untethered Through the Short Grass* (NB, 183), and *After Rereading Robert Graves, I Go Outside to Get My Head Together* (NB, 186). Again, "Aftermath" is the section title for the first twelve poems of *Chickamauga*. The convention is a familiar one. We have, for example, Keats's *A Dream, After Reading Dante's Episode Of Paolo and Francesca*, Robert Louis Stevenson's *After Reading "Antony and Cleopatra,"* Samuel Taylor Coleridge's *Effusion, After Reading the Interesting Account of the Young Savage of Aveyron*, and such variations as Keats's *On First Looking into Chapman's Homer*, Billy Collins's *Reading an Anthology of Chinese Poems of the Sung Dynasty, I Pause to Admire the Length and Clarity of Their Titles*, and Bertolt Brecht's *On Reading a Recent Greek Poet*.

Reading Lao Tzu Again in the New Year

Orig. pub. *Poetry* 155 (January 1990): 253.
C, 6–7; NB, 4–5
Pattern: 4–4 × 4 (32 lines)
Time: End of December 1988–4 January 1989
Place: Charlottesville

Reading the *Tao Te Ching* provides another occasion for stock-taking, this time at the "Snub end of a dismal year" and the beginning of another. The poem begins in darkness, the sky displaying its "undercoat of blackwash" and the darkness indifferently shrugging its shoulders. The image of the burning shirt in section 1 is less apocalyptic or purgatorial than infernal (etymologically, "dismal" is "evil day"). In answering to his life, the poet discovers that nothing much has changed, the old and new years and the old and new songs being more or less the same, even in the face of a changed heart.

In section 2, the poet mediates on the rising and falling of prosodies and poetic structures, concluding that at least when they fall, "Failure reseeds the old ground." Still, the words and structures that that emerge from the ground are wrong, and "Even the questions are compromise," the questions being those Blakean queries in ll. 3–4: "Does the grass, with its inches in two worlds, love the dirt? / Does the snowflake the raindrop." The poet rather despairs of language being able to capture the "essence of all things," but this sense of failure is reversed from his reading in the *Tao Te Ching*. The secret comes in sense of emptiness of Lao Tzu, who writes:

> I do my utmost to attain emptiness;
> I hold firmly to stillness.
> The myriad creatures all rise together
> And I watch their return.
> The teeming creatures
> All return to their separate roots.
> Returning to one's roots is known as stillness [*Tao Te Ching*, chap. 16; trans. Lau].

The enigmatic notion of emptiness in Taoism has to do with restraint, patience, simplicity, and the lack of desire. Its companion is the idea of *wu wei* or nondoing, which means to be still and passive so that the *Tao* can act unhindered. A Western analogue is Keats's Negative

Capability, which removes us from the irritable searching after fact and reason, and removes us as well from the desire to answer to our lives (section 1). This secret of emptiness frees the poet to return in the last section to the description of the new year's landscape in all its glory. The key word here is "affection," a disposition of the heart scattered throughout Wright's poetry, especially in the "journals" of *The World of the Ten Thousand Things*. The poet moves therefore from the darkness at the end of the "dismal year" to the daylight world, which is tumbled by the wind "into the eastern [and Eastern?] countries," as he hangs between the *yin* of now and the *yang* of not-now. As Lao Tzu says, "Standing before it [the *Tao*], it has no beginning; / even when followed, it has no end. / In the now, it exists; to the present apply it, / follow it well, and reach its beginning" (*Tao Te Ching*, chap. 14; trans. Stan Rosenthal).

p. 4. ll. 13–20–p. 5, ll. 1–8. *I've heard ... is emptiness.* "My words are easy to understand / And my actions are easy to perform / Yet no other can understand or perform them. / My words have meaning; my actions have reason; / Yet these cannot be known and I cannot be known" (Lao Tzu, *Tao Te Ching*, chap. 70, interpolation by Peter A. Merel). "Looked at but cannot be seen--it is beneath form; / Listened to but cannot be heard--it is beneath sound; / Held but cannot be touched--it is beneath feeling; / These depthless things evade definition, / And blend into a single mystery. / In its rising there is no light, / In its falling there is no darkness, / A continuous thread beyond description, / Lining what can not occur; / Its form formless, / Its image nothing, / Its name silence" (ibid., chap. 14). On the theme of emptiness, see *Tao Te Ching*, chaps. 3, 5, 16, 22, 45, and 50.

Under the Nine Trees in January

Orig. pub. *New Yorker* 65, no. 9 (17 April 1989): 89.
C, 8; NB, 6
Pattern: 3 × 5
Time: January 1989
Place: Charlottesville

The questions posed by the poet, positioned under the branches of the nine trees in his back yard, are these: What is the proper attitude we should take toward the ultimate void? Should we lament the solitude of death? Should we long for the stillness of paradise? Or should we rather formulate some plan of action ("Give counsel") in the face of the impending darkness, while we continue to inch our way through life?

The questions are never answered, but the poet does leave us with a metaphor of the world as handkerchief. This is an ironic inversion of Whitman's grass as "the handkerchief of the Lord" (*Song of Myself*, sec. 6). Here the handkerchief becomes an emblem of acceptance: today the poet spreads the handkerchief—the cold and snowy world of death—across his knees; tomorrow it will be folded into the breast pocket of his funeral suit.

p. 6, l. 6. *the season's decrease diminishes me.* While passages in italics are generally quotations in Wright's poems, this apparent one is fictitious. It does, however, contain an echo of a line from John Donne's *Devotion XVII*: "Any man's death diminishes me, because I am involved in mankind." The question, then, is whether we should lament the annual death of the seasons as we lament the death of a human being.

After Reading Wang Wei, I Go Outside to the Full Moon

Orig. pub. *New Republic* 201, no. 24 (11 December 1989): 34.
C, 9; NB, 7
Pattern: 3 × 4
Time: Winter 1989
Place: Charlottesville

Wright borrows the last line of the poem from Wang Wei and borrows as well the T'ang poet's characteristic seven-syllable line. Wang Wei wrote in formal couplets. Wright's poem is in tightly controlled tercets, each following the regular pattern of 7–13–7 syllables. The mood of Wright's poem is much darker than what is found in most of the verse of the generally happy and carefree Wang Wei. (Wang Wei's late poems do sound an elegiac note; several are laments.)

The sound of anguish and bitter regret that drones through the darkness reinforces the feelings that arise from the poet's awareness of his afflicted and tired body: "No resting place in the black pews of the winter trees, / No resting place in the clouds." Thus, the appeal for mercy for both the long-deceased Wang Wei and for himself.

In the concluding stanza, the "Isolate landscape" and the "World's grip" are set in opposition to the "absolute," which in another autumn poem Wang Wei, a devout Buddhist, enjoined his readers to study: "I sit alone sad at my whitening hair.... White hairs will never be transformed / That elixir is beyond creation / To eliminate decrepitude / Study the absolute" (*Poems of Wang Wei* [Harmondsworth: Penguin, 1973], 121). "How can we," asks Wang Wei, "escape from these earthly toils / Shake off the dust and leave the noise of the world?" (ibid., 116). In another poem he remarks that his knowledge of landscape "abated my feeling of isolation" (ibid., 72). But not apparently for the poet: the absolute, symbolized here as the bright moon, is "as small as a poker chip" and moves away.

p. 7, l. 12. *Bright moon shining between pines.* G.W. Robinson's translation of l. 3 of Wang Wei's *In the Hills at Nightfall in Autumn*, in *Poems of Wang Wei*, 75.

Wright is a great admirer of the Wang Wei and the other poets of the T'ang Dynasty. For some of his explicit debts to the Chinese poets, see *Chinoiserie* (CM, 19), *Portrait of the Artist with Li Po* (WTTT, 34), *T'ang Notebook* (WTTT, 102–4), *Language Journal* (WTTT, 216), *China Journal* (WTTT, 227), *After Reading Tu Fu, I Go outside to the Dwarf Orchard* (NB, 12), *Cicada* (NB, 14–15), *Looking Outside the Cabin Window, I Remember a Line by Li Po* (NB, 18), *With Eddie and Nancy in Arezzo at the Caffè Grande* (NB, 51), *Waiting for Tu Fu* (NB, 56), *Poem Half in the Manner of Li Ho* (NB, 88–9), *Disjecta Membra* (NB, 129–41), *Reply to Wang Wei* (NB, 166), *After Reading T'ao Ch'ing, I Wander Untethered Through the Short Grass* (NB, 183), *Landscape as Metaphor, Landscape as Fate and a Happy Life* (NB, 189), *Mildly Depressed, Far from Home, I Go Outside for a While,* (SHS, 22), *Body and Soul II* (SHS, 77–9), *There Is Balm in Gilead* (BY, 4–5), *Portrait of the Artist by Li Shang-Yin* (BY, 6), *Sinology* (BY, 70). See also *Halflife*, 77–8, 132–3, and QN, 128–9.

Easter 1989

Orig. pub. *Antaeus* 64–65 (Spring–Autumn 1990): 141–2.
C, 10–11; NB, 8–9
Pattern: 5 × 6
Time: March 1989
Place: Charlottesville

Here the poet represents Easter as a natural, not a revealed, feature of religion. When the darkness is rolled away, what emerges from the cave is not a resurrected body but the "fluorescent shapes" of the peonies. On three occasions the poet pauses for philosophical or religious meditations. In the first (p. 8, ll. 5 ff.) he observes simply that the *elan vital* that rejuvenates nature is the same power that will "divest and undo us." The second (p. 8, ll. 66 ff.) is a dismissal of belief, which is only a block against the invisible that we use to keep the soul from slipping. Finally, there is the confession, by way of Pseudo-Dionysus, that we really cannot speak of the hidden divinity (p. 9, ll. 3 ff), who, in any event, "asks us for nothing."

The focus of the poem, however, is on the slowly developing evidences of spring, with its cowled crocuses and cauled willows. These are represented not as a hallelujah chorus but as an ominous, disquieting, and vaguely threatening force. The Druidic circles of crocus are "morose," the willows are menacing, the "full moon comes // gunning," the hardwoods gurgle and boil like a witch's caldron, and the peonies are fused, ready to explode. Moreover, belief is like "the jonquil's yellow head," which rather than symbolizing new life simply butts into nothingness. Thus, this Eastertide poem has little to do with Easter, except by way of irony. What astonishes is not an account of the empty tomb but the poet's exceptional descriptive power—his startlingly inventive use of language.

p. 9, l. 7. *Pseudo-Dionysus*. According to Pseudo-Dionysus, the Christian neo-Platonist of the 4th or 5th century C.E., "we cannot be enlightened by the divine rays except they be hidden within the covering of many sacred veils" (*Of the Celestial Hierarchy*, I.2)

Reading Rorty and Paul Celan One Morning in Early June

Orig. pub. as *One Morning in Early June* in *New Yorker* 66, no. 17 (11 June 1990): 46–7.
C, 12–14; NB, 10–11
Pattern: 7–7 × 3 (42 lines)
Time: 3 June 1989
Place: Charlottesville

The two people in the title are an unlikely couple. Rorty, a sometime member of the philosophy department at the University of Virginia, is quoted in the poem. Paul Celan is not, and there are only indirect references to some of his poetic themes, such as silence. But what Celan stands for—the paradoxes of his poetic vision, his elliptical and dislocated syntax, his allusive, polysemous semantics—is present in the poem as an antitype for the philosophical pragmatism of Rorty, two snippets of which are quoted in the section 2.

In Rorty's pragmatism, there is no room for a correspondence theory of truth. Ideas are worthwhile if they are efficacious in helping us to solve some problem, not because they can be linked with some prior notion of what is real or true. Similarly, his theory of language holds that meaning is social product: there is no relation between our sentences and something in the world out there those sentences are intended faithfully to reproduce. The first line of section 2 is drawn from the first sentence of Rorty's *Contingency, Irony, and Solidarity*: "About two hundred years ago, the idea that truth was made rather than found began to take hold of the imagination of Europe" (Cambridge: Cambridge University Press, 1989, p. 3). Rorty goes on to affirm this view of truth—that it is created rather than discovered. The second reference to Rorty's position comes on p. 11, ll. 1–4: "If sentences constitute // everything we believe, / Vocabularies retool / Our ability to measure and get it right, / And languages don't exist." This is the view outlined in Rorty's first chapter, "The Contingency of Language," where he maintains that cultures gradually lose the vocabularies they have inherited and replace them with others, the idiom of Romantic poetry replacing the idiom of eighteenth-century rationalism being one example. In this view, languages do not exist: they are made.

Wright is inclined to reject Rorty's theories of both truth and language. He offers his own theory that language discovers truth, an example of such discovery being these lines: "Something weighs on our shoulders / And settles itself like black light // invisibly in our hair ..." Although Wright has obviously created these lines, they are not from a language he has made. He uses the language ready-at-hand to discover and reveal some mysterious force that settles upon us. In fact, the first and third sections of the poem are extended examples of what the poet can discover by pointing the lens of his poetic camera both at what is directly in front of him and, in a cinematic backward glance, at what it can retrieve from the memory of the mind's eye. In the first stanza, he does not make "the little aura between the slats of the Venetian blinds" or Rebecca Munch across the street reading her newspaper; he discovers these things, just as he discovers that the telephone lines form the lines of a musical staff. He does not create the tips of the pine trees that are like E.T.'s sizzling finger; he discovers this analogy. Similarly with the catalogue of things in the poet's room (section 3), including a photo of *Ca' Paruta*, a villa in the Euganean Hills of Italy, and a photo of the church of San Zeno by Carlo Ponti (d. 1893). These are already before the poet's eye, recovered by consciousness, not created. The poem concludes with another mystery, one emerging through the mist of a sticky June afternoon and discovered through a language that does exist: the alabaster and flaming windows of the cathedral of San Pietro, "plugged in / To what's not there"— which is one view of the truth of Paul Celan's and our own "amazing world ... more secret than ever / And beautiful of access."

p. 10, l. 13. *E.T.'s finger*. The magical lighting up of E.T.'s finger in Steven Spielberg's *E.T. The Extra-Terrestrial*
p. 10, l. 20. *substanceless blue*. Cf. the opening line of Sylvia Plath's *Ariel*: "Stasis in darkness. / Then the substanceless blue."
p. 11, l. 17. *Sette Ponti*. A road which connects Florence to Arezzo, built on the Roman road "Cassia Vetus." Outside of Loro one can take the Via di Sette Ponti to San Guistino and then detour by way of the Via Cassia to reach the village of Gròpina, with its High Romanesque Cathedral of San Pietro, begun in 1097.

After Reading Tu Fu, I Go Outside to the Dwarf Orchard

Orig. pub. *Field* 41 (Fall 1989): 98.
C, 15 ; NB, 12
Pattern: 4 × 3
Time: Summer 1989
Place: Charlottesville backyard

At age fifty-four, the poet wonders what he has to look forward to, realizing that each day he becomes "of less use" to himself and aware that "Tomorrow is dark. // Day-after-tomorrow is darker still." He has repaired to his own yard after reading Tu Fu (712–70), regarded by many as the greatest poet of the T'ang Dynasty. Wright is closer to Tu Fu than to the other T'ang landscape poets in sensibility, technical originality, and emotional range. Both poets are anxious about what the future holds. Although both are highly autobiographical, Wright's poems are more centripetal, focusing on his internal imaginative quest. Tu Fu's poems are often centrifugal, representing life in its historical and public contexts. Wright's poems reflect very little of the political and social events of the time. In the present poem, the debt to Tu Fu can be traced to an image or a line drawn from here and there: e.g., "Flitting, flitting, what am I like / But a sand-snipe in the wide, wide world" (*A Night Abroad*, in *Three Hundred Poems of the T'ang Dynasty*, 310); and "The fears that are borne on a little boat" (*Seeing Li Po in a Dream*, 330). Tu Fu writes, "I watch on the horizon / Day after day, the chaos of the world" (*A View of the Wilderness*, 314). In Wright's most explicit borrowing, this becomes transformed into the injunction to go quietly "Into the world's tumult, into the chaos of every day."

p. 203. Wright's note indicates that the translator of *Three Hundred Poems of the T'ang Dynasty* is anonymous and that the book is undated. But the edition he refers to was translated by Xuzhou Ding (Taipei: Wu Chou Chu Pan Shê, 1973). The poems were compiled by Hengtangtuishi (1711–78). *Three Hundred Poems of the T'ang Dynasty* is a pirated edition of Witter Bynner's *The Jade Mountain*, originally published by Knopf in 1929.

Thinking of David Summers at the Beginning of Winter

Orig. pub. *Kenyon Review* 13 (Winter 1991): 29.
C, 16; NB, 13
Pattern: 4 × 4 (16 lines)
Time: 20 December 1989
Place: Charlottesville

Title: David Summers, professor of art history at the University of Virginia, told Wright the Pliny anecdote in stanza 4. The summer/winter word-play comes, of course, from his convenient surname.

The chill of December has forced the poet to discard his poem "Autumn Thoughts," and he turns his energies to winter thoughts instead. The first two stanzas describe the descending thermometer and its material manifestations both inside and outside the house: the electric heaters, the ice in the downspout, and the "snow stiff as a wedding dress / Carelessly left unkempt // all week in another room." All this iciness leads to a vague sense of angst about the distance from us of the objects we desire and the brevity of our days and nights. And what the poet desires (he projects it upon us as well) is the power of art to recreate an illusion. The reference to Pliny's outline is the key to the idea of reinvention. In Book 35 of his *Natural History* Pliny recounts the story of a Corinthian maid, the daughter of Boutades, a potter from Skyon. She drew the silhouette of her fiancé, who was about to go abroad, from the shadow of his head cast on the wall by a candle. Her father then filled in the outlines with clay and modeled the face in relief so that his daughter would have a souvenir of her beloved to console her in her loneliness. The suggestion seems to be that art can provide, in Matthew Arnold's phrase, a consolation and a stay against the disquiet recorded in stanza 3.

p. 13, l. 13. *Pliny's outline*. See also Wright's note in *NB*, 203.

Cicada

Orig. pub. in *Western Humanities Review* 51, no. 1 (1997): 61.
C, 17–18; NB, 14–15
Pattern: 5–5 × 3 (30 lines)
Time: Early September
Place: Charlottesville

Title: For this poem Wright records his debt to Kenneth Rexroth's translation of *One Hundred Poems from the Chinese* (NB, 203). Although cicadas appear in one of the poems (*The Terrace in the Snow* by Su Tung P'o), the influence is to be traced to the general *penseroso* mood in some of the poems, as in these lines of Tu Fu: "Poetry and letters / Persist in silence and solitude" (*Night in the House by the River*, p. 29); "Everywhere men speak in whispers. / I brood on the uselessness of letters" (*Snow Storm*, p. 6); and "The way back forgotten, hidden / Away, I become like you, / An empty boat, floating, adrift" (*Written on the Wall at Chang's Hermitage*, p. 4).

After an initial stanza in which the poet confesses a restless nervousness, he quotes some snatches from book 10 of St. Augustine's *Confessions*. Then in section 2 we have a response to Augustine's account of how he has sought to overcome the temptations of the eye—temptations because the lavish allurement of the world's beauty takes our attention away from its proper object, which is God Himself. In section 2 the poet does redirect his attention away from the eye and toward the ear. He records the whine of the cicada and the wind's rustling leaves in a stanza that is almost completely devoid of images (we have only the indistinct blackness of the cicada's wings, the dark tree, and the simile of the amber husk). But Augustine's advice to abandon the allurements of the eye does not result in the effect Augustine would wish, the raising of the voice in praise of God. In the "dark tree of the self" the poet discovers only an "emptiness at the heart of being."

Images organize themselves in space; sounds, in time. The poet's reflections on time in section 3, beginning with the metaphor identifying time with water, arrive at another response to Augustine, who in book 11 of the *Confessions* remarks, "Time, therefore, is not the movement of a body" (273).

p. 14. ll. 6–10. *This earthly light ... of the eye.* The quotation is composed of selections from St. Augustine's *Confessions*, bk. 10, chap. 34, pars. 4–6. Wright quotes from R.S. Pine-Coffin's translation (Harmondsworth: Penguin, 1961), 240–1.

Tennessee Line

Orig. pub. *Yale Review* 79 (Winter 1990): 246–7.
C, 19–20; NB, 16–17
Pattern: 2–6 × 3 (36 lines)
Time: 25 August (Wright's birthday, as well as his father's), with flashback to California in 1958
Place: Charlottesville

The first section is almost completely a description of the August afternoon, though it reflects a mood of inertia and listlessness on the part of the poet: the afternoon is overcast, August is "limp as a frayed rope in the trees," sounds drift, the orchard is shadowless, the peach leaves are dull, the wind is absent, the birds have disappeared, the rabbit bounds away, and the truck gears downshift. This sense of absence triggers a memory from thirty-two years earlier, when Wright was studying Italian at the Presidio's Army Language School in Monterey, California. The journal he was keeping at the time was, he says, filled with 114 pages of "inarticulate self-pity" as he tried to discover a distinctive voice for his dark, moral moanings. Back in the present (section 3), the poet's *aporia* has not diminished ("A loneliness west of solitude / Splinters the landscape // uncomforting as Braille"), but he *is* able to offer a poetic credo: the self is identical with the words it continues to rearrange, not in order to offer some grand moral vision but simply to describe and then describe again the small things of the world. This is a version of Montaigne's remark that he was consubstantial with his book. Wright is firmly committed to the post-Romantic conception of the self—the isolated body, "Gathering the past against itself, // making it otherwise."

p. 16, l. 6. *the .22 bullet and Amitone.* The bullet was a kind of parody talisman Wright carried around in his pocket. Amitone is an antacid.
p. 16, l. 19. *memento scrivi.* A written reminder.
p. 16, ll. 13–19. The 114-page journal is not extant. The "Tennessee line" (l. 15) appears to refer to the psychological state of affairs described in this section (the tack taken), but it might mean a half-dozen other things as well: the course the poet's life had taken from the Tennessee years, his ancestry, part of a dialogue, an early form of poetic lineation, a source of information, the position about words referring to things (see *Tattoos*, no. 12), the Tennessee state boundary, and a Tennessee railway.

Looking Outside the Cabin Window, I Remember a Line by Li Po

Orig. pub. *Field* 41 (Fall 1989): 97.
C, 21; NB, 18
Pattern: 4-4-4-4-2 (18 lines)
Time: Summer
Place: Montana

The setting now changes from Charlottesville to the Montana high country, where Wright has for many years spent his summers. Here the poet thinks of a line from Li Po's *Bidding a Friend Farewell at Ching-mên Ferry* (the complete poem is reproduced in the note below). Wright's description is much more elaborate and striking in its imagery than Li Po's. The central mood is expectation: the meadow waits expectantly for "the wind to rise and fill it," and the Milky Way waits for the darkness to reveal its "barge of stars." The anticipation permeating the landscape is transferred to the poet whose desire is to "see beyond seeing." But his desire is not fulfilled: all he can see is "language, that burning field," which is the language of the stars. Expectations aside, the remarkable imagery is worth the price of admission: the river "sliding its cargo of dragon scales / To gutter under the snuff // of marsh willow and tamarack"; "the rain's loose silver"; the "Sunlight [that] reloads and ricochets off the window glass."

p. 18, l.1. *The river winds through the wilderness*. From Li Po's *Bidding a Friend Farewell at Ching-mên Ferry*: "Sailing far off from Ching-mên Ferry, / Soon you will be with people in the south, / Where the mountains end and the plains begin / And the river winds through wilderness.... / The moon is lifted like a mirror, / Sea-clouds gleam like palaces, / And the water has brought you a touch of home / To draw your boat three hundred miles" (*Three Hundred Poems of the T'ang Dynasty*, 108; ellipsis in original translation).

p. 18, l. 15. *River of Heaven*. A conventional metaphor for the Milky Way in both Eastern (Japanese, Chinese, Indian) and Western traditions. One finds the phrase in the translations of some of the T'ang poets—for example, Li Ho, Tu Mu, and Li Po.

p. 18, l. 17. *that burning field*. Cf. the "conjectural *Ursprache*" spoken by the inhabitants of Borges's imaginary Tlön, whose language has no nouns and who see a cloud of smoke and a "burning field" as an "example of association of ideas" (Jorge Luis Borges, Tlön, Uqbar, Orbis Tertius, in *Labyrinths* [New York: New Directions, 1964], 9).

Mid-winter Snowfall in the Piazza Dante

Orig. pub. *Poetry* 155 (January 1990): 253.
C, 25–6; NB, 19–20
Pattern: 3 × 11 (33 lines)
Time: January 1959
Place: Verona

In this flashback to Verona, the twenty-three-year-old poet recounts an episode from his age of innocence. The scene is an opulent *caffè* where four games of chess are in progress and a wedding celebration under way. The poet, "Caught in the glow of all things golden" and ready to begin his life, remarks on the immensity of both his ignorance (he has just arrived in Verona) and his happiness. He wanders through the *caffè* with his brandy and double espresso, seduced by and seducing the golden glow, the mirrors, and plush comfort, all the while aware of a contrasting world outside—the snowstorm that is progressively covering the statue of Dante in the piazza beyond the *caffè* windows.

Stanza 9 (p. 20, l. 7 ff.) cuts to the present, the poet proposing to tell us what he had learned in the meantime. But in his typical riddling way he declares that what he has learned in incommunicable, revealing only that the learning took place in the dark. He then adds, "If there is one secret to this life, it is this life. / This life and its hand-me-downs, // bishop to pawn 4, void's gambit." The secret of life, then, is life itself and what we inherit from the past. The bishop-to-pawn gambit is not a report on a chess move that the poet recalls seeing in the *caffè* thirty years earlier, but the initial move taken by the feeling of emptiness in order to gain a more favorable position with respect to the darkness. Still, "hand-me-downs" (a pun) and "void" in the context of a chess game remind us of other literary works—*Alice in Wonderland*, *The Waste Land*, *Gargantua and Pantagruel*, and *The Tempest*—where the chess is connected with narratives of descent into the underworld. *Chickamauga*, we recall, is Wright's *nekyia*, the greatest example of which is by the poet who gave his name to the piazza outside the Verona *caffè*.

p. 19, l. 3. *Dante's bronze body*. Cesare Zocchi's famous statue of Dante was erected by the city of Verona in 1896 during Austrian rule.
p. 20, l. 3. *Tutti maschi*. All males.

Sprung Narratives

Orig. pub. *Southern Review* 27 (Winter 1991): 70–8.
C, 27–35; NB, 21–9
Pattern: 5 × 5, 4 × 2, 4 × 6, 4 × 2, 5 × 5, 4 × 2, 4 × 6, 4 × 2, 5 × 5 (155 lines)
Time: March
Place: Charlottesville backyard, with flashbacks to Kingsport, Tennessee, Italy, and California.

"Sprung Narratives" winks at Hopkins's notion of "sprung rhythm," a line in which an initial stressed syllable is followed by a variable number of unstressed syllables. Hopkins claimed to have discovered this rhythm in folk songs, Welsh verse, Shakespeare, Milton, and elsewhere. As Wright is committed to the syllabic count of a line rather than to the stresses of its metrical feet, the term does not strictly apply to his poems. Still, according to Hopkins, sprung rhythm is designed to imitate the rhythms of natural speech, of which Wright's poetry has a generous serving. "Midnight, cloud-scatter and cloud-vanish, // sky black-chill and black-clear" (p. 22, l. 11) is not natural speech. "What were we thinking of" and "I guess so"—in the opening and closing lines of *Sprung Narratives*—is, conforming quite obviously to the normal patterns of ordinary conversation. Another half-serious suggestion in the title is that the opening and closing sections from the poet's childhood have been sprung apart to insert the narratives that come between.

The structure of the first eight sections of the poem is a kind of thematic counterpoint in which a scene remembered from the poet's past is followed by a reflection, set in the present, about his pilgrimage. The final section combines the two.

Section 1. Kingsport, Tennessee (1945), an episode recalled from the poet's youth. Wright and his brother Winter, aged ten and eight, had missed their school bus, began walking home through the snow without any sense of direction, and eventually ended up five miles from home. How they were rescued by their parents, "abstract with dread," is not recorded, but the poet does see the episode as part of the approach to adolescence, which "loomed/ At walk's end, eager to gather us." The two boys, however, were far from eager themselves to begin a new dance that would carry them away from childhood, believing they had a no-cut contract with the landscape of their youth. (The dance metaphor appears three times in the poem.) Revisiting childhood through memory, however, makes the poet realize that it is impossible to reach the world of innocence, except through the external details of the short story he has written.

Section 2. In this interlude the poet, now in his Charlottesville back yard, urges himself to "Sit still and lengthen your lines, / Shorten your poems and listen to what the darkness says." The dark landscape, then described, reveals to him that he should seize the night, so to speak, for who knows what the immediate or foreseeable future holds?

Section 3. Rome (1963). The poet recalls seeing a movie, during his first year as a Fulbright student, at the Teatro Farnese in Rome, neither the dialogue nor the plot of which he could understand. What he does remember is the lively reaction of the rowdy Roman spectators. The entire episode becomes a parable of our general inability to understand the language of the world: "Speaking in ignorance / And joy," says the poet, drawing on certain ideas of George Steiner, "we answer / What wasn't asked, by someone we don't know, in strange tongues."

Section 4. The consciousness of death in this interlude raises this question: "Will I have become / The landscape I've looked at and walked through / Or the road that took me there // or the time to arrive?" Neither this question nor the one that follows is answered, because they cannot be, though the poet does believe that the identity of the landscape and the journey is a "lovely" idea. In such a radical metaphor (landscape = journey) we have the identification of the two fundamental building blocks of literature, which in turn are rooted in those basic categories of all discourse, space and time: the image or spatial projection of what the eye sees in the landscape and the temporal movement of the pilgrim's journey.

Section 5. Laguna Beach (1966 et seq.). This flashback centers on the poet's seventeen-year sojourn in Laguna Beach, California, where the self-satisfied landscape never changed and seemed to affect the people observed by the poet in the same way, "ghost figures" who appear "Always the same shades // turning their flat, cocoa-buttered faces, unchangeable bodies impatient, unfulfilled." All this has a dulling effect on the poet as well, who stares at a sea that stares back at him and who confesses poignantly, "I never knew anyone." This turns out to be a rather sad chapter in the history of the poet, whose mature efforts to "make it new" depend so deeply on the changing of the seasons. The structure of this section (five five-line stanzas), which repeats the structure of the opening and closing sections, serves as a double mirror, reflecting backward and forward the same lineation (8–25–8–25) and the same stanzaic pattern.

Section 6. Perhaps the sense of absence that pervades section 5 elicits the changed perspective in this interlude, which is that under the "dark prerogatives" of the present text lies a vision of youthful innocence, a dream-like vision in which light poetic lines lie just beneath the dark surface, waiting to burst forth. These lines are identified with a youthful body, whose limbs and eyelids gleam and whose movements ("little dances and paroxysm") stir with energetic abandon.

Section 7. The beach at Ostia, the harbor city of ancient Rome, and two months later Rome itself (September 1963). Here the poet recalls an outing to the beach with a group of student priests and two golden-haired sisters, Maria Luisa and Astrid, whose father had arranged and paid for the trip. They can hardly understand the poet's English. One of the priests-to-be, Esposito, an American who had begun his study for holy orders, is reenacting scenes from his time as an actor, singer, and dancer—pirouetting and singing along the beach. The scene begins with Esposito's dancing, which may have been triggered, in the poet's subconscious at least, with the dances of the youthful body at the end of the previous section. In any event, the poet casts a warm eye on the two girls, whose charms, they think, will extend far beyond their youth. The only dark intrusion into the glow of this carefree excursion is the revelation that in two months the poet will learn from Jerry Jacobsen, a Fulbright friend, that John F. Kennedy had been killed.

Section 8. This interlude centers on the mystery that surrounds us—something that we hear and taste and that "takes our breath away" but that cannot otherwise be exemplified.

Section 9. The antecedent of "it" in the first line appears to be the mysterious "something" of the previous stanza, but whatever "it" refers to is quickly lost in the simile of the imagined photograph of a friend's house or of the poet's own house. The simile is extended for the rest of the section, but our sense of the simile begins to wane as the poet recreates in some detail an imagined visit to his childhood home and town, cataloguing the differences between then and now: by the second stanza the visit and the recollection seem to us literal rather than figurative. The last two stanzas are the poet's interpretation of his reverie: "Seeing the past so // diminishes it and us too," so that both disappear "into the back hole of history." But not quite: what saves "it" is memory, which, even though like a retreating dot of light, nevertheless affirms that the poet is the one obliged to serve memory's function. In stanza 1 of this section the poet's house is said to be "seen from next door / Through the bathroom window, // a curtain pushed to one side." In the poem's clever (Wordsworthian) conclusion, we learn that we are the agents of the retreating dot of light, for it is we, having long forgotten the initial simile, who are "half hidden behind a bathroom window curtain." Section 9, then, recapitulates the structure of the entire poem, a dialectic between recalled events and internal self-reflection, both of which are aspects of the terra cognita, the title of part 2 of Chickamauga.

p. 21, l. 6. *Armour Drug ... Brooks Circle.* Places in Kingsport, Tennessee.

p. 22, ll. 15 ff. In the movie briefly described—Monicelli's *La Grande Guerra* (*The Great War*)—a pardoned criminal (Vittorio Gassman) becomes a reluctant inductee in the Italian army in World War I and joins another soldier in dodging the battlefront. The two comical cowards are so afraid of committing treason that they become heroes. This wartime comedy, co-starring Alberto Sordi and Silvana Mangano, was nominated for the best foreign film in 1959.

p. 23, ll. 5–9. *romanacci* = crude or rowdy Romans. *stronzo* = turd. *Fijo de na mignota* = son of a bitch. *Semmo l'anima de li mortacci tui* = may your dead [ancestors] go to hell.

p. 23, ll. 13–16. *The world is a language ... in strange tongues.* The idea here is expressed in a number of different formulations by George Steiner in *Real Presences* (Chicago: University of Chicago Press, 1989), especially chap. 2, pt. 4. For example: "A sentence always means more.... No enumeration, no analytic ordering of the units of a sentence yields a corresponding sum of sense.... There is always, as Blake taught, 'excess' of the signified beyond the signifier.... [T]he motif of semantic inadequacy is an ancient one. However artful, however inspired, the words of the poet, of the philosopher will fall short of the numinous intensities of certain phenomena and states of felt being. The aura of certain settings in nature, of certain privacies of desire or of pain resists communicative transfer into speech.... Not even the purest tautologist (a lexicographer *in extremis*) has ever held the total sum of essence to be convertible into the currency of the word and the sentence" (82, 91–2). Wright cites Steiner's *Real Presences* (in a note on p. 203)—a book that argues for a transcendent presence as a necessary foundation of all art and human dialogue. Hints of Steiner's thesis are also found on p. 25, ll. 16 ff.

p. 23, l. 18. *Belli and Dante.* The Piazza Belli, named for Giuseppe Gioacchino Belli (1791–1864), is across the Tiber by way of the Via Arenula. Here a monument to Belli sits in front of Dante's house.

p. 23, l. 20. *A li mortacci tui, brutto zozzo, v'a fa'un culo* = To your dead, ugly old scum bag, fuck off. *Zozzo* (dirty old bag of junk) is a rather strange term of affection among Romans.

p. 26, ll. 5 ff. This scene, in which the frolicking Esposito separates himself from the other priests-to-be, likened by Wright to "a fabulous bird," is reminiscent of Stephen Dedalus's separating himself from the Christian brothers in part 4 of *A Portrait of the Artist as a Young Man*, shortly before Joyce likens him to the "fabulous artificer."

p. 26, l. 17. *birreria on Via della Croce.* Maria Luisa and Astrid's father's brewery, located on a street below the Spanish Steps in Rome.

p. 27, l. 9. *Something surrounds us we can't exemplify.* This is another idea that runs throughout Steiner's *Real Presences*.

Lines on Seeing a Photograph for the First Time in Thirty Years

Orig. pub. *Field* 41 (Fall 1989): 95–6.
C, 36–7
Pattern: 6 × 5
Time: 1959
Place: San Vigilio, as described in the poem

This poem, excluded from *Negative Blue*, is another of the flashback-memory poems, prompted in this case by a thirty-year-old picture of the poet and his friend Ingrid at the Punta San Vigilio, a promontory on the eastern side of Lake Garda, almost directly across from the town of Salò on the western shore of the lake. As the poet says, Punta San Vigilio "crooks like a little finger into the lake / Just above [the town of] Garda." Wright, newly arrived in Verona, and Ingrid, standing on the stone steps, are framed by an archway, and the waves of the lake can be seen lapping in the background. The poet has already decided upon his "motif"—"Landscape and memory"—but the photo reveals no signs that a transfiguration, looming in the background behind the unnamed photographer, is about to occur. The poem concludes with a reflection on memories: they "circle the landscape ... their centers cut loose and disappearing, / Tiny cracks in the mind's sky, / Sheenlines, afterglint." These small points of illumination "are the lights we look for."

C, p. 36, l. 13. *Ingrid.* A girl-friend who also makes an appearance with Wright in Milan in *Bar Giamaica, 1959-60*, (*WTTT*, 39, l. 5). She reappears, this time in Rome, in *Scar Tissue II* (ST, 42, l. 16).

Broken English

Orig. pub. as *Sunday at Home at the Beginning of April* in *Amicus Journal* 11, no. 4 (Fall 1989): 23.
C, 41; NB, 30
Pattern: 3-5-3
Time: Spring
Place: Charlottesville

After the brief descriptive opening, we have a series of discontinuous aphorisms, all of which have a linguistic subject matter: speech, part of speech, semantics, and syntax. Some are koan-like. Even the ones that might seem more or less straightforward, such as the first, take us aback. "What matters we only tell ourselves" appears at first glance to require that the poet quit writing, or at least to cease having his poems published. "Every poet's secret desire," he says in his commonplace notebook, "is to be Rimbaud" (*Halflife*, 23). But the point is that for Wright the poetic process is a conversation with himself about the things that matter most. This aphorism could stand as a headnote to the one about privacy: "All speech pulls toward privacy // and the zones of the infinite." But of course all speech clearly does not pull toward anything. The significance of the aphorism is that Wright's poetic speech tends toward the personal, sometimes clandestine, interior life, and to say that it pulls in that direction, rather than pushes, is a spatial conundrum, until we realize that, at least here, the "zones of the infinite" are interior. Such a view underwrites a radically immanent poetic—a self-conscious poetic of a Romantic persona little interested in making connections with other selves. As Wright says in "Bytes and Pieces," "I write from the point of view of a monk in his cell. Sometimes I look at the stones, sometimes I look out the window" (*QN*, 80).

The concluding tercet is something of a riddle. To say that "Truth's an indefinite article" suggests that there is no one absolute truth. There may be *a* truth here and there but no definitive truth (*the* truth). The last line—"One *the* in a world of *a*"—refers, then, not to truth but to the statement by Anna Akhmatova, who wrote, "That day in Moscow, it will all come true, / when, for the last time, I take my leave." The suggestion is that she has bowed out on many occasions before and that her present leave-taking will be the final one. Wright's twist on this is that any life is always the final life: the first and the last are the same. To this he adds that the poet's own self is the definite one in a world of other indefinite and indistinct selves.

p. 30, l. 3. *my long poem*. A purely imaginary poem.
p. 30, l. 8. *Without syntax there is no immortality*. Cf. Nietzsche's remark, "I fear we shall never be rid of God, so long as we still believe in grammar" (*The Twilight of the Idols*, trans. Anthony M. Ludovici [New York: Russell and Russell, 1964], 22).
p. 30, l. 9. *Akhmatova*. The line comes from Anna Akhmatova's *You will hear the thunder and remember me*, in *You Will Hear the Thunder: Poems*, trans. D.M. Thomas (Athens: Ohio University Press, 1985), 86 [ll. 5–6].
p. 30, l. 11. *One the ... of a*. Cf. the line of Wright's mentor, Donald Justice: "The *the* has become an *a*" (*Homage to the Memory of Wallace Stevens*, in *Collected Poems* [New York: Knopf, 2004], 163).

Maple on the Hill

Orig. pub. *Grand Street* 10, no. 2 (1991): 113–4.
C, 42–3; NB, 31–2
Pattern: 4 × 5
Time: October
Place: Charlottesville

The first and last sections of this lyric set up a contrast between two kinds of progression—the cyclical movement of nature and the linear movement of history. They are connected by a stanza from the Carter Family's *Maple on the Hill*. The thematic link among the three parts is death. In section 1 we begin to see the descent of the natural cycle in the description of the October leaves: the pheasant-tail colors of the maple leaves begin to appear, some leaves have already fallen "to cuckold the grass," and the "day saws itself in half." In the bluegrass tune of section 2, the singer recalls an earlier starry night when he and his "little darling" loved each other beneath the maple on the hill. Now that they are growing old and feeble, the singer appeals to his darling not to forget him when he is dead. In section 3 the poet observes that history, in never repeating itself, devours us, no matter what masks we wear, adding that in the City of the Dead no one has an identity. In the final couplet, the dog of history, a kind of hound of heaven, is, unlike the flow of history, discontinuous and discrete.

p. 31, ll. 9–12. *Don't forget me ... on my grave*. These lines are the fourth stanza of a bluegrass tune, *Maple on the Hill*, made popular by the Carter Family, the Stanley Brothers, and others.

p. 31, ll. 15–16. *Plutarch*. The point is implicit in a number of Plutarch's parallel lives. About Callicratidas, Plutarch says specifically: "as general, he united in his life the lives of all, and could hardly be called one" (from par. 1 of "Pelopidas," *Lives*, trans. A.H. Clough).

p. 32, l. 2. *City of the Dead*. Satan's city in the *Inferno*—the city of Dis.

p. 32, l. 2. *Here I am ... boy*. A variation perhaps on Barry Manilow's "I'm what you've waited for / here I am / I'm your man" (*I'm Your Man*), or Paul Westerway's "here I am / I'm your spark" (*Runaway Wind*).

*Black and Blue

Orig. pub. *Poetry* 157 (January 1991): 219.
C, 44-6
Pattern: 3 × 11
Time: Summer
Place: Montana cabin

These tercets are mostly short takes on some feature of the landscape. They are like the shorter works of the T'ang poets in their concision. Occasionally there is a commentary or judgment: "Unseen ... something is always there"; "Our lives are an emptiness." Two of the vignettes spring from actual photographs. The first (section 6) is a photo of the poet in his Levis assuming his Montgomery Clift pose; the second (section 10) is a picture of Wright and his brother on a fishing trip with their father. But there is little to hold the eleven discrete sketches together, which is perhaps why Wright excluded these bits of "broken English" from *Negative Blue*.

p. 44, l. 8. *Basin Creek*. The creek runs through the Wrights' property in Lincoln County, Montana.

Chickamauga

Orig. pub. *Poetry* 157 (January 1991): 219.
C, 47; NB, 33
Pattern: 3 × 5
Time: End of summer
Place: Charlottesville

Chickamauga. A town in the north Georgia hills near Chattanooga, Tennessee. Chickamauga Creek was the site of the famous Civil War battle fought on 19–20 September 1863.

Wright has said that "the poem 'Chickamauga' shows a pretty abstract idea of history. I took it as the title of the book because that's where my great-grandfather was wounded out of the Civil War and I wanted to have some connection, some familial connection with that particular volume, since I had the Dante trilogy in mind" (Turner). The abstract idea of history appears in sections 2 and 4 of this cryptic poem. Sections 3 and 5 have to do with the idea of poetry.

The idea of poetry: "The poem is a code with no message," the poet announces, which is a version of MacLeish's modernist view that "a poem should not mean but be." "Code" here refers to the signals used to transmit something secret. As Wright says in an interview, "as any old intelligence agent will tell you, nothing matters but the codes. Cryptography is all. You get the right code, you discover the secret" (QN, 167). The code is what lies behind the surface mask, which is "incommunicado, // unhoused and peregrine." The secret, we learn in section 5, is that the code refers to a poetic belief. "Structure becomes an element of belief, syntax / And grammar a catechist, / Their words, what the beads say, // words thumbed to our discontent." That is, the old systems of belief have been displaced by a new creed of language: words are our prayer beads, and even though our thumbing them may lead to discontent (poets are never satisfied with what they produce), our catechism contains only syntactic structures. We believe, then, not in the message of the poem but in its linguistic structure. "Without syntax," Wright said in *Broken English*, "there is no immortality" (p. 41, l. 8)

The idea of history. In section 2 we are told that "History handles our past like spoiled fruit," meaning apparently that it dismisses our blemished and insignificant stories. We may be rather self-contented about our lives (section 4), but history will soon enough pluck us out with its fish net into the "suffocating light and air." This is, as Wright says, a "pretty abstract idea of history," and its relation to the Battle of Chickamauga is tenuous at best.

When published in *Chickamauga*, the previous four poems formed a separate section entitled "Broken English," a phrase that suggests Wright's broken, dropped-down lines. But it has thematic implications as well: the discontinuous koans of *Broken English*, the rupture that comes with the ellipsis in *Maple on the Hill*, the separated sketches of *Black and Blue*, and the solving of a linguistic code in *Chickamauga*.

Still Life on a Matchbox Lid

Orig. pub. *New Yorker* 67, no. 10 (29 April 1991): 64.
C, 51; *NB*, 34
Pattern: 3 × 2

This is an abstract verbal painting in miniature. It thus throws the burden of response on the eye of the reader. The still life has no representational details, but at a middle distance the viewer can distinguish two archetypal shapes, both having to do with the journey. The first is anabatic: the gods know there is no shortcut to the other world. The second is linear: "If you want great tranquility," you must undertake the long walk into the future, focusing the priority of the word itself and on minute particulars, like the wind-splitting dog hair, and without brooding on the past.

p. 34, l. 2. *watchers, the holy ones.* According to Wright, this was not intended to be a reference to the divine beings in "The Book of the Watchers," chaps. 1–36 of the Book of Enoch. But the parallel may be instructive nevertheless. In his narrative Enoch reports that some angels have run away from a society called the Holy Watchers. After they are discovered, they send Enoch to carry a request for pardon to the Watchers. The Watchers, then, are a type of the fallen angels in Genesis 6.

Blaise Pascal Lip-Syncs the Void

Orig. pub. *Field* 45 (Fall 1991): 62.
C, 52; *NB*, 35

Pattern: 5 × 3
Time: December
Place: Locust Avenue, Charlottesville

Title: In an interview Wright explains that he was reading Pascal at the time that the music group Milli Vanilli was in the news (*QN*, 125–6). The group had received "Best New Artist" award in 1990, but the prize was revoked because the group's members, Rob Pilatus and Fab Morvan, had not performed any of the songs on the album: they had lip-synced vocals actually sung by Charles Shaw, John Davis, and Brad Howe. In the mid-seventeenth century Blaise Pascal wrote three treatises on the void. And in his *Pensées* he asked, "What is more absurd than to say that lifeless bodies have passions, fears, hatreds,—that insensible bodies, lifeless and incapable of life, have passions which presuppose at least a sensitive soul to feel them, nay more, that the object of their dread is the void? What is there in the void that could make them afraid? Nothing is more shallow and ridiculous. This is not all; it is said that they have in themselves a source of movement to shun the void" (no. 74). On the other hand, Pascal reveals the terror arising from the contemplation of infinite space: "*Le silence éternel de ces espaces infini m'effraie*" (The eternal silence of these infinite spaces frightens me) (*Pensées*, no. 206).

This is a paean celebrating things that are not final, unwinnowed, inconstant, and incomplete. We are caught between the reality and the shadow, between the song sung and the song lip-synched, uncertain about which is which. Thus the poet's appeal for an openness to a nature in which there is continual metamorphosis. We need not lip-sync the void, like Pascal, but rather open our hearts to the relativity of a changing world, accepting its richness, like that described in the last stanza. Or as Wright put it in his commonplace book, "We lip away at the void, like the tide, gaining an inch this year, an inch next year" (*Halflife*, 28).

p. 35, l. 6. *There's change ... Pascal contends.* "All changes with time." "Change is necessary to make the form of the one become the form of the other" (*Pensées*, 294, 512). On succession, see *Pensées*, 651, 710, 737, and Pascal's *Preface to the Treatise on Vacuum*.

p. 35, l. 8. "That nature is corrupt. Proved by nature itself" (*Pensées*, 60). The corruption of both nature and human nature is a refrain sounded throughout the *Pensées*.

Winter-Worship

Orig. pub. *Field* 45 (Fall 1991): 62.
C, 53; NB, 36
Pattern: 4 × 4
Time: January
Place: Charlottesville

This supplication to the Mother of Darkness is for her to rescue us from the dark absence we have lived in too long. In the depths of the dark winter season, there *is* splendor: witness the snowflake. While the journey can be demonic, especially as it passes through the dismal January weather, the poet prays to the goddess of darkness to "darken our disbelief" and show us the radiance that arises from the fires of hell. The prayer is for her to "Inset our eyesight" and thus "End us our outstay." (In Wright's creative syntax, the noun "inset" becomes a verb, and the verb "outstay" becomes a noun.)

l. 13. *A journey's a fragment of Hell.* An ancient Islamic proverb, quoted in Bruce Chatwin's semi-fictional meditation on Aboriginal culture, *Songlines*, where the narrator, who has quit his job with an art auction firm and taken a trip to Africa, remarks, "One night, caught in a sandstorm in the Western Sahara, I understood Muhammed's dictum, 'A journey is a fragment of Hell'" (New York: Viking, 1987), 19. Chatwin's book is cited in Wright's note (*NB*, 203).

The Silent Generation

Orig. pub. *New Yorker* 67, no. 4 (18 March 1991): 40.
C, 54; NB, 37
Pattern: 4 × 3
Time: January
Place: Charlottesville backyard

The "silent generation" refers to those born between approximately 1925 and 1942. In addition to being silent, they have often been characterized as withdrawn, indifferent, and uncreative. The phrase was coined in a 1951 cover story of *Time* magazine to refer to the generation coming of age at the time—the postwar generation, which was of course Wright's own. For the poet, what the silent generation "never had to say" is difficult to remember a half-century later, but it had something to do with social justice. The silent generation, says the poet, was afraid to confront the question, while remaining confident it would escape any world-wide catastrophes. The silence is regrettable, and the poet admits that there was some good in whatever the causes were, but it won't much matter: when the members of the silent generation die, there will be little evidence that they had lived.

For *Silent Generation II* and *Silent Generation III*, see ST, 6 and 66–7.

p. 37, l. 10. *give the devil his due*. Cervantes, *Don Quixote*, pt. 1, bk. 3, chap 3. Cf. the French and Italian proverbs: The French say, "Il ne faut pas faire le diable plus noir qu'il n'est"; and the Italians, "Non bisognà fare il diablo piu nero che non è"—"The devil is not so black as he is painted."
p. 37, l. 11. *We walk ... in the earth*. "And the Lord said unto Satan, Whence comest thou? Then Satan answered the Lord, and said, From going to and fro in the earth, and from walking up and down in it" (Job 1:7 and 2:2).

An Ordinary Afternoon in Charlottesville

Orig. pub. *New Yorker* 67, no. 42 (9 December 1991): 68.
C, 55; NB, 38
Pattern: 5 × 3
Time: Apparently spring
Place: Charlottesville backyard

The title casts a glance at Wallace Stevens' *An Ordinary Evening in New Haven*. Stevens wrote an extraordinary long poem about his ordinary evening; Wright, an extraordinary short one about his ordinary afternoon.

The poet reads the ideograms in the book of nature, cast on the backyard grass by the sun. The message is "*Purgatorio, illuminatio, contemplatio*," which is the three-part process, according to St. John of the Cross, by which one enters the fire of contemplation. First, the divine purgation does its work, cleansing the soul, which is then "brought to light and seen clearly through the illumination of this dark light of divine contemplation." But for the poet, while the light cast on the Charlottesville back yard is "endurable," the divine light is not: we are, alas, "foundered and fallowed" by its sight. The "loving fire" is not just purgatorial; it is sacrificial as well—an immolation. Although the landscape is indifferent to sacrifice, the sun's sprinkling of its "holy grit" across the lawn (*immolare* meant originally "to sprinkle with sacrificial meal") triggers the poet's awareness that "everything starts in fire." "Or so they say," "they" being St. John of the Cross and other mystics, such as Jacob Boehme, with his first principles of fire and light. We would like to believe in this fire of illumination, says the poet, especially as each year we feel more and more the coldness of death inching its way into our bloodstream. The birds, like the afternoon itself, are oblivious to all this, but perhaps their "wise chant, *hold still, hold still*" is the best advice: wait patiently for the "*Purgatorio, illuminatio, contemplatio,*" which is one of the "longed-for lands" about which Stevens speaks in An Ordinary Evening in New Haven (*Collected Poems* [New York: Knopf, 1967], 486).

p. 38, l, 3. *Purgatorio, illuminatio, contemplatio*. This three-part process is found in St. John of the Cross, among others. "Similarly, we should philosophize about this divine, loving fire of contemplation. Before transforming the soul, it purges it of all contrary qualities.... This divine purge stirs up all the foul and vicious humors of which the soul was never before aware.... And now that they may be expelled and annihilated they are brought to light and seen clearly through the illumination of this dark light of divine contemplation" (*The Dark Night*, in *The Collected Works of St. John of the Cross*, trans. Kieran Kavanaugh, OCD, and Otilio Rodriguez, OCD, rev. ed. [Washington, DC: ICS Publications, 1991], bk. 2, chap. 10, par. 2. See also bk. 2, chap. 12, pars. 1–4).

*Tom Strand and the Angel of Death

Orig. pub. *Wallace Stevens Journal* 17, no. 1 (Spring 1993): 64.
C, 56
Pattern: 5 × 3
Time: August
Place: Montana cabin

The first stanza records an episode that apparently occurred some time before—Mark Strand's answer to his son's question about the Angel of Death. Wright's own reaction at the time—that the Angel of Death was swirling on a stem—returns to him during a Montana summer: "I remember her skirt and stem/ In the black meadow grass." Regarding the Angel, the poet professes that he is "Bone of her bone and flesh of her flesh," at which point he turns to remark that the indecipherable code of the vanishing stars reveals nothing about "this life that is handed us." This is a poem that, in Wallace Stevens's words, "must resist the intelligence, almost successfully" (*Man Carrying Things*, in *Collected Poems*, 350).

C, p. 56, l. 1. *my friend's son*. Thomas Summerfield Strand, son of the poet Mark Strand.

Mondo Angelico

Orig. pub. in *Iron Mountain Review* 7 (Spring 1992): 4.
C, 57; NB, 39
Pattern: 4 × 3

Title: *mondo angelico* = angelic world. By an accident of language *mondo* is also the short, pithy dialogue between Zen masters and their disciples in which one might find a response such as "their shadows shadows of shadows." The title of this and the following poem are variations on the famous Italian documentary *Mondo Cane* ("*Dog's World*"), a 1962 film about the barbarism of a world gone insane.

The poem is an extended metaphor that identifies fish with angels: they are always just out of sight and touch ("their shadows shadows of shadows"); their home is the underworld of the Montana landscape; half dark and half light, they signal to us and then disappear; drifting "in the deep ether of their rectitude," they are on the threshold of offering us some response, but then, alas, they disappear, insensitively ignoring us.

Mondo Henbane

Orig. pub. in *Iron Mountain Review* 7 (Spring 1992): 5.
C, 58; NB, 40
Pattern: 4 × 3

Time: Spring
Place: Charlottesville, apparently
Title: *henbane* = a plant belonging to the same order as the potato, tomato, and belladonna; its medicinal uses date from antiquity.

In William Blake's *The Marriage of Heaven and Hell* an Angel shows the speaker, a foolish young man, his eternal lot. They descend into a cavern until they reach a boundless void. Sitting on "the twisted root of an oak," they beheld, the speaker reports, "the infinite Abyss, fiery as the smoke of a burning city; beneath us at an immense distance, was the sun, black but shining; round it were fiery tracks on which revolv'd vast spiders, crawling after their prey; which flew, or rather swum, in the infinite deep, in the most terrific shapes of animals sprung from corruption; & the air was full of them, & seem'd composed of them: these are Devils, and are called Powers of the air. I now asked my companion which was my eternal lot? he said, between the black & white spiders." The speaker goes on to record a hellish vision of a terrifying serpent: "we saw his mouth & red gills hang just above the raging foam tinging the black deep with beams of blood, advancing toward us with all the fury of a spiritual existence" (A Memorable Fancy (no. 4), *The Complete Poetry and Prose of William Blake*, ed. David Erdman, rev. ed [Berkeley: University of California Press, 1982], 41).

This, says the poet, is where the journey ends, but for now the pain of the demonic vision fails to actualize, just as it failed to do so in Blake's *Memorable Fancy*, where the traditional Christian view of punishment by fire is turned upside down: the speaker soon discovers himself "on a pleasant bank beside a river by moon light hearing a harper who sung to the harp." The Angel's metaphysics is all wrong, Blake's speaker reports: the hell-vision of punishment was only an illusion, conjured by the angel. Similarly, in Wright's poem, a lovely Edenic vision comes into view—the "green-backed tree swallows," the "Load-heavy bumblebees," and, finally, the robin listening to the spiders fly away. Wright may not be as convinced as Blake was about the victory of innocence: *Chickamauga*, after all, is his *Inferno*. But at least "for now" the paradisal garden displaces the orthodox illusion of the terror of fire and brimstone: from the garden comes a henbane for pain, as it were.

Miles Davis and Elizabeth Bishop Fake the Break

Orig. pub. *Poetry* 160 (September 1992): 311.
C, 59; NB, 41
Pattern: 3-3-2-5-3
Time: 29 September 1991
Place: Charlottesville backyard

"Break" in the title refers to change in musical phrases by the adding of embellishments (a shout, repeated words or sounds) to emphasize a musical passage. Just as musicians fake the breaking of traditional phrases, so poets subvert literary conventions by improvising.

The poem opens with a reflection on the difficulty of beginning. The imperative "begin" does not help in the face of silence, which one cannot simply set aside in order to get the poem under way. But by stanza 3, with its description of the neighbor's pears, the poet has discovered how to begin. The last half of the poem turns into an *ars poetica*. First, we have the affirmation of Elizabeth Bishop's statement that poetry is "just description." But of course neither Bishop's or Wright's poems are ever "just description." Then in the last stanza, we return to "the top"—the first line with its emphatic "*begin*," about which the poet now has something to say: he begins in ignorance, and he remains there, for the end of poetry is not to deliver knowledge, but to "stick to the melody" that arises from description. How to wring music from the earthly paradise, Wright says in an interview "has always been the only true question" (QN, 120). The poet does not have to worry, then, about where to begin: he need only trust his eye (for the description) and his ear (for the melody).

p. 41, l. 9. *It's just description.* Richard Wilbur reports that Bishop "once said to me rather sadly about her own work: 'It's all description, no philosophy.'" ("A Conversation with Richard Wilbur," *Image: A Journal of the Arts and Religion* 12 [Winter 1995]: 55–68).

p. 41, l. 14. *we stick to the melody.* That is, we don't follow the practice of jazz musicians who advise not to play the melody but to play around it. Miles Davis advised his musicians, "Don't play what's there. Play what's not there."

Peccatology

Orig. pub. *Poetry* 160 (September 1992): 311.
C, 61; NB, 42
Pattern: 2-5-2
Time: Indian summer
Place: Charlottesville backyard

The structure of this little "study of sin" is similar to that of *Mondo Henbane*. In that poem the sensory wonders afforded by nature erase the vision of hell set forth by the Angel in Blake's satire. Here nature performs the same function, supplanting Kafka's sensory notion of sin. The senses have another role for the poet: the hedge ivy and locust pods of Indian summer absolve the idea of sin, not entirely dispelling it, but making it into a small thing.

p. 42, ll. 1–2. "Sin always comes openly, and can at once be grasped at once by the senses. It comes root and all, and does not have to be torn up" (Franz Kafka, "Reflections on Sin, Pain, Hope, and the True Way," no. 7, in *The Great Wall of China: Stories and Reflections* [New York: Schocken Books, 1948], 304).

East of the Blue Ridge, Our Tombs Are in the Dove's Throat

Orig. pub. *Southwest Review* 77 (Spring–Summer 1992): 231.
C, 61; NB, 43
Pattern: 5-3-3-5
Time: A Sunday in winter 1991
Place: Charlottesville backyard

If we are waiting for a sign of salvation, according to Lorca, we wait in vain. Still, as the poet says, "We'd like to fly away ourselves ... into or out of the sky's mouth" and disappear "into a windfall of light." But the problem is that "down here" in our earthly existence, we have no access to the divine calculus where everything adds up. Down here two plus two never makes two plus two: all we have is the world of the ten thousand things, as in stanzas 2 and 4. We therefore experience only the "earthly splendor," never the heavenly one, where two plus two does equal four and where an image, like tombs in the dove's throat, might be something more than surreal.

p. 43, l. 3. *Lorca.* "Behind these poems lurks a terrible question that has no answer. Our people cross their arms in prayer, look at the stars, and wait in vain for a sign of salvation. The gesture is pathetic but true. And the poem either poses a deep emotional question with no answer, or solves it with death, which is the question of questions" (Federico García Lorca, "Architecture of Deep Song," Lorca's own commentary on *Poem of the Deep Song*. The second sentence is qtd. in Christopher Mauer's Introduction to Lorca's *Collected Poems* [New York: Farrar Straus Giroux, 1991], xix, the book cited in Wright's note, C, 95, and NB, 203.) A variation on Lorca's line appears in *River Run* in *SHS*.

"Not everyone can see the truth, but he can be it"

Orig. pub. *Michigan Quarterly Review* 31 (Summer 1992): 361.
C, 62; NB, 44
Pattern: 3-2-1-4-1-3
Time: Sunday, 22 December 1991
Place: Charlottesville backyard

The title is from Franz Kafka's *The Blue Octavo Notebooks*, The Third Notebook, 11 December 1917, ed. Max Brod, trans. by Ernst Kaiser and Eithne Wilkins (Cambridge. MA: Exact Change, 1991), 31. The passages on either side of the one quoted are apposite: "Our art is a way of being dazzled by truth: the light on the grotesquely retreating face is true, and nothing else." "Expulsion from Paradise is in its main aspect eternal: that is to say, although expulsion from Paradise is final, and life in the world unavoidable, the eternity of the process (or, expressed in temporal terms, the eternal repetition of the process) nevertheless makes it possible not only that we might remain in Paradise permanently, but that we may in fact be there permanently, no matter whether we know it here or not" (ibid.).

The key to this poem is the idea of devolution, which comes at the exact center of the poem. The pilgrim poet has descended slowly through the various stages of his quest down "to his one appointed spot," having been guided by something outside himself. This something is perhaps fate. The passage, in any event, has come in "predetermined degrees we've neither a heart nor hand in." The time is the winter solstice, or Saturnalia, the festival of inner renewal. And to participate in this renewal the poet enjoins himself to pause for a while, to rid himself of his traveling baggage, to rip of all his masks, even those, as Kafka says—in the passage quoted in the note below—that hide beneath "the core of the core," and then to let the fire "absorbed by the Holy of Holies" begin to shine. This, as Wright says in his essay on "The Poem as Journey" (where he quotes the Kafka passage), is what the pilgrimage is all about (QN, 38).

> p. 44, l. 14. *Only the fire ... Let it shine.* "Before setting foot in the Holy of Holies you must take off your shoes, yet not only your shoes, but everything; you must take off your traveling garment and lay down your luggage; and under that you must shed your nakedness and everything that is under the nakedness and everything that hides beneath that, and then the core and the core of the core, then the remainder and then the residue and then even the glimmer of the undying fire. Only the fire itself is absorbed by the Holy of Holies and lets itself be absorbed by it; neither can resist the other" (Kafka, *The Blue Octavo Notebooks*, 39).

As Our Bodies Rise, Our Names Turn into Light

Orig. pub. *Michigan Quarterly Review* 31 (Summer 1992): 362.
C, 63; NB, 45
Pattern: 4 × 3
Time: January 1992
Place: Charlottesville

As the poet records the sights and sounds from the usual observation post in his yard, it suddenly occurs to him how strange it is "to have a name, any name on this poor earth." Because names are one of the obvious ways we identify ourselves, having a name appears to relate here to the poet's identity, a distinctive self that emerges amid the sounds from the neighbors and against the backdrop of the salted streets and falling snow. The last stanza leads toward an epiphany—the awareness that "Everything flows toward structure, the last ache in the ache for God." "Structure" here relates to the narrative shape of the pilgrimage, the Dantean *strada sottonarrativa* or the under-narrative of the individual poems that, taken together, form the several trilogies. As "Everything flows toward structure," part of that structure is also the seasonal cycle, the repeated but ever-changing pattern that inches its way along through the cold winter nights. "Structure" relates as well to the poet's religious longing: if fulfilled, this desire, as the title suggests, will transform the bodies of the named ones into light. The poem begins with a view of landscape as *natura naturans*—nature as a vital process—and ends with one of landscape as *natura naturata*—nature as an ordered system.

Absence Inside an Absence

Orig. pub. *Southern Review* 28 (Autumn 1992): 919.
C, 64; NB, 46
Pattern: 5 × 4
Time: Winter 1992

The declaration of the sixth-century ascetic John the Solitary sounds like an inversion of the Derridean claim that writing is prior to speech. "How long," John asked, "shall I be in the world of the voice and not in the world of the word? For everything that is seen is voice and is spoken with the voice, but in the invisible world there is no voice, for not even voice can utter its mystery. How long shall I be a voice and not silence, when shall I depart from the voice, no longer remaining in things which the voice proclaims? When shall I become word in an awareness of hidden things, when shall I be raised up to silence, to something which neither word nor voice can bring?" (qtd. in Gillespie and Ross, 54 [see below]). The poet affirms the claim of John the Solitary and other medieval mystics that while "our lives are language" (i.e., we live in the world of the spoken word) "our desires are apophatic," meaning that we desire to express knowledge of God by what God is not. This is a version of those forms of negative theology known as the *via negativa* that we find elsewhere in Wright.

When the poet says, "The bush in the flame is the bush in the flame," he is referring to the encounter of the burning bush by Moses, which, according to Gillespie and Ross (see note below), "is a classic apophatic image which allows the focusing of the imagination on a single image but which eschews representation of what it communicates" (p. 57). They add that such "strategies of imagistic effacement offer mystical writers a means of counteracting the pull of referentiality in their handling of language" (p. 58), which is also a leitmotif in Wright. But what the poet gives in stanza 1 he takes back in stanzas 2 and 3. Our voices will cause even the angels to recoil, so it is better to forget the apophatic word. Besides we can come to that still point where everything is emptied out by a dialectic of "flame and counterflame": we can, in other words, abandon the voice altogether, achieving the apophatic moment by the various illuminations we see directly before us.

Nevertheless, the poet concludes, John of Solitary provides a powerful insight—that a transcendental presence can come from the *via negativa*—an absence inside and absence, devoid of all images from the natural world, the earth being only "dark syllables in our mouths."

p. 46, ll. 1–3. *John the Solitary.* Wright's note (p. 203) refers to the unpublished paper by Vincent Gillespie and Maggie Ross "The Apophatic Image: The Poetics of Effacement in Julian of Norwich." The book has since been published as vol. 5 of *The Medieval Mystical Tradition*, ed. Marion Glasscoe (Woodbridge, Suffolk: D.S. Brewer, 1992). For the Gillespie and Ross essay, see pp. 53–77.

Still Life with Spring and Time to Burn

Orig. pub. *Southern Review* 28 (Autumn 1992): 918.
C, 66; NB, 47

Pattern: 5 × 3
Time: Early March 1992
Place: Charlottesville backyard

The spring scene in this still life, with its preening buds and the "Blue moan of the mourning dove," gets dispatched after the first two lines, unless a pun is intended by the title (I have some time to burn because I'm yet alive). More abstractly, spring is said to be a time of relief (winter is over), of sorrow (the dolorosa of the Stabat Mater), of uncertainty, and of renewal, and it "holds our affections dear // and asks us to love it." What ensues is a meditation on time and affection, the two things, so we think, we are accountable to. But think again. Time will undo us and hang us out like a coat on a deck chair, and we end up dancing with the *spiritus mundi*, which will "grind us to grain-out." Quite why affection or love will also kill us is uncertain, unless it is the diseased kind associated with the swollen renewal of stanza 3. Or perhaps the idea is a variation on Emily Dickinson's "The Test of Love—is Death."

p. 47, l. 5. In *The Lady of the Lake* Sir Walter Scott speaks of the mountain shadows lying in "bright uncertainty" (canto 3, sec. 2, l. 8).

*Morandi II

Orig. pub. *Yale Review* 81 (April 1993): 26.
C, 67
Pattern: 5-5-2

This homage to Giorgio Morandi pays tribute to him as the artist's artist, devoted only to perfecting his craft, reducing everything to basic shapes, revealing the power of negative spaces ("the losses we get strange gain from"), as he sketched and etched and painted landscapes and bottles from his simple studio in Bologna. "Giorgio Morandi stayed home," says the poet, "And kept his distance and measure. And kept his silence. / No word for anything but his work," meaning that he was disengaged from with the social, political, and cultural currents swirling around in the wider Italian and European communities. This is the image of Morandi that he, to some extent, projected, and which his family nurtured after his death. Janet Abramowicz's biography of Morandi, *Giorgio Morandi: The Art of Silence* (Yale University Press, 2004), published more than a decade after Wright's poem appeared, dispels this myth, showing how Morandi was very much involved with other contemporary European artists and how he was far from being apolitical, having had connections with the Fascist regime.

This does nothing to gainsay the last two stanzas of the poem, where the poet lets Morandi's shapes and objects speak for themselves, remarking only that his scratches were "like an abyss, // a "Mondrian-absence one might descend to." As Wright reported in an interview, "There is a kind of spatial negation, a visual power in absence that painters [like Cézanne and Morandi] understand and employ, and which I'm interested in poetically. It's a sort of white hole that has a kinetic draw to it that the lines of the poem float on and resist" (QN, 173). Or again, in another interview, replying to a question about his interest in Cézanne, Morandi, and Mondrian, Wright said, "Keeping things apart, leaving things out, blank canvas, blank page spaces, not quite completing what is obvious, completing what is not obvious, the idea of knowing what comes next and then declining to say it, or fill it in, determination to keep the circle from touching—one works, as I once said, in the synapse, in the electric field between what is and what isn't, between the beginning and the beginning. It's not so much a desire to keep things tentative as one to keep things from touching, from becoming complete and becoming final. One wants to feel the kinetics, the possibilities, always the what's-left-to-do. If you know what it is, and you know where it goes, the longer you can keep it out, the deeper it will go once you put it in. Exile's the ultimate synapse—from there you can go anywhere. Cézanne, Matisse, Morandi, and Mondrian—negative transcendence, what you take out is stronger than what you put in. There are no Gods, there are only saints" (Spiegelman, 121).

With Simic and Marinetti at the Giubbe Rosse
Orig. pub. *Field* 47 (Fall 1992): 100.
C, 68; NB, 48
Pattern: 6 × 3
Time: 1992, during Wright's tenure as visiting professor in Florence
Place: Florence

    The setting is the Giubbe Rosse, a famous café in Florence where the Futurist movement blossomed, struggled, and expanded. It played an important role in the history of Italian culture as a workshop of ideas, projects, and passions of the Futurists. Wright and his poet friend Charles Simic are in the café, along with the ghosts of F.T. Marinetti, the creative firebrand of the Futurist movement, and others. The poem attempts to recreate some sense of what the café would have been like eighty years before, interweaving the account of the present situation with lines from Marinetti. The form of the poem seems intended to imitate the disjointed syntax of Marinetti.

    Those who are condemned to repeat the Futurists, says the poet, playing on Santayana's well-known maxim about remembering the past, would be anyone who advocated the themes of the Futurists' manifestoes: the dynamic and violent character of early twentieth-century urban life, the force and speed of machines, the glorification of war and (at least in the early days of the movement) Fascism, the denunciation of the past, the denigration of tradition, and the destruction of museums and academic institutions. Not included among the condemned are Wright and Simic, who have in fact remembered the Futurists and are, with their brandies in hand, *sulla traccia*, on the trail.

p. 48, l. 5. *Giovanni Papini* (1881–1956). Journalist, critic, poet, and novelist; his avant-garde polemics made him one of the most controversial Italian literary figures in the early twentieth century. With *Giuseppe Prezzolini* he founded the influential but short-lived Florentine magazine *Leonardo* (1903–07) and *La Voce*.

p. 48, l. 6. *Carlo Emilio Gadda* (1893–1973). Italian novelist, short-story writer, and essayist: one of Italy's most daring experimental writers.

p. 48, l. 7. *Let's murder the moonlight*. The title of the manifesto of the Italian Futurist movement, headed by F.T. Marinetti, in which he reports how he and a group of supporters used hundreds of light bulbs to "murder" the moonlight. For the Futurists the moonlight as a conventional symbol exploited by poets for centuries had to be vanquished.

p. 48, l. 12. *The wind ... muscles*. "3 corrosive shadows against / the DAWN / the winds working away away kneading the sea so muscles / and blood for Daybreak...." The lines are from F.T. Marinetti's *Yes, yes, like this, the dawn on the sea*, ll. 1–4; trans. Richard J. Pioli (*October 24* [Spring 1983]: 100).

p. 48, ll. 15–17. *Little by little ... high plains*. From the Marinetti's Futurist fantasy *Let's Murder the Moonlight*, in which a horde of Futurist artists sets out to lay the great military railroad to the summit of the world. But their advance is interrupted by the midnight appearance of the moon: "suddenly we felt the carnal Moon, the Moon of lovely warm thighs, abandoning herself languidly against our broken backs. A cry went up in the airy solitude of the high plains: 'Let's murder the moonshine!' Some ran to nearby cascades" (*Marinetti: Selected Writings*, trans. R.W. Flint and Arthur A. Coppotelli [New York: Farrar, Straus and Giroux, 1972]).

p. 48, l. 18. *Simic ... ammazzata*. Simic and Wright on the trail. The murdered moon.

To the Egyptian Mummy in the Etruscan Museum at Cortona
Orig. pub. *Paris Review* 34 (Winter 1992): 227.
C, 69–70; NB, 49–50
Pattern: 5 × 4

Time: Spring 1992
Place: Cortona

Displayed in the Etruscan Museum in Cortona, located in the Palazzo Civico in Piazza Signorelli near the eighteenth-century Teatro Signorelli, are two mummies, both adult males. The poet addresses one of them, using his "stranger's eye" to describe to the wrapped body what is going on outside the window and the figures from the past whom he half-expects to materialize and climb up the road "Toward the south gate and you, // pale messenger from the wordless world." The poet then proposes to free the landscape for the mummy, just as Leonardo freed the caged doves in the Florentine marketplace. His desire is for the mummy—removed from his original resting place, taken to a foreign land ("peninsulaed" in the Italian boot), and forever imprisoned in his glass case—to have the freedom at least to see the Italian landscape sailing away into an ever diminishing radiance.

p. 49, l. 11. *Guidoriccio da Fogliano.* Italian soldier who is the subject of a fresco by Simone Martini, in the Palazzo Pubblico, Siena.

p. 49, l. 13. *Malatesta.* Sigismondo Malatesta (1417–68), lord of Rimini. *Marches* = area of central Italy, separated from the Emilia Romagna region by the Marecchia River. Pound's so-called Malatesta Cantos (VIII–XI) are devoted to the life and times of Sigismondo.

p. 49, ll. 16–17. "Leonardo's disposition was so lovable that he commanded everyone's affection. He owned, one might say, nothing and he worked very little, yet he always kept servants as well as horses. These gave him great pleasure as indeed did all of the animal creation which he treated with wonderful love and patience. For example, often when he was walking past the places birds were sold he would pay the price asked, take them from their cages, and let them fly off into the air, giving them back their lost freedom" (Giorgio Vasari, *Lives of the Artists*, trans. George Bull [Harmondsworth: Penguin, 1987], 1:257).

With Eddie and Nancy in Arezzo at the Caffè Grande

Orig. pub. *Field* 47 (Fall 1992): 100.
C, 71; NB, 51
Pattern: 5 × 3
Time: Mid-May 1992
Place: Arezzo, Italy

Title: Eddie and Nancy Conner are Wright's friends, going back to his years in Italy.

The theme of this poem is the passage of time, represented by the "desolate edge" of sunlight that makes its way inexorably across the piazza and reinforced by Po Chü-I's lines about the Fleeting World. The Tao has taught Po Chü-I not to grieve about the flying by of the days and months, but simply to watch their passing. The poet does not grieve either, but he feels the pain: the moving edge of sunlight and shadow pries and cuts whatever it passes over—the children playing soccer, the poet and his two friends—like a knife blade. Opposed to the slicing of the sun is the tapping and sliding of the blind ticket seller, who is of course oblivious to the "desolate edge." At the exact mid-point of the poem we are told that "The pain of what is present never comes to an end," which leads to the ambiguous concluding line: "One life is all we're entitled to, but it's enough"—which is perhaps why the poet began with the image of "Piero in wraps": his *The Legend of the True Cross* is concealed by the restorers' drapes.

p. 51, l. 1. *Piero ... restauro.* That is, *The Legend of the True Cross* by Piero della Francesca in the church of San Francesco in Arezzo is being restored. These frescoes recount the miraculous story of the wood of Christ's Cross. The fifteen-year restoration was finally completed in 2000. On Piero, see note to *Tattoos*, poem 7, CM, 62, and Wright's "Piero," in UP, 7–8.

p. 51, l. 6. "The flower of the pear-tree gathers and turns to fruit; / The swallows' eggs have hatched into young birds. / When the Seasons' changes thus confront the mind / What comfort can the Doctrine of Tao give? / It will teach me to watch the days and months fly / Without grieving that Youth slips away; / If the Fleeting World is but a long dream, / It does not matter whether one is young or old. / But ever since the day that my friend left my side / And has lived an exile in the City of Chiang-ling, / There is one wish I cannot quite destroy: / That from time to time we may chance to meet again" (Po Chü-I, *At the End of Spring*, poem 19 in *More Translations from the Chinese*, trans. Arthur Waley [New York: Knopf, 1919]).

p. 51, l. 13. *Lotteria di Foligno*. The lottery of Foligno, an Umbrian town.

There Is No Shelter

Orig. pub. *Paris Review* 34 (Winter 1992): 228.
C, 72; NB, 52
Pattern: 4 × 2
Place: Charlottesville

This dream-like poem, which could have been entitled *Peccatology II*, is framed by two similes. The first likens "the sins of the whole world" to the evening dew. The analogy here involves condensation (sins "collect here") both as a natural phenomenon and as a symbolic one. Dew as a figure condenses all of the qualities of sin into a single image. "To see a world in a grain of sand," says Blake. To see the sins of the world in a drop of dew, says Wright. This is the evening world. In the morning, the sins of the world explode in flame, and there is no shelter from the fiery burst. The charred residue of sin etches "the edges of our lives and the course of things, filling / The shadows in, // an aftertrace, through the discards of the broken world." Here the process is one of displacement: the omnipresence of sin gets pushed onto something associated with it—fire—and this process is likened in the concluding simile to "the long, slow burn of a struck match."

This exquisite little lyric provides a different view of sin from *Peccatology* (NB, 42), where sin turned out to be a "small" thing in the face of Indian summer with its ivy and hemlock, red leaves and locust pods, making everything else diminish by comparison. But in the present poem, there is no landscape to erase the etchings of sin as it makes its way through the detritus of "the broken world," leaving its traces everywhere. In the familiar hymn, God is said to be our shelter from the stormy blast. There is some respite from sin in the dewy night-time world, but in the daytime vision of this lyric, no shelter, divine or otherwise, is available.

Watching the Equinox Arrive in Charlottesville, September 1992

Orig. pub. *Colorado Review* 20, no. 1 (Spring 1993): 103.
C, 75–7; NB, 53–5
Pattern: 10 × 2 × 6
Time: 22 September 1992
Place: Charlottesville

In section 1 the remarkable descriptions that follow on the beginning of the autumnal equinox reinforce the poet's awareness that each season begins all over again. The death and renewal of the annual cycle is portrayed metaphorically as a process of unlearning and learning: "each year the orchard unlearns // everything it's been taught," and "You've got to unlearn things, the season repeats." This means that "For every change there's a form" (and, one would suppose, vice versa), the dozen or so such forms catalogued in this section serving to illustrate the point.

In section 2 the awareness of the passage of time has become the "monotonous tick of the universe." The Zen Buddhists urge us to detach ourselves from material reality, but the "monotonous tick" reminds us of time's winged chariot, and thus it "Painfully pries our lips apart, // and dirties our tongues / With soiled, incessant music"—not a very efficacious view of the ends and means of poetry. Zen Buddhists also enjoin us to "enter the blackness, the form of forms," but this is difficult to do, given the hum-drum intrusions of flat tires and phone calls. While the poet seems inclined to affirm the Zen teachings, a philosophy of immanence finally trumps transcendence, and he finds it "hard to argue with" the position that God and the imagination are one: "what we see outside ourselves we'll soon see inside ourselves." Thus, the apophatic Buddhist injunction to empty oneself and enter the "form of forms," far removed from the plentitude of the quotidian that we have in section 1, is displaced by the declaration of Jesus in the Gospel of Thomas: "I am the light that is over all things. I am all: from me all came forth, and to me all attained. Split a piece of wood; I am there. Lift up the stone, and you will find me there" (vs. 77). The conclusion follows: "Hard to imagine a paradise beyond what the hand breaks."

Section 3 returns to the theme of section 1—the inexorable turning of the seasons. The anxiety springing from the poet's awareness that the *spiritus anima* is on his trail ("seeking my blood out") comes to the surface, and the poet declares that solitude, surrounded by absence, is "hard work," producing only mouthfuls of silence and air (as on the dust jacket of *Chickamauga*) and realizing that "our own lives drift away from us." At this point to poetic eye takes over: "We keep our eyes on the dirt.... We watch, but we don't move." Again, speculations about the empyrean are trumped by close attention to the landscape's "undergrowth." The number of equinoxes that the poet has yet to experience continue, of course, to diminish. His response to this stark reality is to wait and watch.

p. 53, l. 1. *2:23*. The beginning of the autumnal equinox, Eastern Standard Time.

p. 53, l. 8. *lemon tree*. Not the citrus tree, but a variety of Virginia flora with lemon-shaped fruit.

p. 53, l. 22. "If you open your mouth, I will hit you thirty times. If you close your mouth, I will still hit your thirty times" (Zen Master Seung Sahn).

p. 53, l. 23. *Live ... dust of the world*. "Living in the world yet not forming attachments to the dust of the world is the way of a true Zen student" (advice to his pupils by Zen Master Zengetsu of the T'ang dynasty, in *Zen Flesh, Zen Bones: A Collection of Zen and Pre-Zen Writtings*, comp. Paul Reps [New York: Doubleday, 1989], 65).

p. 54, l. 6. *They say ... form of forms*. "In rain during a black night, enter that *blackness* as the form of forms" (*Zen Flesh, Zen Bones*, 169).

p. 54, l. 7 *No matter ... as light*. "Waking, sleeping, dreaming know you as *light*" (*Zen Flesh, Zen Bones*, 169).

p. 54, l. 17. *Hard to imagine ... breaks*. Cf. the same idea in another context in Wallace Stevens's *Sunday Morning*: "I am content when wakened birds, / Before they fly, test the reality / Of misty fields, by their sweet questionings; / But when the birds are gone, and their warm fields / Return no more, where, then, is paradise? / There is not any haunt of prophecy, / Nor any old chimera of the grave, / Neither the golden underground, nor isle / Melodious, where spirits gat them home, / Nor visionary south, nor cloudy palm / Remote on heaven's hill, that has endured / As April's green endures" (*Collected Poems* [New York: Knopf, 1967], 68).

Waiting for Tu Fu

Orig. pub. Gettysburg Review 6, no. 1 (Winter 1993): 85.
C, 78–80; NB, 56–8
Pattern: 6 × 3 × 3
Time: 22 December 1992
Place: Charlottesville

For the Wright/Tu Fu connection, see the commentary for *After Reading Tu Fu, I Go Outside to the Dwarf Orchard* (NB, 12). Like Wright, Tu Fu occasionally weaves together discontinuous themes and modes in a single poem. See, for example, Tu Fu's *Seven Songs at T'ung-ku*, *Autumn Pastoral*, and *Reflections in Autumn*, referred to in *Waiting for Tu Fu*. Other poems in which Tu Fu makes an appearance—all in *Negative Blue*—are *Cicada* (14–15), *Still Life with Stick and Word* (60), *China Mail* (128), and *Thinking about the Night Sky, I Remember a Poem by Tu Fu* (195). Tu Fu does not appear in Wright's poetry before *Chickamauga* and only once after *North American Bear*.

1. Chickamauga

In section 1 the poet, supine on the "cold grasses," situates his place of repose so that he can see the golden autumn leaves against the sky. Twice he identifies the leaves with the artifice of a goldsmith: "the beaten artifice / Of gold leaf and sky" and "The Greek-thin hammered gold artifacts // and glazed inlay / Of landscape and sky." This golden, fiery world extends beyond "Even the void / beyond the void the clouds cross. / Even the knowledge that everything's fire, // and nothing ever comes back." But the poet shrugs off all of this as belonging to the past or as "somebody else's line of talk." The somebody else would include Yeats, with his vision of gold mosaics, holy fire, and the "hammered gold and gold enamelling" of the Grecian goldsmiths in *Sailing to Byzantium*. It would include as well Heraclitus, who said that "everything is fire," fire being for him the preeminent image for describing the fundamental reality of change. The poet finds himself in a sacred space: the words that rise from his body are "prayer-smoke," which the "glazed inlay / Of landscape and sky" accept as incense.

Section 2 begins with Tu Fu's question about the justification of his life, a question the poet has also asked: "What has it come to, / Carrying us like a barge toward the century's end / And sheer drop-off into millennial history?" Reflecting on the beginning of the millennium, which is still eight years away, the poet remembers his days at the Sky Valley School in the early 1950s, an age of innocence and grace: "O we were pure and holy in those days ... O we were abstract and true." The remembered scene here mirrors the nostalgia of Tu Fu in *Reflections in Autumn*: "A peaceful, long-ago country keeps in my thoughts." But reality intrudes, and the eye that could see so clearly before the fall from grace, "now sees nothing at all." This is the poet's disheartening response to Tu Fu's question.

Section 3 opens with another of Tu Fu's questions, this one from his poem *Adrift*, and again the poet adopts it for himself: "Where is my life going in these isolate outlands?" The answer comes in the poet's identifying, like Tu Fu, with the landscape, "a circle whose center is everywhere / And circumference nowhere." As winter approaches, a dark and ominous mood intrudes, and it is clear that the poet has come to identify not just with the landscape but with Tu Fu as well. The clouds, which are present in the first two sections (once as a simile), are now a "wreckage"; darkness "smokes forth" in the trees, which have emptied themselves of their leaves; and it is now the "Dead end of autumn," which means more than simply the winter solstice (22 December). It is a triple pun. With "everything caught between stone-drift and stone," the poet is at an *impasse*, and the ear hears "dead-end"—having *no exit*. In the last lines of *Reflections in Autumn* Tu Fu says, "I watch / Now, nothing more—hair white, a grief-sung gaze sinking." The white-haired poet too is apparently watching and waiting as he drifts away, like the immortals in another of Tu Fu's poems, into the distant heavens toward the circumference that is nowhere.

p. 56, l. 12. *nothing ever comes back*. Cf. P.D. Ouspensky: "everything passes away, nothing returns!" (*Tertium Organum*, 2nd ed., trans. Nicholas Bessaraboff and Claude Bragdon [New York: Knopf, 1922], 40).

p. 56, l. 19. *What have ... yourself.* "Look closely—where is / This fleeting consequence you've tangled your life in?" (Tu Fu, *Meandering River*, in *Selected Poems of Tu Fu*, trans. David Hinton [New York: New Directions, 1989], 34). "How suddenly it all passed" (*Ballad of a Hundred Worries*, ibid., 58). "The flame flickers / Good fortune over and over—and for what?" (*Day's End*, ibid., 93).

p. 57, l. 3. *I remember ... North Carolina.* The memory of the North Carolina Sunday comes from Wright's time at Sky Valley Camp, between Hendersonville and Brevard, where a Mr. and Mrs. Perry ran two summer camps. The camp was on the shore of Lake Louellen, the surface of which the poet remembers "cutting ... once in a green canoe" (p. 57, l. 16).

p. 57, l. 4. *organ chord.* The reference is to a memory of Mrs. Perry playing, not an organ, but a piano. Wright attended the camp during the summers of 1948, 1949, and 1950. See *Sky Valley Rider*, in CM, 39. In an interview with Michael Chitwood, Wright discusses his time at Sky Valley in some detail (QN, 142-5).

p. 57, ll. 18-19. "Each departure like any other, where is / my life going in these isolate outlands?" (Tu Fu, *Adrift*, in *Selected Poems of Tu Fu*, 68).

p. 57, ll. 21-2. "The nature of God is a circle of which the centre is everywhere and the circumference is nowhere" (an aphorism attributed to Empedocles, Augustine, Pascal, and numerous others).

p. 58, ll. 7–8. See *Reflections in Autumn*, in *Selected Poems of Tu Fu*, 81–4. Chengdu (or Ch'eng-tu in Hinton's translation), the capital of Sichuan Province in the Three Gorges region of Central China, was the home of Tu Fu. The Yangtze River gorges (Qutang, Wuxia, and Xiling), collectively known as Sanxia or Three Gorges, appear in a number of Tu Fu's poems.

p. 58, ll. 11–12. *Immortals ... boats.* "But tonight a dazzling lake / Stretches into distant heavens—as if any moment, / On this raft of immortals, I will drift away" (Tu Fu, *Entering Tung-t'ing Lake*, in *Selected Poems of Tu Fu*, 112.) Tu Fu refers to himself as the white-haired poet in a number of poems, including the final line of *Reflections in Autumn* 984); see also *Selected Poems of Tu Fu*, 60, 75, 89, 91, 93, 94, 106.

The reference to Paul Celan in Wright's notes (*NB*, 204) points not to any direct borrowing or even allusion, but to the general sense of a negative theology that emerges from Celan's private and often idiosyncratic vision.

Paesaggio Notturno

Orig. pub. *New Yorker* 69, no. 22 (14 July 1993): 52.
C, 83; *NB*, 59
Pattern: 4 × 3
Time: 8 March 1993
Place: Charlottesville backyard

Title: *paesaggio notturno* = nocturnal landscape

This pensive little composition, with its simple structure (like the tripartite matins of the Anglican breviary), leads to the lesson at the beginning of stanza 3: "All things are found in all things." This is Wright's version of the idea of interpenetration that we find in, for example, Whitehead, the Mahayana sutras, and Plotinus, who says in the *Fifth Ennead*, "Each being contains within itself the whole intelligible world. Therefore all is everywhere. Each is there all and all is each." For the poet, light is in light. Less cryptically, the "lesson" is illustrated by the poem's metaphors in which things are in fact said to be other things. The tightly structured nocturne (each line has seven syllables) reveals that the moon is an actor, the maple tree is a group of nerve cells, the sky is a Munch painting, the bulb tufts are teeth, the night is a mouth, the wind is time's dust, and so on.

The two concluding lines of the poem need not be read as religious statements, but both are drawn from sacred texts as a way of summing up the mystery of metaphor. The first is from The Book of Thomas the Contender, who has said to Jesus "that those who speak about things that are invisible and difficult to explain are like those who shoot their arrows at a target at night." Jesus replies, "It is in light that light exists" (*NHL*, 202). The last line comes from Psalm 65:2, though the variation that appears Isaiah 66:23 may fit better the moonscape of the poem: "And it shall come to pass, that from one new moon to another, and from one Sabbath to another, shall all flesh come to worship before me, saith the Lord." As a nocturne is a musical composition, Wright may also be echoing the line from the first aria in *You Gates of Zion* (1727), "Drum kömmt alles Fleisch zu dir."

p. 54, l. 4. *Munch sky.* As it is night, perhaps like the dark blue sky in Edvard Munch's *Evening on Karl Johan* or the lighter blues in *Night in St. Cloud* and *Summer Night in Aasgarstrand*. The numerous Munch skies vary widely in color.

Still Life with Stick and Word

Orig. pub. *Colorado Review* 21, no. 1 (Spring 1994): 60.
C, 84; *NB*, 60
Pattern: 5 × 4
Time: May 1983
Place: Charlottesville backyard

The poet decides to repress his apprehension about the number of Aprils that still await him—an unknown number—and focus instead on something nearby (a stick) and small (a word). A week later his description of the stick emerges: "Maple, most likely, fuzz-barked and twice-broken, spore-pocked / With white spots." We then move from center to circumference as the spots are projected as "star charts" for crossing the Milky Way.

As the poet moves from his back yard to inside his house, the second "subject" of his still life is revealed, the word "white." He repeats the word, which is like paint on his tongue, and things begin to materialize, reminding us of the handiwork of God in Genesis 1: "light forms, / Bottles arise, emptiness opens its corridors." What becomes visible on the poet's canvas is a Giorgio Morandi painting—or at least it is like one, the rising bottles suggesting a Morandi still life, where the white space between the bottles forms empty corridors and doorways. In creating negative space, white becomes the "great eviscerator," the absence of color "that form bears," or an emptying out so as to disclose some secret. In the final stanza, the poet moves back outside, where he is confronted with a case in point for both "endless things" and "entrances": the white "yips" of the constellations that mirror the river of heaven (the overburn of the Milky Way) and the light shining through the kitchen window. The poem concludes with a testament to metaphor ("How unlike it is") and simile ("How like"). The escaping houselight *is* a photographic slide; it *is like* a slide. The white spots on the maple stick *are* the Milky Way; they *are like* the Milky Way. The constellations *are* "yips in the dog dark"; they *are like* such yips. The light from the kitchen window is/is like the "window" of the white bottle in Morandi's *Natura Morta* paintings.

The movement of the poet from outside to inside and back to outside is a movement from absence to presence to absence. This mirrors the thematic focus on the power of negative space to create form. As in Genesis, light is formed from the nothingness of the void.

p. 60, ll. 1–5. *April ... This word.* "March gone, now. April's moon. / I age: how many more to meet? / Won't let mind linger on the endless things beyond me. / I'll try to finish this / One small cup" (Tu Fu, *Full of Feeling (Nine Quatrains)*, no. IV, in *Bright Moon, Perching Bird: Poems by Li Po and Tu Fu*, trans. J.P. Seaton and James Cryer [Middletown, CT: 1987], 87).
Natura Morta, cited in Wright's note (*NB*, 204), is one of a number paintings with that title that Morandi did in the mid-1950s. This one is part of the permanent collection of the University of Iowa Museum of Art. It is reproduced in Bonnie Costello's essay, "Charles Wright, Giorgio Morandi, and the Metaphysics of the Line," *Mosaic* 35, no. 1 (March 2002): 168, and in Costello's reprinted essay in *HL*, 315.

Summer Storm

Orig. pub. as a broadside by the *Art Institute of Chicago*.
C, 85; NB, 61
Pattern: 5 × 3
Time: Summer 1993
Place: Charlottesville backyard.

Piet Mondrian believed that there is no way to represent what we perceive in the natural world but that we can approach the reality behind that world through abstract forms. The essence of these forms became for him, after about 1920, vertical and horizontal lines, the primary colors, and the three tones (white, grey, black). The poet says that Mondrian knew that "Art is the image of an image of an image," a variation of the mimetic view that the artist creates forms which, as imitations of imitations, are twice removed from what is really real—the universal, permanent, and unchanging Idea of a thing. "An old idea not that old," says the poet, meaning that it is as young as book 10 of Plato's *Republic*. The focus of the poem, however, is less on a theory of art than on Mondrian's technique of reworking his paintings layer by layer so that the painting becomes "More vacant, more transparent" as "skins" of paint are repeatedly added. In this *both/and* view, vacancy correlates with absence and transparency with clarity.

Behind the approaching storm and the maple tree in stanza 2 is Mondrian's canvas "window" which "gives out [offers a view] onto ontology." In other words, the white spaces in Mondrian's 1935 painting open up onto a continually changing world, each frame dividing itself from the others in some temporal (horizontal) or spatial (vertical) perspective. Not being able to "see the same thing twice" is one ontological point of view. Wright's positioning himself in his Charlottesville back yard and the Montana wilderness means that he is always looking through the same "window," but his descriptions, whether of the sky, the clouds, "that maple" in his back yard, the constellations, or the flora and fauna of the Yaak valley, are always made refreshingly and ingeniously new. Such is the ontology of difference in sameness.

p. 61, ll. 1–6. *As Mondrian ... from 1935.* The reference is apparently to Piet Mondrian's *Composition in Gray and Red* (1935), a painting with double sets of horizontal and vertical lines.

Looking West from Laguna Beach at Night

Orig. pub. *New Yorker* 71 (13 March 1995): 82.
C, 86; NB, 62
Pattern: 6 × 3
Place: Laguna Beach
Time: Summer 1993

In this triptych the looking takes place at three different times and in three different directions. The focus of the first panel is the various lights seen from the poet's mother-in-law's home—the "oil-rig lanterns" out in the Pacific, the lights of the descending airplanes, the stars shining through the eucalyptus trees, and the town lights encircling the bay. In the second panel—a summer scene—dance music wafts up from the hotel below. In the third scene, which is set sometime later, the poet stares at the zodiac with a feeling of regret that he cannot name the constellations. Were he able to do so, he would possess "the mythic history of Western civilization." But, the poet laments, relying on his familiar pun, "I've spent my life knowing nothing."

p. 62, l. 1. *mother-in-law's house.* The house of Hollywood actress Jeanette Nolan (1911–98).
p. 62, l. 9. *Twist and Shout* = a song by the Isley Brothers (1962), remade by the Beatles in 1963. *Begin the Beguine* = a Cole Porter song from *Jubilee* (1935).
p. 62, l. 17. *curry the physics of metamorphosis.* The reference is to the poet's failure to learn what Ovid says about the constellations. His *Fasti* has more than fifty astronomical references. In the transformations in the *Metamorphoses*, human beings are not infrequently changed into constellations.

Looking Again at What I Looked at for Seventeen Years

Orig. pub. *New Yorker* 71 (13 March 1995): 83.
C, 87; NB, 63
Pattern: 5 × 3
Place: Laguna Beach
Time: 1993

Title: Wright taught at the University of California, Irvine, for seventeen years—from 1966 to 1983.

This is the first of four poems in which water is the dominant element, though it does not enter the poem until the last stanza. The poem opens with another of Wright's descriptions of the sunset, represented here with two metaphors: "Soutine meat-streaks in the West" (that is, the meat-like colors in any number of paintings by the Lithuanian expressionist Chaim Soutine [1894–1943]) and "peroxided gums." In between we have the metaphor identifying the ocean and a drop cloth, another figure from the artist's studio. Wright calls these unlikely metaphors "mixed," but they are by no means impermissible, because they serve the same function—to capture the color of the sunset. But the poet then says—in his riddling way—that mixed metaphors are a simile for memory. Memory, however, is represented by other metaphors: "time's drone," suggesting the continuous low hum at the edge of consciousness; gouache (another metaphor from painting), signifying that our efforts to recall the past must break through an opaque and distant ("hovering near the horizon") surface; and a "black / Instinct filling the edges in," still another painting metaphor, meaning the powerful motivation we have to complete the canvas of our memories, which are often hazy at the boundaries and filled with holes.

The second stanza is an elaboration of the role of memory. Without memory we would have no texts or stories. It is both "nerve-net and nerve-spring," catching whatever swims through consciousness of the past and triggering our imaginative sensibilities. Memory, moreover, enables us to make connections (it is fundamentally associative), fills up the blank spaces in our lives, makes and unmakes us, and gives vitality to life, motivating both spirit (breath) and body.

The last stanza is an illustration of the power of memory to take away and then give back, to deconstruct and then to construct us. This power is captured by the metaphor of the sea, which sucks memory "away to where it's unreachable for good / Until it all comes back." But the sea is also a simile for the process: "It's like that," says the poet, repeating his initial observation about the mixed metaphors.

Both of the initial metaphors for the sunset are rather astonishing in their originality—who besides Wright would ever think of dead carcasses or bleached gums as tropes for a sunset? But the unusual, unexpected, and often extraordinary figure is one of Wright's signatures. It might be worth pausing to remind ourselves of his inventiveness in this regard. Here is a sampler of descriptions of sunsets from 1968 to 2006:

> Sunset. The sky, over Arkansas, inflames
> Like the new flesh in a scar [*The Bolivar Letters* (GRH, 34)].

> Heart's coal; hinge to the dark door;
> Tongue that flicks from this blue hill: sunset:
> Snail's track and calf's cover;
> The last wipe of expectancy [*Tongues* (HF, 53)].

> The weightless, unclarified light from the setting sun
> Lies like despair on the ginger root [*Depression Before the Solstice* (CM, 138)].

> The flash from the setting sun
> Is more than a trick of light, where halflife
> Is more than just a watery glow,
>   and everything's fire ... [*Going Home* (CM, 146)].

> Sun like an orange mousse through
> A snowfall of trumpet bells on the oleander [*Dog Day Vespers* (WTTT, 32)].

> Twenty-five years ago I used to sit on this jut of rocks
> As the sun went down like an offering through the glaze
> And backfires of Monterey Bay [*The Other Side of the River* (WTTT, 80)].

And the sun, as it always does,
>> dropping into its slot without a click
>> [*The Other Side of the River* (WTTT, 81)].

Already sundown has passed you and follows me up the road,
Color of dragonfly wings [*Three Poems of Departure* (WTTT, 85)].

Sunset like a girl's robe falling away long ago ... [*T'ang Notebook* (WTTT, 103)].

Sunset like carrot juice down the left pane of the sky
Into the indeterminacy of somewhere else [*Arkansas Traveler* (WTTT, 107)].

Down below Prato, the sun was lowering its burned body
Into the shadows [*A Journal of True Confessions* (WTTT, 140)].

The sunset, Mannerist clouds
>> just shy of the Blue Ridge
Gainsay the age before they lose their blush
In the rising coagulation of five o'clock [*A Journal of the Year of the Ox* (WTTT, 154)].

Clouds slide from the Dolomites
>> as though let out to dry.
Sunset again: that same color of rose leaf and rose water
>> [*A Journal of the Year of the Ox* (WTTT, 177)].

the sun set like a coffin
Into the grey Pacific [*Tennessee Line* (NB, 16)].

I love the way the evening sun goes down,
>> orange brass-plaque, life's loss-logo,
Behind the Laguna hills and bare night-wisps of fog.
I love the way the hills empurple and sky goes nectarine,
The way the lights appear like little electric fig seeds, the wet west
Burnishing over into the indeterminate colors of the divine
>> [*Looking Across Laguna Canyon at Dusk, West-by-Northwest* (NB, 64)].

Sky white as raw silk
>> opening mirror cold-sprung in the west,
Sunset like dead grass [*Poem Half in the Manner of Li Ho* (NB, 88)].

High-fiving in Charlottesville.
Sunset heaped up, as close to us as a barrel fire
>> [*The Appalachian Book of the Dead IV* (NB, 177)].

Orange Crush sunset over the Blue Ridge [*A Short History of the Shadow* (SHS, 39)].

the Indian paintbrush sundown [*Buffalo Yoga Coda III* (BY, 32)].

Sunset soaks down to the last leaves of the autumn trees
>> [*The Gospel According to St. Someone* (BY, 37)].

Lagoon light, sunset and cloud blaze,
>> red of the Cardinal entourage [*Rosso Venexiano* (BY, 44)].

Cloud-gondolas floating in with the east-moving wind-waters,
Black-hulled and gilt-edged,
>> white on white up above, smooth pole.
Later, the sunset, flamingo, great bird of passage [*Nostalgia III* (BY, 52)].

Sunset sheen like old wax on the steps into the sky [*La Dolcemara Vita* (BY, 67)].

Sunset in Appalachia, bituminous bulwark
Against the western skydrop.
An Advent of gold and green, an Easter of ashes [*Appalachian Farewell* (ST, 3)].

The slit wrists of sundown
                          tincture the western sky wall [*Scar Tissue* (ST, 36)].

Sundown. Pink hoofprints above the Blue Ridge,
                          soft hoofprints [*Littlefoot*, part 1].

Sunset, line like a long tongue-lick above the Blue Ridge,
Mock orange, then tangerine, then blush [*Littlefoot*, part 7].

As the sun goes down.
What small light there is drains off into its spikiness.
And glows like a severed head against the darkness [*Littlefoot*, part 30].

p. 63, l. 1. *Soutine meat-streaks*. See the colors in, for example *Carcass of Beef*, *Self Portrait*, *Street of Cagnes-sur-Mer*, and *Ray with Tomatoes*.

Looking Across Laguna Canyon at Dusk, West-by-Northwest

Orig. pub. *New Yorker* 70, no. 18 (20 June 1994): 67.
C, 88; NB, 64
Pattern: 5 × 2
Place: Laguna Beach
Time: Unspecified, but 1993

    We begin with a reversal of the opening line of W.C. Handy's *St. Louis Blues* (1914): "I hate to see that evening sun go down," followed, as in the previous companion poem, by a metaphor for the setting sun—an "orange brass-plaque" descending behind the Laguna hills as the "sky goes nectarine." Although the descending sun is also a logo for "life's loss," the moment is altogether pleasurable for the poet and a prelude to an epiphany. At that point when the sunset and its reflection on the sea are practically indistinguishable and become "indeterminate colors of the divine," the poet wants to pour himself "into the veins of the invisible," which is altogether different from W.C. Handy's lament: "If I feel tomorrow, like I feel today, / I'm gonna pack my trunk and make my getaway." Handy's desire is for escape. Wright's is for exaltation, even apotheosis, so that the poet would become like Dionysus. Wright's note refers us to a book by Roberto Calasso, and the passages the poem alludes to are these: "Dionysus would arrive in Athens for the Anthesteria with the spirits of the dead, then disappear with them.... 'Sovereign of all that is moist' [says Plutarch], Dionysus himself is liquid, a stream that surrounds us.... Dionysus is the river we hear flowing by in the distance ... then one day it rises and floods everything, as if the normal above-water state of things, the sober delimitation of our existence, were but a brief parenthesis overwhelmed in an instant" (*The Marriage of Cadmus and Harmony*, trans. Tim Parks [New York: Knopf, 1993], 42, 44, 45). The poet's wish, then, is to identify (become one with) the watery element, as represented, in Calasso's view, by Dionysus, and thus overwhelm the "sober delimitation" of his existence.

Venexia I

Orig. pub. *Shenandoah* 45, no. 1 (Spring 1995): 105.
C, 89; NB, 65
Pattern: 4 × 5

Time: October 1993, during the time Wright was teaching in Venice.

Title: The Roman numeral after "Venexia" is an exception to Wright's usual practice of not numbering the first of one or more poems with the same title. "Venexia" = the Venetian form of the Italian "Venezia."

The lavish spectacle of Venice at night, with its "light-splints" and "moon-spark," is overwhelmed the following day by the damp and dreary realization that the city will eventually sink to its death by water. The rainy weather, says the poet, "rubs us away," water being the ultimate auto-da-fé. "We husband our imperfections," the poet concludes, "our changes of tune," such as the change that occurs between stanzas 1 and 2. This means that we can still hold our affection for Venice—and for life itself—even in the face of that rising water that will submerge us. Water in the previous poem was an apocalyptic image. Here it is demonic—the auto-da-fé that obliterates everything except affection, which, Wright will later declare, is "the absolute everything rises to" (*Apologia Pro Vita Sua*).

p. 65, l. 17. *Zattere.* Bank in the south of Venice, facing the Giudecca Canal.

Venexia II

Orig. pub. *Shenandoah* 45, no. 1 (Spring 1995): 106.
C, 90; NB, 66
Pattern: 4 × 5
Time: 1993?
Place: Venice

The fourth "water" poem continues the theme of the third: the rising waters begin a slow process of immersion under the statue of the Virgin, whose "stone-stern gaze" surveys the slosh of garbage in the Venetian canals at high tide. The scene induces what the poet calls a "chain of Speculation" in the penultimate line, speculation chiefly about whether the dark Venetian waters are life-giving or life-taking. The waters are cathartic, scouring and emptying us out and, but then they fill us "With sweet, invisible plentitude." This emptying and filling is not without ambiguity, as we see in the second stanza where the dark waters are identified with dark music, "black notes to leave our lives by." The substitution of "leave" for "live" associates death with the dark, water-music. The presiding deity is the Angel of Death on the gondola's prow in stanza 3, but whatever splendor there may be in her shining solitude, darkness finally defeats light. The tolling of the bell of Santa Maria Gloriosa dei Frari signals the terminate hour, which originates in water and ends there as well—another image of death by water. We are reminded that the four "water" poems are part of a section in *Chickamauga* called "Imaginary Endings."

p. 66, l. 1. *Rimbaud's boat.* "Lighter than a cork, I danced on the waves" (Arthur Rimbaud, *The Drunken Boat*, l. 14, trans. Oliver Bernard)
p. 66, l. 3. *Serenissima.* The name given to the Republic of Venice from early days until May 1797.
p. 66, l. 13. *Rio San Polo.* Canal to the northwest of Santa Maria della Salute.
p. 66, l. 14. *traghetto.* Ferry.
p. 66, l. 16. *Salute.* Santa Maria della Salute, the grand, domed seventeenth-century church that guards the entrance to the Grand Canal.
p. 66, l. 18. *Santa Maria Gloriosa dei Frari.* After St. Mark's, the largest church in Venice, located in Campo dei Frari, San Polo.

Yard Work

Orig. pub. *Partisan Review* 61 (Spring 1994): 309.
C, 92; NB, 67

1. Chickamauga

Pattern: 4 × 3
Place: Charlottesville backyard
Time: 1993

Wright's hope that he will be remembered, which is the same as Sappho's hope, is represented as a dialectic of sameness and difference. For Sappho, the word is caught between the beginning of speech and the invisible. For Wright the word is caught between the landscape and the absolute. But the language of Sappho and the language of landscape turn out to be the "same sound," and the invisible and the landscape turn out to be the "same place." These abstractions, says the poet, stick to their own business, and he enjoins himself to do likewise. This means that he must get back to the business of "yard work"—the attentive devotion to what like directly in front of him, such as moving the inchworm "from here to there." The inchworm can perhaps be read allegorically: each poem moves the poet inexorably a little farther along the path of his pilgrimage. The implication is that if he continues to write the matter of being remembered will take care of itself. The poet is sitting in his back yard, just as he was in the first poem of *Chickamauga* and just as he will be in the final poems of both *Black Zodiac* and *Appalachia*. Yard work will turn out to be hard work.

p. 67, ll. 1–2. *I think ... Sappho once said.* "someone will remember us / I say / even in another time" (Fragment 147, *If Not, Winter: Fragments of Sappho*, trans. Anne Carson [New York: Knopf, 2002], 297).

CHAPTER 2

Black Zodiac

Black Zodiac was published by Farrar, Straus, and Giroux in 1997. For that year it received the National Book Critics Circle Award for Poetry, the Pulitzer Prize for Poetry, and the *Los Angeles Times* Prize for Poetry. The fourth printing was issued by Farrar, Straus, and Giroux under the Noonday Press imprint in 1998. The Spanish translation is *Zodiaco Negro*, trans. Jeannette L. Clariond (Valencia: Pre-textos, 2002).

The cover art is identified on the dust jacket as "Autobiographical Essay, by Huai Su, T'ang Dynasty." Huai Su (725–785), the "genius of the cursive script," was sometimes called "Huai the Crazy" because of the unrestrained style of his calligraphy. He was said to have dashed off his scripts as he pleased, often in a state of drunkenness. There are different forms of Chinese cursive (or "grass") script, but the features shared by all cursive styles are a simplified structure, a running together of strokes, rapidly written and flowing lines, and a low level of legibility. The beauty of the cursive script is expressed in a Chinese saying, "The writing stops but the meaning goes on: the brush has been put down but the power is unending." Among the styles of Chinese calligraphy, the cursive script most closely approaches abstract art. It is all rather blithely spontaneous. One can understand Wright's choosing a work with simplified and flowing lines called "Autobiographical Essay," which dates from 777. The cover reproduces a third of a larger portion of Huai Su's scroll, though the reproduction on the cover was mistakenly inverted.

Overview: As a journal devoted to landscape, the details of which are mostly metaphors for the poet's interior life, *Black Zodiac* is an *ars poetica* poem on a grand scale. The goal of his quest is Utopian—a desire for the transcendent light at the end of the journey. The poet may not achieve the vision, what he once described as "what it is I would like to happen"; in fact, he has grave doubts about the possibility of realizing the goal of the quest, which here is a purgatorial journey. But that vision is nevertheless what motivates the journey.

As points along the pilgrimage route, these poems take us to the Tennessee and Carolina mountains, to Verona and Umbria, to the Montana wilderness, and to a few other places. But mostly it is an interior journey: just as Faulkner constructed his vision from his Yoknapatawpha postage-stamp world, so Wright constructs his from a smaller postage-stamp—the garden of his own back yard. We are treated to an extensive tour of that garden: Wright's own "autobiographical essay" takes place in a middle earth, hanging between the zodiac and the world below.

Black Zodiac, then, is a metaphysical and religious quest founded on the description of landscape. Many of the poems have a three-part structure: the question or problem posed or illustrated at the beginning, then a movement into the description of landscape, and a conclusion that is a recognition of some kind. It may be a recognition that doesn't take the poet very far or it may be ambiguous or it may move him ever so slightly toward the light. The three-part structure is not always present, and in the longer poems it is more complicated, but it is typical.

The larger cosmological structure is a version of the familiar chain of being, except the links in the chain have often broken. Still, Wright's universe is one in which the divine powers exist in the heavens (enlightenment is up) and demonic ones somewhere below (darkness is down). There are all kinds of variations on this, the black zodiac itself being an obvious one and the *via negativa* another. The things of this world—Wright's landscape—mediate between the top and bottom of the ladder. For the poet's soul sometimes the mediation works; often it does not.

Apologia Pro Vita Sua

Orig. pub. in part in *Paris Review* 37, no. 135 (Summer 1995): 33–6, and in *Poetry* 166 (April 1995). BZ, 3–19; NB, 71–87

Pattern: As noted in the introduction to the present book, each part of the *Apologia* has nine sections, and each section has nine lines (in three tercets). This yields a pattern of threes and nines: $3 \times 3 = 9$; $3 \times 9 = 27$; $3 \times 27 = 81$ (9×9). The *Envoi* (pp. 86–7) repeats the pattern: nine three-line stanzas, making for a total of 90 (9×10). The ninety tercets, though not *terza rima*, are nevertheless Dantesque in form. The maintaining of equal clusters of lines is typical of Wright's later work.

The title establishes a religious context, recalling our most famous *Apologia pro Vita Sua*, the history of Newman's religious opinions (1864).

Part 1.
Section 1, p. 71. The metaphor of the dogwood as "Spring's via Dolorosa" helps set the tone for this "apologia"—both defense and explanation—of the poet's life. The via Dolorosa is the Way of Sorrows (the Stations of the Cross), and the dogwood is *identified* with the via Dolorosa. The *Stabat mater* ("At the cross her station keeping, / Stood the mournful Mother weeping, / Close to Jesus to the last....") is often sung while passing from one Station of the Cross to the next. Here Wright is drawing on the legend of the dogwood: the blossoms are like the cross, their petals are blood-stained, and the center of the blossom is a thorny crown. The dogwood, a conventional symbol of Christ's crucifixion, is a "myth limb" to be sure, but this poor dogwood is "sap-crippled, arthritic, and winter-weathered." Thus, it inverts the conventional associations that spring calls up, and the reference to April (p. 72, l. 10) reminds us of the "the cruelest month" of Eliot's *The Waste Land*.

The poem begins with another conventional metaphor—the journey, which will soon come to an end—and the poet is accompanied by his "side-kick" failure, more akin to Sancho Panza than Virgil. Like Dante, he is lost ("Nowhere to go but up, nowhere to turn"). In a "dream-light" that was other than flat, one could imagine a *three-dimensional* sidekick. The sense of this complex metaphor seems to be that in failure there can be no "depth": all is a two-dimensional flatness. The poet is at the nadir of the heavy world ("world-weight"). The surreal image of the dogwood's roots becoming the hair of the poet's mother is a haunting metaphor of death. Wright's mother's grave in Kingsport, Tennessee, has a dogwood planted on it. Her maiden name was "Winter." (*Thinking of Winter at the Beginning of Summer* [NB, 116], has the even more haunting image of both dead parents, rocking back and forth in their blackened boats.) "Winter-weathered," then, has triggered the image of the mother below ground, so that she too is linked with the end of the road in line 1. The first section does not provide an auspicious beginning for an *apologia*, in any of the word's several senses.

Section 2, p. 71. Here the mood changes with the possibility of light opening up, assisted by the landscape's lever and the poet's jack-wedge, the first of several examples of this outdoor tool-work (cf. ratcheting in *China Mail* and wrenching in *Lives of the Saints*.) The bead of dew opens out into radiance ("a world in a grain of sand"). Can the pilgrim wedge the landscape sufficiently for an aura of transcendence to accompany his "going forth"? Will the pilgrim step forward through the entrance? We are left with the questions, the poet standing there with the flowers under his feet and the white sky above, hearing the church bells.

Section 3, p. 72. *Vita Sua*. The poet has tried to bring the journal as a form of writing and landscape as a subject back to life through "language and strict attention," but has failed. Both journal writing and landscape, he says, are discredited.

Wright on Wright. In response to an interviewer's question about the meaning of "discredited," Wright replied, "Well, perhaps I didn't choose my word as accurately as I should have. I thought of the journal form being discredited as a conveyor of serious literary ambition. Usually the journal form is thought to encompass shut-in women, old guys trying to make sense of or justification for what they've done or haven't done in their lives, and so on. What I was trying to do was to make the journal form and the idea of a serious look at landscape, which is thought of as a kind of Sunday painterly occupation—I was trying to make both of those into a serious vehicle for saying something that exists possibly beyond each. Since neither is generally thought of as a repository for poetic seriousness, but as poetic gesture, I wanted to take them both and see what I could do with them vis-à-vis ... this sounds pretentious, but the spiritual journey that I felt I've been on for the last thirty years, when I've been trying to write these poems. And I was trying to imbue them, or endow them, or at least inject them with the kind of seriousness that I thought they could contain and could regenerate in poetry. One never knows whether one has done that or not. It's the sort of thing that everyone tells you not to do: don't write a poem about the sunset, and quite properly so, because you can't beat the sunset. Well, probably one shouldn't write serious poems in a journal form, or write landscape that is imbued with something beyond the landscape. But since you're not supposed to, that seemed to be a good reason to try to do it. And since I like looking at landscape, and since my mental faculties seem better equipped for notation and observation rather than flow-through narrative, I thought perhaps these are good vehicles for me to try to get in and drive, and so I did" (Zawacki, 19).

Elsewhere Wright distinguishes nature from landscape. He puts it this way in *Quarter Notes*: "The heart of nature is nature, the heart of landscape is God. Which is to say, the heart of nature is disease (and dis-ease), and the heart of landscape is design (*dasein*)." *Dasein* is a pun—Heidegger's term for being in the world—which he characterizes in terms of affective relationships with people (not Wright-like) and objects (quite Wright-like). Again, Wright says, "Nature is inherently sentimental, landscape is not." Or still again: "Landscape is something you determine and dominate; nature is something that determines and dominates you." Finally, "Landscape is a 'distancing' factor (description of same, identification of self in same) as regards the 'self,' the 'I' in poetry. Nature, on the other hand, is quicksand" (QN, 85). This takes us a long way from Shelley's "I fall upon the thorns of life. I bleed." It takes us closer to the Chinese poets of the T'ang dynasty.

The line from the song in section 3 (p. 72, l. 8), *Verona mi fe,' disfecemi Verona* ("Verona made me, Verona unmade me") is a variation on Dante's "*Siena mi fe,' disfecemi Maremma*" (*Purgatorio*, 5.133), which Pound uses as a title for one of the sections of *Hugh Selwyn Mauberley*. Compare Virgil's epitaph: "Mantua gave me life, Calabria slew me; Parthenope now holds me. I have sung shepherds, the countryside, and wars." The reference—at least *Verona mi fe'*—is to Wright's early Italian sojourn, where he became aware of Pound and began writing poetry.

He was stationed in Verona during the time of his military service, and his experience at Lake Garda outside Verona was, as he has described it on numerous occasions, a Saul-like epiphany that led to his becoming a poet. But, he says, Verona unmade him as well. He has bridged the gap between then and now, between being made and unmade, but it has been to no avail: what the new year ushered in by April means is "beyond words"—in the sense not of something extraordinary but of something outside the power of language to capture. This is a typical self-deprecating ploy on the part of Wright—to announce the impossibility of the poetic enterprise and then to present us with a book containing twenty more poems. As we have seen, Wright has his reasons for believing that the poetic journal is a discredited form and landscape a discredited subject matter. The rest of *Black Zodiac* and all of *Appalachia* illustrate that neither, if discredited, should be.

Section 4, p. 72. We shift quickly to a rather macabre view of the Eucharist ("meat" for "body," "ghostly" for "spiritual"). There's no resurrection of the body ("vessel of life") during this Easter season for the poet. "Vessel" is of course a conventional metaphor: it is Biblical, as in Jeremiah, and the Virgin is identified with the vessel of life in the liturgy. In the context of the Eucharist in these lines, there is perhaps also a hint of the vessel as chalice. But primarily the "vessel of life" is the body. If it is gathered back to the visible, then transubstantiation has failed. The primary sources for this section are two passages from *The Book of Thomas the Contender* in *The Nag Hammadi Library*: "Thomas answered and said, 'It is beneficial for us, lord, to rest among our own.' The savior said, 'Yes, it is useful. And it is good for you, since things visible among men will dissolve—for the vessel of their flesh will dissolve, and when it is brought to naught it will come to be among visible things, among things that are seen. And then the fire which they see gives them pain on account of love for the faith they formerly possessed. They will be gathered back to that which is visible. Moreover, those who have sight among things that are not visible, without the first love they will perish in the concern for this life and the scorching of the fire. Only a little while longer, and that which is visible will dissolve; then shapeless shades will emerge, and in the midst of tombs they will forever dwell upon the corpses in pain and corruption of soul'" (NHL, 203–4). "They [the fools] have always been attracted downwards; as they are killed, they are assimilated to all the beasts of the perishable realm" (NHL, 203).

The poet moves downward, envisioning his own death as assimilation back into the earth. Spring's fragrance is like lust, the darkness begins to seep through, and the world begins to tilt. The syntax of the tercet that begins at the bottom of p. 72 is ambiguous. The movement of all visible things is, here, downward. Are we to read the lines as what the poet sees—the world starting to tilt—from where he sits in his backyard? He doesn't cause us to pause after "sit," and so the verb appears to be transitive, as if the poet is an usher, showing the still point its place. This is perhaps an echo of Eliot's still point of the turning world, or perhaps even Pound's "unwobbling pivot," something permanent and unchanging in the human flux, or a glimpse of order through the mists of "usury." In *The Tripartite Tractate*, another Nag Hammadi text, those who have been restored are said to have been grasped in "an unwavering and immovable way" (NHL, 99). Yet the "unwavering point" and all it represents is unavailable, invisible, below the waves. In this Gnostic battle between light and darkness, the latter is, at this stage, beginning to win.

A number of other Gnostic themes, often sublimated, emerge here and there in Wright's poetry: the battle between the flesh and the spirit; the notion that there are innumerable other worlds that emanate from some Supreme Being and operate in the cosmos; the idea that human beings exist at various stages of spiritual development; and the belief that divine "gnosis" can penetrate this world, as in the prologue to the Gospel of John: "In the beginning was the Word." While the *Apologia* draws heavily on the Gnostic texts in *The Nag Hammadi Library*, Wright's undivided attention to the phenomena of the physical world—nature in the nineteenth-century Romantic sense and landscape in Wright's sense—is far removed from Gnosticism. The word "nature" as referring to the world of living things and the forces of the cosmos does not appear in *The Nag Hammadi Library*.

Section 5, p. 73. We return to landscape, the clouds triggering a series of reflections on how each of the four elements fall. Neither the earth (the here and now) nor the air (the there and then) can redeem us. If there is to be no union of earth and air, no resurrection of the body and spirit (soul), which are moving away from each other, then we are deprived of an "attitude." The word "attitude" here means not so much feeling or disposition as it does a sense of place or position in space. Things in space, like airplanes, have, if bereft of their attitude, no points of reference. The word appears also in the context of form, measure, and spatial position in *Lonesome Pine Special* (WTTT, 72) *Meditation on Form and Measure* (NB, 91), *October II* (NB, 102), and *Deep Measure* (NB, 115). It could be, however, that the poet means that in the absence of resurrection and redemption we are bereft of what one Nag Hammadi text calls "an attitude of amazement at the exalted one who will become manifest" (*The Tripartite Tractate*, NHL, 79).

Section 6, p. 73. *The color purple interlude*. Purple is the liturgical color for Advent, but here amethyst, or royal purple, is associated with magic. It was said by Leonardo and others to have the power to ward off evil (*malocchio*) and storms and to prevent drunkenness (*amethystos* = not drunken). The ancient Egyptians used it for intaglios and the Maya for jewelry and purses. But in this stanza the color purple is also associated with the mind, insight, and remembering. Focusing, however, on the penumbra of the heavens, that shadow between complete darkness and complete illumination, the poet can discover no distinguishing marks. Magic fails, and in the battle between light and darkness, between insight and drunkenness, nothing is gained, as we see in the rhetorical question of the final tercet.

Section 7, p. 74. *The painters' section*. The central theme here is the absence of any reassurance in either art or poetry, with the accompanying feeling of loneliness. Painting and writing are mere gestures hanging between the abysses of darkness and light with nothing to intercede between the opposites. The painters mentioned are three of Wright's most admired: Morandi, Cézanne, and Rothko

Giorgio Morandi (1890–1964) was an Italian painter whose subdued tones and monumental simplicity of form is reminiscent of Paul Cézanne. Morandi (1890–1964) is one of Wright's most beloved artists. See the notes and commentaries above for *Morandi II* (C, 67) and *Still Life with Stick and Wood* (NB 60). For other appearances of Morandi in Wright's poems, see *Morandi* in CM, 114; *A Journal of True Confessions* in WTTT, 143; *Chinese Journal* in WTTT, 199; *Basic Dialogue* in NB, 147; *Giorgio Morandi and the Talking Eternity Blues* in NB, 167; *Looking Around* in SHS, 3; and *Homage to Giorgio Morandi* in BY, 60–1. Except for some very early portraits, his work is centers on (1) the landscape, with windowless houses, of hilly northern Italy, (2) the courtyard of his apartment building in Bologna, and (3) and bottles, bowls, boxes, tins, and other utensils atop a table in his studio. His colors are muted and dusty, and he paints his subjects from directly in front of them. There is almost no drama in Morandi, and the meaning and feeling contained in his paintings and drawings has to be teased out from his sense of structure and his handing of space, issuing in what Wright calls in one interview "the energy of absence" (QN, 173) and in another "negative transcendence" (Spiegelman, 121). Some art critics note that Morandi was influenced by Cézanne.

Mark Rothko (1903–70), the third of Wright's quintessential painters, was an American artist whose style evolved into a very peaceful and meditative form of Abstract Expressionism;

he stained large canvases with rectangular blocks of pure color. His later works became much more somber and darker. "I can say that the dark pictures began in 1957," he wrote, "and have persisted almost completely to this day" (qtd. by James E.B. Breslin, *Mark Rothko: A Biography* [Chicago: University of Chicago Press, 1993], 328). Rothko committed suicide in 1970, as the final line of this section suggests. "Two tone fields, horizon line between the abysses, / Generally white, always speechless" is a description of some of the paintings from Rothko's more or less classic period, such as his *Untitled* (1969–70). "Silence is so accurate," said Rothko. The battle here again is between light and dark. "Rothko could choose either one to disappear into" (p. 74, l. 9). He chose the dark. A short time before he committed suicide, he remarked to Dore Ashton about his paintings, "The dark is always at the top"—that is, black zodiac. Rothko also makes an appearance in *Looking at Pictures* (WTTT, 113), *A Journal of True Confessions* (WTTT, 143), and *Homage to Mark Rothko* (BY, 38–9).

Section 8, p. 74. The Italian quotation is from pt. 2 of Guido de Cavalcanti's *Rime*, XXXV: "Because I expect never to return, little poem, to Tuscany"—a line quoted by Pound in *ABC of Reading* as an example of clarity, simplicity, and condensation (New York: New Directions, 1960, p. 96). Here Wright picks up the themes of section 3 (the wide gap between here and there, now and then) and section 6 (the difficulty of remembering), along with the theme of the poet as exile: Dante, Guido, and Job. The "thingless" allusion (p. 74, l. 15) is to Job 1:21: "Naked came I out of my mother's womb, and naked shall I return thither." Still, the poet grants that even a snowflake of memory is better than no memory at all, and that to have failed is better than not having tried, which is a version of T.S. Eliot's remark in his essay on Baudelaire: "So far as we are human, what we do must be either evil or good; so far as we do evil or good, we are human; and it is better, in a paradoxical way, to do evil than to do nothing; at least we exist" (*Selected Essays* [New York: Harcourt, Brace, 1950], 380). The central image here is the snowflakes of memory. The poem, like Dante's *Commedia*, is the anthem of exile.

Section 9, p. 74. This section begins with the commonplace abstraction of time as both creator and destroyer. (The idea of time "as the type of First Begetter" comes from verse 24 of *Eugnostos the Blessed* in the NHL, 234.) But it then shifts abruptly to the image of the fingernail, and we return to the things of this world, to the poet's consciousness of himself and his place in the little garden, with its birds and flowers. Part 1 of the *Apologia* began in dreamlight and with the desire to jack-wedge the landscape so as to let the light in. Here we end in half-dark, but as half-dark is also half-light, at least all is not lost. The request to St. Stone, a purely fictitious saint, is an invocation for help in continuing the odyssey. Part 1 concludes with the poet wanting to plod along in spite of his discredited form and discredited subject, in spite of important acts being wordless, of the difficulty of distinguishing parts from wholes, of being bereft, of bridging the break to no avail, of not being able to connect past and present, and all of his other travails. If Rothko chose to disappear into the dark tone, the pilgrim does not. This same inclination ("more work to be done" with the ellipsis pointing us to the next page) comes also at the end of the *Envoi*, where the poet opts for the daytime metaphysics of the natural world.

Part 2.
Section 1, p. 76. Following the doctor's hollow prognosis that "something will get you," the *apologia* turns to a complaint about physical ills and psychological *Angst*. The doctor has said not to worry, but this only triggers a catalogue of complaints. The simile in ll. 7–9 is a male version of Albrecht Dürer's *Melancholia* (1514), depicting the winged personification of Melancholy, seated dejectedly and holding a compass in her lap.

"Black dog" as a colloquial term for depression goes back to Horace. In the English tradition, Winston Churchill is said to have coined the phrase for his own melancholy, but it can be traced back at least to Samuel Johnson, who used it a number of times and who said that Robert Burton's *Anatomy of Melancholy* was the only book that ever got him out of bed to read two hours earlier than he wanted to (James Boswell, *The Life of Samuel Johnson*, ed. George Birkbeck Hill [Oxford: Oxford University Press, 1934], 2:121). "Sick and tired" in line 6 is a *double entendre*, meaning, on the one hand, that the poet is thoroughly weary of his own complaints and, on the other, that in addition to being physically ill he is tired of complaining about it ("everyone's had enough"). The symptoms of melancholy are all described as bodily ills, and these in turn are emblematic of a psychological depression.

Section 2, p. 76. This section is a flashback to an East Tennessee golf match with the poet's buddy Chuck Ross. Rotherwood (p. 76, l. 15) is a historic home at the junction of the North Fork and Holston Rivers in Kingsport, Tennessee. The focus here is an *apologia* in its other sense, a mild expression of regret for the various forms of devious golf behavior and a confession of a "teen-age false sense of attainment."

The remainder of part 2 is a series of vignettes from the poet's past, less *apologia* than snapshots from *vita sua*:

- p. 77, ll. 1–9. A portrait of a summer camp-mate, encountered forty years later in Lexington, Virginia, now a rather pathetic cleric. The contrast is between the larger than life camper of an earlier time, sneaking off with his blanket and flashlight each night for a rendezvous with the camp cook, and his present diminished appearance—rabbit-eyed, fumbling, dry-lipped, and apologetic.
- p. 77, ll. 10–18. An account of a 1990 trip to Paris, which turned out to produce ten days of sleeplessness and hallucination in the rainy City of Light. *Le Dôme, La Closerie des Lilas, Le Select,* and *La Coupole* on the Boulevard Montparnesse—all of which are still in business— were, in Montparnasse's heyday (from 1910 to 1920), cafes where starving artists could occupy a table all evening for a few *centimes*.
- p. 77, l. 19–p. 78, l. 7. An experience in 1958 at the Monterey Jazz Festival, especially the conversation between Percy Heath and the drunk, tone-deaf poet. Heath, Jackson, Lewis, Mulligan, and Desmond were all jazz musicians. The ominous image of ocean's eyelid is a metaphor for the impending build-up in Vietnam. Wright was in Monterey in 1957–58 to attend the Army Language School, where he learned Italian.
- p. 78, ll. 8–16. Life in Oak Ridge, Tennessee (1943–45), during which time the poet announces that he learned three things: something unnamed from paper route; something unnamed from breaking-and-entering episode; and resurrection from the water, the only thing that mattered. This World War II experience, along with the knowledge of death-by-water that emerged during these years, is a thematic elaboration of the references to South Vietnam and the "Pacific's dark eyelid" of the previous section. The descent and ascent motif, which the poet declares he didn't and still doesn't know what to do with, is nevertheless what his poetry will continue to explore throughout the pilgrimage. "Nothing even comes close," he says, to mattering as much as resurrection from the depths, and the variations on this theme will turn out to be the real *apologia* for his life.
- p. 78, l. 1–p. 79, l. 7. A 1944 voyeuristic experience from his Oak Ridge childhood that mystifies the nine-year-old. Elm Grove, Pine Valley, and Cedar Hill were all schools in Oak Ridge. The "new world's sun king" is the atom bomb. The Oak Ridge Reservation, where Wright's father worked for a time, was established in 1942 as part of the Manhattan Project.
- p. 78, ll. 9–17. In this flashback to 1957 in Kingsport, the summer following Wright's

graduation from college, the poet and his friend Carter are working for a Sullivan County bank, trying to extract payments from the destitute and delinquent purchasers of cemetery plots. The poet condemns himself for to taking such a miserable job—*apologia* as regretful acknowledgment once more. World War II continues to hover in the background.

- p. 78, l. 19–p. 80, l. 6. The present: 5 June 1994. The poet's reflections on his parents, on the fact that he's older than they were when they died (he is almost 59) and that they never saw their grandson Luke. Wright's mother (Mary Winter) died in 1964; his father (Charles Penzel) in 1972. The pall of death always hangs heavy over Wright's consciousness here, as it does in much of his later work.

This part of the *Apologia*, which began with melancholy, ends with reflections on death ("Some afternoon, some noon, it will all be over"), but like the ending of part 1, not yet: there are more rounds to climb in this purgatorial journey.

Part 3
The dialectic of part 3 is a set of oppositions between the visible and the invisible, the past and the future, certainty and uncertainty, defining and dismantling, ignorance and illumination, forgetfulness and memory, beginning and end, concealment and revelation. Wright's note on p. 204 refers us to the already cited *Nag Hammadi Library*, the dozen or so papyrus books discovered by an Arab peasant in 1945. These manuscripts, hidden for a millennium and a half, are a record of what orthodox Christianity perceived to be its most dangerous challenge, known most commonly as Gnosticism. Several allegorical "characters" in part 3 derive from *The Nag Hammadi Library*: "the Adversary" (p. 81, l. 17), "the Illuminator" (p. 83, l. 2) and "The Unknown Master of the Pure Poem" (p. 84, l. 3). Other borrowings from *The Nag Hammadi Library* are noted in what follows.

Section 1, p. 81. The setting is a hot, muggy Sunday in June in the Charlottesville backyard. Externally, the poet hears his neighbor's roof being shingled, and he observes the grackles, the hedge, the magnolia, the "pie-pan frightener," the trash cans along Locust Avenue, among other things. But the focus is on the poet's internal mood, and what emerges from his self-analysis is anxiety, forgetfulness, ignorance, uncertainty. The "slow ripples of otherworldliness" have come to the poet for forty years, yet they have been ineffective illuminations and the poetry ("screed") ineffectual. Thus the poet's invocation to the mystics—St. John of the Cross and Julian(a) of Norwich—to take him the rest of the way. The appeal is for a vision that is not ineffective or indifferent ("feckless"). Wright is forever on the lookout for a Virgil to assist him along the way. He occasionally appeals to saints other than the two here and St. Stone in part 1, section 9: e.g., St. Xavier (*A Journal of True Confessions*), St. Francis (*Umbrian Dreams*), and St. Catherine of Siena (*Buffalo Yoga Coda I*).

Section 2. The theme here is knowledge—the things that are good to know—and these things turn out to derive from the often arcane Gnostic pronouncements of *The Nag Hammadi Library*.

The first and second tercets are borrowed from *The Concept of Our Great Power*: "Know how what has departed came to be, in order that you may know how to discern what lives to become: of what appearance that aeon is, or what kind it is, or how it will come to be. Why do you not ask what kind you will become, (or) rather how you came to be? Discern what size the water is, that it is immeasurable (and) incomprehensible, both its beginning and its end" (*NHL*, 312–13). "He who will know our great Power will become invisible, and fire will not be able to consume him.... (Those) whom I constrained to gather all that is fallen—and the writings of our great Power, in order that he may inscribe your name in our great light" (*NHL*, 312). The first line of the third tercet is from *The Teachings of Sylvanus*: "What else is evil....

For a foolish man usually puts on folly like a robe, and like a garment of sorrow, he puts on shame" (*NHL*, 383).

In the next line the poet says that it is good to know that time is the Adversary, the demonic force we work against (the same figure we meet in the Book of Job, *ha-satan*, the Adversary or the Accuser). The Adversary appears in four of the Nag Hammadi texts. Section 2 concludes with this enigmatic line: "The clouds are unequal and words are." Unequal to what? Unequal in what respects? And does "words are" require a predicate? *The Tripartite Tractate* of *The Nag Hammadi Library* provides a clue: "He [the Logos] generated manifest images of the living visages, pleasing among things which are good, existing among the things which exist, resembling them in beauty, but unequal to them in truth, since they are not from an agreement with him, between the one who brought them forth and the one who revealed himself to him. But in wisdom and knowledge he acts, mingling the Logos with him(self) entirely. Therefore, those which came forth from him are great, just as that which is truly great" (*NHL*, 80). The sense, then, seems to be, according to the author of the *Tractate*, that the clouds resemble living things in beauty but not in truth, truth being reserved for language, the words that come from the Word. This, in effect, is what the author of the *Tractate* goes on to say: in the beginning the Logos was.

Section 3, p. 82. (There should be a line separating sections 2 and 3 at the bottom of p. 81. The section separator was inserted in the *Black Zodiac* version of the poem, but it was accidentally omitted in *Negative Blue*.) The landscape seems to portend something ominous, says the poet, who proceeds to give us a snapshot of a friend who can no longer speak and concludes by agreeing with a third friend that "life's hard." The focus here is on the inability of language to "set things right."

Section 4, p. 82. The question in this section is what to do about Sundays, this Sunday being a sun day: the sun is at first only a "tongued wafer behind the clouds," but by noon it has become a "laser disk." Wallace Stevens has entered our consciousness in the previous stanza (p. 82, l. 7), and there is more than an echo of his *Sunday Morning* here, the solitude of remembered Sundays chilling us "unto the grave." The speaker in Stevens's poem asks the same question Wright does two stanzas later: "And what of me afterwards?" (p. 83, l. 13).

Section 5, pp. 82-3. This section begins with another borrowing from *The Nag Hammadi Library*: "For you descended into a great ignorance, / but you have not been defiled by anything in it. / For you descended into a great mindlessness, /and your recollection remained. // You walked in mud, / and your garments were not soiled, / and you have not been buried in their filth, / and you have not been caught.... There is in me forgetfulness, / yet I remember things that are not theirs" (*The First Apocalypse of James*, *NHL*, 263-4). Memory is the great savior, redeeming the poet, yet his memory of some things has failed, having forgotten, for example, "Who the Illuminator is" and "Who will have pity on what needs to have pity on it." The Illuminator of knowledge is a vaguely allegorical "character" in *The Apocalypse of Adam* in *The Nag Hammadi Library*. In *The Letter of Philip to Peter* the Illuminator is identified with Jesus ("I am the light"), and in and *The Second Apocalypse of James*, which is Wright's primary source for this section, the Illuminator is the redeemer. The forgotten line about pity comes from *The Second Apocalypse of James*: "For your sake, they will have pity / on whomever they pity" (*NHL*, 273). In any event, without memory the poet will be able neither to complete his purgatorial journey nor to enter whatever phase will follow, once more using the language of *The Nag Hammadi Library*: "And again he shall provide / an end for what has begun, / and a beginning for what is about to be ended" (*NHL*, 274).

Section 6, p. 83. *The Nag Hammadi Library* is filled to the point of obsession with speculations about beginning and ends. Such speculations spur the poet to wax philosophically about the coming and going of "the determining moments of our lives." The contrast between the dark trash cans along the curb and the star between the cusps of the moon (as in the Turkish flag, a white crescent moon and a star on a red background) sets the scene for a defining moment.

The poet appears to be on the verge of an epiphany, but nothing comes of it. Whatever elaboration might have been forthcoming is displaced by another series of queries, and the section concludes in the interrogative mood with which it began.

Section 7, pp. 83–4. This section—on the advantages of anonymity over naming—begins with a paraphrase from *The Gospel of Philip* in *The Nag Hammadi Library*: "'The father' and 'the son' are single names; 'the holy spirit' is a double name. For they are everywhere: they are above, they are below; they are in the concealed, they are in the revealed. The Holy Spirit is in the revealed: it is below. It is in the concealed: it is above.... Echamoth is one thing and Echmoth, another. Echamoth is Wisdom simply, but Echmoth is the Wisdom of death, which is the one who knows death, which is called 'the little Wisdom'" (*NHL*, 145–6). The poet concludes that it is better to write anonymously, letting the words, unencumbered by the writer's name, speak for themselves.

As for the identity of Unknown Master of the Pure Poem (p. 84, l. 3), he is Wright's poetic father, who walks through the backyard garden that his son has laid out. In the various texts of *The Nag Hammadi Library* he is the divine figure called "Unknown One" (*Allogenes*) and the "unknown" Father (*The Tripartite Tractate* and *Zostrianos*). The Pure Poet is a displaced version of the Master of Pure Gnosis (the Logos) in the Nag Hammadi texts.

Section 8, p. 84. The poet revisits the sights and sounds of noontime in Charlottesville, a continuation of the scene in section 1. He finds little to celebrate, what with the stifling heat, the desultory breeze, the evil eye of the garden mojo, and the lives of others whose lurking presence the poet feels. The crucifixion on the back of the grackle is close to an objective correlative of the poet's own state.

Section 9, p. 84–5. The *Apologia* ends with an affirmation that we hardly expect, given the generally negative mood of the *Apologia*. But here the poet declares that everything rises to the absolute of affection and to the devotion to detail, as in the love-lisp of the magnolia's white-tongued petal—what has been off-loaded by the landscape. Again, the similarity to the concluding vision of Stevens's *Sunday Morning*, with the speaker's affirmation of the natural world, is worth remarking.

Envoi. Ordinarily an "envoi" is a conventionalized set of four-line, rhymed stanzas at the end of a poem. The only convention we have here is that the *envoi* closes off the *Apologia*. But an "envoi" can also be a "sending," as in the diplomatic meaning of "envoy" or as in Pound's *envoi* at the end of *Hugh Selwyn Mauberley*, where he dispatches his book. Too, Wright's *envoi* is his beginning, as we are sent off into "the daytime metaphysics of the natural world." The first part of the *envoi* focuses on absence—the absence of delight, of full meaning, of a sense of place, of taut memory. There's no *Angst* in the animal world, but there is in the world of the poet, with ash on his tongue, and in our cybernetic world, where on-lines do not connect, downloads do not deliver, and voice-overs are not recognizable. But, says the poet, we need a sense of the past, present, and future. The poet's solution: he will take whatever wanes and breaks down, including Ryder's paintings, "Language, the weather, the word of God." This is a victory of acceptance, though if it is only waning and darkness and breaking down that are taken, it seems to be a rather small victory. But in the last three lines, the poet takes what waxes as well, for he embraces this "daytime metaphysics of the natural world" as "icon and testament." What he will also take, but which remains unsaid, is the nighttime metaphysics of the natural world, for the black zodiac will turn out to be just as much a backdrop for his rapt attention as what is illuminated by the negative blue of the daytime sky.

The general movement of this journey as *apologia*, or vice versa, has been downward. But at the end of all four sections the poet's verse does manage to turn ("verse" and "turn" mean the same thing) toward the metaphysics of light. The *Apologia* as a whole, then, mimics the movement of the *Commedia*. One is reminded too of a couplet from Samuel Taylor Coleridge's own *Apologia pro Vita Sua* about the gift of seeing beyond the transient or commonplace appearance of things: "His gifted ken can see / Phantoms of sublimity."

* * *

The next five poems in *Black Zodiac* were conceived of as a unit, forming part 2 of that book (the breaks are not indicated in *Negative Blue*). As so often in Wright's poetry, the poems are arranged chronologically. Here we move through the year from December (*Poem Half in the Manner of Li Po*), July (*Meditation on Form and Measure*), August (*Poem Almost Wholly in My Own Manner*), late August (*Meditation of Summer and Shapelessness*), and September (*The Appalachian Book of the Dead*). Wright is very conscious throughout of the seasonal cycle. "I am addicted to the seasons," he says (Spiegelman, 119).

Poem Half in the Manner of Li Ho

Orig. pub. *Field* 50 (Spring 1994): 64.
BZ, 23–4; NB, 88–9
Pattern: (2 × 3) (9 × 2) (2 × 3)
Time: December

Li Ho (791–817) was a Chinese poet of the late T'ang Dynasty. A.C. Graham writes, "Although famous in the ninth century and never quite forgotten, he offended the conventionality of later taste by his individuality and its health and balance by his morbidity and violence.... Li Ho's central theme is the transience of life, a subject which he treats as though no one before him had ever felt the drip of the water-clock on his nerves, in a wholly personal imagery of ghosts, blood, dying animals, weeping statues, whirlwinds, the will-o'-the-wisp" (*Poems of the Late T'ang*, 89). Graham also observes that in Li Ho we get "an unobtrusive change in the relation between subjective and objective. A rigour in seeking the objective correlative of emotion is a strong point of most Chinese poetry in all periods" (91). Wright's poems are not imitations of Li Ho, at least not the ones in Graham's anthology. But one can hear an occasional echo from Li Ho's little lyrics, and the inscrutable God is found in his poem *Don't Go Out the Door*.

The half of the poem after the manner of Li Ho is found in sections 1 and 3, each composed of three couplets. These are interrupted by the poignant story of Li Ho, composed of two nine-line stanzas. Both halves represent, again, the dark, melancholic mood—first, in the account of Li Ho's early death and, second, in "our" disconsolation and pain because we can't achieve what we aspire to (the weightlessness in some "zone of grace"), and because in the mournfulness and despair of the mountain landscape words are of no use. Thus, we land somewhere in middle earth between the zone of grace (something) and nothing. We encounter over and over in Wright's work this notion that we are suspended between the *here* and the *there*, the light and the dark, heaven and hell. Even poetry is what hangs in that white space between the lines, as Wright says in *Poem Almost Wholly in My Own Manner* (p. 94, l. 13). In the same poem we are told that the poet's mother is "layered between history and a three-line lament" (p. 93, l. 4), and we are said to live in the cracks of those spaces where the forces lift and lower. In *The Appalachian Book of the Dead* the poet writes of the "strata our bodies rise through."

The Li Ho half-imitations (sects. 1 and 3) contain parallel movements. The first aspires to get beyond the "lip of language." The third says that "there are no words / For December's chill redaction" (the editing job December has done). In other words, language is powerless to do what we want it to do. But then the poet immediately proceeds to give us two striking images of what is not beyond language: the white sky with the sunset opening up in the west and the image of suspension between earth and heaven. In the first set of couplets we have abstraction–landscape–abstraction and in the second set, landscape–abstraction–landscape.

Wright's account of Li Ho's life appears to be drawn, at least in part, from David Young's account in *Five T'ang Poets*: "Every day he [Li Ho] would go out riding on a donkey, accompanied by a servant boy with a tapestry bag. As he wandered through the countryside, he would compose poems and toss them into a bag. At home in the evening, he would dump out his day's work and finish the poems, allegedly provoking his mother's comment: 'My son will not stop until he has vomited up his heart!'" (*Five T'ang Poets* [Oberlin, Ohio: Oberlin College Press, 1990], 119). Young also notes that Li Ho was "summoned on his deathbed by a heavenly messenger riding a red dragon" (121). Wright occasionally picks up a phrase from Young's translations: "raw silk" (from *Sixth Moon*, 130), "white sky" (*Eleventh Moon*, 135), "no words can describe" (*Dawn in Stone City*, 145).

p. 89, l. 8. *How mournful ... are.* "The Southern hills, how mournful" (Li Ho, *Criticisms*, in *Poems of the Late T'ang*, trans. A.C. Graham [Harmondsworth: Penguin, 1965], 114).
p. 89, l. 12. Cf. Li Ho's metaphor, "the black flag of cloud which hung in the empty night" (*An Arrowhead from the Ancient Battlefield of Ch'ang-p'ing*, in *Poems of the Late T'ang*, 99). There is also an echo in Li Ho's line that the gods are "for ever present between somewhere and nowhere" (*Magic Strings*, ibid., 94).

Meditation on Form and Measure

Orig. pub. *Field* 51 (Fall 1994): 81–2.
BZ, 25–7; NB, 90–2
Pattern: 5 × 2, for each of the five sections
Time: July
Place: Montana

This poem is also a meditation on death: "Of any two thoughts I have, one is devoted to death" (p. 90, l. 2). "We pattern ourselves against the dead" (p. 91, l. 11). "We live among ghosts" (p. 91, l. 15). "Memory is a cemetery" (p. 92, l. 1).

Against death and against the chaos and shapelessness and uncertainty of life, the poet offers the *form* of landscape, beginning with the one on July 13, with its buck robin and doe bird and its Northern sky. The poet opens his palm to block out the stars, confirming their existence. The entire stanza glances upward: creatures of the air, the blue sky, the star-wheels, and the cloud; even the doe bird is "tail-up." The setting is the Montana landscape. The second *form* offered is the extraordinary pictures of the spruce trees and the night scene in section 2. Here the poet's metaphorical imagination gets fully untracked: the spruces form the cloister of an abbey, some of the trees are frocked monks, the grouse hide in the dark folds of the frock, and the two male grouse strut sacrificially, like lords, down the dead log. It is a quiet scene, which is perhaps why verbs are absent: there is really only one verb, "lord down" (though there are several verbals and several implied copulas). The language is religious: cloister, abbey, monk, frock, cross, graced, sacrificial, lord. This and the moon scene that follows are meditations on *form* (a genuine shape thrown up against the shapelessness of life in section 1), and, thus, they are one answer to the question, "what confirms the hand?" (p. 90, l. 1)

"The difference between nothing and not-nothing," says Wright, "is a line drawn on the air. One must try to draw the line" (*Quarter Notes*, 84). This is a poem of the air and the firmament—from the stars and moon of sections 1 and 2, through "Father darkness, mother night" of section 3, to the constellations in sections 4 and 5. The creatures are all creatures of the air: we have three birds in sections 1 and 2 (robin, doe bird, and grouse) and others follow (hawk, jay, swallows, and jack robin). Even the snatches of the Verdi aria (from *aer*, the lower atmosphere) in section 4, though incongruous with the "bird snarl" of the jays, get us airborne.

Form and measure. The central section of the poem is a meditation on these two abstractions. Wright concludes by saying that form and measure become one. This means the unity, or actually the identity of space and time. Measure, as said before, is the form we impose upon time, especially on the movement of the poetic line, but in this poem it is also on the movement from the star-light at the beginning to the life-enclosing stars at the end (sect. 5).

As for syllabic measure, *Wright on Wright*: "I count all the syllables in every line that I write. I try to have them be odd numbers of syllables. I like to think I work in a kind of bastardized quantitative measure, which is to say, I'm more interested in the number and the duration and the weight of the syllables than I am in the stress count or stress patterns in the line. I'm very aware of the stress patterns when they start becoming obvious, and I try to move them around. But, in fact, my main concern is the pattern of vowels. And I listen to them constantly when I write. I used to be very conscious of the number of both stresses and syllables. I have come, now, to be much more interested only in the syllable count. The stresses tend to take care of themselves. If you're working with a thirteen-syllable line, you're going to have somewhere between four and seven stresses in a line, automatically, unless you go 'rock, rock, rock, rock, rock, rock, rock, rock, rock, rock, rock, rock, rock,' until you have thirteen. But basically the stresses will take care of themselves. It is to me an extension, a variation, a going forth from 'the sequence of the musical phrase' where Pound said you should be interested in the shape of the line, and it should move in the sequence of the musical phrase as opposed to the sequence of the metronome. In other words, what he meant by that was don't just write lines in pentameter" (*Halflife*, 163–4).

Otherwise regarding form and measure, there is also a rhythm in the number of lines Wright has in each stanza, the number of stanzas per section (in those poems so divided), and the number of sections in each poem.

The Italian phrase O *vaghe stelle dell'orso* (p. 92, l. 7) is the opening line of one of Giacomo Leopardi's *Canti*—no. 22, *Le ricordanze* (1829)—which Wright translates in the drop-down line. The poet wants to retake from Leopardi the line about the beautiful stars of the Bear (*Ursa Major*) so that he can someday "immerse [himself] in its cold, Lethean shine." In *Le ricordanze* (*Memories*), Leopardi contemplates the beautiful stars of the Bear from a garden, just as Wright contemplates them from the Montana wilderness. Leopardi's memories of his life are anything but pleasant, and he wants to abandon his present life and join the fair star of the Great Bear. It is not so much a suicide wish as it is a desire to transcend his harsh and woeful life for "mysterious worlds" that lie beyond the blue hills and the far sea. The Great Bear's Lethean shine is, thus, the light of forgetfulness. What he wants to forget are all those people—everybody it seems—for "whom strange words, and wisdom and good sense / Are cause for laughter and amusing sport."

Poem Almost Wholly in My Own Manner

Orig. pub. *Gettysburg Review* 8, no. 1 (Winter 1995): 22.
BZ, 28–30; NB, 93–5
Pattern: 2 × 6, for each of the three sections
Time: August

"*Where the Southern cross the yellow Dog*" is a line from W.C. Handy's *Yellow Dog Blues*. The "Southern" is the Southern Railway Company in Mississippi, which crossed the Yellow Dog Railway, a nickname for the Yazoo & Mississippi Delta Railway which ran through the heart of the Mississippi Delta in the early 1900s, at a town called Moorhead, Mississippi. (For a photograph of this famous crossing see http://www.earlyblues.com/Yellow%20Dog.htm.) Why it was called "Yellow Dog" is uncertain. "Dog" was railroad slang for a local line, and one theory is that the name derived from the yellow cars of the Yazoo and Mississippi Delta Railway. Another is that the name comes from the "Y.D." painted on the side of the cars—an abbreviation for Yazoo and Delta. References to the Yellow Dog appear in early blues songs by Charlie Patton, Lucille Bogan, and Big Bill Broonzy. But its most well-known reference is in W.C. Handy's autobiography, where he describes an incident at a train station in Tutwiler, Mississippi. There he heard an old man playing guitar with a knife blade and singing over and over again, "Goin' where the Southern cross the Dog." The man's singing was answered by the moaning sound of the knife sliding across the metal strings of the guitar.

Handy's *Yellow Dog Blues*, originally written as *Yellow Dog Rag*, is about the moaning of Miss Susan Johnson over the disappearance of her boyfriend, a jockey named Lee. The chorus reports that "Easy rider's got a stay away / So he had to vamp it but the hike ain't far. / He's gone where the Southern 'cross' the Yellow Dog." The song, therefore, is an answer to the question posed in an earlier popular blues piece, *I Wonder Where My Easy Rider's Gone Today*.

Wright's mother (p. 93, ll. 2–3), Mary Winter Wright, who grew up in Leland, had hopes that her son would become a writer. Two of her own favorite writers were William Faulkner, whose brother she had dated when she was at the University of Mississippi, and Eudora Welty (Suarez, 53). In the poem, the mother's sheltered life in Leland put her on the wrong side of the tracks from the blues tradition: she was "unfretted" (the pun seems to be intentional) and "unaware," caught between the history of the delta and the lament of the blues.

This is a challenging poem thematically, but its mood is clearly elegiac. It contains a number of haunting themes: the movement of black music north from its home in the Mississippi Delta, the impossibility of having hope and faith and the near impossibility of showing charity (the charitable sky is a "sweet grief" and charity itself—those "malevolent mercies"—disappears once it has made an appearance), the ability of music to do what language cannot ("Poetry is what's left between the lines—a strange speech and a hard language, / It's all in the unwritten, it's all in the unsaid"). There is a certain plaintive feeling because jazz and blues were not left between the lines and they should have been, i.e., between the lines of the Southern and the Yellow Dog and between the lines of the poem. Thus, the scorching of the highway in the journey north (the fire beneath the turning wheels of time later modulates into the whirling wheels of Ezekiel), the black notes that follow us, the scalded flesh and singed hair, the unstrung (another pun) musicians. Wright ordinarily leaves politics alone, but the poem has a subtext of the history of the black experience in the Mississippi Delta, from where the "black notes … follow our footsteps like blood from a cut finger"(p. 94, ll. 1–2) and where time has turned the tenants out (p. 93, l. 11–12). Whatever Robert Johnson and W.C. Handy might now have to say about this offers only cold comfort (p. 95, ll. 1–7).

Meditation on Summer and Shapelessness

Orig. pub. *Colorado Review* 22, no. 1 (Spring 1995): 16.
BZ, 31–3; NB, 96–8
Pattern: 10 × 2, for each of the three sections
Time: Late August
Place: Charlottesville

This is one of the bleaker poems of *Black Zodiac*, at least after the bats have ascended "to their remission." The poet, growing older, is unable to face the day, and so escapes into the darkness. Happiness is in separation, as in the case of Candide, who, in this worst of all possible worlds, decided he would simply cultivate his garden, and in the case of Hadrian (Nero), who exiled himself to the isle of Capri for the last decade of his life (p. 96, l. 11). The poet allies himself with such exiles, with "Sour saints, aspiring aphasiacs, / Recluses and anchorites," with the doubters. All of these stand opposed to Raymond of Toulouse and Hadrian, whom the poet half expects and half hopes will cross the hedge row into his bat-blurred, mythic moonscape. Raymond (1052–1105) was the most prestigious count to go on the First Crusade and Hadrian (Emperor of Rome, 117–138) had Jerusalem stormed as well, though to put down a Jewish revolt against the Romans. Whatever their motives, they were at least men of action who did not crumble under the "moon's pull" and were not beaten down by the "day's doom."

In section 2 we move from the dreamscape of the moonlit back yard to the poet's daytime world, where he explains why he has come to identify with the ascetics and eremites. It is because they understood the power of the nightscape and the shapeless dread of the "day's doom" where everything is shadowed with angst. This dread comes from the poet's awareness of his ultimate extinction and of his inability to recognize the stranger in the mirror. It is a function as well of his having to drag himself through the dreary daily routine of pill-taking, tooth-brushing, and news-watching. O not to be in Charlottesville, now that August's here.

In section 3 we return to nighttime, and here we learn that there is nevertheless something gained from the movement from light to darkness; for it is the "darkened life" with its new moon and star charts that transform the dog-days of August: "To be separate, to be apart, is to be whole again ... the happy life is the darkened life." This is a vision not unlike that of St. John of the Cross (see the epigraph to Wright's *Via Negativa* in SHS, 62). In the Gnostic battle between light and darkness in the poet's consciousness, darkness wins.

The Appalachian Book of the Dead

Orig. pub. *Yale Review* 84 (January 1996): 109–10, and *PN Review* 27, no. 1 (September–October 2000)
BZ, 34–5; NB, 99–100
Pattern: 7 × 4
Time: A Sunday in September
Place: Charlottesville

In Wright's grand Dantean scheme, *Black Zodiac* is his *Purgatorio* and *Appalachia* his *Paradiso*, except that, as Wright remarks in an interview, he lacked the religious zeal to write a genuine *Paradiso* (Suarez, 56; see also *Blackbird*). He determined, therefore, to take as his models the *Tibetan Book of the Dead* and *The Egyptian Book of the Dead*. The *Tibetan Book of the Dead* or *Bardo Thödol* ("Liberation Through Hearing in the In-Between State") has to do with the period that connects the death of individuals with their following rebirth. The process involves a priest reading the book of the dead into the ear of the deceased, who is said to move through different states—such as ego loss, hallucination, and re-entry. *The Egyptian Book of the Dead* is a collection of chapters made up of magic spells and formulas. It served as a kind of guidebook to a happy afterlife, providing clues and passwords for the dead that enabled them to overcome hazards and find their proper path.

There are six *Appalachian Book of the Dead* poems (the five that follow the present one are in *Appalachia*) and references to the book appear as well in *The Writing Life, Giorgio Morandi and the Talking Eternity Blues, Early Saturday Afternoon, Early Evening,* and *After Rereading Robert Graves, I Go Outside to Get My Head Together* (NB, 165, 167, 179, and 186). The *Appalachian Book of the Dead* poems are, according to Wright's own account (Suarez, 56), a more or less secular version of the Tibetan and Egyptian sacred texts. But the present poem, with its references to angels, the Eucharist, "the passageways of Paradise," *ex votos*, altars and sanctuary, God's breath, and the Book of Genesis, is clearly within the Christian orbit as well.

The poem opens with the sights and sounds of a brilliant September Sunday—the antitype of the bug-surfing bat in the opening scene of the previous poem—and with the poet's consciousness of the inexorable tick-tock of time. Then we get the quotation from Pound, *Go in fear of abstractions*. The context of Pound's injunction is this: "Use no superfluous word, no adjective, which does not reveal something. Don't use such an expression as 'dim land of peace.' It dulls the image. It mixes an abstraction with the concrete. It comes from the writer's not realising that the natural object is always the adequate symbol. Go in fear of abstractions" ("A Retrospect," in *Literary Essays of Ezra Pound*, ed. T.S. Eliot [New York: New Directions, 1935], 4–5). "Well, possibly," muses the poet, not wholly buying this bit of advice. The extraordinary linguistic power Wright manifests in representing the natural object in fresh and ingenious ways is sometimes symbolic, sometime not. But he is by no means afraid of abstractions: witness three that shortly follow—"enlightenment," "compassion and affection." Such abstractions are, of course, omnipresent in Wright's poems.

In this poem, compassion and affection, the poet's Eucharist, are identified symbolically with something in the natural world—the tributaries of the river. But it is a river above our lives that "we sense the sense of," which is some awareness of the divine. We can perhaps arise through the strata of rock to gain some enlightenment. But if the "uneasy, suburbanized" poet can get there through abstractions, getting there through landscape appears initially to be more difficult. The garden with its "skeletal altars" and "vacant sanctuary" is no genuine paradise. Still, there is hope, as we see in the last stanza, with its long division metaphor at the end. Landscape can, after all, remeasure "the stations of the dead." What we don't see (enlightenment, compassion, affection, the sacred) is contained many times (the quotient) in what we see. When Adam and Eve walked up and down in the Garden, they heard the voice of God (Genesis 3:8), so the back yard sanctuary turns out not to be vacant after all. The "long division" metaphor is a pun: it is time to get to work on the poetic project so as to discover in the visible more quotients of the invisible, and it is time to begin the project of measuring the poetic line and dividing the poems into their patterned stanzas. Perhaps there is a hint as well of di-vision, Blake's "double vision," the jacking up of the infinite and eternal from the natural and human worlds.

At one of his readings Wright remarked, "This poem is called "Appalachian Book of the Dead IV," which presupposes one, two, three, and foreshadows five and six. I've been working on this, oh God, this project for twenty-seven years, just book after book.... But I was coming to the end of it, and I needed a "paradise," a *paradiso*. I looked deep into my heart, and I said, 'Chuck. Chuck, you are not theologically inclined nor do you have the talent to write a *paradiso*. So what are you going to do to finish off this twenty-seven-year project?' I got the idea for a Book of the Dead, which, as you will recall, if you remember reading of the Tibetan

Book of the Dead, is a bunch of mantras and amulets and sayings and pep talks spoken into the ear of the soon-to-be dearly departed who is a true believer and knows where he's going. I thought, 'Well, I can do that, as long as I'm not the one whose ear is being whispered into.' So I wrote some Books of the Dead, and this is number four" (*Blackbird*).

Umbrian Dreams

Orig. pub. *Ploughshares* 68 (Winter 1995–96): 177; *PN Review* 27, no. 1 (September–October 2000).
BZ, 39; NB, 101
Pattern: 5-4-5-4
Time: Autumn
Place: Charlottesville

This wonderfully rich lyric is the first of eight poems in part 3 of *Black Zodiac* (the book is not divided into parts in *Negative Blue*), and it provides a stark contrast to the two-dimensional, flat-lit life at the beginning of *Apologia pro Vita Sua*. We have moved from the sorrows of spring to the healing of fall.

The poem sets up a contrast between the spectacular, fiery-gold, front-lit, world of autumn light (like frost-fired Byzantine mosaics and Heraclitean fires) and a much softer, misty, Umbrian radiance that has somehow healed the wounded body. "Flat-lit" is a photographic term, flat light occurring when the sky is hazy or overcast, so that it appears white or gray rather than blue. There is no apparent direction to the light, so there are basically no shadows and thus no three-dimensional effect. Some professional photographers prefer such light because they can control the light on their subjects by using a flash. In the first line we have a form of negative metaphor. Nothing is flat-lit: everything is brilliant and fully lit. Nothing is tabula-rasaed: everything is fully inscribed. The landscape, which previously had been like the green heart of Italy, has not been changed into an Umbrian sackcloth but into a brilliant autumn spectacle, as colorful as a Mycenaean mask. In such a lush and spectacular setting, where the October backdrop is like that of a fully adorned drag queen, somber thoughts of the crucifixion implied by the stigmata and the *Stabat mater* are distant ("a sleep and a death away")

At the beginning of the second half of the poem, the reference to Yeats might lead us to expect a continuation of the spectacular artifice, like that, say, of *Sailing to Byzantium*. But the "mythic body" of the poet's dream is the feathery white Zeus in *Leda and the Swan*. Apparently, Wright wants us to bracket out all the violence and eroticism of Yeats's sonnet, and see only the ascetically "honed and horizoned" white landscape (like an anchorite), drawn from the image of the swan-god. In any event, we have pivoted about-face from the first two stanzas, and the poem ends with a vision of the poet as hermit again, withdrawing from the extravagant landscape of October in "full drag" back into the tabula-rasaed world of Umbrian sackcloth, a world where the light is "stretched" and "weightless," the dolorosa world of the saint's stigmata. If you don't believe it, the poet enjoins us in a line that could have been written by Browning, stick your finger in the wound. The oozing in the penultimate line is apparently meant to convey the impression that in the poet's dream world the light is misty, even watery (lambent). But the oozing discharge from the wound in the context of the stigmata simile, opening and closing, flickering and going out, is eerie nevertheless: stigmata are said to heal and disappear as suddenly as they becomes visible. This is clearly not a wish-fulfillment dream. The dream-vision of the crucifixion, lit by a soft and watery radiance, displaces the aureate light of Charlottesville's autumn leaves—mostly, one would guess, those of the sugar maples.

p. 101, l. 1. *tabula rasa*. John Locke's blank slate of the mind, the notion that individuals are born without any mental content so that their identity is completely determined by events after birth.

p. 101, l. 2. *Umbrian*. Umbria is sometimes called "the green heart of Italy."

p. 101, l. 2. *Stabat mater*. Literally, "The Mother stood"; the first words of a thirteenth-century hymn sung in the Stations of the Cross service. It is attributed to the Italian poet Iacopone da Todi, the Iacopo of l. 12. Iacopo (ca. 1230–1306) joined the Franciscan order.

October II

Orig. pub. *Ploughshares* 68 (Winter 1995–96): 178.
BZ, 40; NB, 102
Pattern: 6 × 3
Place: Charlottesville

We begin with "October in mission creep," "mission creep" being the military expression for the process by which a mission's goals change over time, expanding beyond their original objectives. October is also in "autumnal reprise," in the sense of an annual deduction, using the "minus sign" to reduce the coffers. "Stand down" is also a military term, meaning the temporary stopping of an offensive action. So what we have here is autumn in cessation or at least, as in line 2, a loss of the intensity it had in the second stanza of *Umbrian Dreams*.

Why "synaptic uncertainty" in l. 3? "Synapse" is a biological term meaning the space in the nervous system over which impulses are transmitted. If the impulse passes over or through the synapse, then a connection has been made. The suggestion, then, is that the making of connections is uncertain at this particular time of the year. Then we get more noun phrases, also scientific, this time from physics and math: "Electrical surge and quick lick of the minus sign." But as with the opening phrases, there are no verbs and we have to make the connections ourselves: the syntax itself has a synapse, we might say—a space between two things that call for some copula. There is an "electrical surge" in the autumnal scene, associated perhaps with its fiery brilliance, but there's also a "quick lick of the minus sign." "Lick" means to pass quickly, and the single stroke of a minus sign is much more like a lick than a plus sign is. There is perhaps also the suggestion of the guitarist's improvised phrase. This is followed by still another metaphor from physics, the "force field." A field of force is a space under the influence of some electrical or magnetic agent. If October is metaphorically a field of force, then it is a constricting one. The force is drawing in on itself, which is another way of suggesting loss.

By the end of the first stanza we have been confronted with (1) a number of negative suggestions: creep, reprise (deduction), stand down, uncertainty, minus sign, tightening, pare, and (2) the relation of these things to form and shape. Ordinarily, the general sense of loss would work against form and shape. But Wright seems to be saying the opposite. It is only when the season is coming to a close, when autumn has lost the brilliance of it maples, when the sap has begun to run down, that we can shape our forms and form our shapes. This sense of constriction, of making things spare and tight, of cutting out all the excess and the superficial surface decoration, is a common theme in Wright's poetry.

But the central question the poem asks is, Which way to go: plus or minus, gain (taking shape) or loss (losing intensity), salvation or damnation, the multifoliate rose or the dead leaf, presence or absence? Or perhaps the question is this: can the synapse between these binary pairs be bridged? By using arithmetical language Wright invites this kind of mathematical reading, and everything in the poem, except the three six-line stanzas, is based on binary pairs, even the Beckett quotation from Augustine: "Do not despair; one of the thieves was saved. Do not presume; one of the thieves was damned." Beckett once told an interviewer "I am interested in the shape of ideas even if I do not believe in them. There is a wonderful sentence in Augustine. I wish I could remember the Latin. It is even finer in Latin than in English. 'Do not despair; one of the thieves was saved. Do not presume; one of the thieves was damned.' That sentence has a wonderful shape. It is the shape that matters" (Alan Schneider, "Working with Beckett" in *Samuel Beckett: The Critical Heritage*, ed. Lawrence Graver and Raymond Federman [Boston: Routledge, 1979], 173). Even the iambic pentameter that Wright calls attention to is binary: plus accent and minus accent, as the linguists would mark it.

Form might be the absence of all *things*, but it is the presence or power that *informs* all things—the force that can transfigure nature, giving us the "electrical surge" of autumnal brilliance (the garnished season), followed by the disappearance of same (the "quick lick of the minus sign"). And form is the force that transubstantiates us, changes us into another substance. This is *October II*, and the first *October* poem was also about change—the poet's speculations about his own transfiguration (*WTTT*, 24). Both processes—transfiguration and transubstantiation—are loaded with theological overtones. In the transubstantiation of the Eucharist, the material is transformed into the spiritual and so identified with it: bread *is* body, and wine *is* blood.

By the end of the poem, the "synaptic uncertainty" appears to have been overcome. The "shape beneath the shape" is a divine shape, Boehme's *Urgrund*, the force of the divine nothingness, which is an example of the *via negativa* that is omnipresent in Wright. October contains this kind of negative power, but it is also a plus: a negative exponent becomes positive when moved under the division sign. Thus, while October is "minus," it is also "plus." A plus sign is a cross, an archetype of the vertical intersecting the horizontal, sacred history (*Heilsgeschichte*) intersecting the ordinary flux of time (*Weltgeschichte*), as the theologians say. This may seem to be an overdetermined reading, but the image is in Eliot's *Four Quartets*, and the multifoliate rose (l. 14) comes straight out of Eliot's *The Hollow Men* and *Little Gidding*. And from these contexts it is associated with Cantos 31–32 of Dante's *Paradiso* and perhaps also with the rose window of the Gothic cathedral, which is also many-petalled.

There is, then, a very large metaphor at work in the poem—the landscape *is* metaphor. Nature (here the October season) is the locus of the dialectic of plus and minus, and from this dialectic emerges the divine "shape beneath the shape." Wright once remarked, "My mind works synaptically" (Suarez, 43). In this poem the minus sign ("synaptic uncertainty") becomes the plus sign ("synaptic certainty").

Lives of the Saints

Orig. pub. *Poetry* 167, no. 3 (December 1995): 125–9.
BZ, 41–5; NB, 103–7
Pattern: 6 × 3, in each of the five parts
Time: December 1994–January 1995
Place: Hollywood; Charlottesville

Part 1. The first section is a lyric of winter blues: the poet's life is "sliding out from underneath" him and becoming shapeless. It is Christmas Eve in Hollywood for the poet, a sixty-year-old frowning private man. (It will actually be eight months before Wright turns sixty.) As he breathes in the air from the negative "blue abyss" he begins to lose faith in the written word. Whereas voice, memory, and action are permanent, the written word is not. We thus have a turning upside down of the Keatsian "thou shalt remain" convention, for everything written, as Derrida says, is *sous rature*. Exhibit A is the scene described in the last stanza, with its seedy characters, pot-smoking crowds, and lewdly dangling palm fronds—all underwritten with the ironic cliché of the final drop-down line. Life is anything but beautiful in this vignette—a demonic parody of the lives of the saints—and certainly erasable.

The Walk of Fame (p. 103, l. 15) is a reference to the bronze star-plaques, embedded in pink and charcoal terrazzo squares on both sides of the sidewalks of Hollywood Boulevard and Vine Street in Hollywood. The "Walk of Famers" would be the mob of tourists and others strolling along Hollywood and Vine.

Part 2. We confront the theme of absence, loss, and silence, once more. The poet cannot get beyond putting a new tread on old material; he cannot find anything novel to say: the images remain hidden, the sounds refuse to come forth, and the words are asleep. He has hoped that his readers would find the fire behind the smoke, the emotion behind the description. But he senses the inevitability of failure of his quest: "All explorers must die of heartbreak." The section ends in silence ("you do the talking") and the sense of loss in the catalogue of "-esses": "endless effortless nothingness," "measureless," "imageless." Thus, the poet turns over to his readers the business of saying something while he merely looks and listens.

p. 104, l. 7. *face the facts*. In *Brewsie and Willie* (1946) Gertrude Stein urged the GIs she befriended in Paris to remember the last Depression and face the facts of what caused it. "Find out the reason why," she wrote in 1946. "Look facts in the face, not just what they all say, the leaders, but every darn one of you, so that a government by the people, for the people, shall not perish from the face of the earth."

p. 104, l. 8. *Pretending ... shows*. "The emotion comes from pretending that there's nothing there but description" (Adam Gopnik's commentary on Thomas Eakins' overstated and self-conscious investing his unconventional subjects with expressiveness, in "Eakins in the Wilderness," *New Yorker* 70 [26 December 1994]: 84).

p. 104, l. 13. *All explorers must die of heartbreak*. The words of Sir Walter Raleigh.

Part 3. Death haunts the poet, who yearns to be pierced by the occasional void through which the supernatural flows. This notion of the abyss or the *Urgrund*, the nothing that is not there and nothing that is (as Stevens says), is a common thread throughout *Black Zodiac*—a version of the *via negativa* of the medieval mystics. That is the prosaic version. Wright's own version is, first, a math problem that does not work out and, second, the image of "the murder of crows," going to its appointment in the winter trees, described geometrically in the final line. "Murder" carries with it something more than just the collective meaning of "group." A "murder" of crows is based on the folk tale that crows form tribunals to judge and punish the bad behavior of a member of the flock: if the verdict goes against the defendant, that bird is murdered by the flock—echoing the judgment theme two lines above.

p. 105, l. 7. *We live ... our own*. "From this the poem springs: that we live in a place / That is not our own, and much more, not ourselves / And hard it is in spite of blazoned days" (Wallace Stevens, *Notes toward a Supreme Fiction*, pt. 1, sect. 4). This section does indeed spring from such a sense of alienation, even in the face of the "warm wind from the gulf" (chinook) that brings the thaw and meltdown.

Part 4. More darkness, more death. "*Al poco giorno...*" (translated in the next line) comes from one of Dante's so-called *rime petrose*, or "stony" poems, about a hard and ice-cold lady, "la pietra."

The syntax of the last stanza is difficult to paraphrase. Apparently, "light's blank" is the object of "can accommodate" and "shelve," and "vacancy" is the object of "absorbs" and "repents of." The focus is on what the poet sees as he glances upward: in spite of how the eye and heart react, the vacancy of the blank light is displaced by the slowly disappearing and ponderous clouds. But the effect of both statements about the clouds is more or less the same: they begin to blot out the vacancy, and nothing can stop their sweep across the sky. Perhaps God has returned, but the juxtaposition of "negative" and "Nothing" at the end casts a pall over the picture. Disentangling the syntax of the final line and a half produces this: Nothing can keep the clouds, ponderous as a negative, from moving. The simile is from photography, but "negative / Nothing" creates a more general suggestion of absence, and if "Nothing" did not begin the line, we get the sense that it still might be capitalized. In any event, we are left with a sense of the blankness of light and the emptiness of the world. The poet has entered a world where there is no plentitude—only Eliot's vacancy.

p. 106, l. 6. *Black branches, black branches.* A twist on a line in Donald Justice's poem *Bus Stop*: "Black flowers, black flowers" (*Collected Poems* [New York: Knopf, 2004], 100).
p. 106, l. 11. *the dwelling of St. John.* Heaven.
p. 106, l. 13. *Posteriori Dei.* God's back, as translated in the next line.

Part 5. We begin with the urban landscape, which, covered with snow, looks almost imaginary. Whatever is revealed is a black-on-white printout. Three additional metaphors follow: the winter snow is a self-defense and a matrix (a surrounding substance), and winter has designed itself. The actual urban world is there, but it lies hidden behind the "Chinese screen" of the ordinary afternoon. There is an echo here of Stevens's *An Ordinary Evening in New Haven*, which contains a Wright-like theory of the "endlessly elaborating poem": "the theory / of poetry is the theory of life, // As it is, in the intricate evasions of as, / In things seen and unseen, created from nothingness, / The heavens, the hells, the worlds, the longed-for lands" (*Collected Poems* [New York: Knopf, 1967], 486). In any event, it is the ordinariness of the urban afternoon, as opposed to the extraordinary landscape of the backyard garden, that apparently induces the sense of Kierkegaardian dread. We live in dread and we depart in dread, and there is little "wrench room" to effect a change. "*In dread we stay and in dread depart*" is from an anonymous thirteenth-century text.

The alternatives are to stay or to leave; to remain in the here and now, which is bad, or to escape to the there and then, which is worse; to linger inside the building, with its movable floor, or to go outside into the demon-infested world where executions are sanctioned by the Church; to watch out for your frontside or to protect your backside. Our lives are like those of the saints—"contemplative, cloistered, and tongue-tied." It is certainly not because we can perform any miracles. The poet makes no choice: we are left hanging on this urban afternoon between with the alternatives outlined, none appealing.

Wright's note (204) indicates debts to Bertran de Born and Robert Graves, but what he might have borrowed from them to make his poem is uncertain.

Christmas East of the Blue Ridge

Orig. pub. *Ploughshares* 68 (Winter 1995–96): 176.
BZ, 46; NB, 108
Pattern: 5 × 4
Place: Charlottesville

No star in the east appears in this Christmas-time scene—the winter of the poet's discontent. The chief problem is the dissipation in the power of landscape's language: the tongues of the rain are small and their words watery; winter's vocabulary is downsized, its phonemes guttural, gravelly, and scratched. But the poet's language is anything but diminished, displaying its typical precision in expressing the poverty of the winter landscape's "language."

All of this is set against the "dispensation of the desert," which is the time of Christ's nativity, the vexing "first birth." In the beginning was the Word. The second birth, "only one word from now," is associated not with resurrection but with death only, and that is not far away. The Advent season, therefore, brings no cause for celebration. We are reminded of the speaker of Stevens's *Sunday Morning*, who faces a similar dilemma.

The clouds, as with those in *The Lives of the Saints*, serve here too as an "alphabet of our discontent," inscribed on the "black walls of our hearts." The alphabet is identified with the clouds, which have begun to break up, unsettling themselves into tattered rags. The poet, however, has not abandoned his own alphabet, and the gold letters seem to be a pun on illumination, even if its subject is a bleak one. As in so many of Wright's darker poems, there remains a hint of light at the end, which is the reason for the ellipsis: more work to be done.

Negatives II

BZ, 47; NB, 109
Pattern: 1–5–5–5–5–1
Time: February
Place: Charlottesville, with flash backs to Italy, 1959

Negatives, which appeared in *Hard Freight* (1973), began with a photographic simile, and in *Negatives II* the photographic trope is picked up again in the shuttering of memory, the reference to negative space, and the dominating black-and-white winter world. But "negatives" refers primarily to things that are unknown (positions in space, shapes, intelligence codes): the poet is unable to see into or behind the overcast winter afternoon, and his memory both fails and plays tricks with his mind ("massing what wasn't there as though it were"). The idea of erasure begins and ends the poem as a way of answering the question, Why write? And the answer is to fill up the blank space produced by erasure and to repeat this process once the present words have been rubbed out. The first and last lines could replace each other without the point being lost. We encountered the process of erasure as it applies to the poetic trade in *Lives of the Saints*, and it appears as well in *Self Portrait in 2035* (CM, 113), *To Giacomo Leopardi in the Sky* (WTTT, 109), *A Journal of the Year of the Ox* (WTTT, 179), *Buffalo Yoga* (BY, 13). The poem is "written, erased, then written again," as Wright puts it in *River Run* (SHS, 40). Or again, in *Homage to Giorgio Morandi*: "Scrape and erase, scrape and erase // until the object comes clear" (BY, 60).

Hovering in the background of this black and white world is a parody of the entire army intelligence game, the conventional trope that links sight and knowledge having now vanished. As we move back and forth between the bleak Charlottesville landscape, across which winter grinds out its cigarette, and the hazy memories of Verona thirty-six years earlier, the poet does not know because he cannot see. But once again, as the ellipses insinuate, the poet will keep on writing.

p. 109, l. 3. *CIC*. The 430th Counterintelligence Corps Detachment, Wright's army unit in Verona, devoted to security matters for military installations. See *Scar Tissue II* in ST, p. 46, ll.1–18.
p. 109, l. 10. *balloon would not go up*. Colloquial expression for "the action or battle would not begin."
p. 109, l. 12. *John Ruskin ... darkest ones*. "The things to exercise yourselves in are the placing of the masses, and the modelling of the lights. It is an admirable exercise to take a pale wash of color for all the shadows, never reinforcing it everywhere, but drawing ... as if it were in far distance, making all the darks one flat pale tint. Then model from those into the lights, rounding as well as you can, on those subtle conditions" (*The Queen of the Air: Being a Study of the Greek Myths of Cloud and Storm*, sect. 177).
p. 109, l. 19. *Brenner Pass*. An important mountain pass that creates a link through the Tyrolean Alps along the current border between Italy and Austria.
p. 109, l. 20. *Run*. A trip to the train station in Vienna to check out an intelligence source.
p. 109, l. 20. *Trieste Station*. The railway terminal in Venice, at the edge of the town center.

Lives of the Artists

Orig. pub. *Field* 53 (Fall 1995): 90–4.
BZ, 48–52; NB, 110–14

Pattern: 6 × 3 in each of the five sections
Time: March 15
Place: Charlottesville

Part 1. This section begins with the poet's advice to himself: plan carefully before you begin writing; be certain you have something to say; don't just polish up things that are not essential. What the poet himself "says" is embodied, first, in the description of the landscape in stanza 2, where the banging and thumping heat of mid–March begins to resurrect the cycle of nature; and, second, in the poet's identifying everyone with the emanations of Poussin's apocalypse. The painting in question is *The Plague of Ashdod*, which Poussin began in 1630, the year that Italy suffered the century's worst outbreak of bubonic plague. The ravages of the plague depicted in Poussin's "hell-hung heart-screen" are apocalyptic, and indeed the painting is sometimes referred to as Poussin's vision of a seventeenth-century apocalypse. In the last stanza, however, the poet takes his place beside those in another apocalyptic vision of unnamed souls fleeing through the dust and disappearing in flame, the fires in this case being the small, unworldly "fires" of the plum tree blossoms—which appear in all five parts of the poem. The connection between the advice in the first stanza and the little apocalypse beneath the plum blossoms is apparently that Poussin's apocalypse provides the model that enables the poet to "finish things." But the connection is rather tenuous. "Apocalypse" means an uncovering, a revelation, but here the poet disappears. Moreover, there is a world of difference between the imminent total devastation in Poussin's "hell-hung" painting and the plum-tree world into which the poet fades away, however otherworldly its white light. The unexpendable things that call for witnessing have not yet been made apparent.

p. 110, ll. 1–2. *Learn how to model ... hisses.* "In old age, Giambologna used to tell his friends the story of how, as a young man, a Flemish sculptor newly arrived in Rome, he made a model to his own original design, finished it coll'alito, 'with his breath'—that is to say, with the utmost care, bringing it to the very peak of finish—and went to show it to the great Michelangelo. And Michelangelo took the model in his hands and completely destroyed it, and then remodeled it according to his way of thinking, and did so with marvelous skill, so that the outcome was quite the opposite of what the young man had done. And then Michelangelo said to Giambologna: Now go and learn the art of modeling before you learn the art of finishing" (James Fenton, "A Lesson from Michelangelo," *New York Review of Books* 42, no. 5 [23 March 1995], 21).

Part 2. The opening lines from Sappho—a simple message about the inexorable passing of time and the extinction wrought by death—are set beside the ineffectual clutter of Christian rites (the Eucharist is a side-bar) and images (plastic Christ, dull stained-glass) in stanza 2. With Sappho providing the intertextual commentary on the poet's condition, we find him, solitary and suffering pain, in the ashes of time. In stanza 3 we are presented with a genuine altar—the earth itself blanketed with the fallen petals of the plum trees. Here the hands of the dead rise ominously from the underworld, offering prayers of sacramental absolution. "Underworld" and "nightshade" make the context more Greek than Christian, and are reminiscent of the opening of Keats's *Ode on Melancholy*, with its conjunction of nightshade and Propsepine. "Nightshade" inclines toward paronomasia: it is the middle of the night and dark hands are thrusting upward from the underworld (thus night shade), and "shade" is an anagram of "Hades." There is no interaction with the dead, only a quiet attentiveness on the part of the poet to their gestures and prayers.

p. 111, ll. 1–2. *When you have died ... will remain.* Sappho, poem 32 in *The Poems of Sappho*, trans. Susy Q. Groden (Indianapolis: Bobbs-Merrill, 1966), 35.
p. 111, ll. 5–7. *The moon has set ... passing ... I lie alone.* Sappho, poem 42, ibid., 45.
p. 111, l. 12. *Pain enters me drop by drop.* Sappho, poem 61 in Mary Barnard's translation, "Pain penetrates / Me drop by drop." This line is not in the Groden translation, Wright's source for the other Sappho lines.
p. 111, l. 13. *dropped their wings at their sides.* Sappho, poem 19, *The Poems of Sappho*, ibid., 21.
p. 111, ll. 16–18. *gold-amber cups and bittersweet.* The translator of this fragment, neither Groden nor Barnard, is uncertain.

Part 3. If we are to ascend the *axis mundi*, we will ascend by finding the simple signature of the "Big Smoke," something larger than the "little smoke" now wafting through the plum trees. It will only take a few words to liberate the "Last untranslatable text." But such resurrection is unavailable to the poet, who cannot decipher the name of "Something" in the plum branches and so does not know what there is to say. In stanza 2, however, the poet does discover he has something to say, assisted by the *Sentences of Sextus*. "[T]he true word / Is the word about the word," says the poet. The author of *Sextus* says, "The true word about God is the word of God" (*NHL*, 506). Because of the deception all around us, this true word is available only to the few. It will not be discovered, we learn in stanza 3, through the religious chitchat and similes of the deceivers drifting down on the plum blossoms. The knowledge that the poet desires is gnosis—the hermetic word, not to be discerned by the ignorant. Part 3 concludes with a paraphrase from *The Sentences of Sextus*: "The sins of those who are ignorant are the shame of those who have taught them" (*NHL*, 504). Thus far for the poet, then, there is to be no rising, no resurrection, which condition is underwritten by a kind of negative echo of Hopkins: "My heart in hiding / Stirred for a bird" (*The Windhover*, ll.7–8). Hopkins transformed his sense of the absence of God into a sense of God's immanence in nature. Not so for the poet, at least here, where the pieces of the *grand récit* are only "intermittent and flaked."

Lying behind part 3 are perhaps these words from *The Book of Thomas the Contender* in *The Nag Hammadi Library*: "You darkened your hearts and surrendered your thoughts to folly, and you filled your thoughts with the smoke of the fire that is in you! And your light has hidden in the cloud of [...] and the garment that is put upon you, you [...]. And you were seized by the hope that does not exist. And whom is it you have believed? Do you not know that you all dwell among those who that [...] you as though you [...]. You baptized your souls in the water of darkness! You walked by your own whims!" (*NHL*, 205–6). The "Big Smoke" might be traced to *The Teaching of Sylvanus* in *The Nag Hammadi Library*: "But no one prevents him (God) from doing what he wants. For who is stronger than him, that he may prevent him? To be sure, it is he who touches the earth, causing it to tremble and also causing the mountains to smoke" (*NHL*, 394).

p. 112, ll. 4, 7, 8. "The faithful do not speak many words, but their works are numerous." From *The Sentences of Sextus* (*NHL*, 508). "Everything god possesses..." (*NHL*, 505). "Don't give the word..." "Do not give the word of God to everyone" (*NHL*, 506).

p. 112, l. 10–11. *the world ... deceived.* "Guard yourself from lying; there is he who deceives and there is he who is deceived" (*The Sentences of Sextus*, *NHL*, 508).

p. 112, l.18. *The sins ... their teachers.* "The sins of those who are ignorant are the shame of those who have taught them" (*The Sentences of Sextus*, *NHL*, 504).

Part 4. The plum blossoms, falling between two worlds, are an image of the invisible and a metaphor of transcendence. The poet is moving toward an affirmation here, writing the one story in the margins of the earth's landscape, even though here it is connected with gnostic secrecy, and he is repeating a series of "I am's" uttered by the Perfect Mind in the Nag Hammadi text. The poetic treatment of the invisible (a word that appears scores of times in *The Nag Hammadi Library*) through image and metaphor is what authorizes our lives, our walking up and down in the world—an image from Job 1:7 and 2:2 that Wright repeats from *The Silent Generation* (*NB*, 37). What is beyond the power of language to capture (the incomprehensible, belief beyond belief, the insubstantial, the mysterious speech) the poet must nevertheless continue to pursue, writing the one story and writing it still again. "There is one story, and one story only," as Robert Graves says in *To Juan in Winter Solstice*. We are not far from the prosaic announcement of the author of one of the texts in *The Nag Hammadi Library*: "Now we shall proceed to consideration of our world, so that we may accurately finish the description of its structure and management. Then it will become obvious how belief in the unseen realm, which has been apparent from creation down to the consummation of the age, was discovered" (*On the Origin of the World*, NHL, 187).

p. 113, l. 4. *I am the silence ...* and the other italicized quotations on this page are from a poem, "The Thunder, Perfect Mind," in *NHL*, 298.
p. 113, l. 7. *Belief ... beyond belief.* Cf. Wallace Steven's "We believe without belief, beyond belief" (*Flyer's Fall*, l. 6).

Part 5. The poet's opening statement about light could serve as a gloss on *The Nag Hammadi Library*, where the word "light" appears 491 times. The author of the Nag Hammadi text entitled *On the Origin of the World* writes that "the limitless light is everywhere" (NHL, 172). But that is only half of the story, for as the author of *The Gospel of Philip* says, "Light and Darkness, life and death, right and left, are brothers of one another" (NHL, 142). Some artists paint the darkness, but not our poet, whose plum trees know nothing of the dark. They are born of radiance and grace, and they, unlike the poet, continually change through the cycle of the seasons. He thinks he might be "restrung" and so transmogrified, but that story will have to wait until he has learned to model things, as Gyges of Lydia did. His advice to himself, following the anecdote from Vasari, returns us to the counsel with which the poem began.

The title of the poem refers, therefore, to Vasari's book, but it also relates to the different lives of the artist's self represented by the five sections: the one who disappears into his own little apocalypse, who walks quietly on the altars of the dead, who searches unsuccessfully for the true word, who continues to tell the story of what lies beyond, and who learns, as Gyges of Lydia did, that the model or outline can emerge from the light.

p. 114, l. 1. *There's nothing ... light.* The words of David Summers, professor of art at the University of Virginia, and a painter himself.
p. 114, ll. 13–18. "According to Pliny, painting was brought to Egypt by Gyges of Lydia; for he says that Gyges once saw his own shadow cast by the light of a fire and instantly drew his own outline on the wall with a piece of charcoal" (Giorgio Vasari, "Preface, *Lives of the Artists*, trans. George Bull [Harmondsworth: Penguin, 1987], 1:27).

Deep Measure

Orig. pub. *Orion* 15, no. 1 (Winter 1996): 61.
BZ, 53; NB, 115
Pattern: 5 × 3
Time: February
Place: Charlottesville

The poet has been dealt a hand by the sun saint, or rather dealt one card, which is all he can play, and that card is measure. The "patron saint of What-Goes-Down" is a version of Gerard de Nerval's "saint of the abyss" (*Artemis*, l. 14), or, as the dealing of cards, an image of *moira*, suggests a Greek context, perhaps it is Helio who is sinking into the "day's dark niche." We begin with the measure of the "wan weight-light" of the February afternoon, which is the wrong world for words: the cycle of nature has moved through the nadir of its annual journey, and in this cold landscape the poet is left speechless. Then we get the "measure" of the doves, rising bulb blades, and gum trees. But there's another, deeper measure that sets our lives to music, and the pilgrim-poet ("homeboy of false time") instructs himself to listen for that. Measure, for Wright, is both linear and spatial form, but he uses it in a fluid way—see the commentary on *Meditation on Form and Measure* (NB, 90–2). In the present poem measure is something deeper than the single number in the hand that he has been dealt. In the dance metaphor in the last half of the poem, measure is deeper than the long sliding strides of the two-step movement that emerges from the cold, winter landscape. All of this is surface measure and a function of the poet-pilgrim's sense of "false time." Thus, his instructions to himself to "set your foot down" and listen to the deeper measure that "sets our lives to music." "Set your foot down" is a pun, meaning both the take a resolute position, to tread downward into the world of the dead, to begin the dance, and to establish his qualitative meter. The language of the poem infuses it with a sense of descending movement: "deep," "undercard," "the patron saint of What-Goes-Down," "deep measure that runnels beneath the bone," "down under," "death-drawn" all suggest a katabasis into a *via negativa*.

Thinking of Winter at the Beginning of Summer

Orig. pub. *Three Penny Review* 64 (Winter 1996).
BZ, 54; NB, 116
Pattern: 5 × 3
Time: Early summer
Place: Charlottesville

Title: Winter is Winter Wright, Charles Wright's brother and an airline pilot, now retired. The poem dedicated to him.

Like the poetry and screenplays of Prévert (1900–77), this poem belongs to the world of surrealism and pataphysics. The connections among the three stanzas—Prévert's "associations of ideas"—are only hinted at. The "nightdreams and daymares" of Avery and Kahn apparently trigger the vision of the poet's airborne brother, his sister Hildegarde who died at age fifty-one, and his dead parents in stanza 2. Winter Wright's being a pilot explains the reference the "enormous planes" in the blue zones. The poet has been pulled from despair, and the last stanza seems to suggest that the roots that have defined him, though tiny, will get him by for a while. The gaze here is upward toward the sun, which cause his roots to glisten. The poet reverses the commonplace notion that our identities are fashioned by what we accept: "What we refuse defines us // a little of this, a little of that." Still, whatever connection we might have with the symbolic sky—the boxed glaze of an Avery painting—we can be fooled by its "fool's gold for a long time." This last melancholic line is repeated—a parody of Frost's "And miles to go before I sleep."

p. 116, l. 1. Milton Avery (1893–1965) was an American painter who explored simplified areas of flat color, applied thinly. Wolf Kahn (b. 1927) is one of the leaders of a group of painters in the 1950s and 1960s who used Abstract Expressionist techniques in a representational way; he is especially noted for the use of color in his landscapes.
p. 116, l. 11. *Pulled ... bad tooth*. Wright's note refers us to Jacques Prévert's *Picasso's Walk*, a poem about "an unfortunate painter of reality" who has difficulty painting an apple on a porcelain plate because the form of the apple keeps changing. The painter then "suddenly finds himself the sad prey / of a numberless crowd of associations of ideas," which Prévert catalogues at some length. After the painter eventually falls asleep, Picasso happens by, eats the apple, breaks the plate, "and the painter drawn from his dreams / like a tooth / finds himself all alone again before his unfinished canvas / with right in the midst of his shattered china / the terrifying pips of reality" (*La Promenade de Picasso*).

Jesuit Graves

Orig. pub. *Iowa Review* 26 (Summer 1996): 202.
BZ, 57; NB, 117
Pattern: 5-4-5-4
Time: July 1995
Place: Dublin, Ireland

This homage to Gerard Manley Hopkins begins section 4 of *Black Zodiac* (the sections are not indicated in *Negative Blue*). The poet distinguishes Hopkins—a poetic Bird-of-Paradise, a Father Candescence, a Father Fire—from the hundreds of other Jesuits whose memorials in the Jesuit plot in Glasnevin Cemetery, Dublin, are so slight and whose God-gulped souls are hidden away by history. The question in the final two lines is a rhetorical one: for Wright, the poet of white-hot fire is no soldier of misfortune, like the other Jesuits buried in Glasnevin (Tuite, Tully, Lynch, et al.), marching into the oblivion of history. Hopkins is one of Wright's heroes, and to reach his master he must climb the scaffolding of Hopkins' poems, with the hope that everything that rises will in fact converge. This is the-shoulders-of-giants theme, and for another statement of the debt to Hopkins, see Wright's "Improvisations: With Father Hopkins on Lake Como" in *Quarter Notes*, 19–27, written five years earlier.

p. 117, l. 7. *plumage of far wonder*. "Hell wars without; but, dear, the while my hands / Gather'd thy book, I heard, this wintry day, / Thy spirit thank me, in his young delight / Stepping again upon the yellow sands. / Go forth: amidst our chaffinch flock display / Thy plumage of far wonder and heavenward flight!" (Gerard Manley Hopkins, *Author's Preface* to his *Poems* [1918], ll. 1–6).

p. 117, ll. 11–12. *Sacrifice ... cause of ruin*. When Hopkins became a Jesuit in 1868 he felt that he should sacrifice his own ambition as a poet to the life of a Jesuit priest, and so he burned his early poems. Only after studying the writings of Duns Scotus four years later did he decide that there was no necessary conflict between Jesuit principles and the writing of poetry. These two lines might also cast a glance at Hopkins's *The Wreck of the Deutschland*, which is about the heroic sacrifice of a group of German nuns who were crossing the North Sea to England when their boat sank in a storm.

p. 117, ll. 16–17: "*P. Gerardus Hopkins ... And then the next name. And then the next.*" For a photograph of Hopkins's name engraved into the memorial stone in the Glasnevin Cemetery, along with the names of the others, see http://www.findagrave.com/cgi-bin/fg.cgi?page=gr&GRid=5858594.

p. 117, l. 20. *Whatever rises comes together*. The idea derives from the mystical philosophy of Pierre Teilhard de Chardin, who claimed that matter, life, and thought move upward to a union with God-Omega, the beginning and end of cosmic evolution. Flannery O'Connor borrowed Teilhard's idea for the title of one of her short stories, "Everything That Rises Must Converge."

Meditation on Song and Structure

Orig. pub. *New Republic* 213 (18 September 1995): 54–5.
BZ, 58–61; NB, 118–21.
Pattern: 7 × 2 for each of the five sections
Time:
Place: Setting: sections 1–3, Umbria; sections, 4–5, Charlottesville backyard.

The convention of poetry as *melos* or song dominates the poem, song being the first object of meditation here. The songs—which are all bird songs—are set in contrast to various states of the poet's psyche. (We actually do not hear the swallows of section 3, where the emphasis is on movement.) Structure, the second object of meditation, is a function not simply of the shape of the lines, stanzas, and sections, which follow a formal pattern, but also of thematic repetition. Images of light appear in all five sections and images of water in all but the last. The relation of song to silence is a theme explored in all of the sections except the first. The dialectical opposites played off against each other are light and darkness, sound and silence, things seen and unseen, earth and heaven, abhorrence and desire.

Section 1. The liquid songs of the morning's mourning dove have something to say, but not to the poet, who is disoriented in that moment between sleep and wakefulness. He considers the simple precision of the dove's song as symbolic of the structure of everyday reality, its "coo coo" defining the limits ("hash-marks") of the landscape. Between one "coo" and the next there is no darkness—only space for a moment of grace telling him that "everything's all right." But the bird sings another kind of song, "a watery kind of music, / Extended improvisations, liquid riffs and breaks." This is the music that the poet cannot hear or understand in his depressed ("I know that everything's wrong") and half-aware state.

Section 2. The song of the nightingale (*usignolo*) also evokes images of water, as it drifts "easy as watershine, / Ripply and rock-run," providing a moment of illumination before the moment of darkness and silence—"The silence of something come and something gone away." "Fled is that music," as Keats says in his own nightingale poem. But here the poet pleads with the ghost bird of the darkness to "light a candle" for him.

Section 3. The flight of the swallows provide an ineffable "language without words," so here the focus is not on music but on the swallows' movement—their surging and darting like fish against the backdrop of the Guelph hills. The vision induces wish-fulfillment. The poet yearns to be reincarnated as a swallow so as to feed on the "seen and the unseen," another Keatsian echo.

Section 4. The mockingbird's song, recalled from a dark night in the early 1950s, is like a light in the darkness. The scene is Lake Llewellyn (now Louellen) on the campus of Sky Valley School in the mountains of North Carolina, between Hendersonville and Brevard. The poet imagines that the mockingbird's song "contained many songs" and that it is metaphorically a light, like the nightingale's "pentimento of sudden illumination," that leads back to "silence, sound of the first voice," which said "Let there be light." The "mockingbird's got his chops," meaning that its riffs are as technically skilled as those of a jazz improvisation.

Section 5. The poet wonders about the purpose of the cardinal's song—"omit, omit"—and wonders as well about what the bird knows. The cardinal is identified with a medieval prelate, and even his position is one of eminence in the gum tree, "Eminence" being also the term used to address a Roman Catholic Cardinal. The bird's double spondee, surrounded by silence on either side, is followed by the sound of the siren and punctuated with E.M. Cioran's bleak observation: "Nothing Matters" is the motto of the void. The poem ends with an invocation to the cardinal (metaphorically Cardinal) to exhale the poet's sins, which are sins of excess. The poet's plea, then, is that his verse will be spare and compressed, like the bird's own song, which turns out to be onomatopoeic, the sound of the song imitating the object of the poet's plea. In the context of the desire of landscape for originality (p. 120, ll. 22–3), there is perhaps a sidelong glance at Father Hopkins's *Pied Beauty*, with its praise for whatever is "counter, original, spare" (l. 7).

What propels the meditation on song is not simply the music of the lines with their odd-numbered syllables (only three of the seventy have an even number), but the freshness and ingenuity of the imagery: the "slim ingots of daylight" coming through the crack for the Persian blinds, the "square crenelations" of the tile roofs in Guelph, the swallows "against the enfrescoed backdrop of tilled hills," the nightingale needling and threading the night together, the Bible-black Lake Llewellyn—to note only a few.

p. 118, l. 19. *Todi.* An Umbrian hill town in the province of Perugia.
p. 118, l. 6. *For that moment ... grace.* "And now for a little moment grace hath been showed from Jehovah our God, to leave us a remnant to escape, and to give us a nail in his holy place, that our God may lighten our eyes, and give us a little reviving in our bondage" (Ezra 9:8).
p. 119, l.1. *Senti.* Listen, an imperative.
p. 120, ll. 21–22. *The void's tattoo ... Cioran.* "*Nothing matters*: a great discovery, if ever there was one, from which no one has been able to gain any advantage. To this discovery, supposedly a depressing one, only the void, of which it is the motto, can give a stirring resonance" (E.M. Cioran, *The New Gods*, trans. Richard Howard [New York: Quadrangle/New York Times Book Co., 1974], 74–5). "Nature loathes originality, nature rejects, execrates *man*" (ibid., 102).

Sitting at Dusk in the Back Yard after the Mondrian Retrospective

Orig. pub. Bellingham Review 19, no. 1 (Spring 1996): 31.
BZ, 62–3; NB, 122–3
Pattern: 5 × 5
Time: August
Place: Charlottesville

Title: The reference, apparently, is to the 1995 Piet Mondrian retrospective at the National Gallery of Art, Washington, D.C., co-organized with the Museum of Modern Art, New York, and the Gemeentemuseum in The Hague.

This is an interlude on *form* and *structure*: These two ideas are what W.B. Gallie calls "essentially contested concepts": ideas that involve disagreements about their meaning and use. One person's form is another person's structure. And they are slippery ideas in both Wright's poetry and his prose, including the interviews. He clearly wants to distinguish them, as he does in the opening lines of this poem, where form is seen as restrictive and structure liberating. But in an interview Wright says that structure is the overall *form* (*Halflife*, 147). Here are some of the other things Wright says about form. The verse journal is a *form* Discontinuity is a *form*. *Form* is the order and control that comes in the making of a poem or the imposition that sets one free from chaos; a stanzaic unit is a *form*. "Three stanzas is a good form for me" (*Halflife*, 72). The length of the line, which in Wright's work is a function of the number of syllables in each line, is a matter of *form*. The basic number of syllables is seven, and the line expands from there into as many as seventeen or nineteen syllables, almost always an odd number. Visible *form* is a matter of condensing the poetic line and the poem itself (as in much of Wright's early work) and expanding it (as in *Zone Journals*). *Form* is distinct from forms (sonnet, sestina, villanelle, etc.). Wright often associates *form* with formalism—technical mastery, including the strict attention to metrical patterns and other repetitive devices, such as rhyme. His drop-down or low-rider line is also a formal feature, so characteristic of his work that his poems are recognizable at a distance by the pattern they make on the page: "After a while, your style will accrue; it will happen to you whether you believe it will or not. E. B. White said style is the writer, and to a certain extent, I think, he is right. In the same way you can go down a hall in an art gallery and see a Cézanne or a Picasso or a Monet or a Rothko or a Frank Stella or a Mondrian, and just by looking at it you know who it is, I would like someone to read a poem of mine and say, 'Oh, that's Charles Wright'" (*Halflife*, 167)—which is possible to do with most poems written since *The Southern Cross* (1981).

Structure, on the other hand, refers to a larger organizing pattern. Structure is an architectural metaphor, and Wright often uses it in this sense: the overall pattern or design of the poem is analogous to that of a building. So for him it is appropriate to speak of the architecture of form, as it applies to poetry, but not the form of architecture. And structure applies to more than one poem: a series of trilogies would of course be a structural pattern, as would the three-part configuration of many of the individual poems, described above in the Introduction.

The dialectic in the present poem is between contraction and expansion, nothing and something, destruction and construction. The way down, as Eliot says, is essential to the way up: or they are one and the same. The crux comes where the crux should come, at the center of the poem: "There is no essence unless / nothing has been left out." This is like a Zen koan. To leave nothing out is, in our colloquial way of speaking, to put everything in. But the white spaces, the erasures that come from the destructive element in art, mean that if you try to put everything in you will have nothing. This is a version of Stevens's "Nothing that is not there and the nothing that is." Nothing, in the sense of "not anything" and nothing in the sense of "something called Nothing"—those are the two senses operating here. The poet wants "not anything" to be left out, but not "something called Nothing." That is the "destructive element," in Mondrian's phrase, echoing a line near the end of Conrad's *Lord Jim*: "In the destructive element immerse." We are at "maximum awareness" at the nadir of the abyss, where "the gods and their names have disappeared." In a painting like *Broadway Boogie Woogie*, Mondrian left nothing out, but he didn't leave Nothing out—all those white spaces without which the constructive color would hardly exist. We might put it this way: Question: "Is there nothing in the picture?" Wright: "No, there is Nothing in the picture." The countryside, the poem concludes, is an "architecture of withdrawal," with its emptiness set off by the reds and blues, as in Mondrian's *Composition No. 8*. The sacrifice of the plenitude of autumn has begun, the seasonal cycle wheeling, like the swallows and bats, toward the vacancy of winter.

p. 122, l. 1. *Form imposes, structure allows—*. In response to an interviewer's question about the influence of Pound and Italy on his poems, Wright replied: "Pound contributed *Cathay* to listen to and *The Pisan Cantos* to look at. Conversational tone in a high mode in the former, emotional road maps in the latter. Italy prompted a realignment with the world and its attendant possibilities. Actually, I suppose it goes a bit further than that. Which is to say, if form imposes and structure allows, then Pound imposed and Italy allowed" (QN, 96).

p. 122, ll. 6–7. *Mondrian ... neglected*. "I think the destructive element is too much neglected in art" (Piet Mondrian, letter to James Johnson Sweeney, in *The New Art—The New Life: The Collected Writings of Piet Mondrian*, ed. Harry Holtzman and Martin S. James [New York: Da Capo Press, 1993], 357).

p. 122, l. 13. *orate sine intermissione*. The line from St. Paul (1 Thessalonians 5:17) is translated in the next line.

Black Zodiac

Orig. pub. *Paris Review* 38 (Winter 1996): 80–3.
BZ, 64–7; NB, 124–7
Pattern: 12 × 6
Time: August
Place: Charlottesville backyard

Black Zodiac is another explicitly *ars poetica* poem. The question posed by the poet is this: What am I to do in the face of the black zodiac, the heavens' darkness, the dominant X, the inevitability of death, the "unanswerable questions," the "unprovable theorems," the mystery of the infinite and the eternal, "the nothing that's nowhere"? The poet's answer: keep on writing, using what is available. And what *is* available is landscape, memories, and those who have come before—the masters (section 1). Some will cry out in praise. Others, in the face of death, will listen by yammering along, some will revile God, and some (those who hate the flesh) will speak in tongues. All of these are lucky because they have already passed through the shadow of death and are "twice-erased" (section 2). Perhaps this afternoon (section 3) will provide a roadmap for the pilgrim-poet as he contemplates the wide gap between the avenues that lead to dust and the infinity of the blue sky. And even though "the great stories always exist in the past," the poet must continue to write about everything that crosses his eye and confronts his consciousness—which he proceeds to do in the catalogue in section 4: the evergreen, the handkerchief of memory, death's dream, the automobile, God's sleep, the moon, the starless night, the spider, toad, and frog. Just use what's lying around, as Mae West said.

We (as he typically does, Wright brings us all into his pilgrimage) may still experience the great cold gulf between us and the dark heavens, but "we harbor no ill will" about that.

We are calligraphers of the disembodied, using our late summer lexicons, and if we do not give up in the face of the evasions of memory, the spirit of silence, and the Invisible Hand, we can abstract the necessary word by describing the landscape. The letters do undarken and come forth (sections 5–6). "Description" is "the word," the poet affirms, by way of Stevens, in conclusion. If description is not an element, at least it is elemental, with all the mystery and splendor of the rain and the garden and the dwarf orchard that the poet sees and to which he must now give witness, including what is "still lurking behind the stars." The phrase "Black Zodiac," Wright says in an interview, "means that the end result of all one's strivings in my case is going to be only as far as one can see, that one cannot go past the Zodiac, cannot go past the stars, that one is forever here, and that's okay." He then adds, "But one sometimes wonders that perhaps it might be nice to be elsewhere sometimes" (Farnsworth).

We have come almost full circle now. It is 31 August, six days after Wright's sixtieth birthday. (The book *Black Zodiac* traces the seasons through a two-year cycle). The poem's setting moves back and forth between daylight and nighttime, but what we have essentially is a nighttime metaphysics of the natural world to complement the daytime metaphysics of the *Envoi* to *Apologia Pro Vita Sua*.

Perhaps Wright chose a twelve-line stanza to correspond to the number of signs in the zodiac. Although not apparent in *Negative Blue*, the poem is the twelfth one in the third section of the book *Black Zodiac*. This central section, moreover, has six poems on either side of it. Whether intentional or not, cosmology recapitulates poetic structure.

p. 124, ll. 1–12. The source for the references to the mixed and mismatched masters is Roberto Calasso's *The Ruins of Kasch* (Cambridge: Harvard University Press, 1994), a meandering but gripping journey through the works of modern philosophical, psychological, economic, historical, and literary "masters"—masters who reveal a vision that is, in Wright's words, "so dark and so clear at the same time" (l. 5). The ruin of Kasch, a mythical African kingdom, becomes an allegory of the ruin of the modern world.

p. 124, l. 13. *Those who look ... praise of him*. The quotation is from Augustine's *Confessions*, bk. 1, chap. 1, par. 1; it is repeated in bk. 10, chap. 43, par. 70.

p. 124, l. 16. *Will listen ... their mouths*. "...deep in the glowing lacuna / at lamp height in the time hole: / listen your way in / with your mouth" (Paul Celan, *The Trumpet Part*, in *Poems of Paul Celan*, trans. Michael Hamburger [New York: Persea, 1995], 351).

p. 126, l. 3. *Moon half-empty, moon half-full*. In August 1995 the moon in its last quarter (half moon) occurred on 18 August, thirteen days before the date of the previous section.

p. 126, l. 20. *Invisible Hand*. This is Adam Smith's metaphor used to illustrate the principle of enlightened self-interest. Smith, a deeply religious man, saw the invisible hand as the mechanism by which a benevolent God administered a universe in which human happiness was maximized. Here the phrase appears to refer to God.

p. 127, l. 9. *Description's ... air or water*. The quotation is from Stevens's *Adagia* (without the contracted verb).

China Mail

Orig. pub. *Iowa Review* 26 (Summer 1996): 201.
BZ, 68; NB, 128
Pattern: 4 × 5
Time: "deep summer"
Place: Charlottesville

In this poem, addressed to Tu Fu (712–70), the great Chinese poet of the T'ang Dynasty, and written after the expectation that the Chinese poet might arrive, the actual borrowings from the Tu Fu's work are not direct. They consist, rather, of shared images, and both poets have a profound empathy for landscape and a sense of solitary desolation. They are fellow travelers. The poet identifies with his Chinese forebear, likening them both to the drifting cloud emptied of its rain. Wright attributes "*Study the absolute*" to Tu Fu (p. 128, l. 12), but the idea is uncharacteristic of Tu Fu and the tag does not appear in any of the collections of Tu that Wright cites in his various notes. The line does appear, however, in G.W. Robinson's translation of Wang Wei's *Sitting Alone on an Autumn Night* (*Poems of Wang Wei*, 121). In any event, Wright steps back from the studied seriousness of *Black Zodiac* (the previous poem): he is not going to study the absolute too intently. He will rather keep in touch with Tu Fu by the exchange of poems, and it is better that way. The words they trace to each other "upon the air" will be familiar to each—the cicadas in the heat of late August, the oaks, the white hair of the moonlight, and the floating cloud.

p. 128, l. 16, *murdered moonlight*. *Let's Murder the Moonlight* was the title of Marinetti's Futurist manifesto. See notes to p. 48, ll. 7 and 15–17, of *C*.

p. 128, l. 17. *Virgo and Scorpio*. Wright (b. 25 August) = Virgo. Tu Fu = Scorpio = those who seek, among other things, the power of transformation at work in ordinary reality. As for Virgo, these things might be noted: The cycle of the heavens turns to Virgo, the virgin, as summer ends. While Virgo is sometimes associated with Demeter, the Greek goddess of the harvest, Virgo's original symbol was the Sphinx, the mythological poser of riddles. So too do Virgoans question (the astrologers tell us), turning inward to seek larger meanings about causes and purposes in life and looking for worthy goals to pursue. Virgoans are the zodiac's analysts, its critics, its purists. They are the servants, custodians, and perfecters of culture. As for the Virgin, she is a symbol less of purity than of hidden wisdom. She is woman in the fullness of self-possession—the high priestess, the healer, the keeper of life's mysteries. Virgoans seek complete realization of the mind. They have strong senses of order and organization and a love of the minute. Virgoans are also perfectionists. They want their environments, as well as their lives, to be tidy. ("I am compulsively orderly," says Wright [*Halflife*, 148].) Virgoans are usually very serious people. There is an innate refinement about them, but also a nervous sensitivity. They are worriers who tend toward pronounced mood swings. In their negative moments they can be pessimistic. (Wright was chosen "most pessimistic" among the graduates in his class at Christ's School.) They are blessed with powerful creative drives, but they view passion with a highly suspicious eye. (Wright's poetry has only an occasional whisper about Eros.) Connections other than those mentioned between Wright and Virgoan traits should be fairly obvious.

p. 128, l. 18. *Of immortality ... its aftermath*. "...the story of our lives opens away ... vacant, silent" (Tu Fu, *Night at the Tower*, in *The Selected Poems of Tu Fu*, 85. The second ellipsis is the translator's.

Wright's note (204) indicates that he has drawn from various translations of Tu Fu's poems. He read Tu Fu in at least these sources: *The Selected Poems of Tu Fu*, trans. David Hinton (New York: New Directions, 1989) (128 poems); *Mountain Home: The Poetry of Ancient China*, trans. David Hinton (Washington: Counterpoint, 2002) (18 poems); *The Jade Mountain*, trans. Witter Bynner (Garden City, NY: Doubleday Anchor, 1964) (34 poems); the pirated edition of Bynner's translation, *Three Hundred Poems of the T'ang Dynasty*, trans. Xuzhou Ding (Taipei: Wu Chou Chu Pan Shê, 1973) (34 poems); *One Hundred Poems from the Chinese*, trans. Kenneth Rexroth (New York: New Directions, 1971) (35 poems); *One Hundred More Poems from the Chinese: Love and the Turning Year*, trans. Kenneth Rexroth (New York: New Directions, 1970) (1 poem); *Li Po and Tu Fu*, trans. Arthur Cooper (Harmondsworth: Penguin, 1973) (18 poems); *Poems of the Late T'ang*, trans. A.C. Graham (Harmondsworth: Penguin, 1965) (8 poems); and *Five T'ang Poets*, trans. David Young (Oberlin College: Oberlin College Press, 1990) (16 poems).

Disjecta Membra

Orig. pub. *American Poetry Review* 25 (November–December 1996): 3–6.
BZ, 71–83; NB, 129–41
Pattern: 10 × 8 in all three parts (240 lines, three fewer than *Apologia Pro Vita Sua*, the poem that opens *Black Zodiac*). There are no breaks in the stanzas of parts 1 and 3. The breaks in part 2 are irregular: one, two, and three lines in various arrangements. (There is one four-line stanza, though it is hidden by the way the lines break between pages 133–4.)
Time: September through January
Place: Charlottesville
Title: "Disjecta membra" is a clipped form of *disjecta membra poetae*, the scattered members or parts of the poet. Horace uses the phrase to mean that his work is subjected to garbled quotation (*Satires*, 1.4.62), but he goes on to say, referring to the work of the early Roman poet Ennius, that you can tell from the briefest extracts of his work that you are dealing with a true poet. Wright identifies his own source of the phrase as Guido Ceronetti's *The Silence of the Body*, and he quotes Ceronetti: "*These fragments are the* disjecta membra *of an elusive, coveted, and vaguely scented knowledge*" (NB, 205). Ceronetti goes on to say, "I have extracted them from

the darkness of entombed notebooks, where they had been buried for future use and pleasure under the inscription 'Medicine'" (*The Silence of the Body* [New York: Farrar, Straus and Giroux, 1993], 4). The form of Ceronetti's book is somewhat like the "improvisations" and "bytes and pieces" in Wright's two prose collections.

Part 1.
Section 1. The poet in his backyard—"a monk among the oak trees"—is critical of the way we present our various persona to our own advantage. We try to trick the Paraclete (the Holy Spirit, the Comforter) by our gestures and poses; we yearn for "the chiaroscuro of character," but the shading of our portraits is false. The mirror that reveals us is thus faulty as well. In line 10 the negation of the "tried and true" cliché (tested and found to be worthy) gets punningly altered to "a shade untrue and a shade untied"—a false tint and a blind let loose.

Section 2. The voice of a discontented God drones from the clear upper air on this Sunday morning, enjoining the poet—and us, as well—to simplify: the third-person point of view is in effect again. The imperative from the aether is for the poet to "Shaker down," that is, to adopt a style that is simple, unornamented, and well crafted, like that of the approaching winter landscape. When the poet repeats the injunction to simplify (p. 129, l. 18), it gets expanded to include divestiture and an opening of "the emptiness." This is elaborated by what the trees do, emptying themselves of their sap in the autumn. The date is 24 September 1995, the day following the fall equinox. The trees have already simplified by shedding their leaves: they lie dead upon the ground, having been shaken down (an echo of the divine the injunction to "Shaker down"). What replaces the trees' sap is an intravenous drip of darkness, injected from "the infinite." By repeating the divine imperative the poet accepts the command to simplify and to divest, thereby imitating the cycle of nature as it pushes through the September equinox toward the emptiness of winter.

Section 3. The focus here is on the poet's sense of oneness with the things around him. The scene is in the back yard of the novelist Peter Matthiesson in New York. As the poet sits in the morning light he sees Matthiesson's zendo through the privet hedge. (Matthiesson is a practicing Buddhist: his *Zen Journals 1969–1982* [pub. 1986] tracks his practice of Zen to his ordination as a Zen priest.) The noise of the traffic subsides in the background; the morning dew has almost completely evaporated; the ants make their way across the garden; the robin, not yet having fled south, flies in brusquely and settles down ("dust-down" perhaps referring as well to the color of robin's feathers); the wind lifts the leaves and tucks them in again; and light and shadow interplay with each other.

Wright says, "I'm not a student of Buddhism ... but it is a condition of being that appeals to me, it is a search that appeals to me. Something, I might add, I am incapable of achieving. I know that. I cannot find that still, small center in my self or in the world that will make me at one with my world. But I look for it. In fact I look for that more than I would look for, how do I say it, a Christian resolution?" (*QN*, 123–4). In the present vignette, the poet, once he has stopped filing his nails, approaches that moment of quiet Zen meditation when everything is identified with everything else—the state of "emptiness" (*shunyata*) in which one senses the interdependency and interpenetration of all things. As Wright later says, "We all have our ways of keeping the Buddha alive" (*SHS*, 30).

Section 4. Here the poet longs for a second chance in a world of an intense color brought on by another cycle of nature, which will be also a world of idleness and solitude and rest. The journey will be a difficult "deep" one into the darkness (another katabasis), but if the longing for rest is fulfilled, he can rearrange the fabric of his heart.

Section 5. We are constantly, the poet says, being swept away from nature by history, which washes away our desires, hope, and essential qualities, as in the Zen aphorism, which Wright overheard someone saying. The silent movement of time will strip us down to a nub, distracting us from the natural world right before our eyes—the spinning spider web weighted with dew and the sunlight becoming a dead body on the pavement. This section is quite elliptical, but the one sentiment that does emerge is that we do not want to be twisted out of our back yards by history.

Section 6. The relationship between life and death is of course complicated: death may hold the secret of life, or life may hold the secret of death. The poet is reminded of this by his backyard garden—or the original Garden with its myth of the Fall. But the cycle of nature itself is not complicated, as the catalogue of backyard creatures shows. The concluding advice to the rabbit—"sit tight and hold on" amid the guillotines of sunlight and shade beyond the neighbor's hedge—might well be advice the poet offers himself: the smartest thing is not to wander from the garden.

Section 7. The opposition here is between the inclination to surrender to love and to get overly close to beauty, on the one hand, and, on the other, to lie low (as Meng Chiao advises) and go it alone, not worrying about tying the knot in the solitary thread of life. Again, these ruminations are set beside the description of the backyard landscape, and we conclude with a comment on the fleeting and insubstantial quality of things: "Of both, there soon will not be a trace." "Both" here is ambiguous: both ink and word? both the poet's shadow and the trees' shadows? both the poet and his poems?

p. 131, ll. 21–2. *Meng Chiao*. "Keep away from sharp swords, / Don't go near a lovely woman. / A sharp sword too close will wound your hand, / Woman's beauty too close will wound your life. / The danger of the road is not in the distance, / Ten years is far enough to break a wheel. / The peril of love is not in loving too often, / A single evening can leave its wound in the soul" (Meng Chiao, *Impromptu*, in *Poems of the Late T'ang*, trans. A.C. Graham [Harmondsworth: Penguin, 1965], 67). Meng Chiao (751–814) was a symbolic and deeply introspective poet.

Section 8. The theme here is the presumption that language can carry the burden we impose on it. "Can we address a blade of grass, the immensity of a snowflake?" The quotation from Celan implies that we cannot—that we must remain mute, even though Celan goes on to say to Nelly Sachs, "you must not believe words like yours can remain unheard." We end up, however, with only a slight pause between language and silence. The poet does counsel us to bite hard into what is in front of us—in order to get hold of it. What is in front of him at the moment is redness—the October maples, the western horizon, northern skies with their "arterial headway." So, yes, the poet can address such subjects in the landscape, and he closes with an invocation, like the petition to the Lord in an evangelical hymn, to let the autumn come.

p. 132, l. 9. *With what words ... silence.* "I wanted most of all ... to tell you—with what words, with what silence?—that you must not believe words like yours can remain unheard" (Paul Celan, letter to Nelly Sachs, January 1958).

Part 2.

Section 1. Here, in bleak November, the poet enters the dark night of the soul, embarrassed by what he has written and aware that "Nothing regenerates us, or shapes us again from the dust." Confessing that we lack transparency means both that we lack clarity and that we are not free from guile. Still, the poet praises the divine "you." "Nothing" regenerates us and whispers our name, suggesting that "nothing" is not, or not simply, "no thing" but, as before, some form of hidden divinity, as in *The Cloud of Unknowing* or the "nothingness" in the abyss of Boehme's *Urgrund*. The description of November's doom-dangled decay, with its "fitful bone light," seeping pus, and dog rot is as demonic a description as one finds in Wright. Still, the poet's dumb fingers must try to write, even though what he produces is illegible.

Section 2. The first three lines, drawn from scattered passage in *Asclepius* (*Nag Hammadi Library*) about the gloomy fate of the soul in death, are set against the more hopeful claim about restoration, also from *Asclepius*. The poet opts for the latter vision, which includes a spiritual food he has hungered for and the light of resurrection. But no such light is available in the remaining *disjecta membra* of part 2.

p. 133, l. 11. *When death ... the body*. "For death occurs, which is the dissolution of the labors of the body, and the number (of the body), when it (death) completes the number of the body. For the number is the union of the body. Now the body dies when it is not able to support the man. And this is death: the dissolution of the body and the destruction of the sensation of the body. And it is not necessary to be afraid of this, nor because of this, but because of what is not known, and is disbelieved (is one afraid)" (*Asclepius 21-29*, NHL, 336-7). Trismegistus is speaking to Asclepius.

p. 133, ll. 11-12. *its food ... groaning*. "For the souls that are filled with much evil will not come and go in the air, but they will be put in the places of the daimons, which are filled with pain, (and) which are always filled with blood and slaughter, and their food, which is weeping, mourning, and groaning" (*Asclepius 21-29*, NHL, 338).

p. 133, ll. 12-13. *stranglers ... dirt*. "Trismegistus, who are these (daimons)? Asclepius, they are the ones who are called 'stranglers,' and those who roll souls down on the dirt, and those who scourge them, and those who cast into the water, and those who cast into the fire, and those who bring about the pains and calamities of men" (*Asclepius 21-29*, NHL, 338).

p. 133, ll. 15-16. *The restoration ... beginning*. "The restoration of the nature of the pious ones who are good will take place in a period of time that never had a beginning. For the will of God has no beginning, even as his nature, which is his will (has no beginning). For the nature of God is will. And his will is the good" (*Asclepius 21-29*, NHL, 336).

Sections 2-8. The rest of part two proceeds in the same discontinuous way. Each unit is still ten lines long, but the lines are broken up into smaller units of irregular lengths: they can hardly be called stanzas as some are only one line. There are thirty-eight of these small units altogether, twenty-eight of which are two or three lines; nine are couplets, and one a quatrain. This comminution of the ten-line form reinforces and even helps to reveal the distressed and disjointed state of the poet's own mind. Part 2 is almost completely an interior monologue, reflecting the poet's anxiety, guilt, disorientation, and impotence in a world of darkness. The description of the landscape has been replaced by the description of a surreal world, where names hang life flesh from flame trees, where the fingerprints of nothing adhere to the skin like watermarks, and where blood rolls back to its wound. The word "is beyond us," declares the poet, shortly echoing Eliot's *Gerontion*: "word within a word, unable to speak a word." The poet's lost penny that was found (Luke 15:8-10) is unspendable. God has no concern for us, and his name has been cut into syllables and scattered about, like the *sparagmos* of Orpheus. There is no first heaven (the empyrean) and no second heaven (the immanent spiritual heaven that Paul speaks of in Ephesians 6:12)—or perhaps the reference is to Pythagoras' music of the spheres. Prayers are an affliction, substance is absence, identities have been erased ("everyone's no one"), "life is a sore gain," and we are "without mercy." The poet's backyard has become an alien and destitute land, and the poet is without light and hope. All he can do is mutter a prayer at the end for the Lord of the garden and the city to "tweak and restartle" him and to guide his hand. Hope is a purgatorial virtue.

All of these *disjecta membra* are poetic kernels—discontinuous and juxtaposed aphorisms—that move in the direction of fragmentation, so that the links are hieroglyphic, epiphanic, and metaphorical.

Part 3.

Section 1. The poet confesses, as he walks the dogs down Locust Avenue, that the scene is familiar and that he has told the same story over and over. Beneath the altar of the Pleiades on Christmas Eve, like Leopardi and his Great Bear, he is "one-on-one with the visible / And shadowy overhang." He begins to tick off those things he has memorized by heart: the constellations, the dog's bark, "bleak supplicants, blood of the lamb," the ellipsis suggesting that his list had not ended but only stopped. The image of the supplicants before the high altar of the Pleiades and that of the lamb are doubtless triggered by the Christmas Eve occasion.

p. 138, l. 7. *Mrs. Fornier's* [sic] *window*. The reference is to Jeanne Marie Fournier's window; her house was down the block at 960 Locust Avenue.

Section 2. The poet begins by projecting Rilke's line on himself. The focus is on a life undone and time wasted, and just at the time the poet, in late middle age, is beginning to catch on to the fundamentals of language. "Despair is our consolation" ("sweet word," the poet adds ironically) and dreary objectivity. But perhaps he is moving past that now, having learned the "difference between the adjective and the noun."

p. 138, l. 11. *Unfinished ... distracted*. In his *Letters on Cézanne*, Ranier Maria Rilke writes, "One lives so badly, because one always comes into the present unfinished, unable, distracted. I cannot think back on any time of my life without such reproaches and worse" (*Letters on Cézanne* [New York: Fromm, 1985], 10).

p. 138, l. 16. *Splendor of little fragments*. "Are all these millions of [heather] branches really so wonderfully wrought? Just look at the radiance of this green which contains a little gold, and the sandalwood warmth of the brown in the little stems, and that fissure with its new, fresh, inner barley green.—Ah, I've been admiring the splendor of these little fragments for days and I am truly ashamed that I was not happy when I was permitted to walk in a superabundance of these" (ibid.).

Section 3. The poet addresses the old metaphysician, the dead moth, telling it that daily we shrink our lives and that writing poetry bleeds the life out of him. The upshot is that the poet will keep his mouth shut and focus on the landscape.

p. 139, l. 8. *Bremo Bluff*. A town on the James River in Fluvanna County, Virginia.

Section 4. The date is January 8, the day of a deep snowfall in Charlottesville—as cold as the bitter and numbing chill Keats records in the first stanza of *The Eve of St. Agnes*. Meanwhile, inside his house the poet glances at the caricature of Thomas Rowlandson's Dr. Syntax on the wall across the room, alongside a photograph of Wright and his army friend George Mancini, taken in Greece in 1961. At the beginning, snow is metaphorically a shroud covering the landscape, and at the end a cover that obscures both the past, like the blurry photograph, and the present.

p. 139, l. 18. *Dr. Syntax*. For a reproduction of the caricature, see http://www.philaprintshop.com/syntax.html

Section 5. The poet formulates a stark contrast between the hard, certain reality of the snow and the ambiguous uncertainty of the human position—in both space and time. The huge drifts "of soft edge and abyss" resulted from the record-setting snowstorm that paralyzed much of the East Coast on January 8, with winter emergencies declared from Georgia through New York.

Section 6. The poet gets an occasional glimpse of the sharp, neatly crafted, and fiery poem, and he would like to inherit its music. All he wishes for now is a somewhat diminished desire: to follow the "fiery ride" of the January sky and "mind its smoke." This imagery, along with "body of ash, body of fire," is purgatorial.

Section 7. The life we long for is the life of landscape—the silent landscape of the Blue Ridge mountains and the buzzards, crows, and "little birds." Such simple gifts from the natural world will fulfill our desires and enable us "to be at ease in the natural world."

Section 8. There is no cheap grace in Wright's poetry, but in his end is his beginning, and so he is ready to start out once again, emptied—and following his father-in-law's advice to take it easy, to lighten up a bit, and do what the clouds do. What the clouds do is incessantly transform themselves. To be emptied is to be purified of the ghosts of his past, and this poem is, after all, the conclusion of Wright's purgatorial journey. "Taking it easy" will prove difficult, as we see in the first poem in *Appalachia*.

p. 141, l. 10. *John.* John McIntire, Wright's father-in-law, the well-known Hollywood actor and husband of the equally well-known Jeannette Nolan.

* * *

In Wright's poetic vision, purgatory is not otherworldly. It is the pilgrimage through life itself and the things of this world—in Wright's unadorned language, a "step-by-step through the mud of time" (Spiegelman, 119). Wright has remarked that *Black Zodiac* "suffers the purgatorial clear-out of all confessions—self-torture, self-mutation" (Caseley, 23). The poet is afforded occasional, hard-won glimpses of the light, and with the help of his T'ang poets, the Nag Hammadi writers, and the other "saints" who serve as his Virgil, he is able to muster sufficient stamina to continue the pilgrimage. But the overwhelming vision of *Black Zodiac* is indeed black: the omnipresent motifs are failure, absence, exile, amnesia, ignorance, uncertainty, separation, and melancholy—all of which the poet has to confront in order to catharsize.

CHAPTER 3

Appalachia and North American Bear

Appalachia

    Black Zodiac was framed by two long poems, *Apologia Pro Vita Sua* (270 lines, counting the *Envoi*) and *Disjecta Membra* (240 lines). *Appalachia* contains short poems exclusively. Two lines from *Quotations* spill over to a second page, but none of the other forty-three poems, in their layout in *Negative Blue*, exceeds a single page. The pencil drawings on the dust jacket are by Mark Strand.

Stray Paragraphs in February, Year of the Rat

Orig. pub. *Kenyon Review* 19 (Spring 1997): 2.
A, 3; NB, 145
Pattern: 4-2-4-2
Time: 1996
Place: Charlottesville

Title: Why "paragraphs" rather than "stanzas" or "verses"? In *Zone Journals* and *Xionia* Wright began to create longer lines, so that his poetry would move in the direction of prose without becoming prose. In several interviews he refers to Montale's notion that all poetry begins in and yearns to return to prose (QN, 105–6, 136–8; Bourgeois, 55; Zawacki, 24). In *Negative Blue* the lines, as well as the poems become shorter, but Wright is still under the sway of Montale's view.

    Why "*stray* paragraphs"? Paragraphs that are just lying around? Or that got found after having been misplaced? Or wandering around looking for their proper home in a poem like *Stray Paragraphs in February*? Wright has spoken, somewhat jokingly, about titles—his increasing attention to them, their tendency to get longer over time, and his membership in a movement called "Titleism" (QN, 159). We do often get little jokes in Wright's titles. And ironies: these "paragraphs" aren't paragraphs, and they certainly are not stray any more. They are tied up or enclosed within the fence of the poem. They have been given their measure in a tight 4 × 2 structure.

The Metaphorical Imagination. We begin by considering the various ways metaphor works in this poem. To say that "the countryside unwrinkles and smooths out" (p. 145, l. 1) is to identify the countryside with a piece of cloth or other fabric. Skin wrinkles, and we can speak of the skin of the earth, but the metaphorical implications of *fabric* work better than *skin* in this context. "Unwrinkles" is in the present tense, but the process is not one in which the countryside everywhere to the east suddenly becomes flat all at once. The metaphor works only because of our knowledge of the geography east of Charlottesville: the hills gradually flatten out until we get to the coast. "Unctuous," which comes from the Latin for smearing or anointing (thus "oily" or "greasy"), adds another layer of metaphor to the implicit personification: the harsh and surly Atlantic is set over against the personified landscape, which is smug and overly pious, even pretentious.

In the next two lines of stanza 1 the figurative language disappears in favor of abstractions: "love," "landscape," "affection," "regret," "joined," "apart." The sense seems clear enough: if you love landscape then you must have a real affection for regret. One could think of any number of things to fit into the slot occupied by "regret": "a true affection for beauty," say, or "a true affection for the city rather than the country," neither of which is likely to be found in Wright's poetic universe. Why, then, regret? The answer is in line 4: while we are, to be sure, a part of the natural world we are always alienated from it because it is not a part of us. We have no explicit metaphors in these lines, but we do have the principle that lies behind metaphor, the principle of identity. Behind the unwrinkling-countryside metaphor of line 1 is an identification of earth (A) and fabric (B). A is B, we're told. But of course we all know that A is not B—that the land east of Charlottesville is one thing and that cloth is something altogether different. This is not simile at work: Wright is not saying that the countryside like a piece of cloth when we iron it or a piece of paper when we smooth out its wrinkles. In metaphor, identity, not analogy, is what is important. So when Wright says that landscape (A) is "yet ourselves" (B), he means that we are identified with it. A is B. What causes the regret, however, is our awareness that A is not B. We are "forever apart," cut off from landscape, not able to identify with it because it is something "Other," and we are unable to be "joined" to it, to use Wright's verb. It is of some interest, then, that in the least overtly metaphorical part of the poem thus far the principle upon which metaphor is founded is at work.

In the second stanza we are told that "Renunciation ... is now our ecstasy." A number of suggestions are embodied in "ecstasy"—a high-pitched emotional frenzy, a feeling of heightened delight or rapture—and most of them have little to do with renunciation. But the word often has a particularly poetic meaning. Longinus uses *ekstasis* to mean poetic transport, as when we are carried away or put out of our place in the presence of an especially elevated or sublime passage of poetry. This is the suggestion Wright seems to intend. (Longinus' notion of the sublime appears in *Autumn's Sidereal, November's a Ball and Chair*, in *NB*, 164). The primary sense of renunciation here is not the abandonment of worldly pleasure but the repudiation of excess in the poetic line. This is a familiar admonition in Wright's poetry: cut away all the excess baggage. The next metaphor appears in line 6: God is (not "as") swallower. If he had not disappeared, God would swallow our sighs of regret.

Now, if we love the landscape, the poet says, we have a true affection for regret. This is because, while we are tied to it, we are also separated from it. The unity that we desire is difficult or impossible. So, we regret that we feel out of joint with the landscape and we sigh about this in our longing. These sighs would mean nothing to God if he had not died or gotten lost or wandered away: he'd just take them into his nothingness.

"Swallow" is a metaphor that moves in two directions: to make disappear and to completely possess. We find the latter idea in Milton, and Ezekiel fills his stomach with the scrolls God gives him. Wright's friend Mark Strand has a poem called *Eating Poetry*, in which he does just that. So swallowing can be a metaphor for completely internalizing. In this sense, then, God, if he were not dead, would take our meager little sighs into himself along with everything else. As for nothingness, this means more than simply the absence of God. It also means God as the *via negativa*, which implies the notion of God without metaphor—the recognition that "God is Father," "God is Light," "God as the Ground of Being," etc. are identifications that do not really account for the mystery of divinity. According to the mystics, adding just one more metaphor to the equation will not get us very far: what we should do is subtract

("God is not this") until we arrive at the mystical point of nothingness. Different versions of this idea appear throughout *Black Zodiac* and elsewhere in Wright's poetry. Taking God as Nothing in this sense, we can say that our failure to be able to identify with landscape is a part of this large dialectic of "is" and "is-not." Assume that God *were* around. Then he would be defined just as much by our renunciations and regrets as by our ecstasies and celebrations, all of which he swallows.

Next, the poet says that "The dregs of the absolute are slow to sift in my blood" (ll. 7–9). He is slow to internalize this sense of God as sediment or distillate in his blood. The blood image is picked up again in the arterial light of the last line of the poem. To say that we have the absolute, if even the dregs, in our blood means that God may not be completely absent. We are now moving, in typical Wright fashion, to the description of landscape, which becomes the central metaphor. The dregs of the absolute are the dead branches, the dead grass, the undergrowth; and the metaphor is extended by identifying this dead detritus with what is hidden below, as in the "I.V. from the infinite" in *Disjecta Membra*, which lets the darkness drip in.

By saying that what is "not revealed / Rises like snow" (l. 10) the poet reverses the commonplace simile, "falls like snow." Something cold is seen as coming up from underneath to cover the bare ground of the poet's soul, similar to the dead dregs entering his consciousness. The phrase "cross-whipped and openmouthed" refers, at the level of description, to the poet's back yard. The wind has whipped the snow around so that bare places are showing, and these bare places look like mouths opening up out of the snow. But metaphorically the earth is the poet's soul, and the open mouth suggests a yearning to be fed. The idea, then, is that the sense of loss, of death, of the dregs of the absolute begins slowly to infuse the poet, to enter his blood, to fill up, even cover, the bare places of his soul.

The couplet that follows (ll. 11–16) contrasts us with the saints, whose hearts are lit with fiery energy. The concluding stanza is an invocation to February, personified as a head-turner. Now that February has got the poet's attention, his plea is for it to ease up a bit. February is a "grind of bone / On bone," and the poet asks February to provide a little relief from that "melancholy music." This could well be a metaphor for what the winds are doing to the dead branches: lifting up the blanket of the cold, desolate earth and letting a little light in. The light is "arterial" because the arteries carry their payload to the heart. Thus, if the poet cannot have the fire of the saints' hearts, might he not have a little light, deep within his arteries? And the request for the "corner" of the landscape to be lifted takes us back to the fabric image with which we began.

Stray Paragraphs in April, Year of the Rat

Orig. pub. *Kenyon Review* 19 (Spring 1997): 2.
A, 4; NB, 146
Pattern: 2-3-2-3-2-1-1-1
Time: 1996
Place: Charlottesville

To begin again with metaphor, the identifications in this poem include:

- poet is mole
- highest desire is only dog prayer
- cardinals are blood clots
- air is a blood stream

- affliction is a gift
- April is a stylish courtesan; April is a potential mouth-dampener
- soul is air (spirit is breath, air)

The opposition in the poem is between the underground world of the dead and the airy upper world, which sustains the soaring cardinals and maintains the poet's soul. This upper world is called "heaven" in stanza 3. The wish to identify with the mole and the dog, which have no objects of desire, is a wish for diminishment. The progressive contracting of the number of lines per unit, concluding with three one-line (stray) "stanzas" at the end, parallels formally the idea of shrinking into the darkness. The connections between stanzas are tenuous, but the intent of the whole is to suggest that (1) grace cannot be earned (we have to wait to be "gathered") and (2) the negative condition can breed something positive (affliction is not a burden but a gift). The invocation, in any event, is for April to dampen the poet's dry mouth, and the final line, with its identification of soul and air as a nurturing force, has moved the poet up from his underground desires.

p. 146, l. 11. *Affliction's a gift*. This is one of the scores of things, often contradictory, that the French philosopher and mystic Simone Weil says about affliction in "The Love of God and Affliction" in *Waiting for God* and in her notebooks, the latter of which Wright gives as his source in a note (NB, 205): *The Notebooks of Simone Weil*, trans. Arthur Wills. 2 vols. (London: Routledge & Kegan Paul, 1965). Working in London for the French provisional government during WWII, Weil insisted on restricting her diet to the rations of her French compatriots. This, along with exhausting herself with her work, led to her death in her mid-thirties. A deeply religious Christian Platonist, she advocated what she called "decreation"—abandoning self-centeredness through mystical experience. This was the only way she saw to reconcile the conflict between religious expectation and the dehumanizing enslavement of a technological culture.

Basic Dialogue

Orig. pub. *Kenyon Review* 19 (Spring 1997): 1.
A, 5; NB, 147
Pattern: 5 × 4
Time: 1996
Place: Charlottesville

The poet's task is to make what lies outside of objects in time and space less abstract and more vital. In line 4 we again have the pun on "nothing"—nothingness and no thing. Nothing, which is what we cannot see, needs to be made more concrete and less unreal. This task gets illustrated in the next stanza, where loss and death are manifest in the dead crepe myrtle, the splayed and drooping tulips, and the absence of blossoms. "Pure description" can lift "nothingness" into another, visual world: the abstract becomes concrete.

Next we get a typical Wright turn—a *culbute*, as the French say—a life-from-death somersault. It is out of the death of winter that the "jubilant revelation" comes, and it comes through the language of the poem itself, the pure description of the "artificial thing." It is the poem that is resurrected, not the poet, for the poet exists in a state of "self-oblivion." At the same time, the landscape itself is rejuvenated and the poet wants to lie down in his garden, a wish fulfilled in the final line. A revived nature yearns to get itself expressed: it nibbles at the poet's fingers—the fingers holding the pen—and the syllables of landscape begin to search for their proper expression. It is as if the poet has still disappeared, for the landscape is trying to express itself, or at least to find a way of doing so. The "minor Armageddon" is the battle between nothing and something, between the dead bushes and the new growth of the dogwood and pine. It is also the struggle to make what we see less unreal. The "waters of disremembering" at the end, a twist on the opening line of Psalm 137, is another expression of self-effacement.

Let the poem write itself, in other words. The "basic dialogue" turns out to be a monologue: landscape speaks, or is beginning to, which is a version of Simone Weil's "decreation" implicit in the previous poem.

p. 147, l. 4. *Nothing's more abstract ... actually see.* The line is from Giorgio Morandi: "I believe that nothing can be more abstract, more unreal, than what we actually see" (Dore Ashton, ed. *Twentieth-Century Artists on Art* [New York: Pantheon, 1985], 435; qtd. in Karen Wilken, *Giorgio Morandi* [Barcelona: Ediciones Polígrafa, S.A., 1997], 122).

p. 147, l. 12. The "lemon tree" in the Charlottesville yard is a Virginia "lemon," not in the citrus family, but having large, hard lemon-sized balls.

Star Turn

Orig. pub. *Recorder* 9, No. 2 (Fall 1996): 1.
A, 7; BZ, 148
Pattern: 5 × 2
Title: A featured skit or number in a theatrical production.

The central metaphor here is that stars are actors, singing actors, in the theater of the heavens. The secondary metaphor is that light is music. The stars are anything but ostentatious. They are quite modest, secretive, and easily frightened ("gun shy"), and they produce only a "dumb show" (Keats's "unheard melodies"). In addition, these stars are not in the best of health. They are "frost-sealed" invalids with bandaged eyes (cf. "bandannaed" in *Star Turn II*, [NB, 182]), "broken pieces / Drifting and rootless." And they are "lidless" eyes, which is why they have to be bandaged during the day. They do however deliver a message with their melody, although neither is specified. As for the little physics lesson, the "great fire" is perhaps a nuclear fission reaction or the Big Bang that produces alpha and beta particles. Or this may be a reference to Scorpio, which in China is known as "the great fire." The poet does not assume a post-Newtonian view of the heavens as a vast waste-space of indifference. But we learn that only at the very end, where his attitude toward the little night-time singers is captured in the word "companions."

A Bad Memory Makes You a Metaphysician, a Good One Makes You a Saint

Orig. pub. *Kenyon Review* 19 (Spring 1997): 3.
A, 8; NB, 149
Pattern: 6—4—6
Time: Spring
Place: Charlottesville

The title, as indicated in Wright's note (NB, 205), comes for E.M. Cioran: "Regression in memory makes one a metaphysician; delight in its origins, a saint" (*Tears and Saints*, trans. Ilinca Zarifopol-Johnston [Chicago: University of Chicago Press, 1995], 39). Wright's note indicates that two lines in the poem have been "taken and laundered" from Ciroan's book. These are lines 13–14, and the passage from which they come is this: "When I think of all the agonies on this earth, I know there are souls which could not be lifted by cohorts of angels, so heavy they will not be able to rise at the Last Judgment, frozen in the barrenness of their own curses. Only light souls can be saved: those whose weight will not break the wings of angels" (44).

We have moved from the stars down to the back yard. The poem turns on the crucible metaphor: the back yard is "God's crucible," in its in several senses: (1) the vessel (back yard) in which God continuously creates his world; (2) the deep bottom of the furnace; (3) the mechanism for refining away the dross; (4) the trial or test. Perhaps clinging in the margins is also the sense that "crucible" probably derives from the lamp that was placed in front of the crucifix (Latin *crux*, cross). In any event, the resurrection motif lies in the background. The poet says that we rise phoenix-like out of the ashes of our little gardens as darkness comes on. Too bad the landscape has to be so bourgeois and suburban, but that is where we are, and it does not look as if we will be able to renounce all this and become hair-shirted ascetics. But the real question is, How can we rise to another life? How can our souls be saved? The answer is that the dross of memory has to be refined away. "Too many things are not left unsaid," Wright says, negating the commonplace, and they should be. If we dredge them up from our memories and put them into our poems, then we have got nature rather than landscape, philosophizing rather than poetry, suburbanite angst rather than pure description of the garden, personal rather than distanced emotion, story rather than image. Pure description comes from the refining process in the crucible, where all the former of these oppositions are purged. This happens when the poet does his proper job, which is "what the syllables want": compression, concision, contraction, simplification—as in the description of the landscape of the first stanza. Everything else drags us down: the unbearable weightiness of being and, as in the passage from Cioran, the heaviness of dark souls, which will snap the angel's wings. Refine that weightiness away if you want to be saved, like the "light souls" in "another life."

Thinking about the Poet Larry Levis One Afternoon in Late May

Orig. pub. *Poetry* 170 (April 1997): 24.
A, 9; NB, 150
Pattern: 6 × 3
Place: Charlottesville

Title: Larry Levis (b. 1946) taught poetry writing and directed the M.F.A. program at Virginia Commonwealth University. He died unexpectedly in May 1996.

This is an elegy that doesn't tell us anything directly about Larry Levis. It tells us a great deal about the poet's grief (though the emotion comes through the description of landscape) and the poet's uncertainties about death and life. We get both the sense of loss and the feeling of uncertainty expressed abstractly and prosaically ("who's to say it's not true," "We haven't a clue as to what counts," and "We just don't know what matters."). We get it expressed concretely in several ways, the chief of which come through the day's vacillating between rain and sunlight, in the images of nature as flesh (inner and outer, shown and hidden, hello and goodbye), and in the image of the sunlight across the tree limbs. This last image is the crux: "Sunlight suffused like a chest pain across the tree limbs. / God, the gathering night, assumes it." Here the poet's obvious emotional pain is embodied, though detached, in the description of landscape, as it is in saying goodbye to the flesh-colored spring. "Assumes" is used in the sense of "takes up or into" or "receives." God has assumed the light (Levis's life) into the gathering darkness (death). Mentally, the uncertainty of the meaning of death remains: "It's all the same dark, it's all the same absence of dark." Psychologically, the pain, though not removed (there is still more rain coming), is endurable because it has been assumed by God, as in the taking up of Christ's body into heaven.

Wright on Wright: "Larry Levis was a farm boy from the great central valley of California.

Son of a grape rancher, probably the best poet to ever come out of the upper valley. Frank Bidart, from Bakersfield, holds the southern part. I first met Larry when he was very young, as I was. He wrote marvelous poems for thirty years and died of a heart attack at forty-eight in Richmond several years ago. An inestimable loss to his generation. His last book, *Elegy*, is stunningly beautiful and prescient. A major talent at the brink of its majority." This is the headnote to Wright's account of his first meeting Levis in 1967, "Larry Levis and the First-time, One-time, Irvine Manuscript Day," in *UP*, 4–5.

In the Kingdom of the Past, the Brown-Eyed Man Is King

Orig. pub. *Poetry* 169 (January 1997): 187.
A, 10; NB, 151
Pattern: 5 × 3
Place: Charlottesville

This poem is about as directly expressed a confession as we ever get from Wright. Can we deceive ourselves by thinking that all the emblems of our past (the photos, books, etc.) are somehow important? No, because our egos, which continue to flourish in their self-regard, are too strong. But even though these things don't add up to much ("tiny arithmetic"), we retain them nevertheless as shrines to the past, to what we could have been, to the roles we played. The "Brown-Eyed Man" is the mythical hero of Chuck Berry's song, "Brown-Eyed Handsome Man," reincarnated in Led Zeppelin's "Good Times Bad Times." We know that we really were not that kind of hero, but we still worship the kingdom of the past. This produces guilt, and, oh, how we love guilt. This is why we still crawl in on our knees before these shrines to confess, this poem being itself one such confession.

All of this is represented concretely by the metaphors drawn from math, the plants in the garden and the room as religious site: photos and half-read books are a "tiny arithmetic" against the darkness that threatens to engulf us; the self is a hardy perennial, the ego its knotty bulb; the locus of the psyche's self-regard is the damp and dreamy soil; the mementos in the room are shrines, *ex votos*, reliquaries, and the cruxes and intersections of one's life.

Passing the Morning under the Serenissima

Orig. pub. *New Yorker* 74, no. 10 (4 May 1998): 144–5.
A, 11; NB, 152
Pattern: 6 × 3
Time: June
Place: Venice

Title: Serenissima was the name of the Republic of Venice from early days until May 1797. The title means simply under the aura of the old Venetian Republic.

This is a "story" poem: the poet recounts how he passes his time on hot days in Venice reading Buzzi, Nooteboom, and Flaubert, and observing all the while the scene before him, with its insects, cloudy sky, and canal boats. The difference between the big Venetian sun and Heraclitus' view of it triggers the account of Heraclitus' life from Buzzi's book.

Heraclitus was the shadowy Greek philosopher whose one book was lost but from which a number of fragments have been preserved. The italicized passage in l. 12 is one version of fragment 65. The breadth of the sun reference (l. 3) is from fragment 37. Heraclitus was called "the weeping philosopher" because of his gloomy view of life. One can understand Wright's attraction to Heraclitus, for his fragments show his thinking was dominated by the opposition of sleeping and waking, life and death. He finds these opposites both at the level of the human soul and the larger cosmos. The existence of these opposites depends only on the difference of the *motion* of "the way upwards" from that of "the way downwards"; otherwise, they are the same. All things, therefore, are at once identical and not identical, which is a good definition of metaphor. Allusions to Heraclitus appear also in *Umbrian Dreams* (NB, 101) and *Looking Around II* (SHS, 6).

p. 152, l. 1. *Ponte S. Polo.* The Venetian bridge across the Rio San Polo, southwest of Campo San Polo.

p. 152, ll. 2–11. *Aldo Buzzi* = a novelist; trained as an architect; worked in film in Rome for many years. The Buzzi reference comes from his *Journey to the Land of Flies and Other Travels*, trans. Ann Goldstein (New York: Random House, 1996): "Behind the blue of the sky I seemed to glimpse something obscurely clear, as when Heraclitus says that the sun has the width of a human foot.... Heraclitus was nicknamed the Obscure because he wrote in a way that could be read only by the very few capable of understanding him: if he seems clear, as in the case of the diameter of the sun, one must suspect that he is being even more obscure than usual. When he could no longer endure the 'clarity' of his fellow citizens he retired to the mountains, feeding, like a hermit, on grasses and wild greens. He became sick with dropsy. He returned to the city, where, stretching out on the ground, he had himself covered with manure so that the heat of the fermentation would dry him out. After two days of this cure he died. Neanthes of Cyzicum adds that having lost, under the manure, every human semblance, he was devoured by dogs. He was also nicknamed the weeping philosopher, as opposed to Democritus, the laughing philosopher" (80–1). Buzzi's account of Heraclitus derives from Diogenes Laertios, who lived about seven centuries later: his *Lives of and Opinions of Eminent Philosophers* records these biographical—and doubtless apocryphal—anecdotes.

p. 152, l. 14. *Cees Nooteboom.* A Dutch poet and travel-writer.

Venetian Dog

Orig. pub. *Poetry* 169 (January 1997): 187.
A, 12; NB, 153
Pattern: 4 × 5
Place: Venice

The problems facing the poet are these: (1) everyone ignores us, (2) language is our enemy, unremittingly beating against us, (3) fortune seems remote, (4) the sound of the church bells and what that symbolizes disappear like pigeons into the sunlight, and (5) the unseen stars move against us. We are, in short, pitiable creatures. Stanza 1 begins sometime in the morning, with the poet's muttering like a mutt about what the day is going to be like. By stanza 3, it is 6:00 P.M.

The "Venetian dog high-stepper" (p. 153, l. 2) refers to a dog in a painting by Vittore Carpaccio, a Venetian artist (1472–1526) whose canvases are filled with canines of various sorts. The best candidate is the large white dog in *The Baptism of the Selenites*. "A Baron Corvo bad day" means that the day is bizarre, or at least difficult to figure out. Baron Corvo was the *nom de plume* of Frederick Rolfe, a rather self-deluded British writer. D.H. Lawrence, W.H. Auden, and Graham Greene admired him; others saw him as a crackpot. He tried to become a priest, but his bid was rejected. He was the author of historical romances (e.g., *Hadrian the Seventh*) and a schoolmaster who took nude photographs of young Italian males. He ended his days sleeping on the streets of Venice after biting every hand that dared feed him. (See also *Homage to Baron Corvo* in HF, 14.)

The central image of stanza 2 is the Dogana, the Venetian Customs House of the Doge, the chief magistrate of the former Republic of Venice. At its top is a globe mounted with a statue of Fortune. *Dogana / dog* is an accidental visual and phonemic pun. Fortune is a fairly complex metaphor. Figuratively, Fortuna is the Italian goddess of fortune and luck. Literally, she is a statue atop the Dogana. Figuratively, once again, she represents power and money and commerce; she is the patron goddess of Venice, a republic that amassed enormous wealth with its commercial enterprises from the Middle Ages until the sixteenth-century. This is suggested by "golden universe": Fortuna stands standing atop a *sphere*. The "golden universe" also refers to the setting itself, bathed as it is by the bright sun bursting through the few scratchy clouds.

The central question the poet asks, in the face of his depressed state, is "what's the body to do?" (l. 13). The question is another of Wright's colloquialisms—the thing we say when, clueless, we throw up or hands in exasperation about some matter, usually trivial. But the situation of the poet (and us) is *not* of "no great matter." The question becomes "What's the *body* to do?" The dog knows what to do. It doesn't retreat from whatever its invisible adversary is: it just barks defiantly, the hair bristling along his bowed back. Then the strategically placed "But," hanging between the last two stanzas, leads us into a painful description of our current condition. We are, says, Wright, like S. Lorenzo in Titian's painting, *The Martyrdom of Saint Lawrence*, reproduced on the cover of the present volume.

St. Lawrence was the last of the seven Roman deacons to be executed in 258 at the order of Valerian. His burning on a red-hot gridiron came from popular legend rather than from historical records. Titian's extraordinary painting, an altarpiece in the Church of the Jesuits in Venice, depicts St. Lawrence as he is being roasted on an elevated grate, his left arm reaching out toward a radiant burst of light that is breaking through the clouds at the very top of the painting—reaching out "in supplication," says Wright. His prayer is less a petition for relief from his pain (his face shows no anguish) than it is a plea for God to gather him into eternity. This is the way we lie, says Wright: we live in great pain on this earth, and our pain will only get more intense; and all the while we yearn to be transported to heaven. We began, then, with a Venetian Dog, and we end with a supplication to a Venetian God.

This is one of Wright's most powerful ekphrastic poems, but its power is diminished without having Titian's painting before us, which is true as well of Wright's other poems about particular paintings, catalogued in the introduction.

In the Valley of the Magra

Orig. pub. *Poetry* 170, no. 3 (June 1997): 125.
A, 14; NB, 154
Pattern: 8 × 2
Time: June, in the poem's first scene
Place: Blue Ridge Mountains, with flashback to a summer in the northern tip of Tuscany. Pontrèmoli, at the top of the Magra Valley, is the capital of Lunigiana.

Wright's note refers us to Hopkins's intricate sonnet *In the Valley of the Elwy*, but the parallels between the two poems are almost nonexistent except for the similarity of the two titles. Hopkins, in the octet, likens the kindness he received at the hands of some friends to a hood: they had sheltered him as a hood or hat would. Then in the sestet he prays that God, using his scales of justice and mercy, will complete the imperfections of his "creature dear" (humankind). Wright's sixteen-line poem turns on an analogy between Italian chestnut blossoms and the Blue Ridge thunderstorm. The memory of the former is triggered by the reality of the latter. Both scenes end at dusk. In the Italian one, as darkness approaches the chestnut blossoms take on the appearance of stars coming through the roots of the great tree of heaven. In the Blue Ridge scene, the farm lights in the valley below begin to take on a color of their own, "the way I remember it..." The poem ends with one of Wright's frequent ellipses, and this ellipsis invites us to add "in the valley of the Magra."

Returned to the Yaak Cabin, I Overhear an Old Greek Song

Orig. pub. *Poetry* 170, no. 3 (June 1997): 126.
A, 15; NB, 155
Pattern: 7 × 2.
Place: Lincoln County, Montana

Basin Creek runs through the Wrights' vacation retreat in the northwestern tip of Montana, a 320-acre tract about five miles south of the Canadian border and about twenty-six miles east of the Idaho state line. It lies just south of the East Fork of the Yaak River and is traversed by Porcupine and Basin Creeks. (See *Mt. Caribou at Night* in WTTT, 12.) The poem, however, tells us it does not really matter where we are (back yard, Montana, Venice, the Magra Valley, Basin Creek), because the Orphic songs will still arise from whatever river is before us. We begin at Basin Creek and end up in the sea with Orpheus' singing head floating off to Lesbos. Orpheus' song is "overheard" in the monotone of the creek's slurred mantra.

Ars Poetica II

Orig. pub. *Virginia Quarterly Review* 73 (Winter 1997): 72.
A, 16; NB, 156
Pattern: 4-1-4-1

A number of Wright's poems, as we have seen, are *ars poetica* poems. An early example is *The New Poem* (1971), a youthful effort in the tradition of the French *symbolistes*. It is a form of negative poetics: Wright tells us what the new poem is not, implying that what it is is the "pure poem." The first poem entitled *Ars Poetica* (CM, 38) is based on a contrast between the attractiveness of the California setting ("back here") and the unattractiveness of "back there" (Appalachia). But then this opposition is denied, as the voices rising out of the ground "back there" are just as important as the spirits called down from the sky "back here." In *Ars Poetica II*, written sixteen years later, the contrast is between the nothingness of death and the inability to understand what the heavenly code of the night sky reveals about "what's to come," on the one hand, and the job the poet has to do in the here and now, on the other hand. For this job, God the taskmaster is holding the poet's feet to His fire. The poem also opposes what the poet believes (first quatrain) with what the night sky "thinks" (second quatrain). The single lines that follow the quatrains overturn what precedes them. Thus, the belief that death has two reprisals is reversed by the projection of the poet's own death, which will be beautiful and cloud-like, without any reprisal. The second quatrain is also reversed: the mysterious code of the night sky, which is thought to hold the eschatological secret, is nothing but a "Great Misunderstanding." It is not the library of last things but "The Library of Last Resort." So the poet must continue the search for the Great Understanding, which is a bold task, but one, as the final line implies, that God insists on.

As we have noted, Wright has said that the subject matter of his poems is three-fold—language, landscape, and the idea of God (QN, 81, 135; Vadnie). Many of Wright's poems are about the difficulty the pilgrim wordsmith encounters in finding the proper language, about decoding the landscape, about discovering that the divine presence is absent, about instructions from poetic forebears, about the struggle between light and darkness. These poems are self-consciously in the *ars poetica* tradition: they focus on the nature, function, and process of the poetic enterprise.

Cicada Blue

Orig. pub. *New England Review* 18 (Summer 1997): 62.
A, 17; *NB*, 157
Pattern: 5 × 4
Time: Mid-August

This ode to blue begins with a projection: the Spanish poets would probably give a one-word response—"blue"—to the mid-August afternoon, which is like a "sucked-out, transparent insect shell." The color blue spreads itself just under the shell of the afternoon's "hard light." Cicadas come in many colors and even in several colors of blue, but this is a shade of sky blue, the "edged and endless / Expanse of nowhere and nothingness" spread out like a handkerchief. It is this blue to which the poet declares his love, altering a line of Federico García Lorca's poem that begins "Verde, te quiero verde ("Green, I love you green").

In the last stanza the blue sky gives way to the an encroaching evening sky, and the poet's memory of the blue, pressed like a leaf into a book, changes to sepia, then brown. The antecedent of "him" in the last line is ambiguous. Is it God or Lorca, the "poet of shadows and death," that we are asked to press firmly into our hearts in an act of preservation? Blue is an object of love for the poet, but it also signifies certain ominous qualities. To say that it is a "labial" (l. 5), as the Spanish poet might, suggests something more than its initial phoneme or that "labia" is an anagram hidden in the title: blue lips bode ill. Too, it represents an infinite and unidentifiable nothingness, a demonic parody of the heavens.

"I love you, blue" is no understatement: blue is the privileged color in Wright's poetry. The word, excluding its appearance in the omnipresent "Blue Ridge," appears more than 170 times in his poems. It is attached to all manner of objects, natural, human, and divine, and to feelings: "Blue agony of the morning-glory" (*Victory Garden*), "That song again, the song of burnt notes. / The blue it rises into, the cobalt, / Proves an enduring flame: Persian death bow / The bead, crystal / And drowned delta, Ephesian reed. / Blue of the twice-bitten rose, blue of the dove" (*Cancer Rising*), "Your mouth is the blue door I walk through" (*Dino Campana*), "the blue attic of heaven" (*April*), "Finger by finger, above Orion, God's blue hand unfolds" (*Thinking of Georg Trakl*), "October settles its whole weight in a blue study" (*A Journal of True Confessions*), "Blue moan of the mourning dove" (*Still Life with Spring and Time To Burn*), and "God's blue breath" (*Disjecta Membra*).

Blue frequently modifies abstract features of thought and of the self, living and dead: "your soul is starting to shrink; listen, it won't come back; listen, it's blue" (*Cherokee*), "The dead are a cadmium blue" (*Homage to Paul Cézanne*), "blue of redemption" (*Yard Journal*), "substanceless blue" (*Reading Richard Rorty and Paul Celan One Morning in Early June*), "blue of infinity, blue // waters above the earth" (*Black Zodiac*), "The blue abyss of everyday air" (*Lives of the Saints*), "blue immensity" (*Yard Journal*); "encrypted blue" (*Summer Mornings*), and "blue of the infinite" (*Drone and Ostinato*).

Blue sometimes describes one half of a metaphor or simile: "the blue chains of the wind" (*Autumn*), "the sea / Shuffled its blue deck" (*The Southern Cross*), "Blue blank pavilions of the sky" (*Sentences*), "clothed in a blue rust" (*Portrait of the Artist with Li Po*), "iron-blue" lights (ibid.), "blue weave of the Cumberlands" (*Lost Souls*), "The Mincio puddled outside the gates, / clouds tattooed on its blue chest" (*Mantova*), "The carapace of the sky blue-ribbed and buzzing" (*Yard Journal*), "the blue plate of the sky" (ibid.), "blue of the sky blue / As a dove's neck" (ibid.), "the blue aorta of the sky" (*Looking Outside the Cabin Window, I Remember a Line by Li Po*), and "the blue apse of the sky" (*A Journal of One Significant Landscape*).

Wright displays great ingenuity in describing particular shades of blue, some of which are completely subjective: "The sky is scrubbed to a delft blue // in the present tense" (*A Journal of English Days*), "The insides [of the dogfish] were blue, the color of Power Putty" (*March Journal*), "The sky is a wrung-out, China blue" (*A Journal of the Year of the Ox*), "a backdrop of Venetian blue" (*Local Journal*), "December's T'ang blue blank page" (*Poem Half in the Manner of Li Ho*), "Sky-back a Cherokee blue" (*Yard Journal*), "stone-washed blue" (*Meditation on Form and Measure*), "Blue as a new translation of Longinus on the sublime" (*Autumn's Sidereal, November's Ball and Chair*), and, of course "cicada blue."

p. 157, ll. 8–9. *All I have written ... revealed to me.* After his vision (or mental breakdown) on 6 December 1273, Aquinas determined to abandon the scholarly life; when his secretary urged him to complete his *Summa*, he responded with the lines given. See Anthony Kenny, *Aquinas* (New York: Hill and Wang, 1980), 26.

All Landscape Is Abstract, and Tends to Repeat Itself

Orig. pub. *Virginia Quarterly Review* 73 (Winter 1997): 74; rpt. *Southern Cultures* 7 no. 3 (Fall 2001): 83–4.
A, 19; NB, 158.
Pattern: 5-1-5-1-5-1
Time: Late August
Place: Charlottesville

The implication of saying "I was the resurrection" (l. 3) seems to be that after the poet began writing, his life became the opposite of resurrection: his soul descended. Still, there's an uncertainty about the rising and falling of the soul after death ("after the light switch has been turned off"). After this confession of ignorance, we have the poet's reaction to the sacred: fear about whether the sacred is present or whether it is absent. For consolation we can choose either, as Guido Ceronetti writes (ll. 7–8), which is not a very happy prospect. Both belief and disbelief are distant and inaccessible. The poet then speculates on the connection between landscape and the absolute: the language of the absolute is solitude; the language of the landscape is untranslatable. So the poet suffers from the rock-and-a-hard-place dilemma: he "hopelessly" moves both backwards and forwards. The bee stings "hopelessly," because after he stings, he dies. Similarly, the landscapes of memory are left in the poet like a bee sting. If language is hopelessly unable to translate the landscape, what then is the poet to do, since what applies to the landscape also applies to the poet's life? If all landscape is abstract, and if it is untranslatable in concrete terms, then the poet has a serious problem—which is why the only hint we have of the landscape is the reference to the Blue Ridge. All forms of landscape may be autobiographical, but if you have writer's block, no one will ever see. This is as restless an attitude as that of the lecturer in Wallace Stevens's *The Ultimate Poem Is Abstract*, which is echoed in the present poem's title.

ll. 7–8. *The sacred is frightening ... our consolation.* "The sacred is frightening. But so is its absence, so is the desecrated world, void or rules and prohibitions. In freedom we cannot exist. We have to choose which fear is most consoling" (Guido Ceronetti's *The Silence of the Body: Materials for the Study of Medicine*, trans. Michael Moore [New York: Farrar, Straus and Giroux, 1993], 85).

Opus Posthumous

Orig. pub. *Slate* 29 October 1998.
A, 20; NB, 159
Pattern: 5-1-5-1
Time: A Friday at the end of August and then the beginning of September

Title: Literally a "late-born work," the existence of which becomes known only after a writer's death. The title links the poem to Wallace Stevens's *Opus Posthumous*.

This spare poem begins with three Hopkins-like noun phrases that seem to be unconnected: "Possum work, world's windowlust, lens of the Byzantine—." "Possum work" is the antitype of playing possum, the feigning of death or inactivity, that is, assuming a "skeletal life." "Thou Possum" is an anagram derived from "posthumous," hinting that once summer had died away the poet must get back to his business: possum work displaces possum play.

Friday in Appalachia is a window onto the world or, as the word "lens" suggests, a window the world looks into. But the end of August's Byzantine world, seen through the window's lens, makes the poet realize that he must be up and doing. If "there's more to come," then there's more poetic work to do. The "brightest angels" of the seasonal cycle, Byzantine in their glory, will be "darkened by time" and "dulled and distanced" as the advent of autumn approaches. August's candle, having been turned up fully at the end of summer, has now burned down to its "wick-end." The alliterative line 6 contains a visual pun, "wicked," meaning both equipped with a wick (one syllable) and evil (two syllables). In Wright's reading the poem, however, the pun disappears. He pronounces the word <wĭk-əd>, so that the weight of the end of summer (its "sink and sigh") is somehow malevolent.

In the second half of the poem we have the arrival of September, ushering in the next phase of the cycle ("set foot on the other side"). September is personified as mysteriously feminine. She has the big dark secret, and we wish she would whisper it to us. September is an incarnation of Robert Graves's eternal feminine and the wild watery world springing from her lap. There is more than a hint of the erotic here, and we almost expect the last word of the poem to be "desire" rather than "disease," returning us to the lust of line 1. But September is a White Goddess, and so the secret language that can capture her is the language of disease (her hurricane power, sprouting up like daisies, can destroy us) or make us very uncomfortable (dis-ease).

The full effect of the music of Wright's poems, here fundamentally alliterative, comes only from reading them aloud, and in this connection we are reminded of the *opera posthumous* of numerous composers.

*What Do You Write About, Where Do Your Ideas Come From?

Orig. pub. *Green Mountain Review* 9–10, nos. 1–2 (Spring–Summer 1996–1997–Summer 1997): 265.
A, 23
Pattern: 14 lines
Time: September

This is a poetic version of what Wright has said in other contexts—that he writes about "language, landscape, and the idea of God" (QN, 123). In "Bytes and Pieces" he remarks, "My ultimate strength is my contemporary weakness—my subject (language, landscape, and the idea of God) is not of much interest now. But it will be again. How all three configure one's own face is important and must be addressed. Unstable as dust, our lives will find us out" (QN, 81–2).

In the poem we have landscape as a subject in ll. 3–5 and, less memorably, in ll. 10–12. The backdrop of the second vignette may be the sunset, so spectacular that it appears to have been dishonestly manipulated ("jury-rigged"). We have the idea of God in "The Big Empty" or Eternal Nothing, which is "a subject of some note." "Note" is a pun: (1) noteworthiness, and (2) the dark musical note that continues rhythmically and hauntingly to thump out "never again" like a heart beat. The poet does not reveal the missing word that would clear up the opposition between "never" (absence, withdrawal) and "again" (presence, return), unless he means that the springing of his ideas over and over again from the Eternal Nothing is an answer to the question, "Where Do Your Ideas Come From?"

As for language, the repetition of "never again" (the phrase appears five times) is the most obvious linguistic feature, and it may glance at James Tate's poem about a shockingly beautiful sunset, *Never Again the Same*. With its octave of a relatively static landscape and its sestet of a kinetic cosmos, the poem is a kind of parody sonnet: the punch line is a repetition of what we have heard twice already and it fails to close anything off. This lack of closure is perhaps why Wright chose not to include the poem in *Negative Blue*.

Quotations

Orig. pub. *American Poet* 14 (Summer 1999).
A, 24; NB, 160
Pattern: 6-6-6-2

We begin with a little poetic manifesto by way of Renoir—a version of Eliot's "objective correlative": don't emote; show me something that contains the emotion. The poet declares his attraction to the idea and then takes it back. We are next introduced to the theme of the poem (death) by way of Chekhov's words, followed by the quotations from Job and Meng Chiao, which are examples of the Renoir feeling/object notion. The point is that to talk about the theme of death is to miss the point. One must represent it by an objective image, such as "dust."

Wright on Wright, in response to an interviewer's question about what seems to be the looseness of the poem: "It is loose, and, indeed, it is on purpose. I had always, for almost thirty years, wanted to make a poem out of pieces of other poems, but so that it didn't sound, to me, as though it *were* just other poems. As though it seemed to have, if not coherence, a time line and a line of march of its own. This is as close as I've been able to come, going from an illusion to a comment in the first section, to a partial quotation in the second, to a third section made up entirely of another text, and then a final section where it's about half and half, and references back, at least in overall suggestiveness, to the points of the other three. Probably a silly enterprise, but it was all very structured and very calculated on my part and is, by necessity, on the surface seemingly loose to the point of apparent arbitrariness, but underneath, in the structural joints and joists of intention, very related and interwoven. It's easy to quote, but difficult to make a quotation over into your own image. I'm still thinking about it, as I haven't got it quite right yet" (Caseley, 25).

p. 160. ll. 1–2. *Renoir ... objects.* "Everyone puts something of himself [into a painting]. What survives of the artist is the feeling which he gives by means of objects" (James Fenton, "Degas in Chicago," *New York Review of Books* 43, no. 16 [17 October 1996]: 24).
p. 160, ll. 7–12. *Chekhov.* These details of Chekhov's life are reported in Donald Rayfield, *Anton Chekhov: A Life* (New York: Henry Holt and Co., 1997), and elsewhere.
p. 160, ll. 13–18. *My breath is corrupt ... dust.* Job 17:1, 12, 14, 16.
p. 161, l. 2. *For a while ... cloak.* The line from Meng Chiao is A.C. Graham's translation of the last line of *Stopping on a Journey at the East Water Pavilion at Lo-ch'eng* (*Poems of the Late T'ang* [Harmondsworth: Penguin, 1965], 61).

The Appalachian Book of the Dead II

Orig. pub. *New Republic* 219, no. 9 (31 August 1998): 42.
A, 26; NB, 162
Pattern: 6 × 3
Time: Columbus Day
Place: Charlottesville

This appears to be a not very promising Columbus Day, what with all the "-less" suffixes: windless, remorseless, toneless, bell-less. Captain Dog, the poet, sounds as if he might like to bite into a chunk of the sweet-meat of despair. If both the world and heaven are silently indifferent, why not? But then we get a turn-around, not unlike that in the first *Appalachian Book of the Dead* poem, with its "skeletal altars" and "vacant sanctuary." Here it is the altar in the apse of the evening that spreads out its black cloth against the sky (an antitype of J. Alfred Prufrock's evening as an "etherized patient"). The poet cries out quietly to Jerusalem—not unlike Blake's Jerusalem. One hope might be the establishment of the city of God here, in Virginia's green and pleasant land, the proper "home" of us all. But the sanctuary of the evening, with its eastern black shroud, turns out to be not all that inviting, and we are aware too of the fear and dread in the destructive desire to go "home." The desire is destructive because "home" means something other than our proper place in the city and garden of this life. It refers, we come to see, to a post-mortem other world—Hamlet's "undiscovered country." Still, all is not darkness: "the light's still lovely in the west"—which echoes of a line from Browning's *My Last Duchess*.

On the relation between this poem and other books of the dead (*The Tibetan Book of the Dead* and *The Egyptian Book of the Dead*), see the notes for *The Appalachia Book of the Dead* (NB, 99–100). The former is a collection of Buddhist texts about the *bardo*, an intermediate state of extended length between death and rebirth. The journey through bardo takes forty-nine days, and there are various stages through which one's soul passes: unconsciousness, reawakening, the encounter with various deities, and so on. There is little connection between this text and Wright's poem. *The Egyptian Book of the Dead* is something else altogether: a collection of some two hundred spells and prayers that are believed to insure a joyous afterlife for the souls of the dead. Wright's *Appalachian Book of the Dead* is almost a parody of the two other books of the dead. He yearns to know what is on the other side of the river, what happens when we "step over" into death. But he remains very skeptical about the possibility of attaining such knowledge. His Book of the Dead is thumbed through in *this* life.

Indian Summer II

Orig. pub. *New Yorker* 74, no. 32 (19 October 1998): 56.
A, 27; NB, 163
Pattern: 3 × 6
Time: November
Place: Charlottesville

The mood that Wright wants to establish in the first half of the poem, with the turkey buzzard having logged on to the sky's monitor, is the burn and ache of November, not just here but "elsewhere." Then we are confronted once again with an indifferent God. The last two lines of the fifth tercet, which echo Browning's Porphyria and the Eve-Demeter archetype, are rather private—or difficult, in any case, to relate to the rest of the poem. But "an end without a story" seems clear enough: the end is what we find in the final tercet, our living in two worlds, Augustine's city of God and city of man. Spring will come to the city of man; maybe it will come to the city of God as well.

Wright's natural religion is fastened to the myth of the eternal return: its cycle endlessly recurs. Spring's purple will always break through the dead leaves and grass, and the heavens will continue to spin their annual patterns—the idea of repetition fortified by the anaphora in the three odd-numbered tercets. One of the striking features of Wright's poetry is its endlessly fascinating and memorable revelations of this changing seasonal landscape. But in spite of his deadly serious quest for the infinite and the eternal, there is no Apocalypse in the final pages of this chapter of the Book of the Dead.

Autumn's Sidereal, November's a Ball and Chain

Orig. pub. *New Yorker* 74, no. 32 (19 October 1998): 36; rpt. in *Southern Cultures* 7, no. 3 (Fall 2001): 84.
A, 29; NB, 164
Pattern: 6–6–2

If autumn with all of its brilliance is metaphysically suggestive and gives meaning to both astral quest and earthly life, November's a drag. Autumn is sidereal, directing us to look cleanly up into the constellations. We are dazzled by the skyscape, winking at its overpowering blue. The sublime, for Longinus, was *ekstasis*, the condition of being lifted out of oneself. The Longinian blue, then, must be a blue that engenders ecstasy. We draw back and wander around, knowing we are under the power of some metaphorical identity. But if nothing is going on in the heavens, there is no reason to project some metaphysical meaning on the upper world. Meanwhile, November is a back-yard ball and chain, dragging us down to the world where things are far from sublime. If the metaphysical world is meaningless, the physical world is not, and the last six lines of the poem record its clear, intricate, earthy reality, including the endless story whispered by the wind in the alliterative final couplet. The concluding "shhh" injunction is for us (and the poet) to be quiet and let the wind do its work.

p. 164, l. 12. A play on Wallace Stevens's line, "The physical world is meaningless tonight" (*Jonga*, in *The Collected Poems of Wallace Stevens* [New York: Knopf, 1954], 337). Wright identifies *Jonga* as the source in his note (205).

The Writing Life

Orig. pub. *Carolina Quarterly* 49, no. 3 (Summer 1997): 15.
A, 30; NB, 165
Pattern: 5 × 3
Time: December
Place: Charlottesville

This is another overtly *ars poetica* poem. The poet's task is, like Adam's, to give things their proper names, the names that reveal their mysterious essence. The landscape itself cries out for this, wanting to be identified with the poet's affection (heart). But the poet finds it extremely difficult to oblige. His affection for landscape is waning. But then he returns to a dog-eared page in The Appalachian Book of the Dead, where the goal of his quest is laid out: "Restitution of the divine in a secular circumstance." This is his poetic mission. But (another one of those "buts") there is very little restitution in what the poet is able to name—the winter light and the slushy sidewalk. Then darkness wipes out the possibility of the writer doing what he wants to do with his life, and we're left with the image of the stump of the poet's maimed, fingerless hand.

Reply to Wang Wei

Orig. pub. *Field* 57 (Fall 1997): 61.
A, 31; NB, 166
Pattern: 5 × 4
Time: December 15
Place: Charlottesville

    This is a winter dialogue with another of Wright's T'ang friends, Wang Wei (701–61), who, along with Li Po and Tu Fu, was one of the great poets of his time. Also a painter and musician, he spent most of his life in a mountain retreat. Kenneth Rexroth says of Wang Wei that he "is one of those model poets, personally and artistically flawless, who occur very rarely in the history of literature" (*One Hundred More Poems from the Chinese: Love and the Turning Year*, trans. Kenneth Rexroth [New York: New Directions, 1970], 133).

    The poem is about making a connection with a fellow poet, one from an ancient time and a different tradition. Yet the difference in time and space doesn't matter, because Wang Wei still speaks of those universal matters that concern Wright: Is there an exit and an end? Can one achieve peace? Can one achieve fame? What are the virtues of the solitary, reclusive life? How do we relate to nature's eternal cycle? How should our time be used? The poet achieves a certain calm serenity at the end, even though Wang Wei will never come. "Still, I sit still," says the poet, the first "still" meaning both "yet" and "motionless." His mind is tabula-rasaed, to use Wright's neologism from *Umbrian Dreams*, cleared of all the clutter in its "essential solitude." Thus, on this cold winter night the dream of the younger hermit (Wright) for the reclusive life is fulfilled.

p. 166, l. 1. *The dream of a reclusive life*. Wright says in an interview, "In my fantasy life I have dreamed of the perfect reclusion being the best way to think and to write about what one was thinking about. As one gets older, that becomes less and less of an attractive option, and more and more of a possible necessity. Any time it becomes a possible necessity, instead of a choice, anything starts to lose its luster a little bit. My ambition now is to be what John Ashbery once termed himself to be, 'a well-known recluse about town'" (Zawacki, 23).

p. 166, l. 5. "East of the lotus leaves—useless to think about it" (Wang Wei, *Taking the Cool of the Evening*, in *Poems of Wang Wei*, trans. G.W. Robinson [Harmondsworth: Penguin, 1973], 129).

p. 166, l. 9. "In my late years I only like / Tranquility, the world's affairs / No longer exercise my mind / Which I now find unpolicied. / Back into the old woods where / Pine winds flutter my loose sash / Hill moon lights me at my lute— / This is all my knowledge" (Wang Wei, *In Answer to Assistant Magistrate Chang*, in *Poems of Wang Wei*, 97).

p. 166, ll. 11–12. "Where are you off to? / You say you've failed—retiring / To the foot of the Southern Mountains? / Well, go—and no more questions / For the white clouds there'll never be an end" (Wang Wei, *Good-bye*, in *Poems of Wang Wei*, 60).

p. 166, l. 16. "Everywhere everywhere they [the lotus blossoms] are flowering and falling" (Wang Wei, *Magnolia Slope*, in *Poems of Wang Wei*, 31).

Giorgio Morandi and the Talking Eternity Blues

Orig. pub. *Field* 57 (Fall 1997): 60.
A, 33; NB, 167
Pattern: 5 × 4
Time: January, though it is unseasonably warm.
Place: Charlottesville

Title: A variation on any number of "talking blues" songs by Woody Guthrie and others.

    On Morandi in other poems by Wright, see *Morandi* in CM, 114; *A Journal of True Confessions* in WTTT, 143; *Chinese Journal* in WTTT, 199; *Morandi II* in C, 67 (not included in NB); *Apologia Pro Vita Sua* in NB, 74; *Basic Dialogue* in NB, 147; *Looking Around* in SHS, 3; and *Homage to Giorgio Morandi* in BY, 60–1. The photograph Wright mentions is Morandi's wordless entry in The Appalachian Book of the Dead. Morandi's late work focused on four vessels that he painted over and over. This is the way Wright describes them, using the same photograph of the painter, in *Looking Around*, a poem from October–November 1999:

> Over there's the ur-photograph,
> 	Giorgio Morandi, glasses pushed up on his forehead,
> Looking hard at four objects—
> Two olive oil tins, one wine bottle, one flower vase,
> A universe of form and structure,...

The photograph, by Herbert List, is the frontispiece of an exhibition catalogue (New York: Rizzoli, 1988). It can be found in Bonnie Costello's article, "Charles Wright, Giorgio Morandi, and the Metaphysics of the Line," *Mosaic* 35, no. 1 (March 2002): 161, and in the reprint of this article in *HL*, 315.

The Morandi photo is a powerful icon for Wright. He's attracted to the painter's power of concentration—the frozen gaze, the unblinking eye, the painter's concern that the "proper thing [is] in its proper place." One of the poem's themes is the failure of language, an omnipresent motif in Wright: "There is an end to language" and to the naming of things. Eternity turns its back on the things that *are* named—the clouds moving along the mountains—and so it provides little comfort. Perhaps Morandi, who does not have to rely of language, can do what the poet cannot do. Eternity's principal resident, God, takes over at the end, subsuming both landscape and language under his shadow. How then can the poet put the proper thing in its proper place, like Morandi does with his four objects? One can understand that when Eternity turns its back on our feeble efforts, it is time to talk the blues if not sing them.

p. 167, l. 16. *Madonnaless*. The absence of the Virgin Mary in one of her roles as the comforter of the afflicted.

Drone and Ostinato

Orig. pub. *Paris Review* 40 (Summer 1998): 115.
A, 35; NB, 168
Pattern: 4 × 3
Time: Winter
Place: Charlottesville

What is the ostinato here, the constantly recurring melodic fragment (musical phrase or rhythm)? What, for that matter, is the drone, a sustained note that does not change pitch? The drone may be the example we have of the same old story—our paltry insignificance in the grand scheme of things and the equally paltry worth of words from the perspective of the soul. "We disappear as the stars do, soundless, without a trace." But "drone" seems also to refer to the "one/one" and "bare/bare" repetition in the final line, which comes from Meister Eckhart. A variation of this line appears in "From the Tract of 'Sister Katrei,'" which is attributed to Eckhart in Buber's *Ecstatic Confessions*, 153–6). From this "Tract" we know that "one in one united" refers to the soul: "The soul is naked and bare of all things that bear names. So it stands, as one, in the One, so that it has a progression in naked divinity" (156). "Bare in bare doth shine" refers to an existence in the divine light by those who are not clothed with worldly desire and who are in the presence of God only: "I am where I was before I was created; where there is only bare God in God. In that place there are no angels or saints or choirs of heaven.... Know that in God there is nothing but God" (155–6). The first "bare" in the last half of the final line refers then, first, to the naked soul, and second, to the naked divinity, both of which are shorn of all external accoutrements. In such a wordless state the soul abandons all the melodic phrases—the ostinato.

p. 168, ll. 11–12. *Wordless ... shine*. "Wordless is the one thing which I have in mind. One in one united, bare in bare doth shine" (Meister Eckhart, qtd. as the epigraph to Martin Buber's collection of mystical texts, *Ecstatic Confessions: The Heart of Mysticism* [New York: Harper and Row, 1985], [vii]). Eckhart (1260–1327) was a German mystic, interested in the various stages of the soul's ascent to God, for which he developed his own special vocabulary. He was accused of heresy, which means that he doubtless had something important to say. Eckhart affirmed an identity with God and suggested that there was even a stage beyond God, an experience of the Godhead.

Ostinato and Drone

Orig. pub. *New England Review* 18 (Summer 1997): 62; rpt. *PN Review* 27, no. 1 (September–October 2000).
A, 36; NB, 169
Pattern: 6 × 3
Time: Winter
Place: Charlottesville

Epigraph: *The mystic's vision is beyond the world of individuation,[;] it is beyond speech and thus incommunicable.* From the "Editor's Introduction" to Buber's *Ecstatic Confessions: The Heart of Mysticism* (New York: Harper and Row, 1985), xv.

Here we begin with the speechlessness of the radiant infinite, or rather the speechlessness of the poet in the face of the brilliance of the infinite. There are no words to communicate the sense of identity in such a vision (the mystic's vision of "one with the one"). But against this idea that the illuminating vision is incommunicable the poet sets the simple quince bush with its "lush / Day-dazzle, noon light and shower shine." The philosophical point by way of Defoe follows, which the poet adapts to his own distinction between voice, which exists, and word, which does not. The poet's voice, which gives us the description of the quince bush in its fiery brilliance, will have to do in the absence of the speechless, incommunicable word (or Word).

p. 169, ll. 13–14. "It is as reasonable to represent one kind of imprisonment by another, as it is to represent anything that really exists by that which exists not" (Daniel Defoe, Preface to vol. 3 of *Robinson Crusoe*). Albert Camus set this as a motto for *The Plague*, making clear that he intended his story to be read as a parable.

"It's Turtles All the Way Down"

Orig. pub. *Sycamore Review* 9, no. 2 (Summer–Fall 1997).
A, 37; NB, 170
Pattern: 3 × 5
Time: February
Place: Charlottesville

The title is a cosmic joke in defense of infinite time. It comes from the story by a well-known scientist, perhaps Alfred North Whitehead or Bertrand Russell, who, according to Stephen Hawking, "once gave a public lecture on astronomy. He described how the earth orbits around the sun and how the sun, in turn, orbits around the center of a vast collection of stars called our galaxy. At the end of the lecture a little old lady at the back of the room got up and said: 'What you have told us is rubbish. The world is really a flat plate supported on the back of a giant tortoise.' The scientist gave a superior smile before replying, 'What is the turtle standing on?' 'You're very clever, young man, very clever,' said the little old lady.

'But it's turtles all the way down'" (*A Brief History of Time* [New York: Bantam Books, 1988], 1).

The question the poem asks is the turtle question: what lies behind what lies behind what lies behind...? This question is directed at the three principle subjects of Wright's poetry: the idea of God, language, and landscape. The first comes by way of the Borges query about the chess pieces and the other two follow forthwith: "What mask is the mask behind the mask / The language wears and the landscape wears"?

The poet engages in a bit of word-play in the final line, the antecedent of "them" remaining, if not indeterminate, at least ambiguous. The reference could be, first, to the wind and the sunshine, in which the poet luxuriates and which he does not want to contemplate coming to an end. In the context of the Big Empty, of "the other side," and of the "dark unfathomable," a second possibility is that "them" refers to God, landscape, and language. Should they come to an end, the poet would have to stop writing. And third, "them" of course refers to turtles. What particularly interests the poet at this February juncture is not so much the gobbets on the mock-crab apple trees, the bronzed needles, and the medium yellow lightfall, but the statements of the Sufi mystics and the mystery of the infinitely descending turtles. There are other plays on words in the poem, some intentional and others perhaps not: "lightfall," "all over," "fall all over"; "face" vs. "mask"; "mask" and "mock" trees.

One of Wright's typical moves is to say that in the face of the inadequacy of language to carry the true depth of idea and emotion, he will have to remain silent. But of course he continues to write. We get a version of this denial followed by affirmation in this poem. In line 3 the poet reports that the landscape he has just described does not interest him. But this is undercut by the fresh and vivid descriptions of the landscape in stanza 3, which are carried over into stanza 5.

p. 170, l. 1. *book*. This may be *Robinson Crusoe* in the previous poem, but it more likely Martin Buber's *Ecstatic Confessions*. Wright draws on Buber's collection in the two previous poems, twice in stanza 2 of the present poem, and twice more in the poem that follows, *Half February*.

p. 170, l. 4. *Mercy is made ... needs fire*. "Bayezid said, 'When I had reached the level of nearness, I heard someone calling, "O Bayezid! Demand all you have to demand." "My God," I answered, "it is you I demand." I heard, "O Bayezid! As long as the tiniest mote of worldly desire remains in you and you have not yet reached the level of decreation and become nothing, you will not be able to find us." "My God," I said, "that I may not return from your court empty-handed, I would demand something of you." "Very well then, demand it." "Grant me the pardon for all humankind, and have mercy on them." A voice rang out, "O Bayezid! Lift up your eyes!" I lifted up my eyes and saw that the exalted Lord was still more moved to clemency toward his servants than I was. "My God," I cried then, "bestow your mercy on Satan!" "O Bayezid!" the voice answered me, "Satan is made of fire, and fire needs fire"' (Bayezid Bistami, in *Ecstatic Confessions*, 18). Bayezid Bistami (803–75) was a Sufi mystic.

p. 170, ll. 5–6. *It also says ... the other*. "He was asked, 'What is the way to God?' He answered, 'Pull back both your feet, and you will be with him—one foot from out of this life, the other foot from out of the other life'" (Hussein al Halladj, in *Ecstatic Confessions*, 20). Hussein al Halladj (d. 309) was a Persian mystic.

p. 170, l. 10. *What god ... chess pieces*. "God moves the player and he, the piece. / What god behind God originates the scheme / Of dust and time and dream and agony?" (Jorge Luis Borges, *The Game of Chess*, in *Dreamtigers*, trans. Mildred Boyer and Harold Morland [New York: E.P. Dutton, 1970], 59).

Half February

Orig. pub. *Yale Review* 85 (October 1997): 21.
A, 38; NB, 171
Pattern: 5 × 4
Time: 14 February
Place: Charlottesville

This is an ironic inversion of Valentine's Day. The state of the poet's heart is not very loving, being too overcome by the winter's cold. It is difficult to be distressed because the object of affection does not reciprocate ("heart-wrung"). It is no less difficult to be even sentimentally mawkish ("sappy"). The heart, like St. Catherine's, simply isn't there, although one should be able to wring a little affection from it on St. Valentine's Day. No, the themes of the day are unfaithfulness and solitude, the poet's soul being as isolated as the nonbeing of Anna Garcias's silkworm of nothingness. What dominates, then, is not what should be but what is ("the subject for today, down here, is the verb 'to be'"). The poet's real lover is solitude and its icy comfort.

p. 171, ll. 13–15. *I saw my soul ... snout.* "I once saw my soul fashioned like a little silkworm, which had been diligently fed and carefully kept by those who raised it. But when it is grown it begins to spin with its little snout a delicate little thread to make a little hut for itself.... Now my soul saw something similar in itself, for with just such sweetness and quiet it gave the Almighty God everything it had in itself and enclosed itself like a little silkworm in its nonbeing and in the recognition of its nothingness" (Anna Garcias, in *Ecstatic Confessions*, 117). Garcias (1549–1626) was a quietist mystic and prioress of a Carmelite convent in Paris.

p. 171, l. 19. *St. Catherine ... heart removed.* "It seemed to [St. Catherine] that her eternal bridegroom was coming to her in his usual manner, opening her left side, taking out her heart and departing from her, and she was left without any heart at all" (from the notes of St. Catherine of Siena's confessor, Raimund of Capua, in *Ecstatic Confessions*, 106). St. Catherine of Siena (1347–80) was an Italian mystic on whose body Christ's stigmata were said to have been imprinted.

Back Yard Boogie Woogie

Orig. pub. *Yale Review* 85 (October 1997): 20.
A, 39; NB, 172
Pattern: 4 × 4
Time: Late February
Place: Charlottesville

Title: A play on Piet Mondrian's *Broadway Boogie-Woogie*.

Mondrian's late painting called *Broadway Boogie-Woogie* (which sold for more than $21 million in November 2004) came from an urban inspiration, including the syncopation of jazz and the repetitions in city street patterns and buildings in New York City. Wright's "Boogie Woogie" is painted in the first stanza, though the city scene is replaced by a garden one. The nondescript blond grass, the squared-off boxwoods, the veined and hived cherry tree silhouetted against the February sky evoke the verticals and horizontals of Mondrian's painting.

The poem turns on an analogy between what the poet sees in the back yard and his own life. The back yard is indifferent to his presence, and its detritus similar to the "scattered, fallen, and overlooked" things in his past and present experience. He concludes by opposing to the forgotten and disregarded fragments of life what Simone Weil calls perfection. Weil's perfection, however, comes from the identity of the self with Christ. For the poet, perfection is the "early leaf bristle" and the "cloud shadows"—the boogie-woogie of his own back yard, *sur le motif*.

p. 172, l. 1. *sur le motif.* From Paul Cézanne's expression, *aller sur le motif* ("to go out into the subject"). Cézanne and the Impressionists abandoned long sessions in the studio in favor of working outside in nature. Rilke uses the phrase in describing Cézanne's practice (*Letters in Cézanne*, 37, 39). Émile Bernard reports that Cézanne did not to attend his mother's funeral in 1897, choosing rather to paint *sur le motif*.

p. 172, l. 13. *Weil.* "For our true dignity is not to be parts of a body, even though it be a mystical one, even though it be that of Christ. It consists in this, that in the state of perfection, which is the vocation of each one of us, we no longer live in ourselves, but Christ lives in us; so that through our perfection Christ, in his integrity and in his indivisible unity, becomes in a sense each one of us, as he is completely in each host. The hosts are not a part of his body" (Simone Weil, *Waiting for God*, trans. Emma Craufurd [New York: G.P. Putnam's Sons, 1951], 80–1).

The Appalachian Book of the Dead III

Orig. pub. *Poetry* 171, no. 1 (October–November 1997): 96.
A, 40; *NB*, 173
Pattern: 6 × 3
Time: 22 February 1997
Place: Charlottesville back yard

The poem represents a world that is sad and diseased, with the "mind-of-Godish" moon as a potential source of healing. Hieroglyphs spread across the lawn, and the poet hears purgative whispers from the dead suppliants from the other side of the septic world. Plotinus' epigram is then interjected: "The soul is in the body as the light is in the air." The poet is uncertain about the truth of the simile, but what he *is* certain of is the permanent affliction of the human condition and the disorder of the sublunar world.

"Such Egyptology in the wind" is a reference to *The Egyptian Book of the Dead*. We have been prepared for "Egyptology" by "hieroglyphs" and "supplicant whispers," and by Plotinus, the founder of Neoplatonism who was born in Egypt and studied in Alexandria. Plotinus believed that what he called "the One," the absolutely transcendental and unknowable object of worship and desire, overflows, like light from the sun, to create the realm of Intelligence (*nous*), which in turn overflows into the realm of the soul. By contemplating the One, the soul is given form. The purpose of such contemplation is eventually to obtain light and vitality by being absorbed into the One. We clearly do not have a full-blown Neoplatonic vision here because we are not under the sun. The moonlight produces only a "mind-of-Godish" effect, though it does anticipate *some* splendor. There is, in other words, no brightly lit emanation, no Dantean visionary identification with pure radiance. Still, "a small-time paradiso" with its "raw brushstrokes" is better than nothing (or Nothing), and this "small-time paradiso" remains a hope: "Surely some splendor's set to come forth, / Some last equation solved, declued and reclarified." None of the first three Appalachian Book of the Dead poems offers anything approaching a confident affirmation, but all three do leave open the possibility of an epiphany from the "silent deeps." Each allows for a lesser earthly paradise, like Pound's hope for a *paradiso terrestre*: perhaps a genuine garden does lie behind the "hieroglyphs on the lawn." "Surely some splendor's set to come forth" is an echo of Yeats's "Surely some revelation is at hand" (*The Second Coming*). Wright's poem, however, ends on a very different note from the nightmare vision of Yeats's beast that "slouches toward Bethlehem to be born."

p. 173, l. 1. Giorgio Morandi has an entry in The Appalachian Book of the Dead in *Giorgio Morandi and the Talking Eternity Blues* (NB, 167), the entry being the photograph of Morandi staring at his four objects. The letter "M," therefore, may represent more than just an entry for the full Moon of this poem. "Illuminated" is perhaps a *double entendre* as well—meaning both the adorned calligraphic design of the manuscript page and the light of the moon raining down.

p. 173, l. 3. *La luna piove*, as translated, "the moon rains." Cf. Shelley's *To a Skylark*: "The moon rains out her beams, and Heaven is overflow'd" (l. 20).

p. 173, l. 6. *I am pure*. "I am Pure. I am pure. I am pure. I am pure. My purity is the purity of this great Phoenix that is in Heracleopolis" (*The Egyptian Book of the Dead*, chap. 125). These lines are part of the instructions for what the deceased has to say when arriving at the Hall of Justice. The rite, sometimes called "The Negative Confession," is one of purgation preceding rebirth.

p. 173, l. 7. *The soul ... in the air*. "May we think that the mode of the soul's presence to body is that of the presence of light to the air?" (Plotinus, *The Fourth Ennead*, "Third Tractate," sec. 22, trans. Stephen MacKenna and B. S. Page).

Opus Posthumous II

Orig. pub. *Poetry* 171, no. 1 (October–November 1997): 97.
A, 41; *NB*, 174

Pattern: 4 × 3
Time: March
Place: Charlottesville

This is another "late-born work." As in the previous *Opus Posthumous*, the poet, possum-like, feigns that his death has previously occurred. Once again, sitting in his deck chair, he is troubled by there being no regard, no acquittal, no light, no pardon, and no nourishment. But in line 8 the poem suddenly turns, announcing that the starvelings feed from the poet's mouth. This surreal image is apparently a reference to poetic speech. In any event, with the tag from Aquinas the mood promptly changes. The poet affirms his love of the objects before him. Only one object is specified—the "gates of the arborvitae." It is both convenient and symbolically important that this threshold-forming shrub means "the tree of life." This is the tree of the Alpha and the Omega. We meet it in both the opening pages of the Bible (Genesis 4:22) and in the closing pages (Revelation 22:19). The gates of the tree of life are apparently identified with, or at least related to, the "gates of mercy." Given the poet's tendency to self-effacement, it seems too much to suggest that the opening up of the threshold of mercy is nourished by the words coming from his mouth. But if love initiates vision, as Aquinas says, then poetic speech can be food for the starvelings and a means of life and mercy.

p. 174, l. 7. *Ubi amor, ibi oculus.* "Trees die & the dream remains /.Not love but that love flows from it /.ex animo /.& cannot ergo delight in itself /.but only in the love flowing from it. /.UBI AMOR IBI OCULUS EST" (Ezra Pound, *Cantos* 90). The Latin phrase originates with Thomas Aquinas: "Contemplationis desiderium procedit ex amore obiecti: quia ubi amor, ibi oculus" ("The desire for contemplation arises from the love for its object: the desire for love opens the eyes of the beholder") (Aquinas, *In Sententiarum* 3.35.1.2). Wright's literal translation follows in the same line. Metaphorically, the line can be translated, "Where there is love, there is vision (or insight)."

Body Language

Orig. pub. *Nation* 265, no. 5 (11 August 1997): 36–7.
A, 45; NB, 175
Pattern: 5 × 4
Time: "Pre-spring"
Place: Charlottesville

This poem sets up a dialectic between the self (called here the "body") and everything outside the self (the "world"). The latter contains and is contained by the former—a version of Blake's "world in a grain of sand." This is the paradox of identity and difference, the paradox that lies at the heart of metaphor. And yet the identification of the body and the world is difficult because of the great distance between them, "like the distance between the *no* and the *yes,* / Nothing and everything." The grain of sand is so insignificant that it is nothing, and yet it contains the world.

In stanza 2 we discover that it is difficult for the poet to feel at home in the pre-spring landscape, which is semi-dead, shorn, grumpy, stubbed, cankered, and burned. How can he identify with a landscape that is so uninviting, causing the body to becomes something completely other ("the unbody")? The answer, in stanza 3, is that we have to keep at it by looking hard "for its certitude" in the landscape, "for its lesson and camouflage." What the poet yearns for (stanza 4) is a sense of belonging—his own body at home within the body of the world. In such a state he can collapse the "abysmal distance" between self and other. He sees such an integrated body everywhere, though he cannot quite articulate it, as the body lisps and licks itself in its effort to break into and enter an inclusive landscape.

"When You're Lost in Juarez, in the Rain, and It's Eastertime Too"

Orig. pub. *Nation* 264, no. 21 (2 June 1997): 32.
A, 46; NB, 176
Pattern: 5-1-5-1-5-1
Time: 28 March 1997 (Good Friday)
Place: Charlottesville

The title is a play on Bob Dylan's *Just Like Tom Thumb's Blues*, the first two lines of which it duplicates with the sole alteration of exchanging the positions of "in Juarez" and "in the Rain." Wright calls attention to the inversion of the two prepositional phrases with his note—"(SIC)"—on p. 206.

The poet sees his project, inching along by slow degrees, as insignificant and trivial from the perspective of the eternal and the infinite. The wand of words, sadly, calls forth no magic, and language remains desperate in its effort to communicate. The poet does not put much stock in the mystics' claim that "communication is languageless": "there's been no alternative / Since language fell from the sky." As Eliot's Sweeney says, you've "gotta use words," and the poet uses his words in the third cinquain to describe the mysteriousness of the night sky over the Blue Ridge. The annunciation of some miracle comes not from an angel but from the spirit of the Hale-Bopp comet. The first and last of the one-line interludes speak of the inadequacy of language, which is reason enough to sing the blues with Bob Dylan. The second reveals its prophetic sufficiency.

p. 176, l. 1. *Like a grain of sand added to time*. Cf. "How can I design a building in Japan that's reminiscent of something I did in Dallas, Texas? How can it be? It's wrong. The opportunity for originality is there. If you don't learn and grow as an artist, you only repeat. Then you don't make any contribution at all. Each work is like adding another grain of sand to time" (I.M. Pei, speaking in the "Biography" series on the A & E channel.)

p. 176, l. 15. *Hale-Bopp*. The Hale-Bopp comet was closest to the earth on 22 March 1997.

The Appalachian Book of the Dead IV

Orig. pub. *Ohio Review* 64–65 (2001): 492.
A, 47; NB, 177
Pattern: 6-1-6-1-6
Time: April
Place: Charlottesville back yard, apparently

We move from the blues of the previous poem to the gospel song, here inscribed on still another page of The Appalachian Book of the Dead. The description of the Charlottesville sunset and the attendant high-fiving creates a hallelujah mood. The exuberance is underwritten by the miracle chronicled in the gospel tune. The injunction to "harbor" and "snub" Jesus extends the river imagery of stanza 1, "to snub" meaning to secure a vessel with a rope. But for "this one" (the poet) to get across the water it will require both louder singing and whispers about the radiant, resurrected body—a miracle different from walking on water. ("Whispers" is an allusion to the formulas spoken softly into the dead person's ear in *The Egyptian Book of the Dead*.).

In the final stanza we discover in "the lesson for today" that the opposition is between the story of the gospel song (and what it offers) and the landscape (and what it offers). The poet opts for landscape over narrative. The real radiance is in today's "electrified" dogwood. And tomorrow will bring the golden April sunlight, the muscadines, and the mountain laurel.

One is reminded of the speaker in Wallace Stevens's *Sunday Morning*, who declares that no religious doctrine "has endured / As April's green endures." That is the real miracle, though it will not be recognized by all the gospel singers at the river intent on the *story* of the miracle.

p. 177, ll. 3–5. *Let's all go down to the river.... eyes of the blind.* This is a gospel song which, according to Wright's note, was recorded by Mac Wiseman, one of the pioneer's of bluegrass music. It was written by Earl Montgomery and Sue Richards (1972). *Rivanna* = the river that runs through Charlottesville.

p. 177, l. 8. *sing louder.* An echo from Yeats's *Sailing to Byzantium*: "Soul clap its hands and sing, and louder sing / For every tatter in its mortal dress" (ll. 11–12).

p. 177, l. 20. *jack-in-heaven* = the jack-in-the-pulpit. The variation is required for the odd-numbered syllable count.

Spring Storm

Orig. pub. *The Bitter Oleander* 3, no. 2 (Fall 1997): 53.
A, 49; NB, 178
Pattern: 6 × 2
Place: Charlottesville

This poem serves to reiterate the theory of landscape in *The Appalachian Book of the Dead IV*. Everything here is pure description except for two lines: "The Chinese can guide you to many things // but the other side's not one of them" (l. 5), and "The end of desire is the beginning of wisdom." Line 5 glances back to line 9 of the previous poem, *The Appalachian Book of the Dead IV*, about getting to "the other side." In that poem the association is with the biblical "other side of the river" Jordan, or the Promised Land, the goal of Moses being to lead the Israelites back to their proper home, an Eden flowing with milk and honey. In the present poem, "the other side" carries that suggestion as well, but the primary meaning is the other side of life. Thus, the proposition that the Chinese provide little guidance for the dead soul. While *The Tibetan Book of the Dead* does purport to be a guide to the afterlife, Wright seems to have in mind the Buddhist notion that our desires delude us into believing that we have a stable, lasting self. But if we abandon this false sense of self by negating the corporeal body, then the prospect of nirvana or the entry into a state of nothingness presents itself. Thus, in line 9, "the *end* of desire" means not the *goal* of desire but its *extinction*, which, when achieved, is "the beginning of wisdom." This is the contrary of one of Blake's Proverbs of Hell: "The road of excess leads to the palace of wisdom." The focus, then, is not on reincarnation, but on incarnation, the Buddha being enshrined in the present tangible reality of "each water drop" of line 1. In *The Appalachian Book of the Dead IV*, landscape wins out over narrative. Here it wins out over mystical and uncertain speculations about the afterlife. What is important to the poet is what the poem presents directly—the natural world in the essential, immanent reality of the four elements: black earth, sun-fire, water drop, and airy surge.

The poem is not about the spring storm but about what presents itself to the poet's eye following the rainfall. The sun, ruling the scene like a Venetian Doge, is in charge here, incarnating the little Buddhas and the rainbows in the droplets, closing the cloud-shutters of the sky, erasing the movement of the stars, and steering the shadow of the lone crow, crawling across the lawn. The simile of the sun as Doge is reminiscent of Wright's vision of the sun-bathed "golden universe" of the Doge's custom house, described in *Venetian Dog* (NB, 153).

p. 178, l. 8. *a little Buddha in each water drop.* " ... thunderheads the deep blue of Krishna / rise on rainbows / and falling shining rain / each drop— / tiny people gliding slanting down: / a little Buddha seated in each pearl" (Gary Snyder, *The Humped-back Flute Player*, in *Mountains and Rivers without End* [Washington, DC: Counterpoint, 1996], 80–1).

Early Saturday Afternoon, Early Evening

Orig. pub. *Paris Review* 147 (Summer 1998): 115.
A, 50; NB, 179
Pattern: 5 × 3
Time: Spring
Place: Charlottesville

We have now come to section "S" of The Appalachian Book of the dead, with its entries, some potential, on "Saturday," "spring," "shining," "shadow," "soft," "shrift," "squeal," and even a series of alliterative sibilant syllables. The thematic focus is on language forgotten though soon to be recovered. To regain his linguistic memory the poet, representing himself as a shadow, invokes his underground parents (father darkness and mother abyss) to "make me light," and they oblige. Stanza 2 recapitulates the first creation story in the Bible, where light emerges from the dark chaos: "And the earth was waste and void; and darkness was upon the face of the deep; and the Spirit of God moved upon the face of the waters" (Genesis 1:2). The poet's lost voice is restored just as he begins to hear the chant of the neighborhood children. The restoration parallels the rejuvenation of the seasonal cycle—the "new green" showing through the "spring light."

p. 179, l. 14. *Red Rover ... over.* The chant in the children's game in which the members of one team attempt to break through the opposing team's line.

"The Holy Ghost Asketh for Us with Mourning and Weeping Unspeakable"

Orig. pub. *Paris Review* 147 (Summer 1998): 116; rpt. in *PN Review* 27, no. 1 (September–October 2000).
A, 51; NB, 180
Pattern: 5 × 4
Place: Charlottesville

Title: From a version of Romans 8:26. In the AV the translation reads, "The Spirit itself maketh intercession for us with groanings which cannot be uttered."

The context of St. Paul's remark is his view that in the present time of suffering the Holy Spirit will intercede for the early Christians and for the saints. Wright includes the martyrs and contemplatives among those for whom intercession is to be made. It is better to forget about sainthood as a bottomless pit(y), he says, repeating the wag's word play, but he does not forget about the saints as an object of contemplation at a distance. The saints have bled just as the back-yard rose now bleeds, and the poet is content just to sit and watch—or else simply to think about the healing of the golden-gowned and hair-shirted martyrs who have suffered bodily wounds of one kind or another.

The last half of the poem begins with another account of the myth of the eternal return, the great natural cycle beginning all over again. The principle is stated abstractly and then illustrated with the description of the newly emergent rhododendron, azaleas, and tulips. The last stanza constitutes the poet's own intercession on behalf of the "Unseen, unlistened to, unspoken of" saints. Yet the light of their salvation is difficult to affirm. As soon as an affirmation is made, the negative immediately suggests itself: "Light is, light is not." Unlike the natural cycle which continually renews itself, the saints tend to disappear into oblivion, and the distance between these souls and the back-yard landscape, which *can* be seen, listened to, and spoken of, is absolute.

The Appalachian Book of the Dead V

Orig. pub. *Oxford American* 20 (1997): 80.
A, 53; NB, 181
Pattern: 5 × 4
Time: May
Place: Charlottesville back deck; then inside the house

This is a "waiting for God" poem. The poet begins by rather aimlessly recording the sights and sounds from his back deck, the apprehensive languishing of the sunlight corresponding to his own internal mood. He then moves inside, where his mind spins through a vortex of expectation, projecting onto the sounds outside (the power mower and the traffic) a sense of vacancy—the state of emptiness recorded throughout the texts in one of Wright's sources, the *Nag Hammadi Library*. The second half of the poem begins with abrupt transition to the world of death—meditations on a ritual drawn from *The Egyptian Book of the Dead*. (See note to line 11, below.) What might it be like when the sibyl releases the soul from the body's cage? The answer is that the process of "crossing over" is as mysterious as ever: "not knowing how, not knowing where, / Remembering nothing, unhappening." The landscape of the final stanza is the watery world of May. We move from the sunlight of stanza 1 into the dark night of stanza 4, the rain bringing with it a theophany, like that in part 5 of *The Waste Land*. While the angels do not appear, the hermetic Overseer does, though the ellipsis, like that in *The Appalachian Book of the Dead III*, leaves us uncertain about the initiate's next step, yet suggesting there is more to come. The blue vision seems to be connected with the turquoise tablets of Hermes Trismegistus, the overseer of the vision mentioned in the note to line 20 (below), who is placed by God in that blue realm between earth and heaven.

The poet makes a subtle connection between the sounds of the mowing machine and the machine in his head. There are oppositions as well in the sounds of stanza one and the silent expectation of the stilled hare.

p. 181, l. 10. *hare*. Wright identifies the source of the hare image as Virginia Woolf's *Diaries* (NB, 206).
p. 181, l. 11. *When your answers ... forty-two gods*. In *The Egyptian Book of the Dead*, forty-two gods were a tribunal of assessor gods to whom the deceased announced his innocence in the Hall of Two Truths (Hall of Justice). The deceased addresses each of the named gods, and his heart is weighed in the balance (Appendix to "The Chapter of Entering into the Hall of Maati to Praise Osiris Khenti-Amenti," plate 29).
p. 181, l. 12. *When your heart's ... feather*. In *The Egyptian Book of the Dead* the deceased's heart is weighed against the feather of truth (Maát) in order to establish the dead person's righteousness (bk. 3, plate 32).
p. 181, l. 13. *When your soul ... its cage*. "Let the two doors of the sky be opened to me. May Keb, the Erpat of the gods, open his jaws to me. May he open my two eyes which are blinded by swathings. May he make me to lift up my legs in walking which are tied together. May Anpu make my thighs to become vigorous. May the goddess Sekhmet raise me, and lift me up. Let me ascend into heaven, let that which I command be performed in Het-ka-Ptah. I know how to use my heart. I am master of my heart-case. I am master of my hands and arms. I am master of my legs. I have the power to do that which my KA desireth to do. My Heart-soul shall not be kept a prisoner in my body at the gates of Amentet when I would go in peace and come forth in peace" ("The Chapter of Giving a Heart to the Osiris Ani in Khert-Neter," *The Egyptian Book of the Dead*).
p. 181, l. 20. *Overseer*. "There is a great demon. The great God has appointed him to be overseer or judge over the souls of men. And God has placed him in the middle of the air, between earth and heaven. Now when the soul comes forth from (the) body, it is necessary that it meet this daimon. Immediately, he (the daimon) will surround this one, and he will examine him in regard to the character that he has developed in his life" (*Asclepius 21–29*, NHL, 337). In *The Discourse on the Eighth and Ninth* of *The Nag Hammadi Library* Hermes Trismegistus, called the Overseer, instructs an initiate, who has already attained the wisdom of the first seven spheres, into the mysteries of the eighth sphere (the empyrean) and the ninth (the sphere of God). After the initiate (referred to as "the son") confirms that he has had a spiritual vision, Hermes enjoins the initiate to inscribe what he has received in hieroglyphic characters, writing it on turquoise: "My son, it is proper to write this book on steles of turquoise, in hieroglyphic characters. For Mind himself has become overseer of these. Therefore, I command that this teaching be carved on stone, and that you place it in my sanctuary" (NHL, 326).

Star Turn II

Orig. pub. *River City* 18–19, nos. 1–2 (Summer 1998): 72.
A, 55; NB, 182
Pattern: 5 × 2

This poem is less coherent than *Star Turn* (NB, 148), but its focus seems to be on difference between the stars and the human condition. Although these stars, because of the moonlight, are fewer and less visible than those in *Star Turn*, they are nevertheless "inalterably in place." But our chaotic lives are not like that, nor are the stars like the selves we imagine futilely we might become. Even though now partially masked, they will always take their appointed place in the cosmic cycle. The central metaphor here is the mask: the stars are "bandannaed by moonlight"; they are like "highlights" from "Dante's death mask"; we ourselves put on the masks of numerous personae; some stars are still camouflaged in the summer sky; and those that are not have escaped from the mask of an eclipse. Masks, of course, go back to our earliest dramatic performances (the Latin *persona* derives from the Etruscan word for "mask"), so there is a hint of the mask even in the "sequin" simile, which elicits a slang expression of approval—"hubba-hubba." A "star turn" is the most striking performer in a song and dance show. And we ourselves are "star-like" dramatis personae. Human masks are projections of desires or signals of pretence. In the masquerade of human lives they are the means for presenting a false outward show, but the masks worn by the stars indicate only simple concealment by the moon. The idea of the mask appears elsewhere in Wright's poetry: *Roma II, Tattoos*, no. 14, *Chickamauga, Venexia I, Umbrian Dreams*, and "*It's Turtles All the Way Down.*"

After Reading T'ao Ch'ing, I Wander Untethered Through the Short Grass

Orig. pub. *Gettysburg Review* 11, no. 3 (Autumn 1998): 471.
A, 56; NB, 183
Pattern: 2 × 6
Time: Spring
Place: Charlottesville

Title: The wandering motif appears throughout T'ao Ch'ien's poetry. "Ch'ing" is a misprint for "Ch'ien."

"I stand inside the word *here*," the poet says punningly, "here" referring to the word itself as it stands in the sentence and to the place where the word is—amid the "plucked stalks and thyroid weeds" of the dry spring season. The poet is in no mood at this point to make a religious affirmation, religion having been in tatters, like the blue empyrean, for a millennium. What the poet does affirm is the vision of T'ao Ch'ien, whose borrowed lines constitute the last stanza. And this vision is that death ends all. As T'ao Ch'ien says in another poem: "I'm no immortal. I can't just soar away / beyond change. There's no doubt about it, / death's death" (*Form, Shadow, Spirit*, in *The Selected Poems of T'ao Ch'ien*, 39). Or in still another: "And who / expects to end in some celestial village? / My dream is to walk out all alone into a lovely / morning—maybe stop to pull weeds in the garden, maybe climb East Ridge and chant, settling into / my breath, or sit writing poems beside a clear stream" (*Back Home Again Chant*, ibid., 34–5). As David Hinton remarks, "Although [T'ao Ch'ien] grieved over loss and dying because he knew the actual to be all there is, he also knew that whatever is alive, himself included, ceases to be as naturally as it comes to be" (ibid., 5–6). This is the position Wright takes in this poem: "My story and I will disappear together, just like this," the final phrase referring to the blank space that follows the end of the poem. But not yet: there is more yard work to be done.

p. 183, l. 9. "Unable to reach that / golden age Huang and T'ang ruled / I inhabit who I am sad and alone" (*Turning Seasons*, in *The Selected Poems of T'ao Ch'ien*, trans. David Hinton [Port Townsend, Wash.: Copper Canyon Press, 1993], 38). Hinton's translation is in couplets, like Wright's poem. Tao Chi'ien (365–427 C.E.) was the son of an official family who gave up his post in his forties to settle as a farmer at home. He made friends with Buddhist monks of the White Lotus order, which developed into Zen.

p. 183, l. 10. *When it ends ... What else?* "Life is its own mirage of change. It ends / vanished, returned into nothing. What else?" (*Home Again Among Gardens and Fields*, in *The Selected Poems of T'ao Ch'ien*, 22).

p. 183, ll. 11–12. *One morning ... like this.* "Away, ever away / into this hundred-year life and beyond, / my story and I vanish together like this" (*After Liu Ch'ai-Sang's Poem*, ibid., 18).

Remembering Spello, Sitting Outside in Prampolini's Garden

Orig. pub. *Gettysburg Review* 11, no. 3 (Autumn 1998): 470.
A, 57; NB, 184–5
Pattern: 2–3–2–3–2–3–3–2
Place: Flashback to Umbria

Title: Spello is a hill town near Assisi in central Umbria, where Wright's friend Gaetano Prampolini, to whom *Black Zodiac* was dedicated, has a home. The Gates of Propertius, which form the great archway of Via Torri di Properzio in Spello, was perhaps ("so they say") an entrance gate before the time of Caesar Augustus. Spello is a small village on the southeastern flank of Mount Subasio.

The poem is a flashback to a late afternoon and early evening in Spello, Umbria, where the poet, perched on his lawn chair, watches the song birds, stares at the heavens, and listens to the night traffic. The approaching nighttime engenders a reflection about the three things that, for Wright, constitute the subject matter of poetry—landscape, language, and the idea of God: "No word for time, no word for God, landscape exists outside each, / But stays, incurable ache, both things, / And bears me out as evening darkens and steps forth." Although language is incapable of finding ways to express "time" and "God," the longing to discover the proper words nevertheless remains. This desire carries the poet along into the darkness, and there is something about the place ("an old address") and the Italian language that creates a sense of security ("snug in my life"). But such a mood is short-lived, displaced by a feeling of otherworldliness and dispossession. The upshot is that the poet watches everything but sees nothing, "Just under the surface of the earth." Here again we have the suggestion that "nothing" is also "Nothing" and so the poem ends on an ominous note. The poet is without a light to guide him in the darkness, just like the cars that glide by without headlights.

After Rereading Robert Graves, I Go Outside to Get My Head Together

A, 59; NB, 186
Pattern: 5 × 4
Time: 4 July
Place: Charlottesville

Stanzas 1 and 4 depict the landscape of sky and garden, bracketing two *ars poetica* stanzas in which the poet takes issue with Robert Graves's strong assertion that the function of poetry is a "religious invocation of the Muse." Wright, on the contrary, declares that the Muse is dead, and that all the poet can do is invoke her memory "in memory of a Memory." Memory (Mneme), according to Pausanius, was one of the original Muses worshipped at Mt. Helicon, along with Meditation (Melete) and Song (Aoede). This is reminiscent of Dante's invocation to the Muses in Canto 2 of the *Inferno*: "O Muses, O high genius, help me now! O memory that wrote down what I saw, here shall your worthiness appear" (ll. 7–9; trans. Singleton). The appeal is for memory accurately to retrace the journey exactly as it happened. In any event, poetry may serve, if not to invoke the Muse in a religious sense, at least to memorialize her memory. In *Early Afternoon, Early Evening* (NB, 179), The Appalachian Book of the Dead is enjoined to spur the memory.

The poet sees, however, that such a rejection of Graves's theory is an insufficient *ars poetica*, and so he adds to what he has somewhat tentatively offered on behalf of memory. Why write? The answer, but only "in part," is to make leaving life easier. How can that be? How does all that Wright has written make the entrance into death any easier? Has the exploration the dark unfathomable, the absolute, the presence and absence prepared him in a way he wouldn't have been otherwise prepared? Writing as praise is clear enough. Practically every poem has stanzas that are at least implicitly a panegyric. Almost all have hymn-like expressions of wonder, especially in the landscape lines. But there is praise for the past too, usually praise for some aspect of the tradition that Eliot calls "the dead." Then we have the *raison d'être* as adding and subtracting. There is something to be said simply for doing it and doing it again. The sum of the cloudy count of the abacus beads is Wright's collected works, which is an impressive sum. The Appalachian Book of the Dead has existed then in order to create the trilogy of trilogies. The poems provide a tally of the world of the ten thousand things—from the lawn sprinkler beyond the hedge to the taunting cardinal and the nectar-laden bees that lie immediately before the poet's gaze.

"Adding" is another of Wright's mathematical metaphors. Earlier the mathematics of the quest had called for the search for the proper quotient and for the beginning of long division. Implicit here is the desire to "work it out," to solve the riddle. One cannot be as precise about this as one can be with a real mathematical problem: what it all adds up to is still cloudy. But "cloudy" also moves upwards into the zodiac, where things are always in process. Finally, we have the parenthetical warning that we shouldn't forget subtraction. This means that some parts of The Appalachian Book of the Dead have not made it into print. The poet writes it all down in The Appalachian Book of the Dead, but then he begins to purge and refine and constrict and make taut. Those are four of the reasons, then, for The Appalachian Book of the Dead—to memorialize memory, the ease the exit into death, to praise the things of the world, and to add and subtract from the register of these things. We can think of others, such as the "restitution of the divine in a secular circumstance" (*The Writing Life*, in NB, 165).

Wright on Wright, in response to an interviewer's question about what seemed to be a terse dismissal of Graves in the poem: "Is this a passing reference to *The White Goddess*, or are you in reaction to Graves' theories of the Muse?" Wright's reply: "I *was* re-reading *The White Goddess* when I wrote the poem, and enjoying it, actually, especially the early Battle of the Trees [chap. 2]. The poem is primarily in reaction to his theories of the Muse, though in the end, of course, it glancingly bows to them. Like Keats's, however, an awkward bow, and a partial one, partially unkept" (Caseley, 24).

p. 186, ll. 6–7. *According to Graves ... Muse.* "'What is the use or function of poetry nowadays?' is a question not the less poignant for being defiantly asked by so many stupid people or apologetically answered by so many silly people. The function of poetry is religious invocation of the Muse; its use is the experience of mixed exaltation and horror that her presence excites" (Robert Graves, *The White Goddess: A Historical Grammar of Poetic Myth*, rev. ed. [New York: Farrar, Straus and Giroux, 1966], 14).

American Twilight

Orig. pub. *Partisan Review* 65, no. 4 (Fall 1998): 614.
A, 60; NB, 187
Pattern: 5-4-5-4
Time: Summer
Place: Charlottesville

Love calls the poet to the things of this world. Children's voices, lightning bugs, and the encroaching darkness rise to that affection and illustrate that devotion to detail which the poet affirmed at the end of *Apologia Pro Vita Sua*. Here, however, he wonders why he should care about such things, much less write about them, when our lives count for nothing in the grand scheme of things: the world goes on without us. But the skepticism is short-lived, gainsaid by the description of the half-light, trees, swallows, and lawn sprinklers that immediately follows. The conclusion: it is better to celebrate the things of this world, including the sounds of the cicadas and terriers, because the poor souls who have already crossed over to the other side have no voices to mark their weal. The poem begins with the sounds of a children's ball game and ends with sounds of the barking dogs, reminding us that Wright is a poet of the ear as well as a poet of the eye.

The Appalachian Book of the Dead VI

Orig. pub. *Ohio Review* 57 (1997): 11.
A, 61; NB, 188
Pattern: 5 × 3
Time: July or early August.
Place: Charlottesville back yard and then inside the house

We begin once again with sounds—the notes of the young singer, the sound of the ball game next door, the truck noises wafting in from the right. All of the other *Appalachian Book of the Dead* poems open with sounds as well:

[I]. the crow's call, the ticking water
II. the sound from the children's games (even though the day itself is toneless)
III. the whispering supplications of the wind: *I am pure, I am pure, I am pure.*
IV. the high-fiving gospel singers
V. the power mower, the traffic, the violin

Another structural feature in the grammar of Wright's imagery is that all of the *Appalachian Book of the Dead* poems conclude with a reference to light:

[I]. the shining leaves
II. the light "still lovely in the west"
III. the "long shine" of the "small-time paradiso"
IV. the lit dogwood and the (anticipated) returning sun
V. the glint on the window glass and the landscape's flash
VI. the "light slick" for the moonbeams and the rising through the azure

This is perhaps the most hermetic of The Appalachian Book of the Dead poems. We begin with a sense of expectation (stanza 1), but the angel who arrives in stanza 2 brings with her the melancholic message that our brief lives are filled with lost days and that we see even those, as Meng Chiao says, only through a glass darkly. In the cryptic third stanza, where the point of view returns to the first-person, the poet is still in a state of expectation, apparently waiting for the angels to help ease his resurrection through the azure to the third heaven—past the cloudy atmosphere (first heaven) and the realm of the stars and planets (second heaven). The poet, lying on his back, is waiting for the right word, which, he has heard, is breathtaking in two senses: astonishing and life-ending.

p. 188, l. 7–9. *Lost days, as Meng Chiao says, ... darkly.* "Nothing left // here but empty shadows of lost days, / a little window of words is too large" (*The Late Poems of Meng Chiao*, trans. David Hinton [Princeton, NJ: Princeton University Press, 1996], 51). Cf. "For now we see through a glass, darkly" (1 Corinthians 12:13).

Landscape as Metaphor, Landscape as Fate and a Happy Life

Orig. pub. *Meridian* 1 (Spring 1998).
A, 62; NB, 189
Pattern: 4-2-4-2-4-2 (the couplets preceded by a dash)
Time: August
Place: Yaak Valley, Montana

Title: "Landscape as metaphor" is of course a simile, and the poem is dominated by similes: lives lifting like leaf spores, evergreens like Egyptian guard dogs, butterflies like angels, stars like high cotton, poppies and sister's words like lip prints. Tracking the white trail of the tiny insect is like tracking the ink across the notebook's blank page, which is a forlorn enterprise because the "dark / Unknowable" is precisely that.

"Up here" [in northwest Montana], "our lives continue to lift off," but we cannot see behind the guarded evergreens. God, a tough taskmaster holding his knee to our necks, does not let us look upward in the broad daylight. The midmorning glare is too much for the poet, who has got his heart set on darkness. The glare is an iconostasis, a screen that comes between the nave (where we are) and the altar (where the secrets lie). What will become the night sky, now hidden behind the screen of the daylight glare, is "monkish and grand"—the one example in the poem of direct metaphorical identity. What we are to read is the stars at midnight, if only we could see them. The cosmos continues its regular pattern: we, like the moving dogs, do not.

The Fragrant One in the last line is apparently the divine judge. The name may derive from the poetry of Qu Yuan, an early Chinese poet (340–78), whose long poem *Li Sao* (*Encountering Sorrow*) is about the quest for a "counterpart," vaguely referred to as The Fragrant One, among other names. *Li Sao* reveals Qu Yuan's love for his state (which is not Wright-like) and the quest of his poetic soul for the beautiful ideal (somewhat Wright-like). The Fragrant One is hardly an appealing divinity in this context: it judges and then "moves on." In other Eastern traditions and in shamanism the Fragrant One is a term of endearment for divinities.

Opus Posthumous III

Orig. pub. *Ohio Review* 57 (1997): 12; rpt. 64–65 (2001): 491.
A, 64; NB, 190
Pattern: 5 × 3
Time: Mid-August
Place: Charlottesville

As the clouds over Virginia burn and crumble like an ancient kingdom, the poet once again waits for the "smallish light / Starting to seep, coppery blue / out of the upper right-hand corner of things." The image takes us back to the beginning of *Apologia Pro Sua Vita*, where landscape becomes a lever for a little light that will "nimbus" the poet's "going forth." Here, at the end of *Appalachia*, there is a little light inside "the lapis lazuli of late afternoon." Although a full stop comes at the end of stanza 2, the sense seems to require that the four "until" clauses attach themselves to the rising and falling of the light "out of the right-hand corner of things." Normal syntax would require that the adverb clauses modify the main verb in stanza 2, which is "looked," but that would violate the apparent sense, which is that the light will continue to rise and fall until the entire landscape has been engulfed by darkness and silence. The final line—"Until there is nothing else"—is metaphorical, representing death. It is only when the clouds stop, the landscape disappears, the bypass is silent, and the grass grieves that the "smallish light" will cease rising and falling. *Appalachia* ends, then, on a note of projected oblivion—a time when, as with Shelley's Ozymandias, "Nothing beside remains." The poem is of course not a genuine *opus posthumous*, for the poet is still very much alive in August 1998, and, as with *Opus Posthumous* (NB, 159), there is more "possum work" to be done. Most immediately, this is *North American Bear*, which forms the coda of *Negative Blue*.

p. 190, l. 1. *Assurbanipal* (d. 626?). The last of the great kings of Assyria, which reached the height of sumptuous living under his reign.

North American Bear

North American Bear, the brief, fourth part of *Negative Blue*, was published by Sutton Hoo Press (La Crosse, WI, 1999) in an edition of 136 copies. Its seven poems are emblematic of the seven major stars of Ursa Major.

Step-children of Paradise

Orig. pub. *Five Points* 2, no. 3 (Spring–Summer 1998): 33.
NB, 193
Pattern: 2–5–5–2
Time: Saturday in January
Place: Charlottesville

The poem turns on the difference between the form and structure of the constellations (like Ursa Major whose tail is triaged through the winter trees) and the "blurred star chart" produced by our own anxious and formless lives. Bears, of course, do not have tails, and constellations are altogether arbitrary formations. The point is that a form has been imposed on the stars, and the projected designs of the constellations stand in sharp contrast to our own lives, continuously dissolved by time and squandered by doing more or less trivial, unconnected things—"a little of this and a little of that." The stars in the constellations have been gathered together and summoned from the beginning of time, but our lives are "ungathered, uncalled upon." Thus, we are step-children of paradise, unattended and unnurtured. In such a situation, the poet, uncharacteristically, cannot muster a back-yard description beyond the two little snapshots of the first line.

In *Umbrian Dreams* the poet declared, "Nothing is flat-lit and tabula rasaed in Charlottesville." In the present poem everything is tabula-rasaed, and there is little prospect that the poet, his fingers being eaten away by time, will have anything to inscribe on the blank tablet. Rainy January is suffering from the doldrums, and the poet with his toothache and his acute consciousness of an eventual cosmic apocalypse, is no less depressed. There may always be room for another life, as the poet says, meaning the genuine paradise that is our proper home—but not, so far as one can tell, another life for these poor step-children.

Freezing Rain
Orig. pub. *Shenandoah* 48, no. 4 (Winter 1998): 38.
NB, 194
Pattern: 3–3–1
Time: Winter
Place: Charlottesville

Freezing Rain extends the theme of the previous poem—the distinction between the sublunary world and the fixed movement of the starry heavens—but with a new twist. The movement of the stars outside of the constellations exists in another order, "an order beyond form." It is a celestial order separated absolutely from both earthly existence ("here") and the structure of the constellations ("there"). The stars in this "order beyond form" are our escorts and attendants ("outriders").

The description of landscape is also extended beyond the meager picture drawn in the first line of *Step-children of Paradise*: here the poet represents the sounds and sights of winter through what Wright is so skilled at inventing—witty figures of speech: the sleet is a drummer tapping on the skylight, the ice on the trees is like a new hairstyle. "Winter's slick-back and stiff gel" is a perfect trope; the simile comparing the "streetlamp reflections" and "vogueing boys" is less successful.

Thinking about the Night Sky, I Remember a Poem by Tu Fu
Orig. pub. *Five Points*, 2, no. 3 (Spring–Summer 1998).
NB, 195
Pattern: 4 × 3
Time: Winter
Place: Charlottesville

The other six poems in *North American Bear* make reference to the constellations and other stars. This one, as the poet reminds us in the final line, is the exception. It is rather about the distances between the stars, between the sky and earth in Tu Fu's poem, between fame and oblivion, between the beginning of passion and its end, between fire and ash, and between the mind and what teases it out of thought. To collapse these distances would be to resolve large questions of cosmology, metaphysics, psychology, and physics. But the poet at this point is not capable of such resolution, just as Tu Fu received no answer to the question about his poetic status except the one he poignantly provides: "Retired for ill-health." The poet turns away from grandiose speculation, being content simply to complete his poem.

p. 195, ll. 1–4. "By bent grasses / in a gentle wind / Under straight mast / I'm alone tonight, // And the stars hang / above the broad plain / But the moon's afloat / in this Great River: // Oh, where's my name / among the poets? / Official rank? / 'Retired for ill-health.' // Drifting, drifting, / what am I more than / A single gull / between sky and earth?" (Tu Fu, *Night Thoughts Afloat*, in *Li Po and Tu Fu*, trans. Arthur Cooper [New York: Penguin, 1973], 237).

North American Bear
Orig. pub. *Southern Review* 35, no. 3 (Summer 1999): 492–4.
NB, 196–8

3. Appalachia and North American Bear

Pattern: 8 × 7
Time: Early November 1998
Place: Charlottesville, with a flashback to 1948.

The seven vignettes in this poem, imitating the seven poems in the limited edition book, hint at a connection with the seven stars of the Big Dipper, part of the constellation of the Great Bear. The point of view is almost completely in the first-person singular. (The editorial "we" and "us" creep into the third section, and the second-person "you" into the fifth.) The poem contains familiar speculations about the symbolic import of the stars, their linguistic code, and their relation to the poet's identity, particularly to his heart (cf. "heart-weight," in section 1, "pulse" and "hijacked heart" in section 3, and the absent "heartbeat" in section 4).

Section 1. On a dim and rainy November afternoon the heavy-hearted poet invokes the starlight, first, to free his earthly surroundings and then to make him "insoluble." He describes himself as "fallow-voiced" and "night-leaning." The third imperative—to move the shadow sideways across his mouth—is apparently addressed to the starlight as well, though it may simply be an extension of the photographic imagery: a negative resist exposed to light becomes relatively insoluble. In any event, it is an appeal for silence from a voice that is already fallow—inactive and unseeded. "Negative" also describes the poet's general mood as he registers the lingering visual impression ("afterscape") of the unremarkable and depressing scene before him. "Fallow-voiced" is an expression also used by Paul Celan: "Fallow-voiced, lashed / forth from the depth" (*Poems of Paul Celan*, trans. Michael Hamburger [New York: Persea, 1995], 315).

Section 2. The central trope of these lines is the "constellations are syntax" metaphor. Looking at the heavens, the poet remembers staring skyward in 1948 while at summer camp in Sky Valley, North Carolina. The constellations—"North American Bear, / Orion, Cassiopeia and the Pleiades"—were then "as beautiful as the alphabet," pin-pricks in the cylindrical scroll of time. But there is no connection among the "word-strings" of the stars. Their sequence is altogether random, and the language they might have had at one time is lost; thus, their syntax is indecipherable and inarticulate.

Section 3. Contemplating the stars plunges the poet into the interrogative mode. The stanza begins with a genuine question, Why are we drawn so vertiginously upward? Does this flight of consciousness spring from some mysterious connection between systole and diastole, ascent and descent, high and low tide, height and depth? Whatever the force is that spins its line out is, like that of the blind fates, unnamable. The poet concludes with two rhetorical questions: "Who is to say the hijacked heart has not returned to its cage? / Who is to say some angel has not // breathed in my ear?" The answer in each case is "nobody."

Section 4. In the Orpheus section, with its parallels to Rilke's poem, the poet substitutes his own vanished life for Eurydice's. His cloud-like life has often been buried and resurrected. But this time, having looked back for his life before he reaches the upper air of the "stern stars," his life vanishes again, its heartbeat and footfall, like Eurydice's, inaudible.

p. 197, ll. 7–13. These lines have parallels to several lines in Robert Lowell's imitation of Rilke's *Orpheus, Eurydice and Hermes*, in *Imitations* (New York: Farrar, Straus and Giroux, 1961), 102. About Eurydice, Lowell writes, for example: "And this sorrow-world circled about her, / just as the sun and stern stars / circle the earth—/ a heaven of anxiety ringed by determined stars."

Section 5. With winter approaching, the poet, walking along the Charlottesville sidewalk, is almost able to see the Chinese version of Ursa Major, its seven stars representing to an anonymous poet on the Western Front an image of General Kê-Shu lifting his sword. The seven stars of the Big Dipper outline only the back and tail of the bear. Thus, the "long-sword over the bear's back" would be an extension of the imaginary line running from the stars Megrez (or delta) through Dubhe (or alpha).

p. 197, ll. 16–20. "This constellation with its seven high stars, / Is Kê-shu lifting his sword in the night: / And no more barbarians, nor their horses, nor cattle, / Dare ford the river boundary" (*General Kê-Shu*, by the poet identified only as "One at the Western Front," in *Three Hundred Poems of the T'ang Dynasty*, 236). This is the edition identified in Wright's note (*NB*, 206).

Section 6. Dawdling and humming in the back yard, the poet gazes at the constellations while he wonders about the once "bright fire of the world" before it burned out. He forgets "whatever it was [he] had to say."

Section 7. Back again on the sidewalk of his Charlottesville neighborhood, the poet reveals that his real neighborhood is the heavens and that he feels momentarily safe inside the outline of a "final solitude," like a "medieval journeyman enfrescoed with his poem in his hand." The image may be drawn from the fresco by Domenico di Michelino in the Duomo in Florence, with its outline of the empyrean and its five stars, or perhaps the fresco by Andrea del Castango in the Uffizi. In any case, the poet, who in section 1 has asked for his constellated habitat to be unhindered, is still journeying among the stars.

If You Talk the Talk, You Better Walk the Walk

Orig. pub. *New England Review* 19, no. 3 (Summer 1998): 111.
NB, 199
Pattern: 5 × 3
Time: February
Place: Charlottesville

Title: A slang expression meaning that if you say something that appears to be true, you should be prepared to illustrate it through your actions.

The first stanza is a rather faithful rendering of the extraordinary poem by Shang-yin, *Written on a Monastery Wall*—a Buddhist version of the opening lines of William Blake's *Auguries of Innocence*: "To see a World in a Grain of Sand / And a Heaven in a Wild Flower / Hold Infinity in the palm of your hand / And Eternity in an hour." The Buddhist monk favors the interior quest for the Tao over the external world—what is "written all around us." The second stanza is precisely a description of the external world—the rain-drenched trees and garden in their familiar and comforting, though incomprehensible, vocabulary. Finally, because we do not understand this illegible world, we try to climb out of it, even though uncertain of our destination. And "we keep on climbing"; that is, we walk the walk, seeking the Tao.

p. 199, ll. 1–5. "They rejected life to seek the Way. Their footprints are before us. / They offered up their brains, ripped up their bodies; so firm was their resolution. / See it as large, and a millet-grain cheats us of the universe: / See it as small, and the world can hide in a pinpoint. / The oyster before its womb fills thinks of the new cassia; / The amber when it first sets, remembers a former pine. / If we trust the true and sure words written on Indian leaves / We hear all past and future in one stroke of the temple bell" (Li Shang-yin, *Written on a Monastery Wall*, in *Poems of the Late T'ang*, trans. A.C. Graham [Baltimore: Penguin, 1965], 161. Wright's note (*NB*, 206) directs us to this poem.

St. Augustine and the Arctic Bear

Orig. pub. in *The New Breadloaf Anthology of Contemporary American Poetry*, ed. Michael Collier and Stanley Plumly (Hanover: University Press of New England, 1999), 346–7.
NB, 200
Pattern: 5 × 4

The unlikely combination of a saint, a bear, and Bubba's bateau sounds like a recipe for slapstick, but the incongruities lead to Wright's familiar juxtaposition of landscape and theological or metaphysical speculation, the latter deriving in this case from three Augustinian pronouncements. We begin with the poet's gaze fixed on the westward-whirling black zodiac and we conclude with his staring at the black water, imitating the gaze of the artic bear. As *North American Bear* is a series of poems about the constellations, it is tempting to see the artic bear as the circumpolar Ursa Major. In this case, the fixing of both the bear's and the poet's eyes on the black water would be a metaphor for gazing at the sky: the Milky Way is conventionally projected as an underworld river. "Bubba's bateau" is suggestive of any number of mythological boats said to carry the soul across water into the realm of death. It is suggestive as well of the constellation Lepus—the little boat that carries Orion, the god of the underworld, down the long river of the sky—or perhaps even the constellation Argo the Boat. "Bubba," of course, elicits an ironic grin in the midst of all this seriousness.

The arctic bear can operate on a literal level as well, and perhaps this is all the poet intends—a polar bear whose whiteness makes it "invisible in its element." It has "form to burn," having stored up enough seal meat to survive the winter on the ice. It fixes its eyes on the black water, waiting for the seals to surface, just as the poet stares at the black zodiac, looking for his own spiritual sustenance. At the same time he is aware of the "lap and noisome breeze" of the Stygian bateau "always at [his] back," like the wingéd chariot of Marvell's *To His Coy Mistress*. The less extravagant, literal reading fits better with the final line: "Formless and timeless, he wears my heart on his hard sleeve." The antecedent of "he" is the arctic bear, who is, "Like time invisible in its element" and so formless. This is linked to the first and the third of the Augustinian declarations—that time is "a body without form": the past has disappeared into memory, the future is unknown, and the present does not really exist. The poet adds to this an ominous note: "When expectation becomes memory ... We'll live in the past, a cold house on a dark street," the cold house being the grave. The second epigram from Augustine—"None fall who will lift their eyes"—introduces the element of faith or "the substance of things hoped for," in the words of the author of the Epistle to the Hebrews. This is the poet's answer to the cold house of death.

p. 200, ll. 7-9. "But how is the future diminished or consumed when it does not yet exist? Or how does the past, which exists no longer, increase, unless it is that in the mind in which all this happens there are three functions? For the mind expects, it attends, and it remembers; so that what it expects passes into what it remembers by way of what it attends to. Who denies that future things do not exist as yet? But still there is already in the mind the expectation of things still future. And who denies that past things now exist no longer?" (Augustine, *Confessions*, bk. 11, chap. 28, par. 37; trans. Albert C. Outler).

p. 200, l. 12. "Let him who understands this confess to thee; and let him who does not understand also confess to thee! Oh, exalted as thou art, still the humble in heart are thy dwelling place! For thou liftest them who are cast down and they fall not for whom thou art the Most High" (ibid., bk. 11, 31, par. 41). "I lift up mine invisible eyes to Thee, that Thou wouldest pluck my feet out of the snare. Thou dost ever and anon pluck them out, for they are ensnared" (ibid., bk. 10, chap. 34, par. 52). See also bk. 13, chap. 38.

p. 200, l. 13. "Who except such a one would tell me whether, if all form were diminished and consumed, formlessness alone would remain, through which a thing was changed and turned from one species into another, so that sheer formlessness would then be characterized by temporal change? And surely this could not be, because without motion there is no time, and where there is no form there is no change" (ibid., bk. 12, chap. 11, par. 14); "...that the invisible and unformed earth is to be understood as having corporeal matter before it had any manner of form" (ibid., bk. 12, chap. 17, par. 25); "It is true that the formlessness which is almost nothing cannot have temporal change in it" (ibid., bk. 12, chap. 19, par. 28).

Sky Diving

Orig. pub. in *The New Breadloaf Anthology of Contemporary American Poetry*, ed. Michael Collier and Stanley Plumly (Hanover, NH: University Press of New England, 1999), 345-6.

NB, 201
Pattern: 2-4-4-2
Time: Unspecified
Place: Charlottesville

The subject of the final poem of *Negative Blue* is the goal of the poet's thirty-year poetic quest—a search for the "the still, small point at the point where all things meet," a phrase repeated from *A Journal of the Year of the Ox* (*WTTT*, 163). This is Eliot's still point of the turning world, the point of intersection between sacred and secular time, between the vertical ladder of the *axis mundi* and the horizontal movement from time past into time future, between the "ground lights" and the "constellations." In the final poem of *Chickamauga* this still point is the intersection of "the edge of the landscape and the absolute." In the final poem of *Black Zodiac* it is the intersection of emptiness and plenitude. In the final poem of *Appalachia* it is the balance between the "burning heart" and the "burning feather of truth." And here at the end of *North American Bear* the still point, says the poet, is "the form that moves the sun and other stars." This, of course, is a repetition of the final line of Dante's *Paradiso*: *l'amor che move il sole e l'altre stelle*. Wright's "form" and Dante's "love" amount to the same thing: they are both metaphors for God. We are reminded then of the analogy between our pilgrim poet and Dante's Dante.

How addicted we are, says the poet, to the heavens, but he says it in so curious a way ("sidereal jones"), combining a bookish word with slang, as to suggest the ironic deflation that we encounter frequently in the poems. But there is nothing ironic in the poet's declaration, "Immensity fills us," even though "nothing acquits us." This last clause contains a pun once more on "nothing": on the one hand, we are not acquitted of our shortcomings by anything; on the other, the experience of nothing does acquit us.

With the poet's feeling the "arterial pulse" of the constellations and his staring "up at the heavens," we are reminded once again of Dante: each of the canticles of *The Divine Comedy* finds Dante the pilgrim staring at up at the stars, and each ends with the word *stelle*. The metaphors of the final couplet are complex but infinitely suggestive. The "drowning pools" of the heavens seem initially to introduce a death-by-water motif. But this idea is qualified by the swallowing metaphor. What swallows us is not the black zodiac but what lies beyond it ("extra-celestial"), which is "the form that moves the sun and the other stars." Swallowing, as we have seen, is a conventional metaphor for possessing. What we genuinely possess we identify with and take into ourselves. The repetition of "such" suggests the poet is somewhat astonished by this sense of being taken into the heaven beyond the heaven—diving into the sky rather than diving out of it. But the final line with its biblical phrasing indicates the poet's openness to such a possibility, and he invites us to join him in the serenity that comes from lying down together. He invites us as well to open our mouths, the mouth being the receptacle of sustenance and the instrument of the word. It is possible that we all might be gathered up into the artifice of eternity, as Yeats puts it—which gives new meaning to the phrase "sky diving."

p. 201, ll. 7–12. Cf. "The traveling-sickles at the extra- / celestial place / mime themselves whitish-grey / into moon swallows, / into star swifts, // I dip to that place / and pour an urnful / down you, / into you" (*Poems of Paul Celan*, trans. Michael Hamburger [New York: Persea Books, 1985], 283).

PART II

The Fourth Trilogy and Its Coda

CHAPTER 4

A Short History of the Shadow

In 2000 Wright reported to an interviewer that after he finished *Appalachia*, "I saw the end in sight, I saw the conclusion of what I was trying to do. And when I didn't do anything for months and months and months, I realized I really was at the end. I wasn't just kidding myself. I had had something I was trying to do, and I did it, and that was it. Now I can sort of shut up again, I hope" (Genoways, 448). What followed, of course, was not silence, but an unprecedented burst of poetic energy that resulted in four more volumes in the next six years. The first of these was *A Short History of the Shadow*.

The painting on the dust jacket is Milton Avery's *Black Night* (1959).

Looking Around

Orig. pub. *Poetry* 175, no. 1 (October–November 1999): 1–3.
SHS, 3–5
Pattern: 4 × 3 × 5 (60 lines)
Time: 1 March 1998–May 1998
Place: Charlottesville

The titles of the three *Looking Around* poems are what we might expect from a poet who has just completed his trilogy of trilogies. The question we naturally have is one the poet asks, surveying the effects of his attic study on the first day of March 1998: "where to begin again?" (l. 4)—a question repeatedly asked by Samuel Beckett's lost characters. A new seasonal cycle has begun: "Each year it happens this way" (p. 4, l. 1). Wright says in an interview, "I am addicted to the seasons ... I have an almost visceral reaction to, and appreciation of, the changes and the portents each carries on its back and inside its body of mythology. Autumn was always my favorite, the romantic favorite, until recently. Now spring holds the field, and the constant tiny chant and drumbeat of 'begin again, begin again,' succors me in" (Spiegelman, 119). The *Looking Around* poems move from spring to summer and from Charlottesville, in the first two, to Montana, in the third.

Surfacing from the catalogue of various objects before him—the statue of the Buddha, the furniture, the rugs—is the "ur-photograph" of Giorgio Morandi that we met earlier in *Giorgio Morandi and the Talking Eternity Blues* (NB, 167). In the photo Morandi is contemplating the bottles he has repeatedly painted, having constricted the entire universe with its "angelic orders" and "applications" down to his familiar bottles, tins, and vases—the world in his own grain of sand. Announcing to Morandi what he already knows, the poet says that Bologna is the world's "bite" (its incisive feature) and its "end" (goal). In other words, there is no need for Morandi to go wandering very far beyond the confines of his studio. The poet does not say so directly, but the implication is that he is going to "begin again" after the manner of his "friend" Giorgio by looking around at what is under his nose. Charlottesville, my friend, Charlottesville, world's bite and world's end. Or Verona. Or the Yaak Valley.

Stanza 2 reintroduces a familiar theme: light comes only from darkness and plenitude from vacancy. The poet remarks that he read this once in a dream and in a book. The dream could have been any wish-fulfillment emerging from nightmare, and the book, something written perhaps by a Zen master or German mystic. But the idea is an archetypal one, firmly embedded in narratives by countless writers—Heraclitus, Homer, Virgil, Dante, Milton, Eliot, Conrad, and scores of others who have shown us the swirling descent into the inferno and the circular climb up the purgatorial mountain toward paradise. The poet yearns to return to this tradition—the "old fires, old geographies"—and thus he reverses Pound's dictum "to make it new." He ties the movement from darkness to light to the regeneration of the seasonal cycle, which each year brings the "good news" of life from the "other world" of death.

Stanza 3 is a parody of such rebirth. April's twinkle and shimmer, like a high-fashion model, remain nothing but surface ostentation, and God himself is putting on something of a show, breaststroking across the heavens. The thunderstorm gathering from the "rear abyss of things" threatens rather than rejuvenates; thus, the poet projects an escape from this world altogether, as in the glad-morning flight of the gospel song. The genuine rebirth is associated this Easter season less with nature than with what is discovered when the stone is rolled slowly away.

A month later, spring, with its "sonatina in green," is passing, and the poet hears *Eine Kleine Mittagmusik*. Still "looking around," he sees a photo of the Roman arena in Verona, which induces a brief reverie about the ghost of Catullus hovering in the distance toward Lake Garda. Catullus, along with Pound, is of course a *genius loci*, Lake Garda being the site where the muse first stirred the poet's sensibility. Reflecting on his journey since then, he sees his effort to track the myth of the eternal return as "misfortune," adding that whatever the goal of his quest has been, it is "so tiny it can dance in the palm of [his] hand."

Stanza 5 is another account of melancholy and disaffection. "This is the moment of our disregard" is an ironic inversion of the familiar religious expression, "This is the moment of our salvation." The weeds have overtaken the garden, and there is nothing to reply to and "nothing to dress us down." The last phrase is a pun, meaning, on the one hand, nothing to reprimand us for our failure, and on the other, nothing to strip away the adornments we put on to present ourselves to the world. We are, alas, caught in the "understory of our lives"—another pun (shaded growth + basement + dark narrative). To protect ourselves from this dismal state of affairs requires "proper attention," but when the poet does focus his attention on the moon, with its rain-ring aura, nothing comes of it. There are "no hieroglyphs" and "no words to the wise." Bleakness is all: thus far, looking around has provided little impetus to write about anything except the difficulty of writing about anything.

p. 3, l. 18. *Make it old*. The contrary of Pound's injunction, "Make it new," a translation from Confucius, which Pound used as the title for one of his collections of essays (New Haven: Yale University Press, 1935).

p. 4, l. 12. From the gospel song by Alfred E. Brumley: "Some glad morning when this life is o'er, / I'll fly away. / To a home on God's celestial shore, / I'll fly away. / I'll fly away, O Glory, I'll fly away. / When I die, Hallelujah, bye and bye, / I'll fly away."

Looking Around II

Orig. pub. *Poetry* 175, no. 1 (October–November 1999): 3–5.
SHS, 6–8
Pattern: 6 × 2 × 5 (60 lines)
Time: 31 May 1998–June 1998
Place: Charlottesville

The poet's glancing around for a second time generates questions we have met before: Is there anything left for the poet to see from his backyard chair that he hasn't seen before? Is it possible to discover the "tiny crack" that separates this world from the next? Is it likely that the poet will be "used for a higher good"? And then questions about the triple subject matter: "Is landscape, like God, a Heraclitean river? / Is language a night flight and sea-change?" The energy of the poem, however, comes not from these questions but from the fresh and memorable description of the landscape in each of the five stanzas. The poet may not see things he hasn't seen before, but he describes them in striking and decidedly novel ways:

- "Twilight twisting down like a slow screw / Into the balsa wood of Saturday afternoon." Compound trope, simile and metaphor: twilight *is like* a slowly twisting screw. Saturday afternoon *is* balsa wood.
- "Late Saturday afternoon, // a solitary plane / Eating its way like a moth across a bolt of dusk." Personified metaphor and simile: Saturday afternoon *is* a single airplane. The plane *is* a creature eating. The process of eating *is like* that of a moth. Dusk *is* a bolt of cloth.
- "Second-hand light, a dishcloth light, wrung out and almost gone." Metaphor: indirect or reflected light *is* a wrung-out dishcloth light.
- "Sky with its glazed look, and half-lidded." Personified metaphor: The sky *is* a person with glazed and half-opened eyes.
- "cloverheads tight, Seurating the yard, / This land-washed *jatte* fireflied and Corgied." See the introduction to the present volume for a brief discussion of these complex tropes.
- "Sky flat as a sheet, smooth as bedclothes on a dead woman's bed." Double simile, the second expanding the general flatness into a particular form of smoothness.
- "Half-moon like a cleaved ox wheel." Simple simile, though the moon as the wheel of an ox cart chopped in two is kin to the seventeenth-century metaphysical conceit.

p. 6, l. 7. *Ugo Foscolo.* Italian writer and patriot (1778–1827) who was much involved in the politics of the day. On the death of Napoleon he exiled himself to England, where he achieved considerable fame as a man of letters. But he was unable to manage his financial affairs and for a while spent time in a debtor's prison.

p. 6, l. 20. *Is landscape ... Heraclitean river?* That is, how can one capture the landscape if, as Heraclitus says, "everything flows and nothing abides" and if "you cannot step twice into the same river" (frags. 20 and 21; trans. Philip Wheelwright).

p. 6, l. 21. *Is language ... sea-change?* How is it possible for language to do its work if, one the one hand, it flies away into the darkness, and if, on the other, it issues in some dramatic transformation.

p. 7, l. 10. *César Vallejo.* Vallejo left Peru in 1923 for Paris, never to return to his native country. The anecdote about Vallejo's looking for "the tiny crack" is Wright's own invention.

p. 7, l. 20. *Machado.* The idea in the maxim here is found throughout Antonio Machado's poems: "the past has never died / nor is tomorrow—nor yesterday—yet written" (*The Iberian God*, ll. 61–2); "Tick, tock, tick, tock ... Always just the same"; "Another day / gone by like all the rest" (*One Day's Poem*, ll. 43, 186–7); "Today on the way to Tomorrow, / of Yesterday that is Still" (*From My Portfolio*, ll. 26–7), in *Selected Poems*, trans. Alan S. Trueblood [Cambridge: Harvard University Press, 1982], 109,127, 135, 215.

Looking Around III

Orig. pub. *Poetry* 175, no. 1 (October–November 1999): 6–8.
SHS, 9–11
Pattern: 5 × 2 × 6 (60 lines)
Time: Summer 1998
Place: Montana cabin

As we might expect in poems about "looking," we *hear* very little. The dogs whimper in *Looking Around*, they bark in *Looking Around II*, and the creek sings in *Looking Around III*. Otherwise, silence makes space for the image: the eye, as Heraclitus says, is a more accurate witness than the ear. Thus, the focus is on "nature" but not to the exclusion of "culture," as the poet makes room for several poetic friends: Ugo Foscolo, César Vallejo, Antonio Machado, Osip Mandelstam, and Dante. Heraclitus, as poetic as any of these, should be included in the group. Their contributions are noted below.

The poet's attitude contains a good measure of self-deprecation. We have come to expect that when he says such things as "I find I have nothing to say to any of this," he will immediately reveal that he has a great deal to say, even if the scene before him is "radiant in its disregard" (p. 11, l. 10). His confession of ignorance of the hows and whys of the Montana landscape is expanded to include his own melancholy: "I don't understand the black lake that pools in my heart." Nor do the children in the photograph (section 6) register in his consciousness. The black mood disappears, however, in the final section, where we get a succinct account of the poet's mission: "To look hard at something, to look through it, is to transform it, / Convert it into something beyond itself, to give it grace." Grace, then, in Wright's vision of things is decidedly *not* beyond the reach of art, and he anticipates the late-night landscape of meadow and mountain being shortly bathed by the brilliant moonlight and transformed into an earthly Paradise. When the poet says of Paradise, "wherever that is," we are reminded again of the speaker of Stevens's *Sunday Morning*, who asks, "And shall the earth / Seem all of paradise that we shall know?" (sect. 3, ll. 10–11).

p. 9, l. 11. *Osip Mandelstam.* "What used to be within reach—out of reach. / Flowers never die. Heaven is whole. / But ahead of us we've only somebody's word" (Poem 395, in Mandelstam's *Selected Poems*, trans. Clarence Brown and W.S. Merwin [New York: Atheneum, 1974], 100).

p. 9, 20. *Mandelstam.* "I've lost my way in the sky—now where? / Let the one with the sky nearest to him answer" (Poem 378, in *Selected Poems*, 94).

p. 10, ll. 13–15. *Dante, according to Mandelstam.* "Dante's comparisons are never descriptive, that is, purely representational. They always pursue the concrete task of presenting the inner form of the poem's structure or driving force. Let us take the very large group of 'bird' similes, all of them extensive caravans now of cranes, now of grackles, now of swallows in classical military phalanxes, now the anarchically disorderly crows so unsuited to the Latin military formation—this entire group of extended similes always corresponds to the instinct for pilgrimage, the journey, colonization, migration. Or, for example, let us take the equally large group of river similes, portraying the rise of the Apennies or the river Arno which irrigates the valley of Tuscany, or the descent of the Alpine wet nurse, the river Po, into the valley of Lombardy. This group of similes is distinguished by its extraordinary breadth and its graduated descent from tercet to tercet, always leading to a complex of culture, homeland and settled civilization, to a political and national complex, so conditioned by the watersheds and, in addition, by the power and direction of the rivers" (Osip Mandelstam, "Conversation about Dante," in *The Complete Critical Prose and Letters*, trans. Jane Gary Harris and Constance Link [Ann Arbor, Mich.: Ardis, 1979], 410).

* * *

The title of the next ten poems, "Millennium Blues," derived from a project Wright participated in, the National Millennium Survey. The project, conceived and designed by James Enyeart, director of the Marion Center in Santa Fe, NM, involved a number of photographers, writers, and video artists whose work was intended to document the breadth and diversity of American life leading up to the millennium. In 1998 Wright replied jokingly to an interviewer who asked whether the encroaching millennium was making its way into his work, that "the only millennial concern that I have, other than to be as far away from Times Square on the first of January 2000 as I can possibly get" is to complete the third trilogy, adding, "My language has been apocalyptic since 1961. Why should I try the prophet now, for just the millennium? There'll be another one" (Zawacki, 29). Each of the "Millennium Blues" poems has fourteen lines.

Citronella

Orig. pub. *Bellingham Review*, 21, no. 2 (Winter 1998–99): 16.
SHS, 15

Pattern: 4-4-4-2
Place: Charlottesville, apparently
Time: Early summer

Title: Citronella is the oil from a citronella plant, its lemon scent being used in perfumes and, as is the case here, an insect-repellant candle.

The smell of citronella enters the poem only incidentally. The poem is chiefly about things that are blank, endless, empty, and indistinct. We begin with the light on the lawn, which is identified with blank newsprint, followed by the "empty notebook" of the moon. Blankness and emptiness, motifs that continue throughout *A Short History of the Shadow*, prompt the thought of death—"When it's over it's over"—yet the poet is quick to add that death, although far removed from the seeming endlessness of youth, is still a mile or so down the road. This is followed by the metamorphosis of the empty notebook of the moon into a book of moonlight (shelved perhaps beside the Appalachian Book of the Dead), the first page of which is the present poem. The second page is yet to be written, which is reason enough to sing the millennium blues, and the poet invokes the Blessed Virgin not to forsake him before it is written and moreover to transform him into something marvelous.

p. 15, l. 14. *Beato immaculato.* The concluding prayer is addressed to the Virgin, the immaculate or blessed one.

If This Is Where God's At, Why Is That Fish Dead?

Orig. pub. in *Thumbscrew* 14 (Autumn 1999): 64.
SHS, 16
Pattern: 4-4-2-4
Time: Autumn
Place: Unspecified, though flashback to Milan

The conditional clauses that open the poem offer five views of God: as an infinite unity (the abstract philosophical view); as a presence in the empyrean (the view of cosmology and natural religion); as powers and dominions, the visible and invisible things created by God in Colossians 1:16 (creative immanence); as bed (resting place); and as held breath (*pneuma* or spirit). These possibilities do indeed provide reason "to be inquisitive," even about a dead fish. The poet's nose, still active from the previous poem, carries him back to a misty autumnal Milan. The scene in Milan is apparently one of the "twelve pictures thrown from the floating world," the "floating world" (ukiyo) being the world of transient pleasures, especially in Edo. Its images were captured in prints (*ukiyo-e*) by artists such as Utamaro and Sharaku. Japanese brides were often brought a series of twelve erotic pictures together with their wedding furniture. There is nothing particularly erotic in the description of Milan, though we are given the promising announcement that in the floating world "sin is a ladder to heaven." This is a Tower of Babel image—an antitype of Jacob's ladder with its ascending and descending angels. The last stanza returns us to a variation of the question in the title: if this is where God is, why do we live on the margins between the eastern and western gates of light. The poet grants that "that's okay": being marginal is better than being fascinated with fame (star-struck). But being okay is insufficient. Otherwise, there would be no reason for the twice-said "remember us," conventional invocations in prayers to Jesus, Mary Magdalene, and the saints.

p. 16, l. 6. *Sforza gardens.* The gardens of the Sforza Castle in Milan.
p. 16, l. 7. *Villa Gusatalla.* Historic villa in Fiorano, constructed on a plan by the architect Caspar Vigarani about 1659.

Charlottesville Nocturne

Orig. pub. in *Thumbscrew* 14 (Autumn 1999): 67.
SHS, 17
Pattern: 4-4-4-2
Time: Late September

    This nocturne contains a series of oxymorons: wounds that don't bleed, dead grass that's still green, light shining from darkness, and sunlight darkening the earth. The late September night is said to be a complete abstraction: there are no adjectives to describe it. This is one of the two themes that emerge—the faltering inadequacy of language to provide any more names and to produce texts that are not hollow. Moreover, we are unable to see or hear the language of landscape as we lean against the invisible in the waking world: "Evening arranges itself around the fallen leaves / Alphabetized across the back yard, // desolate syllables / That braille us and sign us." The other theme is that light emerges from the darkness. The world of the nocturnal dream is the locus of illumination, but then everything is thrown into darkness when the sun rises. This, then, is a Heraclitean ode to night, another lyric in the songbook of the millennium blues.

It's Dry for Sure, Dry Enough to Spit Cotton

Orig. pub. in *Thumbscrew* 14 (Autumn 1999): 66.
SHS, 18
Pattern: 4-4-4-2
Time: "summer half-gone, autumn half-here"
Place: Charlottesville

    To "spit cotton" is a colloquial phrase, dating from the mid-nineteenth century, meaning to be very thirsty or having a dry mouth, which is the condition of the speaker as he surveys the parched wasteland around him. The desire for rain, like that in Eliot's poem, is more than physical: water here is an emblem of a life-giving spiritual force. The poet wishes for rain to wash "death's birthmark" off our foreheads and rejuvenate us, just as John the Baptist appeared in another wasteland, the wilderness, proclaiming a new Exodus through the ritual of baptism in the clean waters of the Jordan.

p. 18, l. 11. *Giovanni Battista*. See Matthew 3:1–6, Mark 1:2–8, and Luke 3:1–6.

If My Glasses Were Better, I Could See Where I'm Headed For

Orig. pub. in *Thumbscrew* 14 (Autumn 1999): 65–6.
SHS, 19
Pattern: 5-4-5
Time: Autumn
Place: Charlottesville

    Night moves in the direction of the poet, whose heart seems as if it is preparing for a long journey. The passage of time is inexorable: "the days move, one at a time, // always at night, and always in my direction." The journey is toward death, just like the autumn movement toward the cessation of things: the flies and bees have already died, the birds have hibernated, the ants have gone south, and the weevils have bored their way into the trunk. Although the title indicates that the poet does not know where he is headed, the journeyman nevertheless prepares to replace his walking shoes with slippers, ready to ease into that place "where all things are forgot." In the words of the Carter Family tune, alluded to in line 11, he is preparing to cross the River Jordan. Still, there is an uncertainty about the "Gates of Mercy," a phrase floating unattached between the poet's stuttered words and the endless cycle of time. The double drop-down line at the end of stanza 2 is atypical, as is the expanded spacing between the three units in this line, suggesting that the Gates of Mercy are in a state of suspension. The poet is waiting for the end. Meanwhile, he will perform his chores and keep his attention on the drift of things.

p. 19, l. 9. *Gates of mercy.* See Thomas Gray, *Elegy in a Country Churchyard*, st. 17; see also Shakespeare, *Henry V* (3.3.10).
p. 19, l. 11. *slippers.* "I'm going to put on the silvery slippers / Oh, yes / I'm going to put on the silvery slippers / Some of these days (hallelujah) / I'm going to put on the silvery slippers / I'm going to put on the silvery slippers / Some of these days" (Stanza 4 of *River Jordan*, a Carter Family tune).

Lost Language

Orig. pub. in *Thumbscrew* 14 (Autumn 1999): 63–4.
SHS, 20
Pattern: 5–4–5
Time: October
Place: Charlottesville

As the world rumbles along through autumn, the life of the poet moves slowly, one word and one syllable at a time—and moves with difficulty as well, for whatever the poet is looking for is fragmented and distant. The struggle, nevertheless, is to slake a "thirst for the divine." Thus, he wants to settle by the river. But paradise happens to be on the other side of the river, and the "star-colored city"—which is Pound's "city of Dioce whose terraces are the colours of stars" (*Canto* 74)—remains "just out of reach."

On Heaven Considered as What Will Cover Us and Stony Comforter

Orig. pub. in *Thumbscrew* 14 (Autumn 1999): 62.
SHS, 21
Pattern: 6–2–6
Time: All Saints' Sunday 1999 = 7 November
Place: Charlottesville

This poem expands the theme of heaven from the previous one, though the view of heaven, as the title indicates, does not sound very promising. "Stony" undercuts whatever reassurance heaven might offer as a shield or veil. "Comforter" in the context of "cover" suggests the metaphor of bedclothes, but this is hardly an inviting picture of the hereafter either. A stony cover can be a tomb, so the title seems to be casting a glance at Wallace Stevens's *On Heaven Considered as a Tomb*, in which the exegetes are asked to comment on the "darkened ghosts" who walk through the night of the tomb of heaven. Do they carry lanterns to light the way? Or is there rather only a "spirituous passage into nothingness," with no light at all emanating from the lanterns of the host ghosts?

What is "longed-for" is apparently heaven or some other form of a Utopian desire. But it is tiny rather than all-encompassing, fragile rather than substantial, and the ways in which it resembles us as it shadows our pilgrimage does not offer much to recommend it. For the "longed-for" to be as "Interminable as black water, / Irreparable as dirt" makes it more demonic than paradisal, a view reinforced by the "seasonal underwork" and "burn" of the approaching autumn evening. The "longed-for" also, we are told, resembles what we have "passed on" (either bequeathed or rejected or perhaps both) and "shucked off" (either removed or cast off or perhaps both). While it is encouraging to know that the "longed-for" finds us, the fact that it "finds us out" also moves in two directions: it exposes our true nature, and it detects and apprehends us—neither a happy prospect.

If the first stanza foregrounds the insignificance of our hopes, the last foregrounds the sense of the emptiness of the earthly garden. Everyone has disappeared, and no one has left even a footprint. Here at the "last stop" of life, even the angels' wings are rolled up and their swords sheathed. The date is 7 November, All Saints' Sunday, but no saints are in evidence. Only a small light in the west will harass us home.

In the conventional myth, the Garden is our proper home, and what is "longed-for" is a return to that Garden—a state of existence before the Fall. But here it is difficult even to discover the garden when autumn is "in override," and unlike Ezekiel's vision, there are no wheels to support the divine throne—or at least no vehicle to carry us beyond the "unimaginable silence." Stony comfort, indeed.

Mildly Depressed, Far from Home, I Go Outside for a While

Orig. pub. in *Thumbscrew* 14 (Autumn 1999): 63.
SHS, 22
Pattern: 6-6-2
Time: November
Place: Charlottesville

The poet is not far from home (the place where he lives) but he is far from home (his ultimate destination). Taking stock of the moonscape from the yard, he identifies the new moon as a "script-bearer," but "buried beneath our being," no script gets carried to the surface. This awareness results in a nostalgic view, like that of his poetic forebear Mêng Hao-jan, of the wide world of the past when the Orphean song was sweet and when the trees almost touched the heavens. Writer's block triggers a sense of guilt: "Late middle age, what am I waiting for?" The poet thus expresses a wish that what was previously dear to him—the sweet melodies about the boundless and abundant world—will return. The wish is similar to the prayers that are uttered at the end of the first two of the "millennium blues" poems. The Orphean songs are now inexpressible, but they need not be. If only the muse would return.

p. 22, ll. 8–10. *How wide the world was ... eddies of heaven.* Wright's debt here is to Mêng Hao-jan's *A Night-Mooring on the Chien-tê River*: "daylight wanes, old memories begin.... / How wide the world was, how close the trees to heaven, / And how clear in the water the nearness of the moon" (*The Jade Mountain*, trans. Witter Bynner [Garden City, NY: Anchor Books, 1964], 85; ellipsis in original). Bynner's translation of three hundred poems from the T'ang period is recorded in Wright's notes (81).

Mondo Orfeo

Orig. pub. in *Photographers, Writers, and the American Scene*, ed. James L. Enyeart, et al. (Santa Fe: Arena Editions, 2002), 276.
SHS, 23
Pattern: 5-5-2-2
Time: Late November
Place: Charlottesville

The new moon has now entered its three-quarter phase, which is where we began in *Citronella* (*SHS*, 15), and Orpheus is still on the poet's mind, though the present *mondo Orfeo* lacks any of the power of the unending song in Ovid's vision of Orpheus. At the beginning, we are identified with the children of the Hindu god Prajapati, who are devotees of both the material (the tactile and the distinct) and the spiritual: the "infinite festers in our bones." We move from that duality to the poet's song, which is bitter and sour. Unlike Orpheus's, whose tongue continued to sing as it floated down the river toward Lesbos, the poet's song does not cause the trees to move. Like most of the other poems in this section ("Millennium Blues"), the poet projects an overwhelming sense of the waning world and the diminished poetic voice: the month and day are moving on their downward paths toward winter and darkness respectively, the sky is drained of its color, voices are lost, the grass is dry (*Waste Land* imagery again), the poet's song has "come to nothing," and the poem ends both in uncertainty ("what-comes-next") and entrapment ("box canyon") and with a demand for silence ("index finger to puckered lips"), whose patron saint is "Shush." All of which are, again, reasons enough for the blues, millennial or otherwise.

p. 23, l. 13. *box canyon* = dead end

p. 23, l. 3. *Acolytes of the tactile ... The infinite festers in our bones.* "We are devotees of the distinct and the articulate, but the infinite festers in our bones" (Robert Calasso, *Ka*, trans. Tim Parks [New York: Knopf, 1998], 36). These are the words of the children of Prajapati (the Hindu progenitor and lord of all creatures). The context, in Calasso's retelling of the myth, is their plan to build a brick altar of fire. They go on to say that their structure "must be wrapped in the cloud of the immeasurable and enclose the immeasurable within itself. The greatest must be embraced and contained in the smallest" (ibid.).

p. 23, l. 6. In Dryden's translation of the Orpheus story in Ovid: "And list'ning trees their rooted stations leave; / Themselves transplanting, all around they grow" (*Metamorphoses*, 10.144–5).

p. 23, l. 10. Orpheus was the son of the king of Thrace, Oeagrus.

The Secret of Poetry

Orig. pub. in *Thumbscrew* 14 (Autumn 1999); rpt. in *Photographers, Writers, and the American Scene*, ed. James L. Enyeart, et al. (Santa Fe: Arena Editions, 2002), 277.

SHS, 24

Pattern: 6–6–2

Time: Icy winter

Place: Charlottesville

Poetry can be found with a lantern, as the second Chinese speaker in Stevens's play *Three Travelers Watch a Sunrise* asserts, and from the poet's perspective it can also be found by the light of the moon, echoing what the Third Chinese speaker says: "I could find it without [a lantern] / On an August night, / If I saw no more / Than the dew on the barns." What such light reveals is a procession across the landscape, a procession of unmotivated abstractions, of the kind one finds so often in Stevens: "lunar essence, the blind structure of matter, // perfection of pain." But the secret of poetry, as against the claim of both the Chinese speakers and the poet, is that looking for poetry is no guarantee that we will find it. And even if we do hear the song of the wind across the icy landscape, it "fills our ears with no meaning," which conclusion is parallel to that of *Charlottesville Nocturne* and which makes the secret of poetry even bleaker. Lurking in the background of the poet's consciousness is surely Stevens's *The Snow Man*, with its Heideggerean punch line: "For the listener, who listens in the snow, / And, nothing himself, beholds / Nothing that is not there and the nothing that is."

p. 24, ll. 1–2. At the beginning of Wallace Stevens's *Three Travelers Watch a Sunrise*, whose dramatis personae are "three Chinese, two Negroes and a girl," a character identified as "Second Chinese" says "All you need, / To find poetry / Is to look for it with a lantern." The stage direction that follows is "The Chinese laugh" (*Collected Poetry and Prose* [New York: Library of America, 1997], 601).

In Praise of Thomas Hardy

Orig. pub. *Washington Square* 6 (Winter 2000): 13.
SHS, 27
Pattern: 8–6
Time: Winter
Place: Charlottesville

This poem begins a series of nine, published as a chapbook, *Night Music* (Exeter, Devon, England: Stride Publications, 2001), all having to with darkness of one kind or another.

The poet wonders if we can imagine what the little physics lesson in the first line actually means. We then move promptly from physics to metaphysics: the unbearable heaviness of light makes us long for darkness. The dialectic of light and darkness is at play throughout Wright's poetry, light most often associated with knowledge, psychological illumination, and the journey of ascent, and darkness with ignorance, uncertainty, and the descent into nothingness. The forces of lightness and darkness are always doing battle with one another, and neither ever dominates the other. Often, as in the black zodiac, the conventional associations are reversed: we ascend not to light but to darkness. Conversely, in Wright's view, we must often descend into the darkness in order to gain some measure of redemption. The anabatic and katabatic halves of the quest work complementarily. They are not contradictory elements in Wright's metaphysics but contrary elements, to use Blake's distinction, and "without contraries there is no progression." We can understand, then, why the present poem with its longing for inner darkness is a panegyric to Thomas Hardy. For Hardy's poetry is also attentive to the "deep shade" of life and acutely aware that death (as in *The Subalterns*) brings the pilgrimage to an end, and he never forsook his search for the God of darkness and light. So Hardy is to be praised for his generally grave, brooding, and melancholic view of reality, always with a touch of irony—all of which exist in good measure as well in Wright's poems.

The lesson in metaphysics is no less difficult for us to "try to imagine" than the lesson in physics, though the elements of the latter are not abandoned in the former. Space is the central category of the octave, and time of the sestet. We are told in the octave that "they" roll downward, "Hoping for realignment and a space that won't shine." "They" hangs in suspension, not attached to any preceding plural noun, and no candidates present themselves other than the collective souls who, unable to bear the weight of lightness, long for a darkened space.

All of this is opposed to the three negative similes of the sestet, which establish what the deep shade is not like. The October moon in its intersection with time achieves an Ovidian metamorphosis that renders things "ghostly." ("Smalled" in l. 9 is a small debt to Hardy. See the note below on Hardy's coinage, which is quite like Wright's syntactic shifts mentioned in the commentary on *Umbrian Dreams* [NB, 101]. "Deep shade" is perhaps too commonplace for Wright to have borrowed it, but it is a phrase Hardy also used.) Even the moonscape, then, offers too much light for the souls yearning for darkness. So too for the "moon-treated" leaves of the ash tree and our own shrunken selves that have been hung out to dry, apparently having been left on the line overnight. One is reminded of the shrunken "spectral manikin" in Hardy's *His Immortality*.

p. 27, l. 1. *Each second ... pounds of sunlight.* So says Gary F. Moring in *The Complete Idiot's Guide to Understanding Einstein*, 2nd ed. (New York: Alpha Books, 2004), 171.

p. 27, l. 9. *smalled.* When an editor complained of Hardy's use of the non-word "smalled" in one of his manuscripts, he invited the editor to look it up in the dictionary—where the editor found its source in Hardy himself. See Hardy's *The Dead Quire*: "There, at the turning, it was heard / Drawing to where the churchyard lay: / But when they followed thitherward / It smalled, and died away" (st. 21). He also used the word in *The Clock of the Years*.

Night Rider

Orig. pub. *The Literary Imagination* 2, no. 1 (Winter 2000): 104.
SHS, 28–31
Pattern: 5-5-5 × 5
Time: begins 31 January 1999 and moves to the end of February, the beginning of March, and then April: Year of the Rabbit (1999)
Place: Charlottesville

Against the backdrop of the moonlit night, the poet announces that he is ready to offer praise but only in a ghostly and disguised form. Similarly with prayer in the last stanza of section 1: our prayers are offered but unanswered. Between praise and prayer, neither of which is fulfilled, we have a meditation on having been called. A divine call chooses us, but the source of the call is too vague to identify. We are told only that the call comes from something (p. 28, l. 6), elevated to "Something" in the prayer (l. 11), and that the something is "not unlike unbeing"—language reminiscent of the German mystics, *The Cloud of Unknowing*, and even Heidegger. This is the *deus absconditus*. We are summoned as well by the "lure of the incidental" at one extreme, and by "immensity" at the other. However difficult it is to specify the source of the call, none of us can escape being "chosen," no matter whether we have or have not turned our backs on memory. As Lancelot Andrewes said, "He is found of them who seek Him not; but of them who seek Him, never but found" (Sermon preached on Easter, 1620). In the present poem heaven and earth have passed away (l. 14), but whereas Jesus says that after such passage his words shall remain (Matthew 24:35), here in place of that assurance we have only a failure to understand (l. 15).

The rest of *Night Rider* intersperses similar meditations with brief descriptions of the landscape: sunrise and sunfall, the swaying and "unmended trees," more moonlight, the Rivanna River flowing through Charlottesville, silent night with the pagan stars, the frosted grass and the crocus heads. The themes, which the poet advances with help from the unlikely combination of the *Nag Hammadi Library*, Robert Calasso's reading of Hindu and Vedic sacred texts, and a blues song by Robert Johnson, are familiar: the difficulty of the poet's getting it right, the shortness of time in which to get it all done; the lack of preparation; the ironic resolution, in consequence, only to tinker around; and the awareness of "more shadow than light, more shade than dark" on the text of the landscape's page. The poet concludes by saying, "If I could do what I thought I could do, I would leave no trace," but of course he has left more than a trace with this poem and those that follow.

Wright on Wright: Willard Spiegelman began an interview with Wright by asking about *Night Rider*, "You seem to be veering with a bit of wariness toward the millennium, don't you agree? This poem rehearses so many of your perennial concerns, themes, and techniques that I am tempted to call it a summary as well as an introduction to 'Charles Wright.' What would you say to someone reading you—this poem, in this journal—for the first time?" Wright's reply: "Well, I guess I'd say that the poem is representative, or at least indicative, of manners, matters, and motions I have come to believe are important to me (and, I guess, by extension, my work). And which I try to give tongue to. I hope it would show what I think is my trademark system of sound patterns, lineation, and verbal structure. I suppose I would say they should read the 'dropped' lines as extensions of the lines they are dropped from, with a rather pronounced caesura. I suppose I would say that the sound pattern runs from stanza to stanza throughout the whole poem, and not just within each isolated stanza. And I suppose I would say that the concerns the poem is confronting, which it talks about, are, as you suggest, continuing ones for me, and are likely to remain so. When one imagines one has the beast in view, it seems silly and sloppy to suddenly go in another direction.

"As for the millennium, I'm not sure what you mean. It's true the poem seems to lug out toward the end of something, but I'm not sure it's the millennium. One religion's millennium is another religion's lunch. The end is not an abstraction, no matter how much we would like it to be. And no matter how much they keep telling us it is. And as for veering warily toward it, I veer warily toward everything, particularly things with double double consonants.

"But in the end I'd have to agree with you, I suppose, that 'Night Rider' has the trappings, at least, of a summation of some of my more recent, and more sticky, concerns. It certainly doesn't encompass everything I've worked through over the years, but a right smart amount. As to what I would say to someone, I guess I'd say to look upon it as an outpost, not an empire, and don't despair" (Spiegelman, 108–9).

p. 28, ll. 16–20. The "book" referred to here is *The Apocryphon of John* (*Nag Hammadi Library*), and the passage is this: "And the man came forth because of the shadow of the light which is in him. And his thinking was superior to all those who had made him. When they looked up, they saw that his thinking was superior. And they took counsel with the whole array of archons and angels. They took fire and earth and water and mixed them together with the four fiery winds. And they wrought them together and caused a great disturbance. And they brought him (Adam) into the shadow of death, in order that they might form (him) again from earth and water and fire and the spirit which originates in matter, which is the ignorance of darkness and desire, and their counterfeit spirit. This is the tomb of the newly-formed body with which the robbers had clothed the man, the bond of forgetfulness; and he became a mortal man. This is the first one who came down, and the first separation. But the Epinoia of the light which was in him, she is the one who was to awaken his thinking" (NHL, 116–17).

p. 28, l. 1. *finocchio*. A variety of fennel whose blanched aromatic, celery-like stalks are eaten as a vegetable. Also called *Florence fennel, sweet fennel*.

p. 29, ll. 8–9. *I am the undefiled ... exists in me*. From *The Apocryphon of John*, NHL, 105, 106). Jesus speaks these words to John.

p. 29, l. 13. The left-hand/right-hand allusion is perhaps to Matthew 6:2–4, but Wright may well be drawing on saying 62 in the *Gospel of Thomas*: "Jesus said: I speak my mysteries to those [who are worthy of my] mysteries. What your right hand does, let not your left hand know what it does" (NHL, 133).

p. 30, l. 16. *Still night, unholy night*. This is a play on the German title of the Christmas carol, *Stille Nacht, Heilige Nacht*. The night is "unholy" because the stars are pagan, not those of Bethlehem. "*Still*" means both "without movement" and "yet."

p. 30–1. *The sacrifice of the horse*. "As long as it continues to wander, the sacrificial horse is like the young Siddhārtha in the park of his father's palace. He too is escorted, he too is secretly led in order that he not see anything: the horse in order that he not encounter mares or water: the Buddha in order that he not encounter old age, illness, or death. But both will encounter what they should not: the horse on his return to the place of sacrifice; Siddhārtha, by chance, in a corner of the park. The Buddha is Tathāgata, 'He-who-came-thus.' The horse is 'he who has been led' (meaning to the sacrificial pole). In those two verbs ('came,' 'led') lies the difference between the two. One emerges from thick forest, like a common pilgrim: thus does the Buddha reappear to his companions—and risks not being recognized. The horse too reappears from thick forest, to find himself once again in the place of sacrifice from whence he set out, as if he had come back by chance, but behind him, imperceptible, his escort has been guiding his wanderings. Blessed are the footsteps of both the one and the other, the Buddha and the horse" (Roberto Calasso, *Ka: Stories of the Mind and Gods of India* [New York: Knopf, 1998], 136–7). Chapter 7 of Calasso's book is devoted to the strange ritual of the sacrifice of the horse, drawn from the *Mahābhārata* and various other Hindu sutras and Vedic texts.

p. 31, l. 9. In February Venus is only about 15 degrees above the horizon. In the Chinese zodiac, the Year of the Rabbit begins on 16 February, according to the lunar calendar.

p. 31, l. 13. *Robert Johnson* (1911–38). An early blues singer from Mississippi, often dubbed the father of modern rock and roll. "If I Had Possession over Judgment Day" is one of his songs. He traveled from town to town, jumping trains throughout the Mississippi Delta and singing in front of small gatherings. His songs are haunted by apocalyptic and supernatural images.

Is

Orig. pub. *Valparaiso Poetry Review* 2, no. 2 (Spring–Summer 2001).
SHS, 32
Time: March–April 1999
Place: Charlottesville

"Is" serves as the copula that, among other things, identifies the two halves of metaphor. The verb occurs eleven times in the poem—fourteen if we count the plural form—and in several lines where the syntax is clipped "is" is implicit. The poem contains "is" as a metaphorical link ("transcendence is a young man's retreat," "March is our medicine") and as indicating a certain state or quality of existence ("March is cold"). "Is" also functions with the impersonal substantive "it," which fills in the slot ordinarily occupied by nouns ("it is we"). In substantives, nothing is being either identified or predicated by "is." The title calls our attention to the metaphorical function of "is" and to the state of human identity under the burden of consciousness. We speak of human character as "personal identity," and it should not escape our notice that we are what we identify with, which is another form of the X = Y principle of metaphor.

The poem itself sets up a series of comparisons among three things: transcendence, human beings (the "we" of the poem), and the natural world. We think that transcendence, which is in a "place beyond place," is absent, but it is really we who are absent. We are *like* March in being cold, colorless, and present in the material world. We are *unlike* March in that while we await deliverance, the seasonal cycle, as it moves toward April's many colors, anticipates nothing: the seasonal changes recur with no reference to us or to a sense of transcendence. The seasons are *unlike* us in that they are always dressed out in their fine clothes, whereas we have only our "marly shoes" and "grass hair." For nature, transcendence has nothing to do with things that lie beyond ordinary perception but only with the process of moving from one season to the next—the cyclical *ricorso*. For us, however, the idea of transcendence comes with the burden of consciousness—a burden because we never know what to expect (will we be delivered?) from some transcendent power that hums along "without mercy" for us poor souls.

Wright's note cites Annie Dillard's, *For the Time Being* (New York: Vintage, 1999), a source for the poem's motifs of hiddenness and absence and the "young man's retreat" (see, especially, chaps. 5 and 6). For example: "God is spirit, spirit expressed infinitely in the universe, who does not give us as the world gives. His home is absence, and there he finds us. In the coils of absence we meet him by seeking him" (139-40). "We live in all we seek. The hidden shows up in too-plain sight. It lives captive on the face of the obvious—the people, events, and things of the day—to which we as sophisticated children have long since become oblivious. What a hideout: Holiness lies spread and borne over the surface of time and stuff like color" (172).

p. 32, l. 12. The reference is to Joseph's coat of many colors (Genesis 37:3).

Polaroids

Orig. pub. *Five Points* 4, no. 2 (Winter 2000): 13.
SHS, 33-5
Pattern: 6-6 × 5 (60 lines)
Time: Summer 1999
Place: Montana cabin

Title: The primary reference is to instant photographs, a metaphor for the verbal pictures of landscape in each of the five vignettes. The photograph is a spatial representation of a moment in time, time and space being the two fundamental philosophical categories we use to make sense of the world—or try to. ("Space is an anagram of "scape" (scene, view), the kind of accidental resemblance that Joyce would exploit for the surplus of meaning it suggests.)

We are told at the beginning of the poem that landscape is insoluble and at the end that time is insoluble as well, especially as we move into its "growing numbness." Section 1 is about the difficulty of deciphering the landscape, which is "heavy and wan, / Sunk like a stone in the growing night, / Snuffed in the heart like a candle flame that won't come back." Still, we must try to contemplate what we see in the world and what we do not see, resetting the "weight of glory" in our hearts by seeking analogies between the material and the spiritual, or at least between things in the middle world and the worlds below and above, comparing "The stone to the dark of the earth, the flame to the star."

Section 2 is about repetition. The poet opens with a declaration resembling a Zen koan: "Those without stories are preordained to repeat them." If you have no stories, there is obviously nothing to repeat, so what is the poet's point? It is obviously not that he has spent time repeating nothing over and over again. The significance of the epigram turns on the meaning of "stories." In the introduction we glanced at the difference between plot in Aristotle's sense and story as meaning any narrative movement from point A to B. Wright's gnomic utterance, then, means that those without stories in the first sense (*mythos* as story-telling) are bound to repeat their stories in the second sense (*mythos* as linear movement, quest, or pilgrimage). Thus we have in the second stanza of section two the catalogue of mysterious things we tend to repeat, which is a sampler or short history of the subjects of Wright's own poetry: charm, mercy, cross-work, signature, catechism, causes of pain, ghosts of things, and summer's green.

Section 3 carries us to the wilderness area of Lincoln County, Montana, where the poet's reflections on order and permanence lead to a dialectic of nature and culture. Order and permanence are obvious in the starry heavens and the enduring cycles of the seasons. Still, the poet has not been cured of his longing for order, nor has he experienced an epiphany that might be recorded in the "artifice" of his poems. The word "artifice" calls up the images of the Florentine masters and the multi-leveled Fort Belvedere with its ramparts overlooking the city of Florence—one of the most quintessential cities of order and permanence, set against the garden of green hills and bisected by the wandering River Arno. The city, then, with its golden-framed treasures and its architectural structures, is just as much an object of order and permanence as the "night sky just north of Mt. Caribou" and the "Mayfire green" of the Italian hills.

The focus of section 4 is on silence in the "blue cathedral" of the wordless Montana summer. The landscape may be wordless, but it is worthy of words and the rest of the poem gives us a series of polaroids, taken through the unmullioned window of the Montana cabin. A sense of mortality hovers in the wings and then emerges center stage in the concluding two lines: we will die into the "numbness of time," as Mandelstam says, as mysteriously and indistinctly as we presently live in the landscape of landscape.

p. 33, l. 9. *weight of glory*. "For our light affliction, which is but for a moment, worketh for us a far more exceeding and eternal weight of glory" (2 Corinthians 4:17). C.S. Lewis used the phrase for a book title, referring to the Christian's responsibility.

p. 33, l. 20. *mojo*. A charm or amulet thought to have magic powers; power or luck, as of magical or supernatural origin; the word is thought to be of Creole origin; a *misericorda* (merciful) means the relaxation of monastic rules and by extension it refers to a small projection on the bottom of a hinged church seat that gives support to a standing worshiper when the seat is turned up.

p. 34, l. 6. *Mt. Caribou*. Caribou Mountain is just south of the Canadian border between Blacktail and Caribou Creeks, about four miles, as the crow flies, from the Wrights' cabin in Lincoln County, Montana.

p. 34, l. 14. *The Arno, as Dino said, like a dithering snake.... various universe*. The simile comes from Campana's *Oscar Wilde at San Miniato*: "The monstrous river glistened listlessly like a scaly serpent" (l. 11) and *Hoodlum Nocturne*: "the monstrous / River glistened like a scaly serpent" (ll. 3–4). See the two poems from *Hard Freight* that were written "After Dino Campana": *Notes for Oscar Wilde at San Miniato* ("the river / Flashes and burns like a snake" [*HF*, 39]) and *Nocturne* ("The Arno, glittering snake" [*HF*, 41]). The simile does not appear in Wright's translation of the *Orphic Songs*, but note the one place in the *Songs* where the Arno moves away from Florence toward silence: "Here [in Florence] the Arno has fresh ripplings still: later it takes on the silence of deeper places: in the channels between low monotonous hills nudging the little Etruscan cities, level now all the way to its mouth, leaving behind the white trophies of Pisa, the precious duomo traversed with its colossal beams, holding in its nakedness such vast breath from the sea. At Signa in the continuous assonantal musical humming I remember that deep silence: silence of a buried epoch, silence of a buried civilization" (*Orphic Songs*, trans. Charles Wright [Oberlin, Ohio: Oberlin College, 1984], 80).

p. 34, l. 17. *purple lupin* = a spike-shaped wildflower; *dog rose* = a deciduous shrub with strong arching branches that spreads along woodland margins.

p. 34, ll. 18–19. *the folded hands ... gentle monk*. "A gentle monk / Folds dead hands" (Georg Trakl, *Transfiguration*, in *Poems*, trans. Lucia Getsi [Athens, OH: Mundus Artium Press, 1973], 121).

p. 35, l. 16. *Mandelstam*. "I've gone, like the martyr of light and shade, / like Rembrandt, into a growing numbness of time" (Poem 364 in Mandelstam's *Selected Poems*, trans. Clarence Brown and W.S. Merwin [New York: Atheneum, 1974], 91).

Nostalgia

Orig. pub. *Valparaiso Poetry Review* 2, no. 2 (Spring–Summer 2001).
SHS, 36–7
Pattern: 3–1 × 5

The poem turns on an extended metaphysical conceit: nostalgia as a wave. It hits us when we least expect it, it breaks up and re-forms and foams and, after its "dog-teeth" have grabbed us and held on, smoothes out the debris on the shore. We take pleasure in nostalgic moments because they create a sense that the past was better than the present. And we take pleasure as well in the surprise afforded by the shadow of nostalgia's wave. Some say that as we grow older nostalgia will outweigh whatever "living existence" we place on the scales of our hearts—the second conceit. But this is a moment the poet, favoring the reality of the present over the idealizing of the past, prays will never arrive. Nostalgia is really the impetus for memory, which Wright is forever honoring. Memory is the mental repository of the past. As the future is unknown and the present is always fleeting, the rear-view mirror is all we have.

A Short History of the Shadow

Orig. pub. *Yale Review* 88, no. 4 (October 2000): 21–2.
SHS, 38–9
Pattern: 10 × 4
Time: Late November, early December
Place: Charlottesville

In this title poem the black zodiac is turned upside down. The perspective is earthly and purgatorial. "Shadow" and its cognates are familiar words in Wright's poetry, occurring more than 130 times (thirty times in this book), often used figuratively. Its meaning in the present, highly associative lyric is itself somewhat shadowy, and the poem as a whole is difficult, but the following observations seem warranted. Wright's idea of the shadow

• is not related to the idea of illusion, as we find it represented by the shadows on the wall in Plato's allegory of the Cave.

• is not connected to Jung's notion of the Shadow as the dark, repressed aspects of our unconscious.

• does not perform any of the phantom-like roles attributed to the Shadow in Eliot's *The Hollow Men*, even though the poem does echo certain motifs from Eliot (e.g., the purification of "the dialect of the tribe" in *Little Gidding*, sect. 2).

• functions in a purgatorial context. The "underworld" in line 2 is not Hell or Hades but what Wright called "living existence" in *Nostalgia*. This is the "real" world, with its "vague shapes and black holes," far removed from the resplendent heaven, which is only virtual. Or at least the shadow is "one part of us that's real" (p. 39, l. 8).

- is associated, though not identified, with the body. Just as Dante's body in Purgatory casts a shadow, as opposed to the dead shades who *are* shadows, so too in this life the body of each of us is a "shadow of flesh." Again, the shadow is not a matter of the body in some otherworldly form.
- reveals that as the purgatorial light and fire become greater, the shadow does not lessen but increases. Here Wright adapts Leon Battista Alberti's idea on painting for his own ends. Darkness is born of light, which reverses the opposite maxim—light is born of darkness—that we find elsewhere in Wright.
- is visible but carries with it an awareness of an invisible presence. The poet does not yet have the language to describe this presence: "A word I don't know yet, a little word, containing infinity." But he hopes that his utterance, not yet liberated from beneath his tongue, will be purified when there is sufficient fire and light. Even a large purification, of the kind embodied in the lines from The Gospel of Philip, may be forthcoming.

Title: A Short History of the Shadow is also the title of a book by Victor I. Stoichita (London: Reaktion Books, 1997), a study of the shadow as it appears in art.

p. 38, l. 5. *Pantops ... Free Bridge.* Pantops Drive and Free Bridge are in Charlottesville.

p. 38, ll. 9–10. *Through water ... what is hidden.* "It is through water and fire that the whole place is purified—the visible by the visible, the hidden by the hidden. There are some things hidden through those visible. There is water in water, there is fire in chrism" (*Gospel of Philip*, NHL, 144). "Chrism" (lit., "an anointing") = olive oil often mixed with balsam, used in various ecclesiastical rites.

p. 39, l. 2. *L'ombra della carne.* As translated, "the shadow of the flesh." See *Purgatorio* 3, ll. 20–21, where Dante, still in a physical body, is the only one casting a shadow. Dante uses the phrase in *Paradiso* 19: "Lume non è, se non vien dal sereno / che non si turba mai; anzi è tenèbra / od ombra de la carne o suo veleno" ("There is no light but comes from the serene / That never is o'ercast, nay, it is darkness / Or shadow of the flesh, or else its poison"), ll. 64–6. Cf. *Purgatorio* 5, ll. 31–4.

p. 39, ll. 16–17. *Leon Battista Alberti says ... from the sun.* "Some lights are from the stars, as from the sun, from the moon and that other beautiful star Venus. Other lights are from fires, but among these there are many differences. The light from the stars makes the shadow equal to the body, but fire makes it greater" (Leon Battista Alberti, *On Painting*, trans. John R. Spencer, rev. ed. [New Haven: Yale University Press, 1966], 50).

River Run

Orig. pub. *St. Luke's Review*
SHS, 40
Pattern: 5-4-5
Place: Charlottesville

The title is perhaps a nod to Joyce's "riverrun," the first word of *Finnegans Wake*.

The theme of the poem is yearning for—even anticipating—life on the other side of the river, Wright's well-worn metaphor for the hereafter. The longing turns into a projection about the other world, the lights and trees of the Charlottesville nighttime transforming themselves into precious stones and thrones—imagery drawn from the Book of Revelation. In Locra, the waiting is for salvation, though for the poet the longing, as it has appeared in his own verse, cannot be so specified because what is desired in unavailable: it has been "written, erased, then written again" and has apparently produced such abandoned titles as "Lost and Unknown" and "Master of the Undeciphered Parchment."

Variations on a Theme. The metaphor of "the other side" turns up in the title poem of *The Other Side of the River*, and variations appear, for example, in these lines: "Thinking of Dante is thinking about the other side / And the other side of the other side" (*Southern Cross*), "no one could answer back from the other side" (*Italian Days*), "the other side of the sky" (*To Giacomo*

Leopardi in the Sky), "Sky like a sheet of carbon paper // repeating our poor ills / On the other side" (*A Journal of One Significant Landscape*), "set to set foot on the other side" (*Opus Posthumous*), "supplicant whispers for the other side" (*The Appalachian Book of the Dead III*), "The Chinese can guide you to many things, // but the other side's not one of them" (*Spring Storm*), "someone, somewhere, is putting his first foot, then the second, / Down on the other side" (*American Twilight*), "Some poems exist still on the other side of our lives" (*Body and Soul*), "Look for us soon on the other side"; "Past midnight's the other side" (*Buffalo Yoga*), and "Expecting our father at any moment, like Charon, to appear / Back out of the light from the other side" (*Archaeology*).

p. 40, l. 3. *Like Lorca ... the other side.* "Our people cross their arms in prayer, look at the stars, and wait in vain for a sign of salvation" (qtd. in Christopher Mauer's Introduction to Lorca's *Collected Poems* [New York: Farrar Straus Giroux, 1991], xix). Wright first used the line in *East of the Blue Ridge, Our Tombs Are in the Dove's Throat* (*NB*, 43).

p. 40, l. 9. *hushed in a brown study.* Silenced in an idle or gloomy reverie.

p. 40, l. 13. *It's not the bullet ... hole.* The title of Laurie Anderson's first single recording (1977).

Appalachian Lullaby

Orig. pub. *Yale Review* 88, no. 4 (October 2000): 23–4.
SHS, 41–2
Pattern: 3 × 7
Time: Childhood
Place: Kingsport

As the poet is lulled to sleep, what begins and ends as the "sweet repose" of the approaching darkness is interrupted by three reveries. The first is of his parents and sister, contained by their private lullabies, drifting off to sleep in their separate rooms. The second is the poet's vision of death: he hears the gates of life close sharply as he makes his exodus across the Red Sea and into the promised land. The third, which is more ominous and which undercuts the vision of the promised land, comes when the poet is completely enveloped in darkness: time, the highway of life, lies before him, but it is too dark to make any progress, and the destination changes from the promised land to a vague "Somewhere." Hesiod's *Works and Days* flashes across his waning consciousness, but in the poet's version there are only three ages: birth, life, and death, or in the poet's colloquial manner of speaking, "We come, we hang out, we disappear"—a parody of Caesar's well-known tag. This depressing shorthand, with the additional note that the innumerable stars "can't be counted on," is muted by the concluding description of death as a "deep and a sweet repose."

p. 41, l. 2. *shadows in ecstasy.* An echo of the title of Charles Williams's novel *Shadows of Ecstasy*.

Night Music

Orig. pub. *Ohio Review*, Thirtieth Anniversary Issue. 64 (2001): 493.
SHS, 43
Pattern: 7 × 3
Time: Summer
Place: Charlottesville, apparently

This poem is an ironic version of our most celebrated example of night music, Mozart's charming serenade, *Eine kleine Nachtmusik*. There is an echo too of the "everlasting Night" in Novalis's *Hymns to the Night* (1800). The anaphora in stanza 1 begins and ends with thoughts of darkness. The four movements of Mozart's nocturne are here reduced a curious assortment of four sounds: (1) those of the tree frogs, (2) the "voices and little outcries" of anonymous bodies "Graffitied with desolation," (3) a "few rehearsals among the insects," and (4) the voice of the savior from The Book of Thomas the Contender. The two lines quoted from this text in the Nag Hammadi Library are part of a series of interjections predicting calamity for those who have rejected the savior's call to hear the word that will redeem them from their alienation. If "The world's a slick rock we've got to cross" in an abiding darkness, revealing only a "narrow and shapeless place," our chances of making it across are slim at best. Or fat. In any event, the words of the savior fall on deaf ears, as the "thing invisible is brought to naught" amid the darkness, and we are told, "This is the way it all ends," not with a bang or even a whimper. So concludes the series of the nine poems in the "Night Music" section.

p. 43, l. 6. *I think ... miles away.* "And the wind, that has come a thousand miles" (Li Po, *The Moon at the Fortified Pass*, in *The Jade Mountain*, trans. Witter Bynner [Garden City, NY: Doubleday, 1964], 46).

p. 43, l. 9. *The air ... with light.* "Who is this who came / Who makes the air tremble with panting?" (Guido Cavalcanti, the opening lines of Poem 4, in *The Complete Poems* [New York: Italica Press, 1992], p. 11).

p. 43, ll. 16–17. *Woe to you ... in your mind.* "Woe to you within the fire that burns in you, for it is insatiable! Woe to you because of the wheel that turns in your minds!" These are the words of the "savior" in *The Book of Thomas the Contender*, NHL, 205).

Thinking of Wallace Stevens at the Beginning of Spring
Orig. pub. *Field* 63 (Fall 2000).
SHS, 47
Pattern: 5 × 2

This is the first of eleven poems in a section of *A Short History of the Shadow* called "Relics."

To have Wallace Stevens staring over your shoulder can be intimidating. In this case it leads to another *ars poetica* poem, the upshot of which is the failure of language to describe the familiar things around us. The "dark musician chording the sacred harp" recalls Stevens's "metaphysician in the dark, twanging / An instrument, twanging a wiry string" (*Of Modern Poetry*, ll. 19–20). But Stevens's metaphysician, whose sounds pass "through sudden rightnesses, wholly," has greater success than Wright's "dark musician" whose lyric notes are an apocryphon, a book with sealed secrets. Words disguise the identity we try to give to things. Thus, "weather" becomes "abject," "descriptions" become "perverse," and "scales" become "inordinate." So the poem is a virga, evaporating before it reaches the ground, and our reaching up with our palms outstretched to receive it goes for naught.

In *Description without Place* Stevens writes that "Description is revelation ... the thesis of the plentifullest John" (sect. 7, ll. 1, 12), referring to John of Patmos, the author of the Book of Revelation. John's apocalypse contains descriptions aplenty. The Book of Revelation is also an apocryphon, its secret message being symbolized by the seals, though much of what John writes about has to do with the removal of the seals. But in the poem what issues from "the sacred harp" remains a secret, pressed within the pages of the "still darker book of revelation."

p. 47, l. 1. *There is so much ... warm.* Cf. the first line of Stevens's *Debris of Life and Mind*: "There is so little that is close and warm."

p. 47, l. 4. *spittle of notes.* Cf. Stevens's "spittle of cows" (*Depression before Spring*, l. 5)

p. 47, l. 9. *virga.* Wisps of precipitation evaporating before reaching the ground.

Relics
Orig. pub. *New Yorker* 76, no. 22 (7 August 2000): 58–9; *PN Review* 27, no. 1 (September–October 2000).

SHS, 48–9
Pattern: 6 × 5
Time: Late April
Place: Charlottesville

What we write, the poet declares, are relics of things that "are always stronger than the thing itself," such as the incompletely erased script of a parchment or the underlying image of a painting. Our writing, in other words, will always be overwritten by something else and so fade into the background; thus, it does not matter what we write. This is a reversal, like the position taken in *Lives of the Saints* (NB, 103), of the permanence of the word: the usual convention is that we can counter morality by what lives on, as Shakespeare says, in the black ink of our rhymes. But the self-effacing poet has no such confidence.

The connection of relics with saint's bones leads by association, in the second stanza, to the curious odor emitted by the dogwoods, which is like the faint smell left by some passing saint, the odor of Paradise. This in turn triggers to the anecdote reported by Aldo Buzzi, which in the following two stanzas Wright reproduces almost completely from *A Weakness for Almost Everything*. Here "relics" refers to something cherished rather than a corpse. In the last stanza the poet seems to have determined that it does make a difference what one writes, and he gives himself three lines to write it. As in the previous poem, the language of landscape is a foreign tongue, "humming a speech we do not speak." Nevertheless, the reader is enjoined, not to pray for us (poets) in the dark hours of our need, but to listen for us. The injunctions in the last line are intriguingly ambiguous: listen in our stead, becoming our substitutes for hearing things; or else be on the lookout for what we have to say; or both.

p. 48, l. 1. *Hoss.* We are collectively addressed as "Hoss," the nickname of the gentle and good-natured Cartwright son in the *Bonanza* series.

pp. 48–9, ll. 12–24. *As though some saint ... penthouse in Milan.* "Some saints, when they are alive, give off a very faint aroma, which the faithful call the odor of paradise, the odor of heaven, the odor of sanctity. 'What is this odor of paradise like?' someone who had smelled it had asked. 'I don't know how to describe it,' he answered, 'because it doesn't resemble the scent of any flower or spice on earth.' Saint Gaspare del Bufalo was one of these fragrant saints. In addition, he walked in the rain without an umbrella and stayed dry. He transmitted this miraculous talent to his secretary, the venerable Giovanni Merlini. We all know about Saint Gaspare because he lived in a time not very distant from ours: the last century. I know a relative of his, a pianist who lives in a lovely apartment in downtown Milan.... The pianist invited me to dinner. She brought to the table a marvelous veal shank—the part from which the butcher usually gets the osso buco [beef leg]—roasted whole, with a divine sauce" (Aldo Buzzi, "Notes on Life," in *A Weakness for Almost Everything* [South Royalton, VT: Steerforth Press, 1999], 40).

Why, It's as Pretty as a Picture

Orig. pub. *New Yorker* 76, no. 37 (4 December 2000): 52; *Thumbscrew* 18 (Spring 2001).
SHS, 50–1
Pattern: 5 × 5
Time: Late spring
Place: Charlottesville

The trite commonplace of the title, as is often the case with Wright's quirky titles, is belied by the serious subject of the poem, which is about what Aristotle called *melos*, *lexis*, and *opsis*— what we hear in the poem, what we understand from the words, and what we see (music, diction, and image). The poet announces that he is a "shallow thinker" and is attuned not so much to ideas (Aristotle's *dianoia*) as to the music that surrounds him. Such music—the chatting birds, the moaning grass, the barking dogs, the traffic noise—relieves him of having to contemplate some "overwhelming design" in the landscape. The random "dark music," filtering through the dusk, is sufficient, and the point about *melos* is well illustrated in the slow and alliterative melody of the first two stanzas.

Stanza 3 begins with a version of W.C. Williams's "Not ideas but things": write not about your ideas, which may turn out to be shallow, but about the things in the natural world that surround you—what you hear and see. This will issue in "a kind of believing without belief." That is, one can depict poetically the existence of the landscape without avowing anything about its truth or ontological status. As Sidney says, "The poet never affirmeth."

Wright is not saying that the poet is mindless (his own poetry is filled to overflowing with ideas). Rather he is saying, as we see in the postcard simile, that the content of the image is not solely intellectual. Landscape is poised like a postcard, halfway between the mind and what brings the landscape into focus, the mind's eye. But the poet is not satisfied with this account of things, for the idea of the landscape as suspended between thought and image is only half right. (We get three different contexts for "half" in the poem: quantitative, "half again"; spatial, "halfway"; and purely descriptive, "half-moon."). A more fully accurate account of the language of landscape reveals that there is a "place" different from that occupied by the postcard. This is the place of the imagination. The poet began with the Coleridgean idea of the imagination as a perceptive faculty. But Coleridge said that the imaginative is also a creative faculty, and this is what the poet finally embraces: words reveal the place (external nature) inside the place (perceived by the mind's eye) inside the place (the imagination as creative power). The "other eye" and "other ear" are the imagination's perceptive faculties. What enables the dawn and sunset to "radiate from it [the perception of landscape] like Eden" is the creative faculty—what Coleridge called "a repetition in the finite mind of the eternal act of creation in the infinite I AM." This *ars poetica* poem turns out to reject the notion of beauty as a pretty picture (the postcard view) in favor of a much richer idea, one not solely visual or aural or mental but imaginative. If this is a shallow idea, then Blake and Coleridge and Wordsworth were shallow thinkers. The final simile, "like Eden," is not innocent. The imagination can create anything, including the world we would like to live in.

Nine-Panel Yaak River Screen

Orig. pub. *Poetry* 178, no. 3 (June 2001): 125–9.
SHS, 52–6
Pattern: 6–6 × 9
Time: Late June
Place: Montana

We move from Charlottesville to the Yaak River valley, where the poet paints nine scenes, as if on a nine-panel Chinese screen, borrowing an occasional line from Trakl and Mandelstam. A number of separate images from the anguished poetry of Trakl haunt the poem: dead children and other corpses, eyelids and mouths, angels and shadows, blackbirds, swallows, and bats. Beneath the images of the northwestern Montana landscape runs the imagery of death, or at least an awareness of the end of things, revealing the presence of Trakl in the poet's consciousness, is present in each of the nine "panels."

- the murmurs of the creek like the lamentation of women, and the awareness of the heart's thudding inside its chambers
- the mother's "shade" and the creeping of the hands of the clock in the "climb north, toward midnight"; the gathering of their dark robes by the shadows of the afternoon
- the anticipation by the poet of his rising from the dead

- the falling away of the world from us as if we were dead; the child's grave
- the sense of being pulled downward
- the gnawing of time on our necks; the eyelids of dead boys
- the coffin-like illusion that something is missing; the double darkness and "what follows that"
  - St. Thomas's hand in the wound of the dead Christ; the chambers of the afterlife
  - the black voyage; sounds that are like a rising corpse

A second motif is the inadequacy of language. In "panel" three, the poet has difficulty remembering the word he will use to fill "a small hole in the silence" when he is resurrected, and as the sunlight settles across the meadow, he realizes that our language for both sorrow and joy is inadequate. In "panel" five, he observes that as he walks through "the day's dactyls and anapests" there is a "widening caesura with each step"; and he notes as well that he is only an interruption in somebody else's story. In "panel" seven, "Our lips form fine words, / But nothing comes out. / Our lips are messengers, but nothing can come out." And in the final "panel" the poet's mouth begins to open but "No words appear on its lips, // no syllables bubble along its tongue." In counterpoint to the gloomy vision that dominates the poem are the descriptions of landscape with their usual freshness and ingenuity, often startling in their originality.

p. 52, l. 8. *Reeds rustle ... their heads.* "The reeds rustle softly / In the stillness of the moor" (Georg Trakl, *On the Moor*, in *Poems*, trans. Lucia Getsi [Athens, OH: Mundus Artium Press, 1973], 95).

p. 52, l. 9. *Creek waters ... lamentation of women.* "the blue spring murmurs the lamentation of women" (Georg Trakl, *On the Mönchsberg*, in *Poems*, 97).

p. 52, ll. 15–17. *middle arch ... swallow unstill.* Cf. "Beneath the whitewashed arch / Where in and out the swallow flew" (Georg Trakl, *Evening in Lans*, in *Poems*, 95).

p. 53, l. 23. *In some other poem.* The poem is Georg Trakl's *In the Village*, in *Poems*, 67–9, where through the wind and snow of a winter evening "emerges a black angel."

p. 54, ll. 4–5, 9. "Orioles in the woods: the length of vowels alone / makes the meter of the classic lines / ... The day yawns like a caesura" (Osip Mandelstam, *Selected Poems*, trans. Clarence Brown and W.S. Merwin [New York: Atheneum, 1974], 7).

p. 55, l. 1 *The white eyelids of dead boys.* "Silently the myrtle blooms over the white eyelids of the dead" (Georg Trakl, *Springtime of the Soul*, in *Poems*, 143).

p. 55, ll. 10–12, p. 56, ll. 14–17. "You left me my lips, and they shape words, even in silence" (Mandelstam, *Selected Poems*, 78). "The horizon lies open, messenger / of no message" (ibid., 85). See also Poem 129, p. 41, and Poem 387, pp. 97–8.

p. 55, l. 20. *St. Thomas's hand ... wound.* "The hand of St. Thomas touches the wound" (Georg Trakl, *Mankind*, in *Poems*, 45). See also John 20:27–9.

The Wind Is Calm and Comes from Another World

Orig. pub. *New Yorker* 76, no. 28 (25 September 2000): 87.
SHS, 57
Pattern: 5–1
Time: August
Place: Montana

The world does not want to converse with us, meaning that it has nothing to tell us beyond what we see. But the poet knows better, believing that there is something behind the world's mask. We should therefore keep our eyes focused "on the X." The poet identifies the "X" with "the cloud-ridden sky," but the real focus is what lies behind the dominating clouds. What sweeps the clouds along, as the title indicates, is some mysterious power that "comes from another world." This is the symbolic sun toward which we need to turn (*heliotrope* derives from *heli-* "sun" and *tropos* "turn"). There might also be an allusion to the inexpressible X of

Mallarmé's *Ses purs ongles très haut dédiant leur onyx*. It should be added that "X" is *not* an example of Wallace Stevens's "dominant X," which, like "the A B C of being," represents the objective world that shrinks from "the motive for metaphor." In the present poem the motive for metaphor is to see behind the surface of what the eyes take in.

Summer Mornings

Orig. pub. *Oxford American* 37 (January–February 2001): 70–1; *Thumbscrew* 18 (Spring 2001). SHS, 58–60
Pattern: 4–4 × 7
Time: Late July
Place: Montana

This is a seven-panel Yaak screen. The first six visual vignettes focus on a feature of the Montana landscape: the wind, the light, the clouds, the shadow of time, the river, and the empyrean. The seventh, more diffuse in its representation, is a series of representations with minimal predication: there is one participle ("melting") and one verb phrase tucked away in a relative clause ("will not rise").

Section 1. The language of the river is available for those who want it, but "What the river says isn't enough." The poet opts, therefore, for the "Vocalissimo" to "speak his piece." This is an allusion to Stevens's *To the Roaring Wind*, the final, four-line poem in Wallace Stevens's *Harmonium*: "What syllable are you seeking, / Vocalissimus, / In the distances of sleep? / Speak it." In Stevens, the wind, designated by the neologism "Vocalissimus" ("big wind"), is enjoined to speak the syllable from the depths of sleep. In Wright, the poet has already decided that the wind will be his voice. "Lay me down" evokes the disturbing death motif of the children's prayer.

Section 2. The poet searches for the proper simile to capture the "silky and rare" morning light. Two similes refer to the light itself. The light is so untamed and shy, it is as if there is no light at all. And it is like a pentimento, the underlying image of a painting that shows through, usually when the top layer of paint has become transparent with age. Then, two additional similes refer to the effect of the light on us. In the first, it is as if the light removed us from its solitude, thus reversing the idea of its feral shyness. The second returns to the context of painting: the light produces an effect on us like that of a glaze on a canvas.

Section 3. This scene contrasts the "unbearable" lightness shining through the evergreens with the dark river below. Although the clouds "stumble upon each other" and "drift," it is as if their destinations ("appointed stations") have been foreordained.

Section 4. The haunting image of the Hunter Gracchus dominates this vignette. In his short story "The Hunter Gracchus" (1916–17) Kafka projects a view of life through a glimpse into the world of the dead. The protagonist insists he is dead, having died from a fall in the Black Woods sometime in the fourth century (it is now, presumably, the early twentieth), and his spirit boarded a ship for the next world. But the pilot became lost, and thus the boat bearing the Hunter on a bier keeps docking at one port after another, looking in vain for his destination. The short story concludes with the Hunter Gracchus saying, "My boat is without a helm—it journeys with the wind which blows in the deepest regions of death." Whatever one makes of Kafka's enigmatic tale, it is clear that the Hunter Gracchus's death ship will never find its proper mooring, which is a theme that haunts our pilgrim-poet as well. In this poem the theme is embodied in the darkness of the shadow of time, cutting swallow-like across the grass. The image of the Hunter Gracchus's long body will make regular appearances in Wright's next three books. See *Buffalo Yoga* (BY, 17), *Buffalo Yoga Coda II* (BY, 29), *Night Thoughts Under* a China Moon (ST, 21), In Praise of Franz Kafka (ST, 60), and Littlefoot (sects. 9 and 22). Wright's interest in "The Hunter Gracchus" is no doubt connected to its setting: Riva on Lake Garda, which was at the time on the Austrian-Italian border. Kafka and Max Brod had visited Riva in September 1909.

Section 5. The eternal cycle of the river that "mumbles a kind of nothingness," which appears to represent the world of oblivion (sleep), is set in contrast to several surreal images: the river's naked hair and flaming wheel and the swinging spiders of the heart. Sleep, which is, as Virgil has it, death's brother, recalls the language of the nighttime children's prayer in section 1.

Section 6. St. Pablo, the patron saint of horses, materializes from the westward moving clouds over Mt. Henry (several miles north of Wright's Montana cabin), which produces still another invocation for comfort to still another saint. The awareness of both sin and mortality (our lives keep rusting away) produces the appeal for the saint's salve. We lie under the empyrean and under the earth as well, where the storm forces track each leg of our journey.

Section 7. We conclude with a series of discontinuous apocalyptic images: martyrdom; a heaven that we cannot decipher, that will not speak to us, and that turns out to be "God's endgame"; the broken and half-dazed angels. The scene is altogether static, a world of adjective and noun only: the single verb phrase—"rise from the dead"—is negated.

Thinking of Marsilio Ficino at the First Hint of Autumn

Orig. pub. *Euphony* 1, no. 2 (May 2001).
SHS, 61
Pattern: 10 × 2
Time: Early September
Place: Charlottesville

The poet weaves Marsilio Ficino's speculations about the Absolute in and out of his own reflections on death and his descriptions of the early September landscape. Ficino, the most important of the neo-Platonic Renaissance philosophers, believed that the universe should be understood through a direct exploration of nature rather than by calling on the authority of traditional writers. In declaring that Ficino was probably right about the Absolute (ll. 14–15), the poet could be referring to any number of passages in Ficino (see, e.g., *Platonic Theology*, bk. 2, chap. 6) or even to his general outlook on the transcendent. Ficino ordinarily uses the term "absolute" to modify something separated from matter, like the soul. In any event, the poem poses this thematic question: Is death, the ultimate form of exile, deeper than the Absolute. Ficino thinks not, associating the Absolute with grace rather than exile. The poet concedes that this may be the case, grace being something that appears suddenly as a gift, like the ripening dogwood berries, the bowing of the garden flowers, and the rising of the constellations. The dipping of the trees, identified with "processional maidens," and the rising of the stars underwrite the yo-yo metaphor that begins the poem. There is a similar process at work in death—it hides out and so distances itself, all the while "keeping in touch." The difference between the Absolute and death is that the latter waits for us, whereas the former does not.

Via Negativa

Orig. pub. *New Yorker* 77, no. 31 (15 October 2001): 172–3.
SHS, 62–4
Pattern: 10 × 5

Time: Early October
Place: Southwest Virginia and then Charlottesville

The epigraph is from *Dark Night of the Soul*, chap. 16, par. 12: "And if he is to know with certainty by what road he travels, he must perforce keep his eyes closed and walk in darkness" (trans. E. Allison Peers).

   The opening scene focuses on the spectacular autumn foliage of Washington County, Virginia. The poet is driving along I-81, just to the northeast of Abingdon in the vicinity of the tiny town of Emory (population 300), which is, incidentally, where the author of this companion lives. The location is between the ridges of the Clinch Mountains ("the epaulets / To the north") and the Iron Mountains, toward which the "pink-and-greens" and the "leaf-darkened" dogwoods lead. The spectacle of color takes the poet's breath away ("vacuums me out"), leaving him "weightless and unrepentant" of the joy he takes in such beauty.

   The poem alternates between descriptions of the landscape and reflections on the *via negativa*. Thus, in section 2, the poet points to the separation between the abounding gods and our ephemeral words (which are only dust), our ephemeral prayers (which rise disembodied into the heavens), and our ephemeral lives (which are a mere "scratch on the sky"). The human condition is a movement "from not-ness to not-ness," the realization of which may cause some discomfort but not anxiety. It is "pretty to think" these thoughts about our lives which will eventually be released and thus "painless, beyond recall." The *via negativa* appears again in section 3, with the feeling of emptiness brought by the Charlottesville frost and the disappearance of the spirit into the darkness—a necessary part of the journey according to St. John of the Cross. Related motifs are, in section 4, our rejection of all meaning and our repeated sinking to our knees. In the final section death in the natural cycle is foregrounded. In the autumn, leaves fall just as they always have and just as our words do. But unlike the trees, which "bear up their ruin" so as to bear leaves again in the spring, there is no repetition of the cycle in human lives, which are nudged "toward the coming ash." We have moved, then, from the breathtaking and animated brilliance of the Appalachian autumn to the year-ending collapse of that spectacle in dust and ashes. And there is a parallel descent in the poet's consciousness along the *via negativa*.

p. 62, l. 8. "weightless" should be "Weightless."

Ars Poetica III

Orig. pub. *New Republic* 225, no. 20 (12 November 2001): 40.
SHS, 65–6
Pattern: 5 × 5
Time: Thanksgiving Day 2000
Place: Charlottesville, apparently

   The art of poetry is a burden but a necessary one. Each of the poet's four-fingered hands continues to tap (type) out messages lapped up by the "sidereal tongue," but it is "a slow climb to the second life." Rimbaud renounced the poetic life, abandoning his writing altogether. But the reason for Rimbaud's renunciation—an utter dissatisfaction with his work—is the reason for Wright to continue writing. The possibility of discovery remains ("What's lost is not lost"). There are still "Old light, old destinations," and who knows what the clouds will "have to say from the far side of the seasons." Thus, the persistent tapping on the typewriter keys, and thus the imperative mood. The Gates of Mercy, which we remember from *If My Glasses Were Better, I Could See Where I'm Headed For* (SHS, 19), are commanded to "stop breaking down," and whatever is flowing just out of earshot instructs the poet to "be brighter" because his words are "foursquare and indestructible."

p. 65, ll. 11–12. *Rimbaud*. When Rimbaud's employer in Aden, Alfred Bardey, discovered his past as a poet, Rimbaud became distressed and replied that it was all "absurd, ridiculous, disgusting."
p. 65, l. 19. *River of Heaven*. See note to p. 18, l. 15 of *NB*.

'54 Chevy

Orig. pub. as a Melas Press broadside (Salem, Virginia), 2000.
SHS, 67
Pattern: 4 × 3
Time: September, late 1950s
Place: Sam's Gap is on the North Carolina-Tennessee border

The poem recreates the memory of a scene along a stretch of hairpin curves on U.S. Highway 19W/23 just before crossing into North Carolina from Tennessee. The trip described is Wright's heading off to college in North Carolina from Kingsport, apparently for the fall semester of his sophomore year.

The epiphany of the middle stanza, where the heart is identified with the "legless bird, hoping for anywhere to land" is set in sharp contrast to the diseased field and aging orchard. The vision was a momentary one that the poet wishes could have "lasted forever and ever." He cannot tell us what the experience meant because, he says, borrowing a line from T'ao Ch'ien, "I forget the words." But the desire to settle down in green pastures, echoing Psalm 23, clearly suggests what the experience meant. A pastoral Garden of Eden has displaced the Alzheimered apple trees, and the "legless bird" reminds us of the fabled "legless birds of Paradise" in Keats's *The Eve of St. Mark*. The poet is almost saying with Wallace Stevens, "Beauty is momentary in the mind ... but in the flesh it is immortal." All we need do is change "flesh" to "heart."

p. 67, l. 12. *But every time ... forget the words*. "All this means something, / something absolute: whenever I start / to explain it, I forget the words altogether" (T'ao Ch'ien, *Drinking Wine*, in *Mountain Home*, 13).

Nostalgia II

Orig. pub. *Ploughshares* 27, nos. 2–3 (Fall 2001): 234.
SHS, 68
Pattern: 6 × 3
Time: January
Place: Flashback to Verona

Title: "Nostalgia" derives from *nostos* ("a return home") + *-algia* ("pain"). Here the bittersweet longing is for Verona, which is one of Wright's more important poetic homes. The flashback is to a winter in 1959 when Wright's friend Harold Schimmel led to him to a Verona bookshop that had facsimile editions of Ezra Pound's *A Lume Spento* and *Thrones* and books under the imprint of *All'insegna del pesce d'oro*, a Milan publishing house owned by Vanni Scheiwiller. *Thrones* contained Pound's *Cantos 96–109*. The bookshop was on the via Mazzini, a street running northeast from the Piazza Brà and the Arena in the centro storico of Verona.

"Made in Verona" (l. 13) refers figuratively to the poet and literally to the books produced by the famous Verona printing house, Stamperia Valdonega, owned by Martino Mardersteig, a celebrated typographer and book designer. Schimmel, who also became a poet and translator, was also "made in Verona." The two poets were in search of "a language and a place to stand," which they found in Verona. The future offered a forceful and menacing ("like Dostoevsky") warning about the efficacy of such a vocation. They chose not to heed it, and the poet concludes his homesick memory with a flourish of understatement: "It's been okay."

Body and Soul

Orig. pub. *New Yorker* 78, no. 7 (8 April 2002): 70–1.
SHS, 71–3
Pattern: 8 × 6
Time: Midwinter
Place: Charlottesville

Title: The ostensible reference of the title is to Coleman Hawkins's "Body and Soul" (1940), which became the most famous recording of the great jazz saxophonist, to whom the poem is dedicated.

The opposition of the body and soul is present in the earliest philosophical speculations of our tradition. It is a central concern of Plato and gets reflected throughout the poetic tradition from *The Friar's Tale* to Yeats. The "world's body" (l. 1) is the mysterious and complex texture of the natural world that poetry, according to John Crowe Ransom, can especially reveal. It is also the container of the *spiritus mundi* or the soul. But the present poem is more about body than soul, which gets mentioned only in the poem's final word and in what mid-winter in Charlottesville does to the soul, which is to shunt it aside. The poem turns out to be primarily another *ars poetica*, accumulating a series of affirmations about the poetic vocation.

These begin in stanza 2, where we encounter the familiar triumvirate: language, landscape, and the idea of God. The poet reaffirms the convictions that he has held for a long time. First, when we speak the world we speak the truth, even prophetically ("how we said the world // was how it was, and how it would be"). Second, the poetic word is also the divine Logos, which can silence nothingness and "lead us inexplicably to grace." Third, it is as if this word-to-grace movement were a function of a particular geographical landscape, such as Verona, Charlottesville, northern Montana, or Laguna Beach.

There are, however, resplendent poems on the other side of our lives that we will never see and utter—that grace beyond the reach of art (stanza 3). These are the poems of death ("Bone music") and cold suffering: we are unable "to summer them out in our wounds." This leads, in stanza 4, to the extended metaphor of life identified with a painting. We are isolated objects, rather than subjects, frozen in time like the images on a canvas, "beautiful, and hung up to dry." Meanwhile, life in the natural and human world goes on outside the canvas.

Stanza 5 returns to the *ars poetica* theme, which now undercuts the affirmations of stanza two. Language, the poet muses, turns out to be insubstantial after all: our words "will not rise from the dead"; "they lie low and disappear." The poet is therefore mistaken, he confesses, about the power of language: our words "fall down," and "we just don't know what counts."

The poem concludes, nevertheless, with four lessons the poet says he has learned—lessons about walking, thinking, writing, and praying. The writing lesson is easy enough to understand: "Write as though you had in hand the last pencil on earth." The other lessons are also an integral part of the poet's mission: the journey itself (walking), the countless intertextual ideas from "somebody else's brain" (thinking), and the frequent invocations to the saints (praying).

p. 73, l. 1. The Martha Graham lesson is the first one, meaning more or less to watch your step as you walk. It is a version of her remark to Eli Wallach, "for God's sake, walk as if you carry the seed."

Hard Dreams

Orig. pub. *64 Magazine* [Charlottesville], 2, no. 6 (July–August 2001): 78.
SHS, 74–6
Pattern: 5 × 10
Time: March
Place: Charlottesville

The sequence of dreams recorded here is "hard" in the sense of being, like most dreams, difficult to resolve or understand. "We can't get past them," as the poet says in the final stanza, speaking of the dogs that guard the gates of horn and ivory. He does occasionally escape from the inner life of his "nightmemories" to record an observation (as in the description of the March landscape in stanza 7) or provide a commentary (as in his annotation of Caravaggio's painting in stanza 4). Otherwise, what is revealed in these "nightdreams and daymares," as Wright calls them in *Thinking of Winter at the Beginning of Summer*, is an apprehensive reference to the emptiness of the poetic word (in the dead and darkened world of stanza 3), a desire to make oneself invisible (in the anaphora of stanza 5), a genuine perplexity about the meaning of the images that trouble the poet's sleep (in the interrogative stanza 6), and an anxiety about what the "junkyard dogs" of the dream world are guarding (stanza 10). But the poem is mostly a rapid-fire succession of discontinuous images that arise from "Another winter afternoon in the underworld" of sleep. It is as if the poet is at Penelope's gate of ivory, from which issue illusion and darkness, and not yet ready to enter the gate of ivory, the genuine dreams of light and life (*Odyssey* 19, ll. 562–7).

p. 74, ll. 16–18. *Caravaggio.* In *The Beheading of St. John*, perhaps Caravaggio's greatest masterpiece, the severe drama of the scene is devoid of all excessive emotion.
p. 75, l. 2. *Jesus bug.* A name in the southern U.S. for the water strider, so-called because of its ability to walk on water.
p. 75, l. 23. The reference is to Blake's illustration for *Purgatorio* ix.

Body and Soul II

Orig. pub. as *Body and Soul* in *Five Points* 6, no. 1 (2002): 97.
SHS, 77–9
Pattern: 8 × 6
Time: April
Place: Charlottesville

There is very little attention to "body" in the poem, except for the poet's recreation of what his eye sees and then describes in stanzas 3 and 6. As for soul, we have the faith that makes the landscape and music, though not language, cohere; and we have hope as the destination of April's light—"the light we commune by"—in stanza 4. Nothing is offered on behalf of charity, except perhaps by implication in the giving over by Hsuan Tsang and Wang Wei to something larger than themselves—even their identifying with it. But this is muted by the undercurrent of solitude that runs through the poem. First, we have Hsuan Tsang's difficult and solitary journey in search of truth. Next is the Wang Wei's journey inside of the landscape, one that bound him up in a stationary solitude. Landscape may have softened "the sharp edges of isolation" for Wang Wei, but it was still isolation.

As for the poet, he recommends the following of Wang Wei's example, enjoining himself, in a witty reversal of the commonplace, "Don't just do something, sit there." This is more than cleverness: it is Wright's version of the Buddhist concept of *shunyata* or void, the emptying of the self of all desire for action. Assuming this Zen-like posture is what will enable the emptiness of stanza 4 to re-ignite: "Every true poem is a spark, // and aspires to the condition of the original fire / Arising out of emptiness." The poet confesses that he is too old and lazy to write poems (stanza 6), but he has just written one, and the suggestion is if he continues to sit in his back yard, poems will continue to emerge from the curling smoke of the seasons. *A Short History of the Shadow* began with the poet's announcing that he is sitting where he always sits, and it concludes with an imperative to himself to continue the same position. Like Morandi in *Looking Around*, there is no need to have his studio enclose anything other than what is immediately before his eyes, like the "Afternoon sky the color of Cream of Wheat, a small / Dollop of butter hazily at the western edge."

p. 77, ll. 9–17. *story*. Richard Bernstein's *Ultimate Journey* (New York: Knopf, 2001) follows the path of a seventh-century Buddhist monk Hsuan Tsang from China to southern India. Hsuan Tsang set out in 629 on his 5000-mile journey along the commercially active Silk Road in order to find ultimate truth of Buddhism, which he did not believe had survived intact when Buddhism spread to his native China. Bernstein retraces the journey, which took Hsuan Tsang seventeen years.

p. 78, ll. 13–16. "After graduation to the degree of *chin-shih* at the age of twenty-three, Wang Wei was fortunate enough to receive immediately the court appointment of Assistant Secretary for Music.... he was almost at once sent off to a minor provincial post.... he put up with this only for a few years.... About this time ... he bought his famous estate on the Wang River, at the eastern end of the mountains variously known as the Chungnan range or the Southern Mountains, about thirty miles south of Ch'angan, the capital.... He lived there on and off, whenever he was unemployed or on holiday, for the rest of his life" (G.W. Robinson, "Introduction," *Poems of Wang Wei* [Harmondsworth: Penguin, 1973], 14).

p. 78, l. 23. *Getting too old and lazy to write poems*. "With age I am growing too lazy to write verses" (Wang Wei, *Lines*, in *Poems of Wang Wei*, 140).

p. 79, l. 1. *Don't just do something, sit there*. Cf. "Just as you have the impulse to do something, *stop*" (*Zen Flesh, Zen Bones: A Collection of Zen and Pre-Zen Writings*, comp. Paul Reps [New York: Doubleday, 1989], 169).

Chapter 5

Buffalo Yoga

The title suggests the coming together of the landscape of the American West and the Eastern tradition of meditative practice. The iconic buffalo is a shorthand way of representing the northwestern Montana setting that forms the backdrop of the title poem and its three codas, and yoga is an abbreviation for the desire to identify the self with something outside of it. The title also juxtaposes something from the natural world—a creature from the landscape—and a discipline that aims for spiritual insight. Language is the mediating force between the Lincoln County landscape, where the buffalo once roamed, and the idea of God.

The painting on the dust jacket is Mark Rothko's *Untitled* (1968). The title of the British edition of the book is *Snake Eyes* (Exeter, Devon: Stride Publications, 2003).

Landscape with Missing Overtones

Orig. pub. *Five Points* 7, no. 2.
BY, 3
Pattern: 3
Place: Charlottesville

This three-line poem, imitating the concision, style, and mood of the T'ang poets, is the first of three "Proems." Its companion piece is the third, *Portrait of the Artist by Li Shang-Yin*. Between the setting sun and the rising moon, we have the striking image of the disappearing light—"evening with its blotting paper / / lifts off the light." The landscape is represented only by images—the setting sun, the Blue Ridge mountains, the shadowy yards, and the moon shining through the pine trees. "Overtones" here means ulterior meanings, but the missing overtones, which have to do with the aging of the poet, remain missing until we come to the mirror poem, *Portrait of the Artist by Li Shang-Lin*, three pages later.

There Is a Balm in Gilead

Orig. pub. *Oxford Poetry* 9, no. 3 (Winter 2003): 31.
BY, 4–5
Pattern: 4 × 5
Time: End of January
Place: Charlottesville

Title. "There is a balm in Gilead / To make the wounded whole; / There is a balm in Gilead / To heal the sin-sick soul. // Sometimes I feel discouraged, / And think my work's in vain, / But then the Holy Spirit / Revives my soul again" (African-American spiritual).

The poet's desire is for a balm to ease the "Landscape's local affliction" and the more general sense of diminishment he feels in the face of a Godless cosmos. If "our poems ... neither hinder nor help," the temptation is to remain silent and affirm "the ultimate hush of language." The end of a cold January offers no trace of our coming and going. On this "morning lit with regret," where, then, is the balm announced in the title? If there is a balm in Gilead, there appears to be none in Charlottesville. Wright's note (p. 81) cites the poetry of the ancient Chinese, so perhaps there some consolation in the companionship he shares with his T'ang comrades, many of whom dwell on the themes of silence and absence. See especially the poems of Li Po, Liu Tsung-yüan, and Cold Mountain in David Hinton's *Mountain Home: The Wilderness Poetry of Ancient China* (Washington, DC: Counterpoint, 2002), the book referred to in the note. Hinton's "Introduction" outlines the cosmology of the Chinese poems and the riddling matter of absence and presence—ideas hovering in the margins of the poem.

p. 4, l. 13. *I write, as I said before, to untie myself.* "I write poems to untie myself, to do penance and disappear / Through the upper right-hand corner of things, to say grace" (*Reunion*, in CM, 141).

Portrait of the Artist by Li Shang-Yin

Orig. pub. *Five Points* 7, no. 2.
BY, 6
Pattern: 3
Place: Charlottesville

The two poems that bracket *There Is a Balm in Gilead* imitate, as said above, the concision and simplicity of the Chinese poets. Li Shang-Yin (812?–58) was a poet of the T'ang Dynasty, known for his subtle allusions and metaphorical complexity. Wright read his poems in *Five Tang Poets*, trans. David Young (Oberlin, OH: Oberlin College Press, 1990); *The Jade Mountain*, trans. Witter Bynner (1964); *Three Hundred Poems of the T'ang Dynasty*, trans. Xuzhou Ding (Taipei: Wu Chou Chu Pan Shê, 1973), which is a pirated edition of *The Jade Mountain*; *Poems of the Late T'ang*, trans. A.C. Graham (Harmondsworth: Penguin, 1965); *One Hundred More Poems from the Chinese: Love and the Turning Year*, trans. Kenneth Rexroth (New York: New Directions, 1970); and elsewhere.

The missing overtones of the previous T'ang proem are made explicit here, where the setting sun over the Blue Ridge is an objective correlative of the poet's having come almost to the end of the line. This book, then, becomes the "Book of White Hair," and the sunset, like life itself, is "a minute of splendor" while, at the same time, "a minute of ash," a temporal version of Li Shang-Lin's spatial image—"One inch of love is an inch of ashes" (untitled poem [ii] in *Poems of the Late Tang*, 146).

Buffalo Yoga

Orig. pub. *American Poetry Review* 32, no. 1 (January–February 2003): 17–20.
BY, 9–22
Pattern: 57 stanzas of various lengths, Wright having abandoned his usual convention of stanza and line symmetry : 1 stanza has 1 line; 11 stanzas have 3 lines; 3 have 4 lines; 24 have 5 lines; 12 have 6 lines; 2 have 7 lines; 1 has 8 lines; 2 have 9 lines, and 1 has ten lines. The poem has 30 sections, separated from each other by a short rule.
Time: July 2001
Place: Montana

Title: See headnote to the book, above.

The poem is a series of thirty meditations (fifty-seven stanzas) on, once again, language, landscape, and the idea of God. God mumbles and mutters and remains largely hidden, except for an occasional glance at his backside (p. 9, ll. 19–20). Nevertheless "The natural world, out of whose wounds the supernatural / Rises, and where it longs to return, / Shifts in its socket from time to time // and sparks come forth" (p. 17, ll. 15–17).

The landscape of the north country, which is said to be "immediate," "more essential," and "more severe" than elsewhere, is the backdrop against which our "earlier lives" play "hide-and-seek" (p. 11, l. 1). In another game-playing metaphor, the evening with its black game pieces and the stars with their white ones are locked in a chess match that moves inexorably toward check-mate (p. 11, ll. 7–12). Interspersed with the description of the landscape is a series of loosely connected meditations on God, the soul, time and mortality, the past, poetry and the poetic vocation. The poet continues his effort to read the world and to understand his role in it. The world is a "magic book" (p. 22, l. 15) inscribed with an alphabet of "radiant lettering" in "the registry of light" (p. 22, l8. 8, 12), sometimes with a mysterious cuneiform (p. 9, l. 10), and sometimes with a "false-front calligraphy" (p. 13, l. 8).

God. The representation of the divine is minimal at best, and knowledge of what is "beyond" is almost intractable (p. 9, l. 12). "God with his good ear to the ground" (p. 9, l. 5) has difficulty hearing the earthly sounds, and it is his ghost that is tapping on the window and dragging his chains on the ground in an effort to catch our attention. Yet, as the poet says, "Everything tends toward circumference," one of the conventional metaphors for God. St. Augustine described the nature of God as a circle whose center was everywhere and its circumference nowhere. Emily Dickinson wrote to Colonel Higginson, saying "My Business is Circumference," thus indicating her characteristic move from the quotidian to the otherworldly (*The Letters of Emily Dickinson*, ed. Thomas H. Johnson [Cambridge: Belknap, 1958], 412). What tends toward circumference, says the poet, is "the world, / This life, and no doubt the next" (p. 12, l. 18–19). He returns to the geometrical metaphor toward the end of the poem, where circumference is less a containing form than a constraining one and where idle detail, like linearity, is to be erased by darkness. Only then does our resurrection toward the stars begin to make sense (p. 22, ll. 1–4).

Soul. Two sections of the poem are devoted explicitly to the soul. In the first (p. 10, ll. 1–5), we are presented with a complex set of identifications. The soul is a "rhythmical knot," according to Mallarmé, which form releases and remakes. This recalls the original meaning of *rhuthumos*: schema, type, form. Each soul, the poet then says, "is its own music," a trope that is then extended to the air-walking spider. This startling metaphorical complex goes back to the myth of Ariadne's thread, and we are reminded too of the gossamer thread of the soul in Whitman's *A Noiseless Patient Spider*. The spider punningly "chords" (extends a segment between two points *and* produces a harmony) and "frets" (worries *and* ornaments with interlaced parts *and* constructs a fingerboard for strings). "Unstringing" and "stringing" are puns as well, referring both to the making of the web and to the preparation of the instrument. Later, "the great spider of light" is the god of the end of things to whom the poet prays for mercy and forgiveness (p. 13, l. 11). The first two identifications (soul = rhythmical knot = music) are explicitly joined by the copula. The items in the predicateless second set (soul = spider = instrument = lamentation = seductive poem) are identified by implication only. The music of the soul is a conventional metaphor. In Marsilio Ficino it is the *humana musica* that results from the proper arrangement of the planetary spheres. The "long lamentation" even hints at "soul music," a combination of blues and jazz, and the "poem whose siren song we're rocked by" introduces another pun: soul music, some forms of which were influenced by rock music, can rock us to sleep. Or does Wright use "rocked by" in the sense of stunned or deeply moved?

The quick succession of associations here are private, and any paraphrase strains to establish the semantic links.

The other "soul" section (p. 18, 1–12) begins with a riddle: "The soul ... begins to know each other." In this grammatical double-take "each" turns out to refer to the two halves of the soul, one directed downward to the material world (the "dirt" from which we are made and to which we return) and the other upward toward the heavens. It is difficult for us to hear the voice of either, but whatever thoughts we have of forgotten things—"The stained glare of angel wings, / Radiant Sundays, / Austere, half-opened chambers of the half-opened heart, / Sun-clustered meadow"—they are surrounded by the soul, which is "a shimmering, speechless lash of light."

Ars poetica. Scattered throughout *Buffalo Yoga* are variations on the omnipresent *ars poetica* testimonials. Section 6 is an account of the poet's having listened all his life for "the dark speech of silence" (p. 10, l. 18). This is the language of the landscape, or at least the more ominous "words" that issue from the black zodiac. But it is now also the "language" of the inexorable tick-tock of the poet's heartbeat with its death-murmur of "blood setting out on its long journey beyond the skin" (p. 10, ll. 19–20).

In sections 8 and 9 the speaker assumes a distanced, third-person perspective. The poet is said to become the poem himself (p. 11, ll. 18–19), identifying the maker with the thing made, as in Montaigne's remark that he was consubstantial with his book. In a disparaging judgment about his effort, the poet thinks to himself that he "didn't have much to say ... but at least he knew how to say it" (p. 12, l. 6). This is a witty reversal of what Wright has no doubt heard countless times from his students—that they knew what they wanted to say but didn't know how to say it. The "winds of forgetfulness" overcome the "waters of deep remembering" (p. 11, l. 21–p. 12, l. 2). Doubts about the poetic enterprise creep into the poet's consciousness: "Who thought that words were salvation?" (p. 15, l. 2). Returning to the first person point of view, the poet says, like the deer silently disappearing into the words, "I would gladly close my mouth // and whisper to no one" (p. 14, l. 12). But of course he does not close his mouth, because he still itches "for ultimate form" and still waits "for the consolation of the commonplace" (p. 15, ll. 14, 19).

The journey. In the stanza about the "red bug" (p. 16, ll. 2–9) the poet says that "we travel back and forth" on a "journey beyond the wide world's end." This last phrase is a variation on the sixteenth-century ballad *Tom o' Bedlam*, the character that Edgar disguises himself as in *King Lear*. In the last stanza of the ballad Tom o' Bedlam says, "By a knight of ghosts and shadows / I summoned am to tourney / Ten leagues beyond the wide world's end, / Methinks it is no journey." Tom, more an ecstatic shaman than a madman, knows, as does the poet, that there is something beyond the end of the journey. The narrative movement may end, but there is something beyond that "is no journey." This is the end of "the deep journey" that the body gathers itself for in stanza 24 (p. 19, l. 10), an echo of Tom 'o Bedlam's song. "Beyond the world's end," like "beyond the skin" (p. 10, l. 20), is a stage of existence—a point of epiphanic stasis—that is a destination but not journey.

The journey records, of course, the passage of time and the inevitable awareness of mortality. The poet is aware of Time as a gradually eroding force, like bootheels and footfalls, and he requests Time to release him: "walk behind me along the corridor, the endless one, / That leads to the place I have to go" (p. 13, ll. 1–7). The awareness of death is represented by the body of Kafka's Hunter Gracchus that makes its annual appearance (p. 17, l. 5). The immediacy of death is introduced with the poet's thoughts of "Tom, just dead, in a foreign land," and the last nine sections of the poem—elegiac in temper—are haunted by thoughts of death. "Tom" is Tom Andrews, Wright's friend, a poet himself, and editor of *The Point Where All*

Things Meet: Essays on the Poetry of Charles Wright (Oberlin College Press, 1995). During the summer of 2001 Andrews fell ill in Athens, Greece, and died in London on 18 July, at age thirty-nine. The refrain about the burial of Andrews interrupts the description of the sounds and sights of the birds and butterflies, the horses and dogs in the penultimate section (p. 21, ll. 13–21). In connection with Andrews, Wright's note (p. 79) cites Goethe's "Alles Nahe werde fern." Borges quotes this line in his lecture "Blindness," and then comments: "Goethe was referring to the evening twilight. Everything near becomes far. It is true. At nightfall, the things closest to us seem to move away from our eyes. So the visible world has moved away from my eyes, perhaps forever" (Jorge Luis Borges, *Selected Non-Fictions*, ed. Eliot Weinberger [New York: Penguin, 2000], 483). As the last stanza of the poem is dependent on an essay by Borges, the source of Wright's quotation from Goethe doubtless comes from the same volume of Borges's essays.

The poet wants to walk under the water like an ouzel to bring Andrews back and lay his body above the water. The thought of Andrews triggers in the stanzas that follow a series of reflections on the gathering of the body for a deep journey (p. 19, ll. 9–10). Other images of the end of things are "the descent of the fiery wheels" (from Ezekiel) and the "ghost-gazed" bodies of the "recently resurrected" (p. 19, ll. 17–18). The poet speaks of the ease by which we are gathered into the artifice of eternity (p. 20, l. 6), of the stars as offering comfort to the dead (p. 20, l. 7), of the long journey on "the other side" of midnight (p. 20, ll. 10–12), of life's brevity—"the length of a struck match"—and of the dark confusion that surrounds our last days (p. 20, l. 20). In the poem's final section on the afterlife, we learn that the journey is "a black voyage / To rediscover our names" (p. 22, ll. 6–7). Life is a matter of reading the book of both the world and the self. After we finish reading the "magical book," "We close it and turn the page down / And never come back, / Returned to what we once were before we became what we are. / This is the tale the world tells, this is the way it ends." We go gently into that good night without a bang or even a whimper.

p. 10, l. 1. *Mallarmé.* "Every soul is a rhythmic knot" (Stéphane Mallarmé, "La musique et les lettres," in *Oeuvres complètes* [Paris: Gallimard/La Pleiade, 1945], 644). The context is Mallarmé's discussion of *vers libre*.

p. 10, l. 9. Cf. "I have forgotten what to say" (Liu' Chang-ch'ing, *While Visiting on the South Stream the Taoist Priest Ch'ang*, in *Three Hundred Poems of the Tang Dynasty*, 194), and "All this means something, / something absolute: whenever I start / to explain it, I forget the words altogether" (T'ao Ch'ien, *Drinking Wine*, in *Mountain Home*, 13).

p. 11. *Georg Trakl blue.* The shade of blue here is uncertain. The word "blue" is omnipresent in Trakl's poems, but he seldom describes its shades. Perhaps Wright had one of these passages in the back of his mind: "A blue deer / Gently bleeds in a thicket of thorns"; "You, a blue deer gently trembling"; or "The eyes of a blue deer follow, / Watching over these darker paths" (Georg Trakl, *Poems*, trans. Lucia Getsi [Athens, OH: Mundus Artium Press, 1973], 89, 101, 127).

p. 15, l. 6. *Rimbaud's piano.* "Madame X set up a piano in the Alps" (Rimbaud, *After the Flood*, l. 10).

p. 17, l. 5. *the Hunter Gracchus.* See the commentary for section 4 of *Summer Mornings*, in *SHS*, 58–60. The image of the Hunter Gracchus's long body appears also in *Buffalo Yoga Coda II* (BY, 29), *Night Thoughts Under a China Moon* (ST, 21), *In Praise of Franz Kafka* (ST, 60), and *Littlefoot* (sects. 9 and 22).

p. 18, l. 13. *Crash ... ouzel.* Crash is one of the locals in the Montana community. He makes an appearance in Tim McIntire's song, reproduced in *Sun-Saddled, Coke-Copping, Bad-Boozing Blues* (BY, 69). The water ouzel or dipper bird can feed under the water, walking along the bottom of the creek, using its wing to assist its progress.

p. 19, l. 14. *the sound of two hands clapping.* This is a parody of Zen koan, "the sound of one hand clapping." The allusion seems to be to Yeats's line in *Sailing to Byzantium*, "soul clap its hands and sing," and perhaps as well to Yeats's source, Blake's report that he witnessed the soul of his dead brother rising and clapping his hands.

p. 20, l. 3. *hemophiliac.* Tom Andrews was a hemophiliac.

p. 22, ll. 5–19. This section is dependent on as passage from Léon Bloy's *L'Ame de Napoleon*, which as indicated in Wright's note (p. 79), was quoted in an essay by Borges: "There is no human being on earth who is capable of declaring who he is. No one knows what he has come to this world to do, to what his acts, feelings, ideas correspond, or what his real *name* is, his imperishable Name in the registry of Light.... History is an immense liturgical text, where the i's are not worth less than the versicles or whole chapters, but the importance of both is undeterminable and is profoundly hidden" (Jorge Luis Borges, *Selected Non-Fictions*, ed. Eliot Weinberger [New York: Penguin, 1999], 361–2; the ellipsis is Borges's).

Buffalo Yoga Coda I

Orig. pub. *Field* 68 (Spring 2003): 5–7.
BY, 25–7
Pattern (6–6) 6 (6–6) (4–4) 8 (5–5) 4
Time: Summer 2001
Place: Montana

 The first coda opens with a striking view of the wet and windy Montana landscape and a no less striking account of the poet's desire to stop "time," a word he slips into his shirt pocket "to keep it back from Forever." This is, of course, a futile gesture: like the cicada, time slips from its case and goes on about its business, its shell serving as a memento mori. The six other sections are rather like discrete short poems, though they are loosely linked by a kind of desperate hopelessness: we, the self-deceived, have no hope of resurrection (stanza 3), our intercessory prayers go unanswered (stanza 4), the light does not illuminate (stanza 5), and the distance between this world and the world of the dead is absolute (stanza 6).

 "Silence breeds," we are told (p. 27, l 4), but it never breeds very successfully: the poet, as always, continues to speak. Silence gets extended treatment in section 2, with its parade of similes. What we "leave unspoken" is *like* the hail not yet reached by the sunlight. Then the comparison is reversed: hail is *like* unuttered words in that it eventually melts into nothingness. Such nothingness is then said to be, first, *like* any failure to act and, second, *like* undifferentiated liquid, impossible to grasp and thus beyond giving and taking. One can understand that the unutterable is nothing(ness) and vice versa, but some things are utterable, as we see in the description of the bullbat and swallows that immediately follows.

 If, however, the poet leaves some things unspoken, the world continues to speak, and the generally dark mood of the first six sections is erased in the four-line conclusion: "I think I'll lie down just here for a little while ... And listen to what the world says." The world has now become "luminous" and "transubstantiated," an antitype of the macabre daydream of section 3, where St. Catherine of Siena is enjoined to drink "something from me." St. Catherine, who practically starved herself, could doubtless abide a bit of nourishment, though blood spurting from pus-filled wounds, an altogether demonic parody of the Eucharist, would not do much for her frail condition. Finally, the possibility that the poet will receive some sublime message from the world is left provisional in the concluding line: the transubstantiated world, which holds the poet "like nothing in its look," is ambiguous: it holds him like nothing else can or it regards him as a nonentity. Or both.

p. 25, l, 19. *bullbat* = nighthawk
p. 26, l. 5. *St. Catherine of Siena*. Roman Catholic mystic, humanitarian, activist, and counselor (1347–80). In her late teens she gave up normal sustenance, living intermittently on bread, water, and raw vegetables. Later she gave up bread, surviving on Communion wafers, cold water, and bitter herbs.
p. 26, l. 12. *Fifteenth Station of the Cross*. The Resurrection. Only fourteen stations, which have to do with the passion or suffering of Christ, are prescribed by Roman Catholic authority, the fourteenth being Christ laid in the tomb.

Buffalo Yoga Coda II

Orig. pub. *Field* 68 (Spring 2003): 8–10.
BY, 28–30
Pattern: (7–7–7) (3) (7–7–7) (3) (7–7)
Time: Summer 2001
Place: Montana

Wright begins by positing an alternative to the narrative structure of Kafka's little parable of the hunting dogs and the hare. Kafka's version is this: "The hunting dogs are playing in the courtyard, but the hare will not escape them, no matter how fast it may be flying already through the woods" ("Reflections on Sin, Pain, Hope and the True Way," in *The Great Wall of China*, trans. Willa and Edwin Muir [New York: Schocken, 1948], 139). The parable assumes that the woods form a confined space from which the hare cannot escape. Therefore, the story will inevitably end with the hare's death—a classic tale of the pursuer and the pursued that ends tragically for the hare. But in the poet's alternative scenario, if the dogs never leave the courtyard, then the narrative will never achieve closure: the hare "will always be slow enough / To outlast the ending." Without a conclusion the parable is an endless succession of episodes with no definable "story and story line." The second parable is like the cycle of the sun, with its "chords and variations" in endless repetition, just as in section 3 the long body of Kafka's Hunter Gracchus ceaselessly circumnavigates our lives.

Stanzas 2 and 3 of section 3 (p. 29, ll. 11 ff.) incorporate four jottings by Kafka, recorded in April 1924 when his tuberculosis made it so painful for him to speak that he communicated by writing on scraps of paper. The first, which creates an alternative ending to the story of Noah, sets the tone of hopelessness: the dove brings back no olive leaf, meaning that the flood waters have not subsided. The forecast is as bleak for Noah as for Kafka's last days. But Kafka also wrote of the wonderful lilacs that drink even when they are dying, and this is the image the poet focuses on in the last stanza, where we have the apotheosis of Kafka. He materializes briefly in "a splotch of sunlight" beyond the Montana creek, refuses the bread, wine, and cheese offered him by the poet, and is then changed back into the sunlight, released in an Ovidian metamorphosis, from the *via dolorosa*.

p. 28, l. 20. *Nijinsky*. Vaslaw Nijinsky (1890–1950), Russian ballet dancer celebrated for his virtuosity.

p. 28, l. 21. Their conversation about death and immortality is described in Chekhov's letter to M. Menshikov: "We had a most interesting conversation. Interesting mainly for me, because I listened more than I spoke. We discussed immortality. He recognizes immortality in its Kantian form and assumes that all of us (human and animals alike) will live on in a principle (such as reason or love), the essence and goals of which are a mystery to us. As for me, I can imagine that principle only as a shapeless, gelatinous mass with which my 'I,' my individuality, my consciousness will merge. I have no use for that kind of immortality, I do not understand it, and Lev Nikolaevich was astonished I didn't" (*Letters of Anton Chekhov*, ed. Avrahm Yarmolinsky [New York: Viking Press, 1973], 286).

p. 29, l. 4. *Hunter Gracchus*. See the commentary for section 4 of *Summer Mornings*, in SHS, 58–60. The image of the Hunter Gracchus's long body appears also in *Buffalo Yoga Coda* (BY, 17), *Night Thoughts Under a China Moon* (ST, 21), *In Praise of Franz Kafka* (ST, 60), and *Littlefoot* (sects. 9 and 22).

p. 29, ll. 11. *The dove finds no olive leaf, so it slips back to the darkness of the ark*. "As in the Bible, the dove has been sent forth; but it has failed to find an olive leaf, so it slips back for the present into the darkness of the ark" (Johann Bauer, *Kafka and Prague*, trans. P.S. Falla [New York: Praeger, 1971], 167). The other three lines from Kafka (ll. 14, 16, 21), which are exact quotations, are also reproduced in *Kafka and Prague*, 167. All four passages come from Kafka's *Briefe 1902-1924* and *Briefe an Milena*.

Buffalo Yoga Coda III

Orig. pub. *Field* 68 (Spring 2003): 11.
BY, 31–33
Pattern: (5–5–5) (10) (6–6–6) (6) (4–4–4)
Time: 27 June 2001
Place: Montana

This third concluding movement is almost wholly a description of the Montana landscape. The exceptions are, first, the anaphora of section 2—ten enigmatic questions, reminiscent of "Thel's Motto" in William Blake's *The Book of Thel*; and second, the interlude in section 3, announcing that the poem is an elegy for Wright's father-in-law John McIntire, whose birthday was June 27 (p. 32, l. 17), and for the poet himself. The interrogative section 2 contains some melancholic notes, but the rest of the poem is anything but pensive. Rather it is celebratory of the Montana landscape, precise in its observations of the local flora and fauna and remarkably original in its figures (e.g., the dark cutlery that the future uses to set the table of the underside of the landscape [p. 31, ll. 11–15], the blades of sunlight appearing momentarily and then being resheathed into the clouds [p. 33, l. 4], "the June clouds / Like Navajo rugs on heaven's floor" [p. 32, ll. 7–8], and "East-inching shadows like black tongues licking themselves up" [p. 33, l. 14]). What better way, then, to memorialize the poet's father-in-law than to celebrate the astonishing landscape bequeathed to his daughter? The elegy is really a panegyric to the "luminous, transubstantiated world," a world to which the poet yields himself as he lies down in its green pastures (final stanza). He tells us in the concluding line that the world holds him "like nothing in its look," which repeats the final line of *Buffalo Yoga Coda I* and which means, as we have seen, either that the world holds him in a very strange way or that the world regards him as altogether insignificant. In either case, the elegy, which the poem is only "in part" (p. 32, l. 20), almost completely disappears in the concluding stanza as the poet continues to remain open "to what the world says."

p. 31, l. 8. *boia* = jerk, fool, rascal.
p. 33, l. 22. *Koo Koo Boyd or Solo Joe, French Garver or Basin Creek.* These are all roads in Lincoln County in the northwest tip of Montana. They lie to the north of Troy, Montana, in the Kootenai National Forest, bordering Idaho and British Columbia.
p. 33, l. 2. Porcupine is a creek in the Kootenai National Forest.

The Gospel According to St. Someone

Orig. pub. *Oxford American* 42 (Winter 2002): 157.
BY, 37
Pattern: 5 × 3
Time: November 2001

The poet projects our lives as occupying a middle space, hanging like bats between the earth below and the forking road of the sky above. We are further disengaged or unattached by being only a "reflected radiance ... clothed in our flash dreams." In such a condition we are doubtless in need of some saint to offer us the Eucharist and to succor us. In the unusual last stanza with its triple apostrophe—"Eternal penny," "Buried November," and "Salvation"— we are still in the individuated dream-world, cut off from the collective, the world we share with others. The poet's concluding appeal is to be laid down so he can continue to inhabit the surreal dream-world, where St. Someone will administer the elements, not from the chalice and tray, but from his mouth and tongue. St. Someone's gospel appears to be something of a stunt rather than a genuine account of good news.

Homage to Mark Rothko

Orig. pub. *Yale Review* 90, no. 4 (October 2002): 16–17. Phi Beta Kappa poem at Harvard.
BY, 38–9
Pattern: 8 × 5
Time: Early December 2001
Place: Charlottesville

This is one of a series of homages by Wright. Others are written to honor X (CM, 16), Ezra Pound (HF, 11–12), Arthur Rimbaud (CM, 13), Baron Corvo (CM, 14–15), Paul Cézanne

(*WTTT*, 3–10), Claude Lorrain (*WTTT*, 82), Cesare Pavese (*WTTT*, 98), and Giorgio Morandi (*BY*, 60–1). Here, the poet begins with a confession that his imitation of the ways of others was to no avail: "nothing was ever revealed." But what was revealed and, therefore, deserving of thanks was what came from memory and the devotion to landscape, with its language of light. Also deserving of thanks is the rag-tag end of early December, with its detritus, dark imagery, and absence of light.

The Celan passage comes from his "Bremen Address" (1958), delivered on the occasion of his receiving the city's Literature Prize. Celan notes that Heidegger had addressed the relation between thanking and thinking in *Was heist Denken?* (1954). Celan picks up on the idea, saying that another context for thinking about the relation is provided by the coordinates or "fields" of *Andacht* (devotion or mindfulness) and *Andenken* (memory). He then asks his audience to permit him to thank him from *there*—that place where devotion and memory originated. Celan's riddling point seems to be that he is speaking to an audience from *here* (*von hier aus*, i.e., Bremen), a place he remembers, on the occasion of his remembering a place *there*. The issue raised, in other words, is the separation between *there* and *here*. Wright's point is much simpler: his devotion to both landscape and memory has been continual even when no revelation ensued (stanza 1).

The dialectic of light and darkness is mirrored, one assumes, in the panels of presence and absence in Rothko's paintings, like the untitled one on the dust jacket. Rothko spoke of an indestructible eternal form. What is distant, shadowy, wordless—the world of "deep subtractions"—is worthy of form, which is "the light that shines without shadow," and this, the poet confesses, is what he has attempted to create, thereby giving "form to the formless."

p. 38, l. 10. *Celan.* The "Bremen Address" can be found in Celan's *Collected Prose*, trans. Rosmarie Waldrop (Manchester: PN Review/Carcanet, 1986), 33–5, and in *Selected Poems and Prose of Paul Celan*, trans. John Felstiner (New York: Norton, 2001), 395–6. For a commentary on the "memory and devotion" passage, see Ian Fairley, "Inunhabited: Paul Celan and the Ground of Translation," *Critical Quarterly* 45, no. 3 (December 2003): 69.
p. 39, l. 6. *Form cannot deconstruct or be annihilated.* This and the other three statements attributed to Rothko (ll. 10, 11, and 13) are actually projections by Wright of what Rothko might have said.

Portrait of the Artist in a Prospect of Stone

Orig. pub. *Poetry* 189, no. 1 (October–November 2002): 89–90.
BY, 40–2
Pattern: 12 × 4
Time: Flashback to 25 March 1961
Place: The Greek isles

Title: A composite of James Joyce's *Portrait of the Artist as a Young Man* and John Ashbery's early self-portrait, *Picture of Little J.A. in a Prospect of Flowers*. The portrait is a subgenre in Wright's poetry. In addition to his seven *Self-Portraits*, we have *Portrait of the Poet in Abraham von Werdt's Dream*, *Portrait of the Artist with Hart Crane*, *Portrait of the Artist with Li Po*, *Portrait of the Artist by Li Shang-Yin*, and the present poem.

This portrait of the poet, which is about the difficulty of remembering the past, is reconstructed from a photograph from the end of Wright's time in the army. He and his friends are enjoying a holiday on the Greek island of Hydra in the Aegean Sea. The poet identifies the people in the photo: George Mancini, his army friend, who first appears in *A Journal of True Confessions* and reappears in *Disjecta Membra* (in another 1961 photo from the Greek Islands), Merle, Eric, someone remembered as the Great Dane, and the poet himself. It is Mancini's last day of duty. Also on this excursion, though not in the photograph, is Axel

Jensen (1932–2003), the Norwegian novelist and author of screen plays. He lived on the Greek islands in the 1960s with his wife Marianne (who later lived with Leonard Cohen on Hydra). Jensen had actually already published the novel mentioned, *Icarus: A Young Man in Sahara* (1957).

The poem also refers to an oil painting by Mary Sims, Wright's friend, based on a photograph of Via del Babuino in Rome. The red thumb smudge came from her having touched the photo that she was using to paint her picture. This vignette is interrupted by the poet's recalling a remark Tom Andrews made much later, and then he recreates two dreams—his own wish to be on permanent leave and then a reverie about the Axel Jensen novel. He says he was attracted by the romance of these expatriates, but he laments his failure of memory: "the past a hiding place / Beyond recall or recovery, no matter our wants or our diligence." The portrait of the artist against the stone barrier of the breakwater is largely one of a poet who regrets this inability to remember. Yet the details he is able to resurrect after forty years, including the precise words of the general staff officer back in Verona and the subject of Jensen's novel, means that certain features of the past are not in fact "Beyond recall."

p. 41, l. 5. *John* = St. John the Divine, author of the Book of Revelation
p. 41, l. 9. *Ricordo di Roma* = Memory of Rome
p. 41., l. 11. *You're blocking my view of God*. This is from a repeated line—"You block my view to God" in a poem by Tom Andrews (*The Temptation of St. Augustine: Left Panel*, in *Random Symmetries: The Collected Poems of Tom Andrews* [Oberlin, OH: Oberlin College Press, 2002], 180, 182). Wright wrote an introduction to this volume—"Tom Andrews: An Appreciation," 1–2.

Rosso Venexiano

Orig. pub. *Hotel Amerika*, 1, no. 1 (Fall 2002): 73.
BY, 43–4
Pattern: 5 × 7
Time: Flashback to end of March 1969.
Place: Venice

Title: "Venetian Red." "Venexiano" is Venetian dialect for "Veneziano."

This is another poem triggered by a photograph, this one taken in Venice, probably in March 1969, the year Wright was a Fulbright lecturer at the University of Padua. The poet describes the mirrored image of him and his wife and then recreates the scene in the floor below their quarters and the wider Venetian landscape. He judges the recollected sights and events to be "unreal" and "silly" and then wonders what, in addition to the remembered "detritus," was "bereft in the camera's lens, or the mirror's eye?" Memory has been dispossessed once more. At this point the poet appropriates the lines from the interview with John Berryman (see the passage below) about why he writes. This is answered immediately by the five examples of "Rosso Venexiano": the red of Mary's gown in Titian's *Assumption* (in the Santa Maria Gloriosa dei Frari, Venice), slightly darker than the red of the flag of the "Serenissima" Republic of Venice and not so bright as the robes of the Cardinals and even less bright, one assumes, than the red of the Doge's fingernail or that of the sunset. This catalogue of the shades of Venetian reds is an example of memory repossessed: the lens of the mind's eye can recapture what the camera's lens and mirror's eye cannot.

p. 43, l. 5. *shelved in two*. That is, the mirror was in two sections, so that the reflections produced the appearance of their being in two pieces.
p. 43, l. 8. Wright and his wife were living in the house of the American abstract expressionist, Timothy Hennessy (b. 1925), also inhabited by Luke Hodgkin (l. 7), the well-known British mathematician, and Dale Chihuly (l. 7), the artist who revolutionized the Studio Glass movement. In 1968 Chihuly became the first American glassblower to work in the Venini Fabrica on the island of Murano.

p. 43, l. l. 7–10. *acqua alta* = high water
p. 43, l. 8. *schifo* = junk. The high water in the place where the Wrights were staying had now subsided, carrying the boxes and flats and stench with it south toward Lido.
p. 43, l. 10. *Malamocco.* Historic town near the southern end of Lido.
p. 43, l. 12. *Veronesi.* The paintings of Paolo Veronese in San Sebastiano.
p. 43, l. 14. *Phantom Turk.* The name comes from a nineteenth-century photograph of a ship on the Grand Canal.
p. 43, l. 66. *Corvo.* For Baron Corvo see the note for p. 153, l. 4 of *NB*.
p. 44, l. 3. *Guardi and Canaletto.* Francesco Guardi = Italian Rococo painter, 1712–ca.1793; Canaletto = Giovanni Antonio Canal (1697–1768), Venetian painter, best known for his picturesque views of the city.
p. 44, l. 4. *Dogana.* See commentary for *Venetian Dog* (NB, 153).
p. 44, l. 8. *Sabo ... scuro* = Saturday, when it gets dark (at sunset).
p. 44, ll. 10–13. The italicized passages come from an interview with John Berryman in *Antaeus*, which Wright quotes in a note on p. 79.

Words Are the Diminution of All Things

Orig. pub. *Field* 66 (Spring 2000): 49.
BY, 45
Pattern: 6 × 3
Time: December 2001
Place: Charlottesville

This poem hinges on the problematic relation between *res* (thing) and *verba* (word), especially as the poet moves into the year's end and moves as well toward the end of his own journey: "There isn't much time ... There isn't a lot to add." Words may be, as the title informs us, the diminution of all things, but things themselves, because they are unspoken, mute, and unutterable, diminish also as a result. If we cannot name things, then they sink down into invisibility and silence. The only things that escape diminution are the things the poem does name—the wheeling turkey buzzards, the afternoon clouds, and the scuttling leaves. "All things," then, is an overstatement by the word- and world-weary poet: the last stanza, in which silence is given voice, turns the claim of the title on its head.

Arrivederci Kingsport

Orig. pub. *New Yorker* 78, no. 31 (14–21 October 2002): 176–7.
BY, 46–8
Pattern: 6 × 8
Time: Flashback to late 1940s and early 1950s
Place: Kingsport, Tennessee, and environs
Title: "Farewell Kingsport"

This is another poem of nostalgia. It resurrects memories of the poet's school years in Kingsport, Tennessee, in the late 1940s and early 1950s. Fourteen contemporaries are named. Who will remember them, the poet asks, "now that I'm gone.... Now that the nameless roads // have carried us all from town?" Well, the poet will remember, even though some of the named friends have not been carried from Kingsport. Naming them reinforces the memory. "And what is the point?" the poet asks. The answer is that Kingsport has not in fact been bade farewell. The friends will never forget their own song (*Goodnight, Sweetheart*) even though the song tells them that it is time to go.

p. 46, l. 12. *WKPT.* Kingsport radio station.
p. 47, ll. 18–21. C.B. (Boots) Duke is a private investor and former owner of the Holston Glass Company in Kingsport. Karen Beall and Champe Bachelder married; he died in February 2006 in Nashville, Tennessee. Sara Lou Ring is a member of First Presbyterian Church. Kay Churchill (Colette) lives in San Rafael, California. Some of the

contemporaries named were Wright's classmates at Dobyns-Bennett High School before he left for Christ School in North Carolina for his junior and senior years.

p. 48, ll. 4–5. *Goodnight sweetheart*. A 1954 rhythm and blues song, originally performed by the doo-wop group The Spaniels.

January II

Orig. pub. *Field* 66 (Spring 2000): 50.
BY, 49
Pattern: 3 × 5
Time: January 2003
Place: Charlottesville, apparently

The first *January* poem was published in *Colophons*, and reprinted in CT and CM.

The poet, reflecting on "monuments in the high desert," concludes that life is "a one-way street" between birth and death. We take mortality on our shoulders, and our journey is an effort "to get back." The desire is not so much to return to our proper home in Eden as it is to identify with the power of the natural elements, all four of which are named in the third stanza. But such identification is "not in the cards," and the rough beast of future, at year's end, pursues us from the past.

p. 49, 3. *monuments in the high desert*. Here we have an echo of Shelley's *Ozymandias*.

Dio Ed Io

Orig. pub. *Poetry* 181, no. 3 (January 2003): 191–2.
BY, 50–1
Pattern: 4 × 8
Time: Sunday in January 2003
Place: Charlottesville, apparently

Title: "God and I"

The object of the poet's exploration here is not just "the idea of God" but his own relationship with God. It is a strained relationship at best, because God, unlike the God of the poet's fathers, is a *deus absconditus*. It the first stanza, God is a distant and impersonal "it." "What ash," the poet asks, "has it come to purify?" Ash, a word that appears more than forty times in Wright's poetry, is a multivalent image, associated both with death and with the Phoenix-like site of rebirth. Sometimes it is apocalyptic, sometimes penitential. Here it is purgatorial, the object of divine purification. But the possibility of being cleansed is remote because "it" has disappeared into the clouds. God is addressed more familiarly as "you" in stanza 2, but He is still the one addressed as absent: "There is a disappearance between us as heavy as dirt," and this makes for an "Unbearable absence of being," says the poet, playing on Milan Kundera's *The Unbearable Lightness of Being*. The poet's condition is contrasted with the carefree teenagers in front of the pharmacy for whom everything is bearably weightless: "Nothing is disappearing in their world. Arrival is all."

With the disappearance of God, the poet leaps into the void, as in the photo-collage of Yves Klein (stanzas 5 and 6). "One of them's you," says the poet, "the other is me." "One of them"—the man disappearing on his bicycle—symbolizes the disappearing God, and Klein represents the poet. In *Quarter Notes* Wright remarks that this famous photo is a metaphor for the poetic journey: "every poem [is] a leap from a high wall by the poetic body.... most journeys are, perforce, of this kind in poems" (39). In the last stanza it is we too, the sidekicks of the poetic Lone Ranger, who will disappear into ash. Only then might we be "taken back," or, as Emily Dickinson says in a note written a few months before her death, "called back."

The theme of disappearance dominates. God has disappeared. The poet effaces himself with his leap into the void, and it takes only a slight change in the spacing of the title for the poetic "I" to vanish completely—*dio e dio*.

p. 50, ll. 17–19. *picture of Yves Klein.* "A Leap into the Void," a 1960 photo-collage by Harry Shunk and John Kender that appeared in *Dimanche* with the caption *Un Homme dans l'espace! Le peintre de l'espace se jette dans le vide.* For a copy of the photograph, see http://www.edit-revue.com/index.php?Article=133.

p. 51, l. 8. *Tonto.* In the *Lone Ranger* radio series, Tonto, saved by the Lone Ranger when they were boys, becomes the Lone Ranger's faithful companion.

Nostalgia III

Orig. pub. *Roanoke Review* 27 (Spring 2002).
BY, 52
Pattern: 3 × 5
Time: Spring, following a dry autumn and winter
Place: Charlottesville, apparently

With age (Wright is approaching his sixty-seventh birthday) comes nostalgia. The other two *Nostalgia* poems date from the previous year (*SHS*, 36 and 68). An impetus for memory, nostalgia, in the first poem with that title, produced pleasure; in the second, the memories of Verona were bittersweet. Here, as the poet traces the day's passage from morning to night, the "music of memory" barely intrudes into the striking descriptions of the landscape. Its mantras produce only indefinite bits and pieces that are called "affections." These are not simply fond or tender feelings but "bleak, unappointed rounds," symbolized ominously by the driverless car in the final line. Nostalgia brings with it an awareness of the passage of time. Whether the journey will take the poet upward or downward is as yet unknown, as the doors to those stairways remain shut.

In Praise of Thomas Chatterton

Orig. pub. *Hotel Amerika* 1, no. 1 (Fall 2002): 72.
BY, 53
Pattern: 6–5–6
Time:
Place: Charlottesville, apparently

This panegyric to Chatterton (1752–70), the precocious bohemian poet who is remembered chiefly for his forgeries of medieval documents, is perhaps prompted (the poet is unsure) by the moon outside his window, which is like the one in an engraving of Chatterton's death. The focus is entirely on Chatterton, except for the hum of the helicopter and the sight of the full moon at the beginning. Wright repeats the praises of Keats and Wordsworth, describes the engraving (the memory of which was triggered by the moon), and wishes the boy prodigy, who committed suicide at age seventeen, happiness in death. The final clause is from Thomas Rowley's *Epitaph on Robert Canynge*: "Whanne Mychael's trumpe shall sounde to rise the solle, / He'll wynge to heavn wyth kynne, and happie bee hys dolle" (ll. 9–10). Rowley was a fictitious fifteenth-century monk created by Chatterton.

p. 53, l. 8. The line is from John Keats's letter to George and Georgiana Keats, 17–27 September 1819.
p. 53, l. 9. *Wordsworth.* The line is from William Wordsworth's *Resolution and Independence*, l. 51.
p. 53, ll. 11. *inked engraving.* Which engraving Wright had in mind is uncertain. It may have been *The Death of Chatterton* by Francesco Bartolozzi, an 1801 engraving, after an etching, *The Death of Chatterton* by Raphael Lamar West, or an etching based on Henry Wallis's oil painting, *The Death of Chatterton* (1856), the most well-known image of Chatterton, which has the dead poet sprawled on a bed, though without the creatures circling overhead.

Charles Wright and the 940 Locust Avenue Heraclitean Rhythm Band

Orig. pub. *Hunger Mountain* 1, premier issue (Fall 2002): 90.
BY, 54–5
Pattern: 6 × 5
Time: Unspecified
Place: Charlottesville

Title. A play on Charles Wright & The Watts 103rd Street Rhythm Band, the first rhythm and blues group signed to a Warner Brothers recording contract. Their best-known hit was *Express Yourself.* Wright lives at 940 Locust Avenue in Charlottesville.

This extraordinary lyric arises from a free association of several motifs: desire, the rocking of the lights in the darkened trees, the movement toward "home," and the mysterious devolution of desire into memory.

The title appears to be a joke, with its "Charles Wright" double entendre, its substitution of 940 Locust Avenue in Charlottesville for 103rd Street in Los Angeles, and its insertion of Heraclitus into the mixture. But the poem itself illustrates that these apparent incongruities all fit together. Charles Wright the poet, as opposed to the funk musician, is the one making the music as he looks out the window of his Locust Avenue home. The central metaphor is the song of life, or rather the songs of life, since the same song, like the same lights and the same life, is never repeated. This is a version of Heraclitus' fragment 21: "You cannot step twice into the same river, for other waters and yet others go ever flowing on." The stars sing their songs too, even though we who live in the world below are not their audience. As for rhythm, that comes from the repetition of words and images, especially the rocking motion of lights in the trees. Interposed into the "tides of darkness" and the floating lights are the phrases from Roy Acuff's *Streamlined Cannonball*: "A long steel rail a short crosstie, I'm on my way back home." Home is where the flame is—the light of the empyrean accessible through the sacred doors—which is an echo of another line from *Streamlined Cannonball*, though in a secular context: "the lights I love are home sweet home to me." The obstacle to getting back home is that we are traveling in the world of darkness "down below," which means that our internal language is only a "shadow music" or what Heraclitus calls the "vision extinguished" (fragment 65).

The poem opens with a wish for the extinction of desire, praise, and lisp, all of which have a muted reference to the poet's own career, the lisp being his view of the imperfect words of his own poetic voice. But desire is not finally extinguished. It is transformed into memory in stanza 4, and what follows from that remark is a vision of the stars that do not sing to us. If we substitute stars for mermaids, this is a version of Prufrock's sentiments in the concluding lines of *The Love Song of J. Alfred Prufrock*. Prufrock is drowned by the human voices that awaken him. The poet finds himself in a similar position of solitude, traveling the earth "without sisters, without brothers" and aware that he cannot live his life over.

Saturday Afternoon

Orig. pub. *Yalobusha Review* 8 (2003): 89–90.
BY, 56–7
Pattern: 5 × 5
Time: Summer
Place: Montana

The description of the Montana landscape begins with a certain slant of light, though not oppressive like Dickinson's, and then surveys the creatures in the foreground, from the dragonflies, "like lumescent Ohio Blue Tip matchsticks" puzzling the irises, to the "horses ablaze in the grained light." It then focuses on the bees that are trying to find something in the "inner sumptuous rooms" of the dead lilac. But the bees have to satisfy themselves with the lilacs' "lesser mansions" and "smaller rooms." The conclusion is a reflection on the language the poet has just used. He declares that his calling the sites of the bees' quests "mansions" and "rooms" is not a metaphor: it is rather "the way it just is." But of course what a metaphor asserts is precisely that, "is" being the decisive verb. To say that the lilac blossoms are mansions is to say what the relationship between the two "just is"—a relationship of identity. The final four lines, about the machinery of the nether world, may or may not be a metaphor. The creaking wheels and pulleys may refer literally to underground mines, or they may refer metaphorically to the "cells" with their "instruments" that the bees have descended to. The former seems more likely, as it provides a better explanation of "This is no metaphor." The poet seems to be saying this: if you think it is metaphorical to say that bees enter "rooms," that is not so strange because we are walk atop mine shafts all the time. Still, he cannot escape metaphor: "We walk on the roofs of great houses." The use of simile at the beginning (three appear in the first two stanzas) is abandoned until the final line, where we have the strangely surreal image of the underground roofs, some alive and some dead, spinning in a vortex like a river. Oh, what the imagination can do on a Saturday afternoon.

Wednesday Morning

Orig. pub. *Meridian* 10 (Fall–Winter 2002): 58.
BY, 58–9
Pattern: 6 × 5
Time: Summer
Place: Montana

This is a meditation on stillness, on the presence of absence, and on the awareness of nothing. When the poet says, "We can see nothing, or take nothing in" because things are so still, we are tempted, as we are elsewhere in Wright's work, to translate "nothing" as "Nothing," rather than as "not anything." Nothingness is represented by the "dark erasures" that stillness imposes on the landscape. The word "nothing," in any event, comes at that crux in the poem where Wright moves from the exterior to the interior landscape, where there is an "Essential stillness at the center of things." This is not at all like Eliot's "still point of the turning world" in *Burnt Norton*, where time and eternity intersect. The interior stillness here yearns to flash a light into "our vague solitude."

The exterior and interior stillnesses are different. The former will eventually change (morning will recover her balance and arise), but the melancholic fact is that the latter will not, stillness being a permanent part of the human condition, on the one hand, and our failure to act ("all that we do not do") and to be (all "that we are not") being a symptom of stillness, on the other. Wright may have in the back of his mind the poetry of Wei Ying-wu, which often heightens the themes of stillness and emptiness. This is, of course, a common motif through Wright's work (the word "emptiness" appears twenty-three times in his poems; "empty," twenty-eight times).

p. 59, l. 8. *blue lady* = a flower, member of the buttercup family

Homage to Giorgio Morandi

Orig. pub. *Ploughshares* 29, no. 1 (Spring 2003): 194–5.
BY, 60–1
Pattern: 5 × 6
Time: Unspecified but with flashback to 1964, when Wright was a Fulbright student in Italy

This homage continues the theme of the presence of absence, which is "always stronger," says Wright, "than the absence of presence" (*UP*, 14). Wright pays homage to Morandi in a number of other poems. See the note to *Giorgio Morandi and the Talking Eternity Blues*, in NB, 167 and the commentaries on the poems listed there. Morandi (1890–1964) is one of Wright's most admired artists. His *Landscape* appears on the cover of *Country Music*. It is a drawing done in 1960, shortly after Wright had arrived in Italy for the first time. Some of the central features of Morandi's work are catalogued in the notes for section 7 of *Apologia Pro Vita Sua* (NB, 74).

A great deal of Morandi's work is like Wright's poetry. As observers and readers we have to fill in the blank spaces with connective tissue. The present poem requires little commentary, but here are three prose statements by Wright himself that could stand as glosses on the final line: "You looked as hard as anyone ever looked, // then left it out."

1. *Wright on Wright*: "As Morandi did in his paintings, we should stake our art on the persistence of continuous perception. As Cézanne did as well, we should have a 'tenderness toward the mundane,' a gathering to us of the quotidian. By concentrating on things that are, we can put meaning where it should be—in direct reconstruction, in the picture itself, in the world as it is when we look at it.... Morandi's drawings, toward the end of his life, resemble the poems of certain masters of style: each line tends to be a statement, self-sufficient, self-contained, where no elaboration is needed. The famous bottles and compote dishes begin to be drawn back into the paper, become larger the more they dissemble. It's almost as though they were drawn on the air, that masterly, and in that instant starting to be borne away, the statement having been made, the design now lodged in the memory, tactile and unremovable. Redemptive on the redemptive air. These are Platonic drawings, their form and architecture already seen and palpable, their decisive indications and linear notations traveling like impulses down the arm and out through the pencil. There's ... a landscape from 1960 [see cover of *Country Music*] consisting of a house, a palm tree, the suggestion of a second house, and possibly a third with some intervening trees or shrubbery, apparently all on a slight hillside, which does for his landscapes what the blue drawing [from 1958] does for his mystical still lifes. In both, the windows into the invisible are lit; in both, what is not there is at least as powerful and tactile as what is. If great art tends toward the condition of the primitive, as I believe it does, and toward the mysteries, as I believe it does, then the late drawings tend toward the same condition. They are full of wonder and singularity, lifelines to the unseen" (*Halflife*, 8–9).

2. *Wright on Wright*: "There is a kind of spatial negation, a visual power in absence that painters understand and employ, and which I'm interested in poetically. It's a sort of white hole that has a kinetic draw to it that the lines of the poem float on and resist. Part of my interest in the dropped line ... is that it sets up a bit of this power field within the line itself; a rhythmic jolt sometimes might appear, small as it is, that kicks the line and the poem along,

keeping it alive over the top of a force that would founder and sink it at any time. But everybody knows this. You keep the composition apart just a little to let this energy in and out, and to let the poem in and out of the energy generated by this emptiness. It's all about the same thing, the power and domination of what's not there, the energy of absence" (QN, 173).

3. Asked in an interview to comment on his appreciation of artists like Morandi, Cezanne, and Mondrian, Wright replied: "Keeping things apart, leaving things out, blank canvas, blank page spaces, not quite completing what is obvious, completing what is not obvious, the idea of knowing what comes next and then declining to say it, or fill it in, determination to keep the circle from touching—one works, as I once said, in the synapse, in the electric field between what is and what isn't, between the beginning and the beginning. It's not so much a desire to keep things tentative as ... to keep things from touching, from becoming complete and becoming final. One wants to feel the kinetics, the possibilities, always the what's-left-to-do. If you know what it is, and you know where it goes, the longer you can keep it out, the deeper it will go once you put it in. Exile's the ultimate synapse—from there you can go anywhere. Cézanne, Matisse, Morandi, and Mondrian—negative transcendence, what you take out is stronger than what you put in. There are no Gods, there are only saints" (Spiegelman, 121).

p. 60, l. 8. *Bob Koffler and Wolf Kahn*. Koffler became a faculty member in graphic design at the Art Institute of Philadelphia. Kahn (b. 1927) became an internationally famous painter.
p. 60, l. 10. *coccodrillo*. Obituary. From the practice of writing obituaries in advance; they remain in the files until such time as they are needed, sleeping down in the basement like crocodiles.
p. 60, l. 12. *Grizzano* = after World War II, the town in the Appenines near Bologna where Morandi regularly sojourned, and where he and his sisters eventually built a modest house and studio.
p. 60, l. 15. *la stessa storia*. The same story.
p. 61, l. 1. *Bologna made you*. A variation on Dante's "Siena mi fe,' disfecemi Maremma" (*Purgatorio*, 5.133). Cf. Wright's own declaration *Verona mi fe,' disfecemi Verona* ("Verona made me, Verona unmade me") in *NB*, 72.

Little Apocalypse

Orig. pub. *New Yorker* 79, no. 13 (26 May 2003): 63.
BY, 62
Pattern: 5 × 3

An apocalypse is a disclosure or, as in the Bible, a prophetic revelation. Wright's "little apocalypse" does not belong to biblical genre, its revelation centering on the busy insect life down below, the clouds above, and the other features on the landscape in between. The last stanza, however, does represent what is often preliminary to an apocalypse—a cataclysm of some sort. The thunderstorm with its drops of fire is foreshadowed by the shuddering ground and mumbling clouds of stanza 1. The one clearly apocalyptic image is that of the four horses of the apocalypse (Revelation 6:1–8), which, in the final line, rear up in the foggy aftermath of the storm. This signal of the end of things is foreshadowed by the Day of Death imagery in stanza 2.

p. 62, l. 10. *sugar bones* = bone-shaped candies used in Day of the Dead ceremonies.
p. 62, l. 13. *drop of fire*. Cf. Christina Rosetti: "Now from my heart, love's deathbed, trickles, trickles, / Drop by drop slowly, drop by drop of fire, / The dross of life, of love, of spent desire" (*Soeur Louise de la Misericorde*, ll. 11–13). In *On the Cliff* Robert Browning uses the phrase "drop of fire" to describe butterfly wings (l. 20).

Snake Eyes

Orig. pub. *New Yorker* 79, no. 1 (17–24 February 2003): 119.
BY, 63
Pattern: 2 × 7

The title, which is also the title for the twenty poems in this section, takes its meaning from the roll of two ones with a pair of six-sided dice. As this is the lowest possible roll, the phrase has come to stand for bad luck.

Wright says, "Some poems are better read than understood" (*UP*, 14), and this is perhaps one of them. Whether the phrase "snake eyes" sets up a binary pattern that resonates throughout the two-line stanzas or that is reiterated in the "mystical twos" of the final couple is uncertain. What is certain is that the poem embodies a central *ars poetica* theme about the difficulty of writing: the indecipherable skyscape will not reveal its secrets, idleness preempts accomplishment, the desire to reach "the radiant root of things" is unfulfilled, and the imagination, while it can open the door, guarantees nothing. Thus, "we" simply wait between the beginning and the end, "whistling the half-remembered tune." The clouds do open up to let "the light come down on some" (good luck) and "taking it back from others" (snake eyes of bad luck), so that the chance of our rolling "boxcars" is exactly equal to the chance of rolling "snake eyes"—one in thirty-six.

p. 63, l. 15. *mojo* = the staple amulet of African-American hoodoo practice, a flannel bag containing one or more magical items.

My Own Little Civil War

Orig. pub. *Shenandoah* 53 (Fall 2003).
BY, 64–6
Pattern: 12 × 5

This is as explicitly autobiographical as Wright ever gets in his poetry. A good deal of the material comes from papers that Wright has kept in an old tin footlocker. When J.D. McClatchy asked Wright what he kept in the tin box, he replied: "Family things, mostly. Old letters, land grant deeds in Arkansas, a couple of family trees. That sort of stuff. Actually, the land grant deeds are interesting, one signed by James K. Polk, one by John Quincy Adams, and one by Andrew Jackson. Simpler presidencies in those days, when you could spend time signing grants for the territory. The whole lot was in a bottom drawer of my father's desk when he died and I've just rather unceremoniously stuck it in this tin box I bought in an antique shop in California. Family letters in almost indecipherable hands from the mid-1800s in Arkansas, a couple of documents from a great-aunt of mine tracing the family lines on my father's side, from Maryland through Virginia to Tennessee and finally to Arkansas. A lock of Robert E. Lee's hair, if you can believe that!" (*QN*, 91). Wright's decision to major in history at Davidson College can perhaps be traced, by his own account, to his interest in the Civil War.

The poem begins as a rather prosaic sketch, but by about line 6 it picks up its poetic rhythm. Its ostensible intent is to reveal the connections with the Civil War of Wright's ancestors: his great-grandfather William Wright, who ended up as one of Robert E. Lee's staff officers; his great-grandfather Penzel, who was wounded at the Battle of Chickamauga; his slave-owning ancestor Isaac Wright, who was too old to serve the Confederate cause (he was in his mid-eighties when the war was over) but whose sympathies are obvious; and an unnamed relative who served as a Confederate quartermaster. Several other relatives get mentioned in passing: Isaac Wright's son Moorehead, who had left North Carolina for Arkansas; Moorehead's wife Elizabeth and their children; a great-aunt Marcella Penzel, one of Charles F. Penzel's three daughters, buried in the Mt. Holly Cemetery in Little Rock.

The poet reveals that he came from the only county in Tennessee that did not secede from the Union. The irony, however, is that his ancestors supported the doomed Southern cause, this irony starkly underwritten by the most unlikely thing contained in the tin box, a lock of Robert E. Lee's hair, which the general had inexplicably sent to Wright's great-grandmother. The poet, then, is left with the tin-box memorabilia and, because there is no connection with the Union cause, with "half the weight and half-life // of a half-healed and hurting world."

p. 64, l. 6 *I was born ... Shiloh churchyard*. Wright was born in Pickwick Dam, Tennessee. The Battle of Shiloh, which began 6 April 1862 by the Shiloh churchyard, was one of the bloodiest battles of the Civil War, leaving more that 3,400 Rebel and Union troops dead.

p. 64, l. 21. *horse and white tomb*. The reference is to Lee's marble tomb in the Chapel of Washington and Lee University. His horse Traveller is buried on the grounds of the University.

p. 65, l. 13. *green hills of Bohemia*. Charles F. Penzel (1840–1906), from whom Wright and his father take their middle name, had emigrated from "the archduchy of Upper Austria" at age sixteen. Soon after he found himself fighting for the Confederacy in the Civil War. He was wounded at the Battle of Chickamauga, eventually became a banker with the Guaranty Trust Company in Little Rock and later was president of the Exchange National Bank, and he served as the chairman of the board of trustees of Arkansas College (now Lyon) from 1899 to 1901.

p. 65, l. 14. *Isaac Wright* (1780–1865) was one of the largest slave owners in Bladen County, North Carolina: he owned more than 300 slaves in 1860. His plantation was on the northern banks of the Cape Fear River. The son mentioned in l. 16 was Moorehead Wright. He died suddenly in April 1857 at age fifty while on his way from Red River to Little Rock, Arkansas. Isaac willed a number of his slaves to his five children.

p. 66, l. 2. *Elizabeth ... children*. Moorehead and Elizabeth Wright had five children: William Fulton, Elizabeth Moorehead, Imagene, Isaac, and Matilda Amelia.

p. 66, l. 6. *Fulton families*. Wright's great-great-great grandfather was William Savin Fulton (1795–1844). In 1829 President Andrew Jackson had sent him to be secretary of the Territory of Arkansas. When Arkansas was admitted as a state in 1836, he became one of its first Senators, serving in Washington until his death. Fulton County, Arkansas, was named for him.

p. 66, l. 10. *wife*. Wright's great-grandmother, the wife of the captain who served on Lee's staff.

La Dolceamara Vita

Orig. pub. *Appalachian Life* 62 (December–January 2003): 28; rpt. in *New Millennium Writings* 14 (2004–2005): 167.
BY, 67
Pattern: 2 × 8
Time: Winter
Place: Charlottesville

Title: The bittersweet life, which is a play on *la dolce vita*, the luxurious, self-indulgent way of life. The phrase was made popular by Federico Fellini's 1960 film, *La Dolce Vita*.

The poet's registers his observations as he strolls down Locust Avenue from his home to the hospital and back. The rains have just ceased. Part of what he sees is *dolce*: the way the rains have "settled like feathers from wild geese," the light on the maple trees, the redness of the dogwood. Part, on the other hand, is *amara*: the chimes of the churches "where nobody goes," the disappearing rainwater that "nobody notices," and the "dying leaves, and the cold flowers." The overall mood is melancholic, what with the poet's "rote" stroll and the darkness behind him becoming darker in front. The desire to "pull the light toward" him if he had it to do all over again is ambiguous, and is as much nightmare as wish-fulfillment, given the juxtaposition of light and death in the final couplet.

p. 67, l. 12. The Martha Jefferson Hospital, 459 Locust Avenue, Charlottesville.

Sun-Saddled, Coke-Copping, Bad-Boozing Blues

Orig. pub. *Southeast Review* 22, no. 2 (Spring 2003): 9.
BY, 68–9

Pattern: 6 × 5
Time: Flashback to the 1960s
Place: Montana

Thoughts of Tim are triggered by a glance at a photograph of the poet and his son on the porch of the Montana cabin. "Tim" is Tim (Timothy John) McIntire, whose dates are given at the end of the poem. He was a talented actor, a musician, a coke addict, and an alcoholic. The son of well-known Hollywood actors John McIntire (1907–91) and Jeanette Nolan (1911–98) and brother of Charles Wright's wife, Holly, Tim died at age forty-two from heart disease. He had begun his acting career as a teenager in his father's *Wagon Train* series. (Holly appeared with her brother in the 1963 Bleeker Story episode of *Wagon Train*). The poem is a sympathetic tribute to a musically talented "Renaissance boy" who is reincarnated by the memory of his music.

Wright on Wright: This "is an elegy of sorts for my brother-in-law, who died in 1986 at the age of 42. He ... lived hard and died young.... And he was also a musician, had his own band. His great unfortunate talent was he could do voices—he could do any voice in the world. And he made his living by doing voice-over commercials ... all the Honda commercials, he did for years. And of course they'd pay him $90,000 a week, and he'd go out and put it all up his nose, which is very unfortunate. Anyway, he was a great guy, and I miss him very much" (*Blackbird*).

p. 68, l. 8. *Billy Myers*. A friend of Tim McIntire.
p. 68, l. 8. *Johnny Rubinstein*. Musician and Hollywood actor (b. 1946); son of piano virtuoso Arthur Rubinstein.
p. 68, ll. 7–12. The lyrics of "Stockman's Bar Again, Boys," one of Tim McIntire's songs. The characters mentioned are Montana old-timers (Big John Phelan, d. 1964; Billy Mitchell, d. 1968).
p. 68, l. 18. Stockman's Bar, long since closed, was in Eureka, Montana, a Lincoln County town five miles south of the Canadian border.
p. 68, l. 21. *American Hot Wax*. 1978 film in which Tim McIntire played the part of the pioneering rock and roll disc jockey Alan Freed.
p. 68, l. 21. *George Jones, type-casting*. McIntire also played George Jones in *Stand by Your Man* (l. 20). Jones, the famous country singer, also had his battles with alcohol and drugs.
p. 69, l. 8. *roll in your sweet baby's arms*. The title of one of George Jones's hits, sung with Tammy Wynette.
p. 69, l. 30. *And lay your body down ... all alone*. The final line of one of McIntire's songs, "A Long Way."

Sinology

Orig. pub. *Pagine* 14, no. 39 (Settembere–Dicembere 2003).
BY, 70
Pattern: 4 × 4
Time: Beginning of winter
Place: Charlottesville

These four little "studies of China" begin with the image of the floating life, a phrase found in one of the poems of Han Shan (Cold Mountain): "Once you realize this floating life is the perfect image of change, / it's breathtaking" (Cold Mountain [Han Shan], Poem 205, in *Mountain Home: The Wilderness Poetry of Ancient China*, trans. David Hinton [Washington, DC: Counterpoint, 2002], 135). Perhaps the phrase also casts a glance at *A Floating Life: Adventures of Li Po*, a biographical novel on the life of the legendary Chinese poet by Simon Elegan. For the poet "floating" translates mostly into an undifferentiated sameness and being adrift in the world. Thus, the memory of his mother "ruffs like an egret and settles back"; nothing sets apart the whiteness of life "back here" from "there." We find that we are "not yet alive" and "not yet dead"; we cannot detect our destination; and so we hang suspended, in this winter season, "between half-empty and half-full." Such a blurry and nebulous state of mind is not conducive to the writing of poetry, though it may be a prelude to the remembering of words and the picking up of the pen once again: "The way to whatever matters begins after that." In the context of "Sinology" it is tempting to hear in the last line the word *Tao*, often translated as "the way."

Images of clouds, dark lakes, and winter landscapes are scattered throughout the Chinese poems in *Mountain Home*. Specific phrases borrowed from *Mountain Home* are in: l. 4, "An egret /startles up, white, and then settles back" (Wang Wei, *Golden-Rain Rapids*, 64); l. 9, "In these twilight years, I love tranquility alone" (Wang Wei, *In Reply to Vice-Magistrate Chang*, 73); l. 14, "and even a single dusk and dawn up here / shows you the way through empty and full" (Hsieh Ling-yün, *On Thatch-Hut Mountain*, 37); and l. 14 again, "Today, things seen becoming thoughts felt: / this is where you start forgetting the words" (Meng Hao-jan, *Sent to Ch'ao, the Palace Reviser*, 43).

p. 70, l. 10. *j-stroke*. Used by paddlers as a correction stroke to keep their boat on a straight course.

Little Apokatastasis

Orig. pub. *Five Points* 7, no. 2.
BY, 73
Pattern: 2 × 2
Time: Winter
Place: Charlottesville

Apokatastasis means a restoration to an original condition. It is the name given to the Christian doctrine that a time will come when all free creatures, including lost souls, will share in the grace of salvation. Acts 3:21 contains the only instance of *apokatastasis* in the New Testament. It is translated as "restitution" in the AV and as "restoration" in the NRSV. In the poem the "little restoration" is the homecoming represented by the cars returning "across the lost highway." Czeslaw Milosz's poetry contains a number of direct references to *apokatastasis*, redefined in broader terms to mean a desire to return to an original wholeness for the object of the poem and, ultimately, for the poet himself. Wright's note (BY, 81) reproduces Milosz's comment: "Apokatastasis: 'That word promises reverse movement.'" The context is this: "Yet I belong to those who believe in *apokatastasis*. / That word promises reverse movement, / Not the one that was set in *katastasis*, / And appears in the Acts, 3, 21" (The title poem of *Bells in Winter* [New York: Ecco Press, 1978], 68). *Katastasis* is the dramatic climax, the settled state before the catastrophe in tragedy. Milosz means that the verse in Acts, which indicates that Jesus is in a holding pattern in heaven until the final universal restoration occurs, is more a *katastasis* than an *apokatastasis*.

In commenting on the apokatastatic idea, Wright said, "What we have, and all we will have, is here in the earthly paradise. How to wring music from it, how to squeeze the light out of it, is, as it has always been, the only true question. I'd say that to love the visible things in the visible world is to love their apokatastatic outline in the invisible next. I think all this, you understand, in my better moments. In my darker ones I'm afraid I rather think the way Philip Larkin did—not anxious for an 'endless extinction.' But we are defined by our better moments, aren't we? Surely we are. Otherwise, God help us" (QN, 120). This means that the people coming home from work, seen through the "tangled branches across the lost highway," are emblematic of a spiritual homecoming.

Star Turn III

BY, 74–5
Pattern: 4 × 5
Time: December
Place: Charlottesville

The first two *Star Turn* poems, which are in NB, 148, 182, turn, so to speak, on the theater metaphor, the "star turn" being the most entertaining item in a show. Here the stars do put on something of a show in the first and third sections, splashing us and thrilling our ears. But the turkey buzzards and crows do as well (section 2). Except for the last four lines, the poem is pure description, and as is the case in practically all of Wright's descriptions of the landscape, their precision and ingenuity dazzle. Exhibit A: "A snail's track of light where earth and clouds seam together." Exhibit B: "Meanwhile, the crows, like floating black stars, drag through the underwinds."

The speculation in the concluding lines is about the eternal mysteriousness of the stars' performance, which is both present and absent. We can never "break their codes" down here on earth, where whatever paltry things we accumulate (pocket change, dried flowers) pale by comparison.

p. 75, l. 3. *where all things are forgot*. Cf. Spenser's *The Faerie Queene*: "In balefull night, where all things are forgot; / All be he subject to mortalitie, / Yet is eterne in mutabilitie, / And by succession made perpetuall, / Transformed oft, and chaunged diverslie" (bk. 3, canto 6, st. 47).

In Praise of Han Shan

Orig. pub. *Five Points* 7, no. 2.
BY, 76
Pattern: 2 × 2

The riddle of the opening couplet is solved by the knowledge that the T'ang poet Han Shan was also known as Cold Mountain, which was also the place where he lived much of his reclusive life. Thus "first" refers to the poet and "second" to the mountain with which he became identified. What little is known about Han Shan comes mostly from legend. He was an eccentric hermit who, along with Li Po and Tu Fu, emerged from the chaos of the An Lushan Rebellion (755–63). He eventually fled for his life for political reasons, escaping into the Tientei Mountains. One can understand how Wright would be drawn to a poet whose name is so closely identified with a particular place and whose self-effacement brings his poetry into high relief. The details in the first three lines of the poem come from David Hinton's introduction to Han Shan (noted below). The final line is a variation of a description of two sages in Chuang Tzu: "They roam at ease beyond the tawdry dust of this world, nothing's own doing / *wu wei* / wandering boundless and free through the selfless unfolding of things" (qtd. in David Hinton, *Mountain Home*, 275). Herein is the justification for the panegyric. "Nothing's own doing," which Wright alters to "Nothing's undoing," is a translation of the Taoist and Zen idea of *wu wei* (nondoing). Lao Tzu describes *wu wei*, the attitude of the Taoist saint, this way: "In the pursuit of learning one knows more every day; in the pursuit of the way one does less every day. One does less and less until one does nothing at all, and when one does nothing at all there is nothing that is undone" (*Tao Te Ching*, trans. D.C. Lau [Harmondsworth: Penguin, 1963], 109 [chap. 48]). *Wu wei*, therefore, does not mean complete inaction but action that is free from desire or motivation. *Wu wei* calls for the Taoist initiate not to intervene in the course of external events but to let things unfold in their normal and inevitable way. R.B.

Blakney's translation of the second half of chapter 48 of the *Tao Te Ching* puts it this way: "By letting go, it all gets done; / The world is won by those who let it go! / But when you try and try, / The world is then beyond the winning" (*The Way of Life* [New York: Mentor, 1983], 101). Which is reason enough to praise the identity of the poet and his place.

p. 76, l. 1. *Cold Mountain.* "Cold Mountain emptied out the distinction between Cold Mountain the poet and Cold Mountain the mountain. This is the essence of the Cold Mountain poems, so it is fitting that almost nothing is known about Cold Mountain the poet.... mostly he roamed the mountains alone, a wild Ch'an sage writing poems on rocks and trees" (David Hinton, *Mountain Home*, 128).

p. 76, l. 2. "According to the legend, Cold Mountain the poet was last seen when, slipping into a crevice that closed behind him, he vanished utterly into the mountain" (ibid.).

p. 76, l. 4. The description of the Taoist sages who "roam at ease beyond the tawdry dust of this world, nothing's own doing" has an uncanny resemblance to e.e. cummings's description of the Canterbury pilgrims: "drifting through vast most / nothing's own nothing children of dust" (*Xaipe*, poem 63, in *Poems 1923-1854* [New York: Harcourt, Brace, 1954], 463).

CHAPTER 6

Scar Tissue

The book is dedicated to the memory of Wright's father- and mother-in-law, John McIntire and Jeanette Nolan, and of his parents, Chuck and Ditty. Twenty-two of the poems were published in a chapbook, *The Wrong End of the Rainbow* (Louisville: Sarabande Books, 2005).

Appalachian Farewell

Orig. pub. *New Yorker* 79, no. 32 (27 October 2003): 78.
WER, 7; ST, 3
Pattern: 3 × 6
Time: Winter
Place: In or around Kingsport, Tennessee

This poem, about the sense of place, begins as a valediction to the native Appalachian home of the poet's early years and ends up being a prayer to the wintry *genius loci* (the Goddess of Bad Roads and Inclement Weather). We begin with four noun phrases that set the scene: "Sunset in Appalachia, bituminous bulwark / Against the western skydrop. / An Advent of gold and green, an Easter of ashes." Here the Church calendar is imposed upon the seasonal cycle but with a reversal of the green and golden world of spring (the Easter season) and the ashen Appalachian mountains of late December (the Advent season). The poet has returned to the place that he and his contemporaries abandoned years ago (for him, Kingsport; for the others, the towns named in the last line). The stories of their lives have been spelled out in the meantime, and yet the invocation to the Goddess is an appeal not only that they might not be forgotten but that she may "Help us never to get above our raising, help us / To hold hard to what was there." "Our raising" means "our rearing"—here in this place where we grew up. The petition that they may never "get above" their raising is an appeal for humility and for maintaining a connection with beginnings. What precisely the poet wants to "hold hard to" is not specified, save for the three places named in the final line, but whatever it is, it is a part of his identity and that of the others who left. The poem, therefore, turns out to be not a farewell but a plea that the Appalachian sense of place, dimmed in memory by the intervening years, be restored and maintained.

p. 3, l. 18. Orebank. A small town east of Kingsport, Tennessee, just to the south of East Stone Drive (Highway 11W). Reedy Creek runs through Kingsport, Tennessee, encircling the Kingsport Greenbelt Park and flowing into the Holston River approximately two miles from the Western border of Sullivan County, Tennessee. Wright lived on Old Stage Road, just to the southwest of Orebank. Surgoinsville is a town in east Tennessee on Highway 11W, southwest of Kingsport about seventeen miles.

Last Supper

First journal appearance in *Daedalus* 135, no. 1 (Winter 2006): 115.
WER, 8; ST, 4

Pattern: 5 × 3
Time: Wednesday before Easter, i.e., sometime between March 18 and April 21.

The magic of the Easter season, its floral display in "full drag," is a spectacle that could engender sentimentality, but the poet rejects that possibility. The background of his consciousness is weighed down by thoughts other than the Easter season. These emerge from an extended metaphor cluster, which includes the last supper (and the Last Supper), the crosses of the dogwood blossoms, the bowed heads of the lilies and jonquils, the reliquary bones, and the spring snow personified as a Grim Slicer. All of these images have symbolic overtones, in this week of the Passion, to the endless "other world," which is introduced at the exact center of the poem (l. 8). The poet senses that he has "come to the end of something," adding that he doesn't know what it is. But by the time we get to the final lines, we know that the end of something is the end of life. So we move from the Last Supper of Christ (the setting of the poem is Maundy Thursday) to an imminent last supper of life. It is not the poet who is holding the cutlery, but "Spring in its starched bib," having materialized out of the late spring snow that fell several days earlier. Our fathers have told us, says the poet, "it's either eat or be eaten." But as spring is holding winter's cutlery, it is not the poet who is going to be eating at this last supper. "Cold grace" indeed to be sliced and forked in this way—a rather demonic parody of the Last Supper.

Inland Sea

Orig. pub. *Blackbird* 3, no. 1 (Spring 2004). Online journal.
WER, 9–10, ST, 5–6
Pattern: 5 × 5
Time: Spring, apparently.

This gloomy meditation takes place under the sway of Sagittarius, the Archer, who was placed in the skies to guide the Argonauts. Pelagus, the star on the arrow at the Archer's hand, was known in antiquity as "The Star of the Proclamation of the Sea." Sagittarius of the Classical legend originated in Mesopotamia, the land between the two rivers. Intentional or not, all this is apposite in a poem focusing on the "waters of memory" and the rains of nostalgia. The central metaphor is that the earth beneath the "Little windows of gold paste" is an inland sea. The problem is that the "waters of memory" are not life-giving waters but bitter, like those in the Book of Numbers; so we are advised to stuff our "heart with dead moss" in this wasteland world of "dry dreams" and to remember Babylon (appropriately in Mesopotamia on the Euphrates, Sagittarius' homeland). Babylon, reports the Psalmist, was the city by whose waters the Israelites sat down and wept (Psalm 137), a line that Eliot inserts into part 3 of *The Waste Land*. Nostalgia, which "arrives like a spring rain" and then dissolves "like a disease," is no more promising than "the waters of memory." Thus, we are rather lost souls: we are dogged by nighttime, the heavens ignore our moans, and we hear no "holy, holy, holy." In the hymn we are told that all God's works will praise his name "in earth and sky and sea," but there is no such praise on the lips of the poet, who can only repeat the stanza with which he began—a repetition, incidentally that is unique in Wright's work.

The Silent Generation II

Orig. pub. *Irish Pages*, 2, no. 1 (Spring–Summer 2003): 173.
WER, 11; ST, 7

Pattern: 3 × 5
Time: May

For *The Silent Generation I* and *The Silent Generation III*, see *NB*, 37, and *ST*, 66–7.

The first poem with this title had to do with the inability, apparently because of fear, of "the silent generation" to confront questions of social justice. The present poem asks, "Who knew we had so much to say, or tongue to say it?"—indicating that the silent generation was not so silent after all: they were "garrulous, word-haunted, senescent." Still, they took their lumps, and the wind crumpled their pages. The poem concludes on a note of Stoic endurance. Throughout it all, the silent generation has kept a stiff lip and has continued to write, with the hope that its "small words," which have already proven the word "silent" false (l. 15), will remain permanent. We find one story of the silent generation here in the book we are holding "at the end of the last page" (l. 2), where the final three words are "sing the song." The third *Silent Generation* poem (below) has a much less sanguine view of that generation's words.

High Country Canticle

Orig. pub. *Notre Dame Review* 18 (Summer 2004).
WER, 12; ST, 8
Pattern: 5 + 1
Time: Late May
Place: Montana

The message of this canticle from the high country is *carpe diem*: you can't stuff anything in your pocketless shroud and your soul will encounter only darkness in the grave: embrace, therefore, the benediction (blessings) offered by the "bright wingrush of grace" moving through the Montana landscape. (In a poem about our seizing the day before we grow old and die is it a coincidence that the first letters of the six lines form the word "oldest"?)

p. 8, l. 1. *The shroud has no pockets.* That is, you can't take anything with you to the grave. The proverb is found in the German tradition as well.
p. 8, l. 5. *bright wingrush of grace.* The phrase is reminiscent of the "bright wings" of the Holy Ghost in Hopkins's sonnet *God's Grandeur*, an image of the beauty of God's grace. It is also suggestive of canto 32 of Dante's *Paradiso*.
p. 8, l. 6. *Spring moves ... poling it.* Cf. "On the spring flood of last night's rain / The ferry-boat moves as though someone were poling" (Wêi Ying-wu, At Ch'u-Chou on the Western Stream, in *The Jade Mountain*, 169).

The Wrong End of the Rainbow

Orig. pub. *Poetry* 183, no. 6 (March 2004): 319.
WER, 13; ST, 9
Pattern: 3 × 6

The poem begins with a recollection of various liaisons with women during the poet's Italian sojourn in 1959: in Rome or perhaps Naples with What's-Her-Name, in Florence with Yes-of-Course, in Milan with That's-the-One, and in Venice with Come-on-Back. The last half of the poem is a nostalgic celebration of an earlier day when passion held sway. The young lovers were at the right end of the rainbow and oblivious to everything except, as we see in stanza 4, their assimilation into the four elements of the natural cycle. In an echo of Theodore Roethke, they measure time by how their bodies sway with the world (earth); they identify with the "river-run" that opens and closes *Finnegans Wake* (water); they soar with the hawk's breath (air), and they live at the "center's heat at the center of things" (fire). This, says the poet, is the way he would like to be remembered, not as he currently is at the wrong end of the rainbow with his feet, rather than his head, in the clouds. The poem celebrates the nostalgia of memory: memory is worth hugging when its "full lips" tell "us just those things // she thinks we want to hear." Recollection, a source that Wright mines repeatedly, tells us many other things as well: the words "memory" and "remember" appear more than 220 times in his poetry.

p. 9, l. 1. *Forio d'Ischia.* Forio is a municipality that occupies the west side of the island of Ischia, southwest of Naples.
p. 9, l. 2. *Pensione Margutta.* A pensione on the Via Margutta in Rome, a bohemian quarter below the Spanish Steps.
p. 9, l. 5. *S. Maria Novella.* The oldest of the great Florentine basilicas, begun in 1246 and completed in 1360.
p. 9, l. 7. *Bar Giamaica.* An artists' bar in Milan that Wright frequented in 1959–60. See *Bar Giamaica 1959–60* in *WTTT*, 39.
p. 9, l. 12. *Remember us as we were.* Cf. *Gate City Breakdown:* "Remember me as you will, but remember me once / Slide-wheeling around the curves, // letting it out on the other side of the line" (*WTTT*, 40).

A Field Guide to the Birds of the Upper Yaak

Orig. pub. *Virginia Quarterly Review* 80, no. 2 (Spring 2004): 114.
WER, 17–18, ST, 10
Pattern: 7 × 3
Place: Montana
Time: Fall, apparently.

The birds of the Upper Yaak make their appearance only in the final three lines. Their presence is recorded rather matter-of-factly, except for the simile that captures perfectly the unfolding wings of the great blue heron, whose wheeling and folding we meet later in *Little Landscape* (*ST*, 64). What we have is less a field guide to the birds than a window onto the misty morning of the evergreen back country, where the poet is a solitary observer. Twice he tells us he is the only person present, and then he adds, "there is almost never another soul around," unlike what is often found in the T'ang poets. The absence of human presence means that "nobody gives a damn." But the poet gives a damn. Even though he tells us that everything is "out in the open," the word "iconostasis" at the exact center of the poem suggests that something is hidden in the altar behind the evergreens. "Iconostasis" is the crux. The screen itself is dark, innocent, and virginal, and its icons "ungazed upon" by anyone other than the poet, who views them from the landscape's nave. There may be "no secret lives" in the foreground of the evergreens, but the poet intimates that something invisible may well lie behind the screen in the sanctuary or on the altar.

p. 10, l. 5. *two lips away.* "Say you'll never stray / More than just two lips away." The lines are from "Near You," words and music by Francis Craig. The song was recorded by the Andrews Sisters in 1947 and by numerous others in the meantime.
p. 10, l. 11. *iconostasis.* A large screen in Greek churches, running from side to side of the apse, separating the sanctuary from the body of the church, thus shutting off the altar and the sanctuary from the worshipper. The analogue in Roman churches is the rood screen.

A Short History of My Life

Orig. pub. *New Yorker* 79, no. 44 (26 January 2004): 68–9.
WER, 14–15; ST, 11–12
Pattern: 3 × 10
Time: Early June
Place: Montana

This brief autobiography has three chapters. They record (1) the poet's birth in Pickwick Dam, Tennessee; (2) the discovery of his poetic mission and therefore his rebirth in Verona,

Italy; and (3) forty-five years later his second rebirth in the dark grace of a Montana June, the vision of which he has tried to record.

p. 11, ll. 1–3. *Laotzu*. Witter Bynner reports on the legend that Lao Tzu was immaculately conceived to a shooting star, carried in his mother's womb for sixty-two years, and born, white-haired, in 604 B.C.E. (*The Way of Life, According to Lao Tzu*, trans. Witter Bynner [New York: Perigree, 1980]).

p. 11, l. 11. *Like Dionysus*. Dionysus, according to one myth, was the son of the god Zeus and the mortal, Semele (daughter of Cadmus of Thebes). Semele was killed by Zeus' lightning bolts while Dionysus was still in her womb, but Dionysus is rescued and undergoes a second birth from Zeus after developing in his thigh.

p.11, l. 17. *S. Zeno*. The church of San Zeno Maggiore in Verona.

p. 11, ll. 19, 20. *Dolomites*. The Alpine mountains to the north of Lago di Garda, the largest lake in Italy, located between Lombardy and Venetia.

p. 11, l. 22–p. 12, l. 1. *the poet ... Alluding to something else*. "DIGONOS, Δίγονος but the twice crucified / where in history will you find it?" (Canto 74, ll. 5–6, *The Cantos of Ezra Pound* [New York: New Directions, 1970], 445). Pound was alluding to Mussolini's being hanged by his heels in Milan, which is what Wright means by "Alluding to something else."

Waking Up After the Storm

Orig. pub. *Notre Dame Review* 18 (Summer 2004)
WER, 19; ST, 13
Pattern: 3 × 2

The poet, wakened by a storm, records the end of a dream but decides it is futile to try to interpret it or to search the stars for enlightenment. The light of the stars, anyway, has begun to disappear under the full moon.

Images from the Kingdom of Things

Orig. pub. *Blackbird* 3, no. 1 (Spring 2004). Online journal.
WER, 20; ST, 14
Pattern: 4 × 3
Place: Montana

The site of the first and third of these image clusters is the Yaak country meadow at nighttime. The second is the afternoon spectacle of Mt. Henry, with its leaning fire tower, rising beyond the meadow to the southwest. The first snapshot reveals the world as "a desolate garden," surreal in its desolation: metaphorically the sunlight is the wind and the nighttime is water. In the second the poet's eye moves from snow-capped Mt. Henry down to the lodgepole pine in the foreground. The third, an adaptation of a stanza from Wang Ch'ang-ling, is a midnight vision of the meadow bathed in the "blanched bones" of the moonlight. This example of "waste and ruin," anticipated by the desolate garden of stanza 1 and the abandoned watchtower of stanza 2, is a wasteland vision of death and vacancy. It raises the question: "How many word-warriors [poets] ever return" from such a scene? The answer is at least two, and they have the same initials: Ch'ang-ling Wang and Charles Wright.

p. 14, l. 5. *Mt. Henry*. One of the mountains in the Kootenai National Forest in northwest Montana.

p. 14, l. 8. *detonators*. In extreme heat (as from a forest fire) the cones of the lodgepole pine explode to release the seeds.

p. 14, l. 9. *The blanched bones*. Cf. Tu Fu: "The moonlight shines cold on white bones" (*Travelling Northward*, in *One Hundred Poems from the Chinese*, trans. Kenneth Rexroth [New York: New Directions, 1971], 10).

p. 14, ll. 9–12. "The stream is cold and the wind like a sword, / As we watch against the sunset on the sandy plain, / Far, far away, shadowy Lin-t'ao. / Old battles, waged by those long walls, / Once were proud on all men's tongues. / But antiquity now is a yellow dust, / Confusing in the grasses its ruins and white bones" (Wang Ch'ang-ling, *Under a Border Fortress*, in Witter Bynner, *The Chinese Translations* [New York: Farrar, Straus Giroux, 1978], 212; rpt. from *The Jade Mountain*, trans. Witter Bynner [Garden City, NY: Doubleday Anchor, 1964], 149).

p. 14, l. 11. The return from the land of the dead is reminiscent of the scene between Dante and Guido de Montefeltro in the *Inferno*, canto 26, which Eliot uses as an epigraph to *The Love Song of J. Alfred Prufrock*. We are perhaps reminded as well of Prufrock's fantasy about Lazarus, who comes back from the dead to tell all.

Confessions of a Song and Dance Man

Orig. pub. *Meridian* 13 (Spring–Summer 2004): 115.
WER, 21–3; ST, 15–17
Pattern: 5 × 8
Place: Montana

The confession comes in stanza 3, where the poet reveals that he is a "God-fearing agnostic." This oxymoron appears to be a joke, as does the mumbling address to the Lord, "O three-in-none." But at the same time, the poet identifies himself as an acolyte, and, thus he is, if not an assistant in the liturgical rites, at least a devoted follower of the faith. The point is that the poet is uncertain about his beliefs. He continues to look for the hidden God, going out of his way to face and pin down the *deus absconditus* behind creation in order to insure that He is absent, and whispering to the Lord even when he knows He is not present. This is the stance of the dance man, shuffling from one point to another, slip-stepping and gliding, affirming and denying, "balancing back and forth" like the red-winged blackbird of the final section, or like the landscape's giving and taking back of illusion in section 2.

Why does the blackbird, the poet wonders in the self-revelatory climax, continue to dive down into the marsh? The answer is that bird needs the "same thing I need up here, I guess, / A place to ruffle and strut, // a place to perch and sing."

Images of the dance alternate with music throughout the poem. The music of the wind sets the poet's "feet to twitching" in section 1. In section 2 the background hum of the mist is like dancers lifted by the wind, and "holding the measure still, holding the time" could refer to the arrested movement of both music and dance. The song and dance come together in the final stanza in the strutting and singing of both the poet and the bird.

p. 15, l. 11. *narcissus poeticus*. A type of iris that Wright's wife Holly planted by their Montana cabin steps.
p. 15, l. 18. *A little landscape's a dangerous thing*. A twist on Alexander Pope's "A little learning is a dangerous thing" (*Essay on Criticism*, pt. 2, l. 15).
p. 16, l. 9. *kyrie eleison* = "Lord have mercy," an expression used frequently in Christian liturgies.
p. 17, l. 3. *Make my bed ... bye-bye*. From *Bye Bye Blackbird*, words by Mort Dixon and melody by Ray Henderson (1926).

Against the American Grain

Orig. pub. *Harper's Magazine* 309, no. 1851 (August 2004): 25.
WER, 24; ST, 18
Pattern: 5 × 3
Place: Montana

The key to what runs against the American grain is provided by Wright's note: "As Hopkins might have called it, an 'inscape of being'" (p. 75). Inscape for Hopkins was what defined the essence of poetry. "Poetry," he wrote, "is in fact speech employed to carry the inscape of speech for the inscape's sake" (*The Journals and Papers of Gerard Manley Hopkins*, ed. Humphry House and Graham Storey [Oxford: Oxford University Press, 1959], 289). Inscape is a cluster of features that gives each thing its unique character. It is similar to Joyce's epiphany, Rimbaud's *illumination*, and Wordsworth's "spots of time," except that for Hopkins inscape was decidedly religious. It refers to the distinctive character of things given to them by the Creator, and thus things with inscape reflect an aspect of God. For Wright, these things are fundamentally objects in the landscape, such as those described in the first two stanzas. They are the things in which the "unordinary persists" and which are "just possible past reason." Such a view is against the American grain, insofar as there is a general resistance, or at least reluctance, in the American grain, including its poetic culture, to speak or write about religious matters. This would include those whom Hopkins labeled "Parnassian"—competent poets but completely uninspired.

The inscape of a thing is sometimes barely perceptible ("flecked"). At other times, as in the experience of plentitude provided by the "evening's overflow," the inscape is completely visible. The "something unordinary" does not reflect a vision of sweetness and light. It includes the sun-pocked afternoon as well as the fragrant lilacs.

Wright on "inscape": "Reading through the journals [of Hopkins], one is constantly struck by the faith GMH has, and the absolute certainty of that faith: that when he decides to describe something—a leaf, a wave, a series of waves, a bird, a landscape sweep—minutely or particularly, he is able to transcend it, through language, and enter whatever it is he is describing; that the inscape is knowable and tactile through language. That the heart of the mystery, the pulse at the very unspeakable center of being, is apprehensible through writing about it. Thus the lovingly, intricately laid down musical strings of language. One no longer believes this is possible. One more often now knows that the only answer to inscape is silence" (QN, 24).

College Days

Orig. pub as a broadside on the occasion of a reading by Wright at his alma mater on 15 April 2004.
WER, 25–6; ST, 19–20
Pattern: 10 × 4

Time: Memories of September 1953 and following

This poem is about the mind's ability to resurrect shards of past experience long forgotten. It centers on Wright's experience at Davidson College, located seven miles from Mooresville, N.C., a small mill town at the time. The date given in the first line—September 1953—was the beginning of Wright's freshman year. Stonestreet's Cafe (l. 5) was located on Main Street in Mooresville, several blocks south of the center of town. It has since disappeared, as have the cotton mills.

The poet is initially puzzled by the material fragments that float through his mind as he recalls the "lay by" (rest stop) of his college days—Pabst Blue Ribbon beer, several novels, "the myth of Dylan Thomas," the academic chapel, the parking lot, and his laundry number. Why these things, the poet wonders. And is it only the material reality of such things—random, trivial, disconnected—that endures? He is as mystified as the rest of us about why some things are retained in memory, but he seeks to illuminate the matter through the simile of small pieces of broken glass that lodge themselves under the skin: we think that these images from our past have disappeared, their sharp edges having been rounded off by the body, but then they reappear when the occasion presents itself, like the occasion of reading a poem at one's alma mater. Images, such as those in stanza 1, really have no meaning, deep or otherwise: they trigger only a little sadness of a world that has disappeared and a little nostalgia. They are not, however, objective correlatives for anything but themselves. The world of memory "floats in the aether of its own content" somewhere between nothing and nothingness.

p. 19, l. 2. *Hearts made of stone.* From *Hearts of Stone*, a popular tune by Rudy Jackson and Eddy Ray. The Fontane Sisters' release climbed to number three on the charts in 1955, and The Charms' rhythm and blues version made it to number fifteen on the R & B charts the same year.

p. 19, l. 8. *myth of Dylan Thomas*. At the time, Thomas was on a stormy tour of the U.S., promoting the publication of his *Collected Poems*, lecturing, appearing on television, and drinking heavily. Two months after Wright began college, Thomas was dead at age thirty-nine. The first poem Wright wrote in college was an imitation of Dylan Thomas.

p. 19, l. 11. *academic chapel*. Davidson College students were required to attend "chapel" services in the Chambers Hall auditorium, where each undergraduate had an assigned seat.

p. 19, l. 12. *laundry number*. The college provided on-campus laundry service for students.

p. 19, l. 16. *Cavafy*. The reference is to ll. 34–8 of Constantine P. Cavafy's *Waiting for the Barbarians* (1904): "Why are the streets and squares emptying so rapidly, / everyone going home so lost in thought? / Because night has fallen and the barbarians have not come. / And some who have just returned from the border say / there are no barbarians any longer."

p. 19, l. 20. *Is sin ... more tactile than a tree?* That is, a question Wright once asked himself. It is not a line that appears in one of his poems.

p. 20, l. 16. *objective correlative*. The term coined by T.S Eliot in his essay "Hamlet and His Problems": "The only way of expressing emotion in the form of art is by finding an 'objective correlative'; in other words, a set of objects, a situation, a chain of events which shall be the formula of that *particular* emotion; such that when the external facts, which must terminate in sensory experience, are given, the emotion is immediately evoked" (*Selected Essays*, rev. ed. [New York: Harcourt, Brace, 1950], 124–5).

Night Thoughts Under a China Moon

Orig. pub. *Notre Dame Review* 18 (Summer 2004).
WER, 27; ST, 24
Pattern: 4
Place: Montana

"Night thoughts" seems intended to put us in the context of the eighteenth-century graveyard poets (Edward Young and others), and "China Moon" reminds us of the lunar predilections of practically all of the T'ang poets. But what stands out in the four-line poem is the image of the Hunter Gracchus. The poet observes that as one walks through the Montana wilderness one will eventually reach water cutting across the trail, and it is perhaps the image of water that calls up the story of Gracchus. In any event, we have the juxtaposition of a rather unexceptional description of the trail-walk beneath the infinitely passing clouds and the exceptional image of the Hunter Gracchus "approaching along the waves / Each time in his journey west of west." There is also a contrast in *The Hunter Gracchus* itself between the ordinariness of life in its opening scene and the extraordinary events that follow.

This is the fourth appearance of the Hunter Gracchus in Wright's poems, and he will appear again—once in *In Praise of Franz Kafka* and twice in *Littlefoot* (sects. 9 and 22). In each case his body is "long," apparently because in Kafka's story he is described as stretched out on a pallet, and in the other six instances he is described as sailing by (SHS, 59; BY, 17; L, sect. 9), sliding through (BY, 29), floating again (ST, 60), and "passing" (L, sect. 22). The juxtaposition of the ordinary with the extraordinary mirrors Kafka's absurdist tale. The hunter Gracchus died from a fall in the Black Forest, and when the boat carrying his body arrives in Riva, he tells the burgomaster, "My death ship lost its way—a wrong turn of the helm, a moment when the helmsman was not paying attention, a distraction from my wonderful homeland—I don't know what it was. I only know that I remain on the earth and that since that time my ship has journeyed over earthly waters. So I—who only wanted to live in my own mountains—travel on after my death through all the countries of the earth."

Kafka's death-haunted parable contains echoes of Wright's own poetic quest. Gracchus says that the boat was supposed to carry him "to the other side," and when the burgomaster asks Gracchus, "And have you no share in the world beyond?" Gracchus responds, "I am always on the immense staircase leading up to it. I roam around on this infinitely wide flight of steps, sometimes up, sometimes down, sometimes to the right, sometimes to the left, always in motion." Wright's journey, which began at the other end of Lake Garda from Riva, is, like Gracchus's to the "west of west"—an effort to get to the other side. Paradise is a matter about which the poet cannot speak, but the idea that in death, as in life (Gracchus insists he is alive as well as dead), we are on a journey to get there is the underlying narrative pattern in Wright's pilgrimage. Both writers would agree that death is not a state of existence to be dreaded. "I had been happy to be alive and was happy to be dead," says the hunter Gracchus. The horror for him is the interminable process of dying: he is no doubt still "approaching along the waves."

Bedtime Story

Orig. pub. *Poetry* 183, no. 6 (March 2004): 318.
WER, 28; ST, 22
Pattern: 5x3
Place: Montana

The narrative in this bedtime story comes in the second stanza, where a mysterious and ominous "Something" is making its way into the meadow and "into our hearts." The noumenal hum of the distant generator sets the tone, and the setting of the story follows in stanza 1. The story is being told to "my small one," who is apparently the same person addressed as "love" in the last stanza, where the issue becomes how "we" should respond to this Something, which is both ushering darkness in and "licking the shadows up." While the Something is filling in the blank spaces, which is a worthy enterprise, at the same time it is "scratching its blue nails against the wall" of our hearts, a less inviting prospect and even bestial in its implications. So what's a body to do? Should the mysterious presence be let in and greeted with astonishment? Should it be accorded a more matter-of-fact but cordial reception? Or should it rather be welcomed with music, hand-clapping, and the "Something Dance?" As the three possibilities are mutually exclusive, the answer in the last line—"I think we should"—must refer to the last of the three possibilities. The moral of the bedtime story seems to be that we should embrace joyfully the mysterious Other. That is the climax. As for the denouement, we are left hanging.

p. 22, l. 1. The *ding an sich* (thing in itself) is an object as it is (or would be) independently of our awareness of it; the noumenon, as opposed, in Kant's distinction, to an object as it appears to us (the phenomenon).

Transparencies

Orig. pub. *Paris Review* 167 (Fall 2003): 150.
WER, 29–30; ST, 23–4
Pattern: 6 × 4

The meaning of the title emerges from the third stanza with the image of the translucent amber, but the issue confronted in the poem—the nature of metaphor and its relation to memory—is anything but transparent. The poet is anxious about the loss of memory over time, which is a corrupting force (p. 23, l. 12). Can we be certain that we remember things as they really are? And do they continue to be the same thing they once were? Even perception itself is questioned: are the trees really trees and the clouds really clouds? In stanza two, the issue is transferred to metaphor, a figure the poet would like to have escape the ravages of time as well: "I wanted the metaphor ... to remain always the same one." This somewhat curious desire, favoring identity over difference, is understandable on one level, since metaphor always asserts the sameness of things: sunlight *is* a rag to be wrung out, as in the previous poem, or sunlight is an impulsive speaker, as in the present one. But the principle of identity is complicated in the second stanza, where the poet says that he "wanted to walk in that metaphor," that metaphor being the idea that time stops. In other words, the poet prefers permanence to change, change being the result of "time's corruption." In such a condition, the poet's own identity would be defined by the principle of identity. Put even more abstractly, in the context of *poetic identity* the desire is for time to equal intransience, and in the context of *personal identify* the desire is for the self to equal stability as well. Similarly, with memory, the poet wishes that it would be "never-changing," a point he illustrates by developing the extended metaphor of the piece of amber. Amber is a fossil resin that traps within itself and preserves plants and insects that are more than 100 million years old but appear as if they were captured only yesterday. If the poet could be trapped within amber's translucent swirls, then he would be able to transfigure exactly nothing. Again, the desire is for time to stop: if it were to stop, then things could not change.

This whole line of thought is upset in the third stanza, where the poet comes to realize that both memory and metaphor cannot be so constrained. Memory is not static: "it moves as it wants to move." The same with metaphor, which constantly changes the predicates of its subjects: a Grecian urn can be a "still unravish'd bride of quietness" at one moment and "a foster-child of silence and slow time" or a "sylvan historian" a moment later. Rather than being incased in amber then, our lives, like our memories, are—here is the metaphor—"summer cotton," which means, far from being "adamantine," they are always subject to transfiguration by the wind, waves, and any number of other forces.

The conclusion reached by the poet is this: "Memory's logo is the abyss, and that's no metaphor." The last clause produces a double-take because the first clause is, in fact, a metaphor: there is no literal sense in which memory sports an identifying symbol. Logo is clearly a figure when it is attached to memory, and the figure is extended (and complicated) by equating the logo of memory with the abyss, which recalls the metaphor of the sun as "life's loss-logo" in *Looking Across Laguna Canyon at Dusk, West-by-Northwest* (NB, 64). It is not too difficult here to translate the metaphor: memories fall into a deep hole and are practically impossible to retrieve. That much is transparent.

Morning Occurrence at Xanadu

Orig. pub. *Notre Dame Review* 18 (Summer 2004).
WER, 31; ST, 25
Pattern: 3 × 2
Place: Montana

Xanadu is the name Wright gave to his Montana cabin. Whether he intended the name to suggest the Xanadu in Coleridge's *Kubla Khan* is uncertain. If he did, then perhaps the epiphanic moment described in the second stanza is parallel to the enchanted opulence of Kubla Khan's sunny pleasure dome—and to the speaker there, who has fed on honey-dew and drunk the milk of Paradise. In any event, the reader is called on to discover the connection that obtains between the two tercets, a connection primarily of opposition. In the first stanza, the focus is on the death of the young swallows, which parallels the green-to-grey transition of the aspen leaves. In the second stanza, the mood turns from somber grief to happy enlightenment. Perhaps the Socratic confession of ignorance follows from the poet's awareness that he knows little about the mysterious workings of the natural cycle and so cannot answer the questions about why young birds die and leaves turn grey. Whatever the case, knowledge of his ignorance is no cause for long-faced melancholy. Such knowledge is *like* the happiness of the man who comes suddenly upon the gleam of light that penetrates the forest clearing. The setting is not unlike the "forests ancient as the hills, / Enfolding sunny spots of greenery" in Coleridge's poem. *Kubla Khan*, which is a dream-vision, is based on a least a score of oppositions. The fewer oppositions in *Morning Occurrence* are based on negative simile—X is unlike its contrary Y: the natural vs. the human, the grey vs. the light, grief vs. happiness, simple sight vs. recognition. The poem is a "little anagnorisis," a companion to *Little Apocalypse* (BY, 62) and *Little Apokatastasis* (BY, 73).

Saturday Morning Satori

Orig. pub. *Blackbird* 3, no. 1 (Spring 2004). Online journal.
WER, 34; ST, 26
Pattern: 5 × 2

Title: *Satori* is the spiritual goal of Zen Buddhism. It roughly translates as individual enlightenment or a flash of sudden awareness.

The poet's Saturday morning *satori* is an insight into the nature of the poetic image. He begins by wishing that the Chinese poet, Wêi Ying-wu, had extended his meditation on the mind-body relation to include a simile, or at least to extend the one in his adage. There are three parts of Wêi Ying-wu's aphorism: first, an exalted mind, and, second, a lightened body produced by the exalted mind. Both are metaphors, one having to do with elevation in space and the other with lack of weight. In part three, the Chinese poet says that the lightened body feels *as if* it could float in the wind (a simile). But as the Chinese poet neglected to say what such *floating* is like, the poet proceeds to provide a simile from what is directly in front of him—a feather, which he had initially believed to be a leaf.

These reflections lead to speculations—in the second stanza—about poetic language: there is a difference between a thing (for example, feather) and an image (a feather used figuratively). The image is said to be "imagination's second best," no imagination being required in our direct experience of things. This means apparently that "imagination's best" is the language of landscape that speaks directly to us, as in the metaphor of the final line, where the gutteral sounds of the heavens (God's voice) "call out to us // each day." All three of the poet's subject matters come together, then, in the second stanza: landscape, language, and the idea of God

p. 26, l. 1. "When the mind is exalted, the body is lightened / And feels as if it could float in the wind" (Wêi Ying-wu, *Entertaining Literary Men in My Official Residence on a Rainy Day*, in Witter Bynner, *The Chinese Translations* [New York: Farrar Straus Giroux, 1978], 233; rpt. from *The Jade Mountain*, trans. Witter Bynner [Garden City, NY: Doubleday Anchor, 1964], 171).

Wrong Notes

Orig. pub. *Virginia Quarterly Review* 80, no. 2 (Spring 2004): 115.
WER, 35–6; ST, 27
Pattern: 5 × 4
Place: Northwest Montana

The poet opens with an instruction to himself, borrowed from a poem by Li Tüan, to "strike a wrong note from time to time." In the Chinese poem a female harpist intentionally plucks an occasional wrong note in order to draw the attention of Chou Yu, evidently someone she admires. This is a literal musical phenomenon, and one for which the Greeks had a word, *parakrousis*. But "to strike the wrong note" also has the expanded meaning of saying or doing something that is unsuited for a particular occasion. That both meanings are present in the poem is suggested by line 2, where striking the wrong note is done "Half for the listening ear, half for the watching eye." The musical meaning, moreover, is implicit in the phrase "lapped scales," referring to the two creeks that flash through the meadow. The sunlight makes them appear to be like the "lapped scales" of a fish, but as the two creeks come together the sound made by one overlaps that of the other, so that two musical scales coincide. The poet may also intend "slides" to carry a musical meaning—the slight portamento or glide that occurs when the voice or a stringed instrument passes from one note to another. This, then, would be the sound of the creeks as they pass between the beaver breaks.

The focus of the poem, however, is less on the literal musical meaning of wrong notes than on the expanded figurative meaning of things that seem incongruous or out of place. The wrong notes of the poet's ear and eye are these: first, the constellations are closer to the poet than the rushing stream, or at least seem to be so; second, the creeks influence the heavens, troubling the sunlight and sparking the moonlight; and third, the meadow and the creeks seem to be invisible, even though the poet is able to describe the deer, coyotes, and clouds, as well as the path of the streams through the trees in the meadow.

p. 27, l. 1. "Her hands of white jade by a window of snow / Are glimmering on a golden-fretted harp— / And to draw the quick eye of Chou Yu, / She touches a wrong note now and then" (Li Tüan, *On Hearing Her Play the Harp*, in Wittner Bynner, *The Chinese Translations*, 132; rpt. from *The Jade Mountain*, 68).

p. 27, l. 3. *Cabinet Mountains*. A range in the wilderness area of northwestern Montana, so named by early French explorers who observed that the mountains resembled a series of closets or cabinets.

p. 27, l. 7. *two creeks*. The two creeks that traverse the meadow of the Wrights' vacation retreat are Basic and Porcupine Creeks, which after coming together run north and empty into the East Fork of the Yaak River.

p. 27, l. 9. A photographic metaphor may be hidden in "flash scales." A flash scale on a camera's flash unit indicates how the f-stop should be set for different distances.

The Minor Art of Self Defense

Orig. pub. *Virginia Quarterly Review* 80, no. 2 (Spring 2004): 113.
WER, 37; ST, 29
Pattern: 3 × 2

This is still another *ars poetica*, though as a self-defense it appears to be partially motivated by a misunderstanding on the part of someone about what Wright has said about landscape. It begins, in any event, with a denial that landscape is a poetic subject matter, which is apparently the position in need of defense. In some of Wright's many remarks on landscape—in his prose reflections and in interviews—he does contend that landscape is a subject matter. He says, for example, "When your subject matter ... is language, landscape, and the idea of God, your aims are different from everybody else's" (QN, 135). Or again, "My ultimate strength is my contemporary weakness—my subject (language, landscape, and the idea of God) is not of much interest now" (QN, 81). A similar remark, though one that does not use the phrase "subject matter," is this: "There are three things, basically, that I write about—language, landscape, and the idea of God" (QN, 123). In common parlance, what one writes about is one's subject or subject matter. What does Wright mean, then, by saying, "Landscape was never a subject matter"?

A partial answer is contained in the distinction Wright makes between "subject matter" and "content" that we glanced at in the Introduction. Wright would apparently want to maintain, then, that the content of landscape is its meaning. But we are still left with the commonplace Horatian distinction between the "what" and the "how." The "how" of poetry we ordinarily associate with "technique," which, along with "method," is the word Wright uses to define the efficient cause. How then can landscape be a technique? From what Wright has said elsewhere, the answer is, or at least appears to be, that landscape is primarily the exterior setting in which the poet happens by more or less random circumstance to find himself—the world into which he is thrown, as Heidegger puts it. This is what Wright calls exterior landscape or "outerscape" (Suarez, 45). The poet's technical skills are the means of recreating the exterior landscape into an interior one—into what Hopkins called "inscape."

What is involved here is the work of the imagination, which for Wright, as for Coleridge, is both a perceptive faculty and a creative one. As Wright says, "I suppose, more than anything else, I'm trying to convince myself that the way I perceive the world is the way that I should perceive the world, that I can recreate the exterior landscape into an interior landscape in which I feel comfortable. The exterior landscape is not always comfortable to be in, but it contains all the elements of comfort. If you can take it inside, if you can transfer it into your own perception, or being, then I suppose one could live more at ease in one's life. I'm not consciously trying, as I say, to establish a mode of perception, or a way that everyone should look at the world. I am only trying to establish for myself a way that acknowledges not only an exterior world and an interior world, but an *It* which is a combination of the two" (*Suarez*, 40). This may not mean in any literal sense that landscape is technique, but landscape is the "scaffold," as Wright says in the poem, whose silences the poet steals and structures into an *It* in a way that reconciles, to use Coleridge's word, the exterior and the interior worlds. To achieve that is more of a major art than a minor one.

Scar Tissue

Orig. pub. *Field* 70 (Spring 2004): 56–62.
ST, 33–39
Pattern: 15 sections; 29 stanzas with an irregular number of lines, though 17 stanzas have 4 lines
Time: July
Place: Montana, with flashbacks to Italy

Scar tissue is what results after the healing of a wound. It leaves a mark and is usually stronger than the original tissue though less able to perform the functions of that tissue. For Wright the scar tissue is, as he says in the rhymed couplet that concludes *Scar Tissue II*, "New skin over old wounds, colorless and numb. / Let the tongues retreat, let the heart be dumb" (p. 45). Several "old wounds" emerge in the poem, but the focus is on the "new skin," and certainly in the poem we have neither a retreating of the tongue nor a silence of the heart. The chief old wound is the inability of language to do its job: "What must be said can't be said ... nobody has a clue" (section 1); "Such destitution of words" (stanza 7); the poetic urge toward God is "unhinged" and unutterable" (section 11). But the urge is, of course, utterable, and while the poet contends once more that his powers are inadequate to meet the linguistic challenge he has set for himself—to represent the ineffable by describing what is in front of him—he nevertheless pushes on, trying to say "what must be said." This is one of the many forms of irony in Wright's poetry. It arises from what the Renaissance rhetoricians called contraries, and the form it takes here, as elsewhere in poems where inadequacy is confessed, is the denial of the assertion by what the rest of the poem does, which is to credit the contrary.

The first two sections establish a contrast between the significant and the insignificant.

In the first, the magnitude of what must but cannot be said comes to the poet from the voices of the unconscious, the prophets, and the God out of the whirlwind. It is the blurred whisper, difficult to recall, that the poet thinks he once heard in his epiphanic moment at Lake Garda. For any of these voices to say "what must be said" requires a crack in the scar tissue's membrane. The "it" in lines 2 and 9 are substantives or noun substitutes and thus have no referents. But the antecedent of "it" in lines 3, 5, and 10 is "what must be said." The pronoun references in the final line of this section are something of a conundrum, but the meaning seems to be this: "it" ("what must be said") is what "it" (the breath that comes through the tiny crack in the scar tissue) has to say, and what seeps through the crack is the "sad stain of our fathers"—the gloomy, perhaps even bloody, past of our ancestors. In the context of the Job allusion in line 4, the "sad stain" might also refer, if not to original sin, at least to the cause of Job's plight advanced by his so-called comforters. Section two proposes that we should listen not simply to the oracular voices but to the cries of the insignificant creatures of the insect world. Even though they are without tongues, they nevertheless offer a message about the dark infinitude of the land of the dead.

Section 3 (p. 34) changes direction. It is a paean to the obvious features of the landscape, as opposed to the picturesque and the ugly, neither of which endures but momentarily. The meaning of the obvious features—the cloudy sky, the summer wind, the shadowy evening—is overdetermined. The final quatrain is difficult, but the point seems to be this: the danger of focusing on the obvious is the creation of a false love for the landscape, but what the obvious can properly do make us aware of the phoenix-like rebirth that can emerge as a fresh fire from the ashes of our words. An example of such regeneration comes in the three-line section that follows, where the poet projects a nighttime vision of lunar replenishment: the moon will refill the woods after the sun has disappeared.

What also tries to emerge through the crack in the scar tissue is the "unutterable" word (p. 37), already mentioned. Here the "wind urge" (the force of air; the Hebrew *ruah* and the Greek *pneuma* = spirit) merges insensibly into the "word urge" or the poetic impetus to achieve the "last form and the final thing, the O." The "O" in infinitely suggestive, symbolizing the perfect form (like Giotto's O), the cycle of time and the cosmos (uni + verse = "one turning"), the contrary of the Alpha (o + *mega* = the large O), the resolution of the narrative cycle which brings the poet back home to the apex of the "O," the explosion of a center into a circumference, and the antitype of the chilling "zero-zero" in section 5 (p. 35, l. 5). "The urge toward form," says the poet, "is the urge toward God." In the familiar proverb, we are told that God's center is everywhere but his circumference is nowhere, which is perhaps what the poet means by saying that the perfection of God is unutterable. Still, the Word is the end toward which the word aims.

The world of *Scar Tissue* is a shadowy world, a world of "charcoal and deeper shades" (p. 35, l. 2), the most extensive description of which comes in the exceptional section devoted to the "almost hour" of dusk and dark contentment. Otherwise, we have the "black night" in section 1 (p. 33, l. 7), the "shadowy overkill // of the evening sun going down (p. 34, l. 12), the "black grass" of section 5 (p. 35, l. 7), the "drained body of daylight" in section 8 (p. 36, l. 8), the "thread that dangles us // between a dark and a darker dark" in section 10 (p. 37, l. 1), the night sky in section 11 (p. 37, l. 11), the blackness of the Lethean waters in section 14 (p. 39, ll. 1–2), and the "dark points" of the ravens in the final section (p. 40, l. 10). It is not altogether a colorless world: there is the scar tissue "stain" (presumably red), the poet's "green itch" and the grasshopper's "green armor," the reddish "tincture of the western sky wall." But primarily the poem is a dialectic of darkness and light.

Wright never permits light, however fragile, to be completely extinguished. Here it is manifest as the "luminous line" that is twice said to prevent us from being completely marooned in the dark world of zero-zero. It is the metaphorical thread "that dangles us // between a dark and a darker dark." And in the poem's one flashback—to the setting sun at Lake Garda in 1959—the glitter of Sermio and the gradual appearance of the lights of Garda coming on are set against the sponging out of the other features of the landscape (p. 37, l. 17–p. 38, l. 9.).

The energy of the raven–blackbird battle in the final stanza dissipates as the birds eventually become invisible, but the poet concludes by asserting to the Lord that he is working hard. A good portion of his hard work comes out in the descriptions strung throughout the poem, as in the picture of the creatures in section 9 (p. 36, ll. 11 ff.) and the "bulging blue of July" in section 13 (p. 38). These are the known things, felt on the pulse and represented with remarkable originality, and they are set over against the poet's "desperation for unknown things" (p. 38, l. 23). When the poet says that the "slit wrists of sundown // tincture the western sky wall" and that this sunset "trumps the Ecclesiast," we know that all is *not* vanity and that language has done its job once again.

p. 33, l. 6. *Dolomites.* See note to l. 19 of *A Short History of My Life* (ST, 11).
p. 37, l. 19. *Harold's wallet.* The wallet of Harold Schimmel, poet and Wright's army friend from the late 1950s and early 1960s.
p. 37, l. 20 ff. Garda, Gardone, Sirmio, and Riva del Garda are small towns along the shore of Lake Garda.
p. 38, l. 8. *Taverna.* A pub.

Scar Tissue II

Orig. pub. *Kenyon Review* 27, no. 2 (Spring 2005): 79–84.
ST, 40–5
Pattern: 5-5-5-5-5-5-5-6-3-3-3-6-6-5-5-5-5-10-7-18-3-3-3-3-2
Time: December–January, with flashbacks to Italy and Hanover County, Virginia
Place: Charlottesville

The poem begins with an opposition between two conceptions of time, the linear sequence that underlies narrative and the cyclical movement of the turning seasons. The former provides a horizontal structure for the telling of our stories, always with the accompanying realization that, unlike the things of the world, we ourselves disappear into oblivion. The latter reveals a permanent circular structure: although nature relentlessly consumes itself, like an ouroboros, it nevertheless endures, shedding its seasonal garments and reclothing itself in endless succession. As we count for nothing, there is little wonder that the poet would call on the Lord to pity his people with the "sumptuous barricades" they throw up "against the dark" and their presumptuous belief in some reward beyond the present.

The poet, however, does not abandon the "story line" of linear time. In three of the sections that follow he recalls events from his past. The first—in section 2—brings together four recollected scenes, all of which have to do with regret and guilt and some having to do with lost love: two scenes from Italy, first with his girlfriend Ingrid in Rome "under the archway of the Via Giulia," and then with his army friends Goldstein and Winfrid Thorp in Verona; an incident in the fire-tower on Mt. Anne in the Sky Lake area of Henderson County, North Carolina (Wright had been sent twice to do repair work on the tower); and a shadowy episode with Betsy Smith at Sweet Briar College near Lynchburg, Virginia. These snapshots are presented without commentary, but they do have a preamble: "Names, and the names of things, past places, / Lost loves and the love of loss, / The alphabet and geometry of guilt, regret / For things done and undone, / All the packaging and misaddresses of our soiled lives" (p. 42, ll. 11–15).

The second narrative—section 6—is a memory of a December bird-hunting trip with his son Luke and the owner of the soybean and millet fields in Hanover County, Virginia. But except for the description of the place, the immediacy of the experience is past recall: "you can't keep anything you can't keep your hands on." The third "story line" comes from an altogether pleasant recollection of life in Verona in 1959 with the Counterintelligence Corps Detachment, where Wright was a security officer. "Great duty," says the poet of his clandestine assignment, and then repeats the epithet at the end of the section: the duty was great because it gave him ample time to cruise "the culture and its sidebars" and to experience a world, new to him, "in its purity and grace, / at least for the moment."

Outside of these three episodes in the "story line," the poem is a series of objective correlatives: the wind and sunrise in section 4 (p. 43), the moon and stars and winter trees in section 5 (p. 44), the feathery rain and grey winter clouds of section 7 (p. 45), the moon again in section 8 (p. 45), and the panorama of the backyard landscape in section 10 (pp. 46–7). The objects described in each of these vignettes have their own emotional suggestions: the sense of being adrift in section 4, astonishment in section 5, calm serenity in section 7, the feeling of mystery brought on by the darkness in section 8, and the awareness of the world's "infinite beauty," which may or may not have a meaning for us, in section 10.

More intriguing is what Wright calls the "subjective correlative." With the objective correlative—in Eliot's words, the "set of objects, a situation, a chain of events" that represent an emotion—the correlation between the object and the emotion is ordinarily transparent. But not so for the subjective correlative, which lies deep beneath "the skin of every story line." The subjective correlative, says the poet, is spirit, adding that it is "correspondent," moving "like water" beneath the object or event. The imagery here is similar to Wordsworth's "correspondent breeze" (*The Prelude*, 1.35), the imagination's response to the inspiration that comes from landscape, and the metaphor behind *spiritus*, we recall, is breath. The difficulty in articulating the spirit as subjective correlative is that "there are no words for these words," or at least whatever language the poet discovers to define spirit quickly erases itself. But as is always the case in Wright's poetry, such skepticism is itself erased. Thus, the continuing quest to represent "immensity and its absolute" (p. 44, l. 7), the love of darkness, which is a mystery, and "what lies behind it," which isn't (p. 45, ll. 16–17).

p. 41, l. 13. *Ingrid*. Wright's girlfriend from his army sojourn in Italy. She also appears in *Bar Giamaica, 1959-60* (*WTTT*, 39) and in *Lines on Seeing a Photograph for the First Time in Thirty Years* (*C*, 36–7). The Via Giulia is a street in Verona, southeast of the Centro Storico.

p. 41, l. 14. *Quel ramo del Lago Como*. "One arm of Lake Como," from the opening sentence of Alessandro Manzoni's *I Promessi Sposi*: "One arm of Lake Como turns off to the south between two unbroken chains of mountains, which cut it up into a series of bays and inlets as the hills advance into the water and retreat again...."

p. 41, l. 16. *Goldstein and Thorpe* [Thorp]. Arnie Goldstein and Winfrid Thorp, friends from Wright's army years. Thorp was a chief warrant officer

p. 42, l. 5. *sunrise is never late, // some Buddhist must certainly have said once.* Perhaps so. The British poet Titus Llewellyn did say it: "sunrise in the morning, never late" (*Sunrise to a Settling Cup of Tea*, l. 3).

p. 42, l. 8. *Obsit omen*. Wright meant to say "*Absit omen*" ("May there be no ill omen").

p. 43, l. 6. *Hanover County*. Located in the east-central Piedmont and Coastal Plain areas of Virginia, between the Chickahominy and Pamunkey Rivers, Hanover County is approximately ninety miles south of Washington, DC, and twelve miles north of Richmond.

p. 44, ll. 10–14. *Via Mantovana ... 430th CIC Detachment*. On the Counter Intelligence Corps Detachment, see note to *NB*, 109, l. 3. Via Mantovana was southwest central Verona.

p. 44, l. 22. *Ed DiCenzo*. An army friend, whose first appearance was in *Driving to Passalacqua* (*WTTT*, 84).

Appalachia Dog

Orig. pub. *Visions-International* (Black Buzzard Press).
ST, 49

Pattern: 6 × 3
Time: Flashback to 1952
Place: Kingsport, Tennessee

This is a poem in praise of a legendary, customized 1949 Ford (the "Appalachia Dog") that has long since disappeared into oblivion—but not from the mind's eye of the poet. The car would cruise the streets of downtown Kingsport, Tennessee, its teenage admirers speculating that it otherwise ran moonshine. The image of the car remains in the "dark drawers" of the poet's consciousness, along with other signs of the times—tapered pants and 78 rpm records.

p. 49, l. 5. *J. Fred's.* J. Fred Johnson Department Store.
p. 49, l. 10. *Zeke Cleek* . A local moonshiner, well known at the time.
p. 49, ll. 10–11. *Junior Johnson's ... North Carolina.* The Grey Ghost was the name of one of the cars Junior Johnson used to run bootleg in Wilkes County, N.C., before he began racing stock cars.
p. 49, l. 15. *Mr. B. collars.* In the 1940s and 1950s big band leader Billy Eckstine wore dress shirts with a large, roll collar that formed a "B" over his tie. It soon became hip to wear "Mr. B. collars."
p. 49, l. 16. *Les Paul and Mary Ford.* Popular musicians of the 1940s and 1950s. Paul invented the solid body electric guitar. He and Mary Ford, his wife, had a number of hits in the 1950s, including *Vaya Con Dios* and *How High the Moon.*

Get a Job

Orig. pub. *Appalachian Heritage* 32 (Spring 2004).
Pattern: 7 × 3
ST, 50
Time: Flashback to 1952
Place: Kingsport, Tennessee

The title mimics the hit song *Get a Job* by a doo-wop group, The Silhouettes, although the song did not actually appear until six years after the time of the flashback.

This reminiscence about a summer construction job focuses on the difference between the sixteen-year-old boy and the other workers—slackers, fecund propagaters ("multipliers"), and ex-felons—on whom he depended. Each day the teenager sought them out for their ritualistic instructions ("their laying on of hands"). But nothing momentous came from these initiation rites, except "cold grace" for the workers, like that afforded by the winter cutlery of spring in *Last Supper* (ST, 4). The poet does admit, however, that he left a skin at the work site, meaning apparently that shed an old outer covering for a new one and so moved through another stage of his growing up. At the time Wright was working for his father's construction company.

p. 50, l. 14. *God rest ... offended.* The line is borrowed from Gerard Manley Hopkins's sonnet about a Liverpool farrier who died at age thirty-one, *Felix Randal:* "Ah well, God rest him all road ever he offended!" "All road" is Hopkins's North Country phrase meaning "all ways."

Archaeology

Orig. pub. *Poetry* 184, no. 4 (August 2004): 304.
ST, 51
Pattern: 5-5-4-5
Time: March, with a flashback to 1942
Place: Charlottesville

As we age, says the poet, we dig into our past, hoping to discover a moment of golden radiance that will clarify and cleanse. Could one such moment have been around a campfire in 1942 when Wright and his brother Winter awaited expectantly for their father to appear across the lake with a boatful of fish? The poet is unable to answer the question, and other incidents that memory resurrects are too fuzzy to see clearly. Therefore, he turns to an archeological dig into the March landscape of the present. But as "Sunlight flaps its enormous wings and lifts off from the backyard," he discovers he cannot dig deeply enough.

p. 51, l. 6. *Hiwassee Dam, North Carolina*. The Wrights had moved from Corinth, Mississippi, to Hiwassee Village, North Carolina, in 1941.

p. 51, l. 9. *Charon*. The ferryman of the dead.

p. 51, l. 13. *cross-eyed, horizon-haired*. Wright reported to one reader that these compound adjectives refer to "the foxfire of memory and its half-false illumination. The two double adjectives mean out of focus and myopic, regarding the viewer trying to look back. I know 'horizon-haired' sounds odd but it's part of myopia; one sees little light spikes above everything. Anyhow, that's what I had in mind" (http://www.aisna.net/rsajournal14/rsa14bacigalupo.pdf)

The Sodbuster's Saloon and Hall of Fame

Orig. pub. *Meridian* 13 (Spring–Summer 2004): 114.
WER, 16; ST, 52
Pattern: 3 × 3
Place: Montana

This is a group portrait of ranchers in the Sodbuster's Saloon, where their drinking and gambling makes them oblivious to their proper jobs. Later they move slowly away from town, letting their horses make their own way while dreaming of rodeo fame. Wright remarked at one of his readings, "I've always thought the sodbuster got a bad press in the movies, and really didn't get his just desserts, and so I wrote [this] poem this summer [2003] in Montana." There are several Sodbuster Saloons throughout the west, but this one is fictitious.

Heraclitean Backwash

Submitted for a *Festschrift* for Helen Vendler, which has not been published as of August 2007.
ST, 53
Pattern: 5 × 3

Heraclitus said that everything flows and that you cannot step into the same river because it is continually moving (Fragments 20 and 21). But for the poet this is a half-truth, because the river can backwash, revealing where one has been before ("back there"). Such backwash provides an occasion for the poet to get some distance on his past life, peering through the window of the world. The glass sends back a faint image of himself, and this self-reflection produces an odd feeling. "Strange flesh in a stranger land," he tells us twice. Moreover, the first three lines of the second stanza sound an ominous note: "Absence," "Nothing," "Silence." But then we get the reversal emerging from the secret whispered by nothing—that out of silence comes healing for some and for others the beginning of a greater light at the end of the dark road. For the poet this greater light comes in chronicling the passage of the clouds and the random pattern of the dandelions. "Like moist souls, [the clouds] litter the sky on their way to where they're not," and the "Dandelions scatter across the earth, // fire points, small sunsqualls." Heraclitus said, "It is pleasure to souls to become moist" (Fragment 72). He also said that the "hidden harmony is better than the obvious" (Fragment 116). If the poet wonders about what he was doing back there, up here he reveals that his function is to call our attention to the spectacle of landscape's hidden harmony.

The imagination for Wright, as for Coleridge, reveals itself in reconciling discordant qualities, which is a primary feature of metaphor. It is a primary feature is well in Heraclitus' philosophy of becoming. In this poem we are presented with several oppositions: here and there, darkness and light, the abstract and the concrete, the strange and the familiar, the living and the dead, the idea and the image. In the imagination, such oppositions interpenetrate. "Opposition," says Heraclitus, "brings concord. Out of discord comes the fairest harmony" (Fragment 98). In the poem something does emerge from Nothing, and one of the secrets that Nothing whispers is captured in the image of the dandelions—the Heraclitean "fire points."

p. 53, l. 11. *Or so the Egyptian thought.* In chap. 87 of the *Egyptian Book of the Dead*, Osiris Ani speaks in the form of both a crocodile and a fish. In chap. 151 the Perfected Soul speaks from the holy egg of the *abtu* fish. The reference may be to a passage in *The Gospel of Thomas*, discovered in the Egyptian desert in the last century: "And he [Jesus] said, 'The person is like a wise fisherman who cast his net into the sea and drew it up from the sea full of little fish. Among them the wise fisherman discovered a fine large fish. He threw all the little fish back into the sea, and easily chose the large fish. Anyone here with two good ears had better listen!'" The implication of the parable seems to be that the big fish—the true Gnostic or even Jesus himself—will speak.

p. 53, parenthetical note. *H.V.* Helen Vendler, a critic Wright admires and for whose *Festschrift*, ed. Nick Halpern and Stephen Burt, the poem was written.

High Country Spring

Orig. pub. in W.T. Pfefferle, *Poets on Place: Interviews and Tales from the Road* (Logan: Utah State University Press, 2005), 193.
ST, 54
Pattern: 3 × 2
Time: Late May
Place: Montana

The little lyric opens with a distinction between description and what is described, but this difference collapses immediately as we get, first, a picture of late May's imminent explosion, and, second, a version of the world in a grain of sand—in this case, in a drop of pine sap, as amber as a robin's beak.

China Traces

Orig. pub. *Rivendell: Native Genius* 4 (Spring 2007).
ST, 55
Pattern: 2–3–3–3–1
Time: Spring
Place: Montana

"Traces" in the title is a pun, meaning both roads and shadowy imprints or outlines. Lines are used to trace, so there is a suggestion too that these poetic lines imitate those of the Chinese poets. The title calls to mind Wright's third major collection, *China Trace* (1977), the epigraph for which was from T'u Lung (T'u Ch'ihshui): "I would like to house my spirit within my body, to nourish my virtue by mildness, and to travel in ether by becoming a void. But I cannot do it yet.... And so, being unable to find peace within myself, I made use of the external surroundings to calm my spirit, and being unable to find delight within my heart, I borrowed a landscape to please it. Therefore, strange were my travels" (trans. Lin Yutang).

The opening couplet contains several riddles. "Nature," says the poet, "contains no negatives." This is both a visual statement (we see nature like we see the positive print of a photo, not the reversed image of a negative) and a statement of natural law (nature may change forms but its elements do not disappear, or, as the poet says, "Nothing is lost there," "there" meaning in nature). As we have seen on several occasions, "Nothing" can mean either "not anything" or "nothingness" (the void, empty space, nonexistence). And it is possible to read the phrase in both ways: all things in nature endure, or the sense of nonexistence may arise in human consciousness but not in nature. Now we come to the real enigma: "The word is. Except the word." The clipped syntax requires us to fill in the blanks. Does the poet mean that the word is lost in nature? Or does he mean that the word simply exists, as in the opening of the Gospel of John: "In the beginning was the Word"? And how are we to understand "Except the word." It appears to be a prepositional phrase, but if the word is lost in nature it makes no sense to exclude the word from what is lost. What we expect rather is "Accept the word." The phrase therefore appears to be not really a phrase after all but an imperative clause. The sense, then, seems to be this: the existence of the word cannot be denied; therefore, the word must be excluded from those things that are lost.

What we are to make of these mental gymnastics is not altogether certain, but we *can* say that in the second stanza—the first of three tercets—the poet expresses a desire for his spirit, which is outside of nature but similar to nature ("like slow mist in the trees"), to vanish. He is searching for a place where this might happen. Spring, the season of renewal, brings only a despondency to the poet: he is out of season, as it were, having autumn in his heart. In the second tercet, we have one answer to what follows "the word is." Here the word, with its poetic charms and spells, is thrown up as a buffer against the inexorable passage of time. It does not work, of course: each evening the darkness hands back to the poet what he has written. On the other hand, the very act of writing is evidence that the word must be excepted from things that are lost. In the third tercet, the disconsolate mood continues, reinforced by the continual, bitter, and boundaryless rain. In such a condition, nothing emerges except the self-devouring "word" of the rushing creek. And we conclude with a somber image of the black zodiac assembling itself. If "nature contains no negatives," it can nevertheless engender a subjective correlative of gloom in the poet's consciousness.

As for the traces of China, this poem, like a number of others, embodies some of the features of Wright's beloved T'ang poets: the focus on both interior and exterior landscape, the compression of language, the sense of solitude that we find, say, in Han Shan and the late Li Po, the feeling of emptiness that is transferred from the landscape, the attentiveness to the world of the ten-thousand things (here the misty trees, the passage of light, the falling rain, the monomorphemic creek, and the assembly of the stars). Too, there is the absence of presence, as in the epigraph of T'u Lung, quoted above. In a world where spiritual presence is hard to come by, the poet can only offer the presence of landscape.

Matins

Orig. pub. *Shenandoah* 55, no. 1 (Spring–Summer 2005): 6.
ST, 56
Pattern: 7 × 2
Time: Early morning in spring or summer
Place: Montana

The description in the opening stanza of the morning sunlight's rejuvenating the landscape is reason enough for a morning prayer. The vital energy of the natural light, one might expect, would induce a corresponding psychological illumination in us and thus be good cause for celebration or thanksgiving. Such might have been the case in a nascent religious sensibility. But as we are aged "nobodies" of Nature, we would do well to abandon self-consciousness and assume the attitude of "nondoing" (*wu wei*). This does not mean to do nothing. It is rather the attitude of the Taoist saint who permits things to unfold according to their own nature. As Lao-tzu says, "The world is ruled by letting things take their course. It cannot be ruled by interfering" (*Tao Te Ching*, chap. 48). This seems to be what Wright has in mind in the image of our "sinking like nothing through the timed tide of ourselves"—a Taoist matins of quiet contemplation.

North

Orig. pub. *Iowa Review* 34, no. 3 (Winter 2004): 185.
ST, 57
Pattern: 10 × 2
Place: Montana

The north is the high country of Lincoln County, Montana, the "landing zone" to which Wright returns each summer. Although we are told that the afternoon is "One part water, two parts of whatever the light won't give us up," the scene described here is nevertheless largely dark and wet, the tatters of the clouds ("fog-rags") trailing through the evergreens with only occasional "sun spurts." This brooding and heavy atmosphere is transferred to the poet himself: his heart is not uplifted, and his desire is repressed, dragging itself "sullen and misty-mouthed through the trees." The north, says the poet, "is our dark glass," a speculum reflecting the north as a place of last resort, where the rhythm of the natural cycle keeps repeating itself; a place of incongruities ("St. Augustine in blackface"); and the locus of the altered and unrecognizable self. The north on this day is without apparition, and the northern light, alas, refuses to surrender any illumination.

In Praise of Franz Kafka

Orig. pub. *Verse* 22, no. 1 (2005): 148.
ST, 58
Pattern: 11
Time: Summer
Place: Montana

This is the fifth appearance of the Hunter Gracchus in Wright's poetry, and he will appear two more times in *Littlefoot* (sects. 9 and 22). His other appearances are recorded in the note to section 4 of *Summer Mornings* (SHS, 59). See also the commentary for that poem and for *Night Thoughts Under a Summer Moon* (above).

The seven poems in which Gracchus appears are all set in Montana. As the poet returns to this site each summer, he is reminded of the hunter of Kafka's fable, whose spirit "passes each year" and whose world of "pure circumference" we are enjoined to follow if we can. Kafka's story concludes with the Hunter Gracchus's telling the burgomaster, "My boat is without a helm—it journeys with the wind which blows in the deepest regions of death."

Vespers

Orig. pub. *West Branch* 56 (17 May 2005).
ST, 59
Pattern: 6 × 3

Time: Summer
Place: Montana

This lyric is built on the familiar "yes ... but" structure, in which one view of life is proposed only to be followed, in this case deflated, by another. Here the contrast is between desire and reality. The desire is embedded in the words of an allegorical figure in Hildegard of Bingen's prophetic and visionary *Book of Divine Works*: "I am the fiery life of divine substance, I blaze above the beauty of the fields, I shine in the waters, I burn in sun, moon and stars" (*Selected Writings*, trans. Mark Atherton [Harmondsworth: Penguin, 2001], 172). Who wouldn't wish such a fiery life, the poet declares. But, alas, the reality is that "we are the children of the underlife," called by "the world in its rags and ghostly raiment ... With grinding and green gristle ... we are its grist, and we are its groan." ("Gr-r-r," says the speaker in Browning's *Soliloquy in a Spanish Cloister*, who is also rooted in the word of grey paper, gripes, groveling, and greengages, and who is called to a vesper service of his own.)

The nighthawk's chortle holds us firmly to the world of the ten thousand things, a half dozen of which are catalogued in the last stanza. "Not much of a life," concludes the poet wryly, "but I'll take it." Still, the desire for the "life of divine substance" has not been erased.

The Narrow Road to the Distant City

Orig. pub. *Rivendell: Native Genius* 4 (Spring 2007).
ST, 60
Pattern: 5 × 3

The juxtaposition of this poem with *Pilgrim's Progress* reminds us that in Bunyan's tale Christian sets out on a journey to the Celestial City on a road that is narrow, as Goodwill reminds him, plagiarizing a line from Matthew's gospel (7:14).

We do not really mean the pleas we make to the Lord to overwhelm us; we mean rather that we would like to be laid down gently and pampered. We are naturally undeserving, which is why the poet asks to Lord to pay attention to us. But at the same time he asks, somewhat brazenly, for the Lord to be Himself, which is followed by what looks at first glance like a variation on the ending of Wallace Stevens's *The Snow Man*, where the listener, who is "nothing himself," is said to behold "Nothing that is not there and the nothing that is" (ll. 14–15). But in Wright's poem the issue is not whether the Lord is called "nothing." The final verb phrase, "called for," is ambiguous. "Called for" can mean summoned or requested (the Lord is called for so that he can receive applause, recognition, or to be Himself). But the sense might also be, "Is the word 'nothing' required as the name of the Lord?" In other words, does being Himself call for the name "nothing"? Still, again, it may refer to the reason for which the Lord is called "nothing," in which case "for" means "because." We are left here with an enigma, just as we are left with an unresolved tension between the request to the Lord to pay attention to us and with the subsequent request for Him to be "a hard wind // that understands nothing."

Pilgrim's Progress

Orig. pub. *Literary Review* 48, no. 3 (Spring 2005): 49.
ST, 61
Pattern: 5 × 3

Wright first referred to himself as "Pilgrim" in *Skins*: "And what does it come to, Pilgrim, / This walking to and fro on the earth...?" (CM, 101). He also uses the word as a self-reference in *Three Poems of Departure* (no. 1) (*WTTT*, 85–93), *T'ang Notebook* (*WTTT*, 102–4), *Sprung Narratives* (*NB*, 21–9), "Not everyone can see the truth, but he can be it" (*NB*, 44), and *Deep Measure* (*NB*, 115). In other poems he refers to his poetic project as a pilgrimage. In the present poem the three stanzas trace the three ages of the pilgrimage—beginning, middle, and end. Childhood was beautiful and elusive, moving untamed through the forest of youth. During the middle years, the power of the sacred places (Delphi and Italy) takes hold, and during the passage through the woods, the trees begin to differentiate themselves. Much during this period is now but half-remembered. In the later years, the Pilgrim has arrived not at the Celestial City but on his own front porch, and we get a portrait of the artist as a dog, "Barking, poor thing, barking, / With no one at home to call him in, // and with no one to turn the light on"—like the barking dog at the Wicket-gate in Bunyan's allegory. We conclude, then, with a kind of parody of the Pilgrim's progress—a *Pilgrim's Regress*, we might call it.

Little Landscape

Orig. pub. *Shenandoah* 55, no. 1 (Spring–Summer 2005): 7.
ST, 62
Pattern: 4 × 3
Time: Midsummer
Place: Montana

In *Confessions of a Song and Dance Man* Wright declared, "A little landscape's a dangerous thing." Here, facing the landscape, the poet is confronted not with danger but with two conundrums. The first is a dilemma, the second a riddle. The dilemma is whether the poet should "lighten the language up," saying "what is true and clean," or "to dark it back down," saying "what is secret and underground." The difference is between a direct and precise clarity, on the one hand, and a shadowy and mysterious apocryphon, on the other. Then we are presented with what looks like still another option—to say well what joy cannot repay—but the other half of the opposition coyly disappears into an ellipsis.

The second conundrum is "like unto" the first insofar as it once more presents the poet with two options, described in this way: "the world is a link and a like: / One fall and all falls." This is a genuine riddle. One answer to the first half of the riddle is this: language presents us with two major alternatives for representing the world. In the first, we link things together metaphorically, thus identifying them. In the second, we represent their likenesses, thus relying on simile. For the next part of the riddle we have to decide whether "falls" is a noun or a verb. The verb seems to be precluded: in the pronoun-plus-verb pattern, ordinary syntax requires "all fall"—though if we translate "all" as "everything," then "fall" could take the –s affix. The more likely possibility, especially in the context of Basin Creek, is that we have two noun phrases, "falls" meaning "cascading water." In this case, all falls are identified with each other (a-world-in-a-grain-of-sand metaphor) or they are similar to each other. The question for the poet is which option to choose, the way of identity or of analogy. But the conundrums disappear in the final stanza, where the poet abandons all philosophical questions in favor of a direct description of the great blue heron, whose knowledge has nothing to do with the dilemmas faced by the poet. What the heron knows is "just is," which is a testimony to being over becoming, existence over essence—Stevens's "things as they are" or Hopkins's "inscape."

Ghost Days

Orig. pub. *Verse* 22, no. 1 (2005): 149.
ST, 63
Pattern: 10 × 2

The theme of the poem is about the difficulty of remembering the details of an experience years before in Rome when the poet and five others, one of whom was his first Italian friend, drove around Rome. Thus, "ghost days"—days that leave only a faint trace or a haunting image. But the poet, as it turns out, does remember quite a few particulars—the model of the car, five of the six people in the car, the precise time that he and his friends were circling the Colosseum, how many inches of snow fell, and the cars that had crashed into the retaining wall of the Tiber.

The second stanza picks up the mosaic image of the first line. The image of his friend Giancarlo comes and then disappears from the "eyeball's golden dome," and their world was like the mosaics in that great monument of Byzantine art in Ravenna, S. Apollinare in Classe. In those days past, says the poet, "How high we all hung, // artificial objects in artificial skies," echoing Yeats's first Byzantium poem, and he looks back on the time as a shining moment in the darkness. This projection from the memory more than compensates for the poet's inability to remember some of the details, and the metaphor identifying the poet and Giancarlo with shining saints gives another meaning to the "ghost" of the title, which is "spirit."

p. 63, l. 8. *macchine*. Cars.
p. 63, l. 9. *What year was that?* Feigned ignorance on the part of the poet. It would have been New Year's Eve, 31 December 1959.
p. 63, l. 12. *marinaio*. Sailor, mate. The Via Margutta is a street in the Centro Storico of Rome.
p. 63, l. 17. *S. Apollinare in Classe*. A Byzantine basilica in Ravenna, its mosaics dating from the sixth and seventh centuries.

The Silent Generation III

Orig. pub. *Irish Pages* 2, no. 1 (Spring–Summer 2003): 173.
ST, 64–5
Pattern: 4 × 3 + 2

The first *Silent Generation* appeared in *Chickamauga* (NB, 37) and the second one in this volume (ST, 7). The present version is a series of five discontinuous sections, each a stanza in length. Together their central thrust is self-critique. The generation that grew up in the 1950s was not all that silent after all, having "had too much to say," like those in *The Silent Generation II*. "Our voices," says the poet, were used "to love your daughters" and "to love your sons." Their wagers failed and their Utopian visions were dashed. They were not overtly immoral, but whatever moral visions they had they internalized, so that "goodness and mercy declined to follow" them. And they lived outside of the mainstream and were misunderstood ("Too strange for our contemporaries ... Not strange enough for posterity"). Thus, in the concluding couplet, the poet advises the next generation to take another course. This is a poem of pure pathos: the love songs of the silent generation turned out to be as ineffectual as that of the garrulous J. Alfred Prufrock.

p. 64, l. 5. *bet on the come*. An expression in poker, meaning that one has not yet had a hand that is likely to win but now has an opportunity for a very strong hand. "On the come" almost always means one is trying for a straight or a flush.
p. 64, l. 10. The allusion is to Psalm 23:6: "Surely goodness and mercy shall follow me all the days of my life; and I shall dwell in the house of the Lord for ever."

Time Will Tell

Orig. pub. *Literary Review* 48, no. 3 (Spring 2005): 49.
ST, 66
Pattern: 7-4-7

    The first two stanzas set up an opposition between innocence and experience. In the early days (the time of innocence), the poetic task was undertaken in towns and cities and foreign countries without any self-consciousness: "Words formed and flew from our fingers. // We listened and loved them all." In the latter days, however, the consciousness of finitude and the passage of time, which begs no one's pardon, loom ominously. The vision of the latter world (experience) is embodied in the metaphor of the wind, which in turn is identified with the breath of murderous Time. Time pushes and pulls our breath in and out, and what "time will tell" is that we move inexorably toward the pulling out of the last breath.

Hawksbane

Orig. pub. *Lasting: Poems On Aging*, ed. Meg Files (Tucson: Pima Press, 2005), 258.
ST, 67
Pattern: 2-1-2-1

    "Hawksbane" is Wright's neologism, based on an analogy to plants such as "dogbane," "wolf's bane," and "henbane." "Bane" is apparently used in the sense of ruin or hapless fate, which is what the hawks suffer—a natureless eternity, where there is "no wind shift." "Hawksbane" may be an allusion to Bashō's haiku about a solitary hawk he saw above the promontory of Irago (*The Narrow Road to the Deep North and Other Travel Sketches* [Harmondsworth: Penguin, 1966], 75).

    The poem is a string of abstract negatives, showing us to be as hapless as the poor hawks: things that cannot be written about; journeys that cannot be taken; eternity without nature, wind shift, and weeds; and our identities determined not by anything new or by anything we have discovered. In the second couplet we are given the reason for our plight: we have been looking in the wrong places and looking for the wrong things.

    Wright's note (p. 75) refers us to Bashō, though he does not borrow from the great haiku poet directly. His debt rather is to the general shape of Bashō's own long and sacred journey. Both poets have the deep desire, in Bashō's words, "to obey nature, to be one with nature, throughout the four seasons of the year" (*The Narrow Road to the Deep North*, 71). Both have doubts about the efficacy of writing poetry. There is a general parallel between the first two lines of the poem and Bashō's summary statement about his experience on Mt. Yudono: "I saw many other things of interest in this mountain, the details of which, however, I refrain from betraying in accordance with the rules I must obey as a pilgrim" (ibid., 126). He also remarks that to say more about the shrine on Mt. Nikkō "would be to violate its holiness" (ibid., 100).

The Woodpecker Pecks, but the Hole Does Not Appear

Orig. pub. *New Yorker* 80, no. 42 (10 January 2005): 26.
ST, 68
Pattern: 6 × 3
Time: July
Place: Montana

The poem turns on one of Wright's familiar oppositions: the fleeting nature of human achievement versus the landscape, which quickly subsumes everything we make and do. From the human perspective, all is empty, as in the *hebel* refrain in Ecclesiastes (*vanitas* in the Vulgate). We come to realize, like Hamlet in the grave, that even the greatest come to naught, their dust good for nothing but stopping up the hole of a beer barrel. What we achieve is like a hole, surrounding nothingness and soon to be forgotten. But not for the woodpecker and the rest of the landscape, which do not have to worry about oblivion. One might think that the anxiety arising from the consciousness of death would lead the poet into a state of dismal disillusionment. But what we get rather are two stanzas celebrating the landscape—the grasses and the winds and especially the birds (swallows and ravens, three kinds of finches, and whatever tweety bird is atop the evergreen stumps). These examples of the "sweet oblivion of the everyday" are an antidote to the consciousness of death, dressing the landscape up in "a warm waistcoat / Over the cold and endless body of memory." Thus, the pure Romantic testament of the final line: the glory of the July Montana morning "Is all that the world allows, and all one could wish for." This is a much happier prospect than the vision we get in *Time Will Tell* and *Hawksbane*.

Singing Lesson

Orig. pub. *Shenandoah* 55, no. 1 (Spring–Summer 2005): 8.
ST, 69
Pattern: 5-4-5
Place: Montana

The first two stanzas draw an exceptional picture of an arrested Montana landscape, which begins to stir slightly at the end of the second stanza. The first two stanzas are almost completely visual. The landscape is presented to us as a canvas to see, and except for the barking dogs and perhaps the "miniature exhalations," we hear nothing. This, then, is a poetry of the eye. But when darkness enshrouds us, the eye, of course, loses its function, the ear must take over. Thus, the concluding stanza, where the imagery is vaguely biblical and its diction decidedly so, focuses on the ear.

The crux is the "Therefore" that opens the third stanza. This is not an Aristotelian "therefore": the imperative that we should suffer the singsong of the darkness does not follow from the premises in the previous description. What we have rather is a poetic logic that is a rally cry for poetry. When, the poet says, God (the Great Mouth) requires that we should allow or submit patiently to the darkness, then we ourselves should suffer (allow) the music of the darkness. If we do, we will abide. The first two "suffers" are imperatives that come from the Great Mouth. But the syntax seems to require that the injunctions that follow—"suffer its singsong, ... Listen to what the words spell, listen and sing the song"—come from the poet's mouth and are his "lesson" to us. It is also a lesson about the elements of poetry: *lexis* is planted firmly in the middle (what the words spell), flanked on one side by *opsis* (what we can see) and *melos* (what we can hear). Which is an appropriate *ars poetica* theme on which to end this volume.

p. 69, l. 10. *Great Mouth.* God. Cf. "[T]ruth is the mouth of the Father. His tongue is the Holy Spirit, who joins him to truth attaching him to the mouth of the Father by his tongue at the time he shall receive the Holy Spirit" (*The Gospel of Truth*, NHL, 44).

CHAPTER 7

Littlefoot: A Poem

Parts 1–7 of Littlefoot orig. pub. as *Appalachian Autumn* in *American Scholar* 74, no. 4 (Autumn 2005): 75–83. Parts 8–12, in *Five Points* 10, nos. 1–2 (2006): 261–7. Part 15 as "16" in *Appalachian Heritage* 34 (Spring 2006): 120. Parts 16 and 17 as *Spring, I* and *Spring, II* in *Yale Review* 95, no. 2 (April 2007). Part 18 in *Front Porch* [Texas State University], issue 1. Part 19 as "22" in *Appalachian Heritage* 34 (Summer 2006): 99. Parts 20–21, *Laurel Review* 40, no. 2 (Summer 2006): 248–54. Parts 13, 22, 26, *Subtropics* 3 (January 2007). Parts 23–24 as "XXVII" and "XXIX" in *Poetry Northwest* (Fall 2006–Winter 2007): 10–12. Parts 27–31, with two additional parts, as *Littlefoot* in *Virginia Quarterly Review* 82, no. 1 (Winter 2006): 190–201, though Wright has excised Parts 36 (five lines) and 40 (a couplet) from that version. Part 32, *New Yorker* 83 (19 and 26 February 2007): 142–3, and Part 34 *New Yorker* 83 (2 April 2007): 54–5. Part 33, *Ploughshares* 32, no. 4 (Winter 2006–7): 151–3. Parts 14 and 25 were not previously published.

The title comes from the name of a yearling horse in part 28.

Just as *Zone Journals* and *Xionia* moved in a different formal direction from that of *Southern Cross* and *The Other Side of the River*, so the shape of *Littlefoot* departs from that of the three previous volumes, the discrete lyrics of which all have their separate titles. In *Littlefoot* the separate parts are untitled, and it is by far the longest poem in Wright's published work, having more than five-and-a-half times the number of lines of the longest of his previous poems, *Apologia Pro Vita Sua*. The poem has thirty-five numbered parts and contains 270 stanzas in 157 sections, amounting to almost 1400 lines. Most of these parts were published elsewhere, though, as indicated above, in the *bricolage* of the present poem several parts were cut.

Parts 1, 3, 5, 7, and 9, which range from 36 to 68 lines, are followed by five even-numbered poems, which have five or six lines. This long poem/short poem pattern is abandoned after part 10. Even though I refer to the thirty-five parts of the long poem, each of the parts is not unlike the separate poems in Wright's other volumes. The main difference is the absence of titles. Because the parts themselves are separate poems, in the commentaries that follow I often refer to the numbered parts as poems.

The thirty-five parts move, with a few exceptions, chronologically through the seasonal cycle from June 2004 through October 2005.

Part 1.
Orig. pub. as part 1 of *Appalachian Autumn* in *American Scholar* 74, no. 4 (Autumn 2005): 75–8.
L, 3–6
Pattern: (6 × 5) (6) (6) (5) (4 × 4) (5)
Time: June–October
Place: Charlottesville

The first poem, which progresses from summer through the hurricane season to fall, is a series of discontinuous vignettes that begin with the poet's taking stock. He first records the dilemma he faces: the impossibility of his reliving the past and yet his urge to do so, especially at this late stage of his life when there is nothing else to say. He gives the impression that it's time to call it quits: "Whatever it was I had to say, I've said it.... / Time to pull up the tie stakes. / Time to repoint the brickwork and leave it all to the weather." But against the awareness of advancing age, memories of the mimosa tree and the hemlock hedge emerge, and the poet decides not to put away his notebook and pencil after all, opting instead to reset the timer so that he can "retrench and retool." Because life it short ("We're not here a lot longer than we are here"), we are advised "to windrow affection" and "not be negligent," so that our hearts, unlike those of our broken-boned friends in nursing homes, will sparkle and the disregard we fear will evaporate. We return to the theme of affection in section 5 after three interludes:

• As he watches the sunset, the poet muses that if dying were like the slow movement of the evening into darkness, it would be easy to die. As the clouds are is still visible at 9:00 p.m., the date must be close to the summer solstice.

• The metaphor behind this meditation on the solitude of a shapeless, rainy Sunday is photography. Monday is the photographer who stares backward in time, one arm hidden under the black hood, ready to snap the shutter and capture a wet scene of "the poem without people," which is what Sunday represents. Wright is a "Sunday" poet: references to that day appear forty-six times in his poems, which is exactly the number of references to the six other days of the week combined.

• In stormy weather—it's the hurricane season—the poet is haunted by questions about the dead. Can their bodies arise from such a sodden world?

Returning to his major motif, the poet declares that "In the affinity is the affection, // in the affection everything else / That matters." Love is a frequent motif in Wright's poetry. Affection, a less ardent form of regard, is less frequent, but widespread nonetheless, occurring two-dozen times. In *Apologia Pro Vita Sua* the poet declared that "Affection's the absolute // everything rises to." In the present poem affection is said to lie in affinity, the natural attraction or likenesses between things, and the affinity present is between the poet's sensibility and the October landscape. This does not make discovering the significance of the connection any easier, for nature is either silent or inarticulate—as we are, and as the gods are. The poet is therefore aware that he must accept a *both/and* world: compassion and cold comfort, emergence and disappearance, internal and external acceptance. Even in his memory of the reflections on the currents of the Adige in Verona, the sunlight was both "Translucent on the near side, // spun gold on the other."

The final section is a variation on the same theme. Is the heaven above actually higher than the earthly paradise? Our intermediary, the moon, should be able to reflect a proper answer, but she too is silent. So we are simply left with the existence of the two worlds and with "No choice." As we will see, this is not the final answer: later the earthly paradise wins out.

p. 3, ll. 11–12. *children ... wife.* Wright's son Luke was living in England at the time. His wife Holly had retired from teaching photography at the University of Virginia in May 2000.

p. 5, l. 15. *It's all music.* A.P. Carter used to remark when he was song-hunting in the Clinch Mountains, "Buddy, it's all music, y'know."

Part 2.

Orig. pub. as part 2 of *Appalachian Autumn* in *American Scholar* 74, no. 4 (Autumn 2005): 78.
L, 7
Pattern: 5

This poem is composed of selected borrowings from *The Thunder, Perfect Mind* in *The Nag Hammadi Library*. For example, "I am the sign of the letter"; "I am the silence that is incomprehensible"; "I am the speech that cannot be grasped" (*NHL*, 303). In some cases Wright negates the last half of what is found in the Nag Hammadi text: "For many are the pleasant forms which exist in numerous sins ... which (men) embrace until they become sober and go up to their resting place. And they will find me there, and they will live, and they will not die again" (*NHL*, 303); "I am the one whom you have scattered, and you have gathered me together" (*NHL*, 299). *The Thunder, Perfect Mind* is an elusive Gnostic text, narrated by a woman from whose gnomic utterances come a recognition of the divine light in all areas of human experience. It consists of numerous paradoxical statements of identity, e.g., "I am the whore and the holy one. / I am the wife and the virgin" (*NHL*, 297). Some of the paradoxes in the text embody a negative theology. In one of her Wright-like utterances she says, "I am a mute who does not speak, / and great is my multitude of words" (*NHL*, 301). In the present poem, Wright identifies with some of the proclamations of the Gnostic speaker; others he reverses.

Part 3.

Orig. pub. as part 3 of *Appalachian Autumn* in *American Scholar* 74, no. 4 (Autumn 2005): 78–9.
L, 8–9
Pattern: (6 × 2) (6 × 4) (3 × 2)
Time: November
Place: Charlottesville

The structure of the first two sections is familiar: a description of landscape that triggers a meditation. In the first, the poet's gaze fastens upon the moon, which as it moves across the Milky Way, provides us our "last instructions." Whether "last" means most recent or final does not matter because we cannot understand them. Nor can we understand the roadmap or the password.

In section 2 the poet resurrects childhood memories of the Holston River, which becomes a metaphor for "negative time" and a simile for memory. The essence of the river is difficult to capture as it is always "undoing itself" and is, like memory, always either "too deep" or "too shallow." "Negative time" is said to be the "pure presence of absence." Similarly, the river "remainders itself // and rises again / Out of its own depletion."

Section 3 returns to the November landscape, which hovered in the background of section 1. As opposed to what St. Cyprian says about salvation (there is none outside the church), the poet affirms that there is no transformation "outside of nature." Yet the November landscape pays no attention to us and does not acknowledge the hope we have of returning to our proper home. If negative time is embodied in the passing of November, the dying of the end of another cycle embodies negative space: "Leaf ends curled up like untanned leather, // grass edges bleared back from emerald ease, / Light-loss diaphanous in the bare-backed and blitherless trees."

p. 8, l. 1. *hard drive*. Wright, who has not schooled himself in computers, nevertheless borrows a number of other computer terms in the first section: screen, scroll, deletable, password. Note also "powers on" in l. 35.

p. 9, l. 13. *Saltville and Gate City*. The North Fork of the Holston River runs through Saltville in Washington County,

Virginia, and Gate City in Scott County, Virginia, the latter just north of Kingsport, Tennessee. It then meanders southwest from Kingsport through Churchill, Tennessee, and about three miles to the north of New Hope, both in Hawkins County.

p. 9, l. 19. *St. Cyprian*. "Qui salus extra ecclesiam non est" (*Letters*, 72).

Part 4.

Orig. pub. as part 4 of *Appalachian Autumn* in *American Scholar* 74, no. 4 (Autumn 2005): 80. L, 10

Pattern: (3 × 3) (3 × 3) (3 × 3) (3 × 3)

This brief interlude picks up the image of darkness from the light-loss of the previous poem. "In a dark time," says Roethke, "the eye begins to see." But not for our poet, who sees no disclosure of light in the black wings of passing time. In line 3 "it" refers apparently to light, which is hidden deep within whatever lies beneath the imagination. The wind-wings association (ll. 1, 5) intimates that the light of light is beaten by the black wings of time back into the darkness.

p. 10, l. 5. *light of life*. "Light, seeking light doth light of light beguile; / So, ere you find where light in darkness lies" (*Love's Labours Lost*, 1.1.77–8). In the Nicene Creed Jesus is identified with the Light of Light." Cf. the metaphor for Christ in *The Teachings of Silvanus*: "the light of the Eternal Light (NHL, 393).

Part 5.

Orig. pub. as part 5 of *Appalachian Autumn* in *American Scholar* 74, no. 4 (Autumn 2005): 80–1. L, 11–12

Pattern: (3 × 3) (3 × 3) (3 × 3) (3 × 3)
Time: November
Place: Kingsport

This poem contains Wright's threefold subject matter: landscape (section 1), language and its relation to time (sections 2 and 3), and the idea of God (section 4). November is a time of radiance and stillness, conducive to revealing nature's minute particulars—the identities of things in themselves. The poet is one such thing, and he invokes the Lord to designate him as a separate identity: "Finger me, Lord, and separate me to what I am."

There are no pronouns or verbs, according to the poet, for capturing the past and future of nature. The implication seems to be that we have only nouns and adjectives for such an enterprise. The eternal present of nature is another matter. It is precise, just as words are, "each singular, each distinct." But since the present in indefinable because non-verbal, the words we seek to capture the landscape, as it presents itself to us "now," drift away from us like petals. Again, the theme is familiar: the inadequacy of language to do what we would like it to do. The language of landscape may be immaculate but it is nevertheless mute. All that the November moon can do is punctuate this sense of absence: "First character in the celestial alphabet, the full moon, / Is a period, and that is that. / No language above to aid us, // no word to the wise."

In the final section the sense of absence is represented by a blank space, about which we know only that it of consists of four syllables. This could be the previous phrase "word to the wise," but in the context of "thrones" and "assisting angels" perhaps the missing syllables are the Tetragrammaton (Yod, Heh, Vav, Heh—the Yahweh of the Old Testament, usually translated "Lord") or some other four-syllable designation for God: The Almighty, Ancient of Days, Holy Spirit, King of Heaven, Rock of Ages, and the like. The last two stanzas are a move we have seen Wright make many times before. After having confessed the inadequacy of language to represent the "now" of landscape—what confronts the poet at the present moment—he proceeds to describe the Kingsport landscape: "the winter-waxed trees / Are twiggy and long-fingery, fretting the woods-wind," whose songs float back to him from sixty years earlier, including lines from the Carter Family's *Wildwood Flower* and *Will You Miss Me When I'm Gone*. The language of landscape turns out not to be mute after all.

p.12, l. 15. *Moccasin Gap*. A natural gap in the sprawling mountains of Southwest Virginia and Northeast Tennessee, north of Kingsport, Tennessee, toward Gate City, Virginia. Chestnut Ridge is on the east side of Kingsport, just south of Highway 11W, near the house where Wright grew up.

p.12, l. 17. *fretting the woods-wind*. The metaphor, a reversal of woodwinds, is musical: the limbs of the trees are a stringed instrument for the wind, like an Aeolian harp.

p. 12, ll. 19–20. *I will twine ... black hair*. The first line of *Wildwood Flower*, a Carter Family tune, recorded in 1928. The line has several variations: "and raven black ..."; "of waving black ..."; "and waving black...." "Mingles" is an archaic British word for the ribbons that girls used to braid into their hair, though some say that "mingles" arose as a mispronunciation of "ringlets," as in Maude Irving's 1859 tune, *I'll Twine Midst the Ringlets*. Maybelle Carter reported that, as a child, she heard her mother sing the song. *Will You Miss Me When I'm Gone* is another Carter Family tune, also recorded in 1928. It is reproduced in its entirety as part 35 of *Littlefoot*.

Part 6.

Orig. pub. as part 6 of *Appalachian Autumn* in *American Scholar* 74, no. 4 (Autumn 2005): 81–2.
L, 13
Pattern: (5)
Time: December

The question asked by the poet in this brief interlude is a rhetorical one. He asserts that nature is sacred, forever bidding us "To sit still and say nothing." The phrase "latches of Paradise" suggests that the gates of heaven are closed to us, and that life in the natural world is "all of paradise that we shall know," as Wallace Stevens puts it.

Part 7.

Orig. pub. as part 7 of *Appalachian Autumn* in *American Scholar* 74, no. 4 (Autumn 2005): 82–3.
L, 14
Pattern: (6 × 3) (1) (6 × 4) (2)
Time: Early December
Place: Charlottesville, with a flashback to a summer camp experience in Hiwassee Dam, North Carolina, in the early 1940s.

Section 1 moves from sunset to darkness, as the poet's consciousness moves correspondingly from an outdoor view of the Charlottesville streetscape to the anteroom of his Locust Avenue home, with its various archaic artifacts. Night, says the poet, is a distant sea, the depths of which are almost an afterlife, and the sea itself is "remembered / As half-crossed."

The one-line section 2 is an image of the poet's mother in a blue dress—an image that bursts into memory or is perhaps precipitated by a photograph. Wright's mother died in 1964.

Section 3, the thematic center, opposes nothingness and plenitude. The poet wonders when he first heard of nothingness and absolution, with its attendant feeling of emptiness, saying that he can remember nothing about either. But he attaches value to nothingness. It is not just a "blank" but a salve that soothes, and it produces a creative ("engendering") attitude. Moreover, what generates the feeling of emptiness is "the liquid of absolution," so that the holy water of a rite of remission hovers in the background of the poet's consciousness. He may not remember the precise moment when he became aware of nothingness and absolution. All that he can say is that he was "Not young." The experience of plenitude, however, did come to him quite early, and stanzas 3–5, represent in rich detail features of the natural world that produced a knowledge of "the deep weight of the endlessness / Of childhood." These "sacred scenes," rather than the quizzical reflections on nothingness and emptiness, form a body of "precious memories."

p. 16, l. 5. *Precious memories ... scenes unfold.* The chorus of *Precious Memories*, a traditional tune by J.F.B. Wright recorded by many country music performers.

Part 8.

Orig. pub., along with parts 9–12, in *Five Points* 10, nos. 1–2 (2006): 261–7.
L, 17
Pattern: 3 × 2

The two tercets of this short lyric are connected by the idea of good fortune (locked up in stanza 1 and unlocked in stanza 2) and by variations on the *axis mundi* image (the ascending and descending footsteps on the stairway of memory; the mirrored connection between earth and heaven). The paradox of the shadowless things of heaven nevertheless having shadows suggests the contrary state of the shades of the underworld. The point is, as Blake says, that without contraries there is no progression, and an entire lifetime, according to the poet, "isn't too much to pay // for such a reflection." The word "reflection" is of course a pun, meaning both the speculation on the contrary states and the mirror image. We are reminded that "speculum" (mirror) and "speculation" derive from the same Latin verb. The poet says that "water mirrors the moon," and of course the moon itself is a mirror of the sun. The moon appears in each of the odd-numbered poems up to this point, as does memory. Neither appears in parts 2, 4, or 6, but both come together here.

The poet's hearing footsteps going up and down the stairway anticipates the Hunter Gracchus, whom we meet again in the next poem. In Kafka's story, Gracchus tells the burgomaster, "I roam about on this infinitely wide flight of steps, sometimes up, sometimes down, sometimes to the right, sometimes to the left, always in motion."

p. 17, l. 4. *earth mirrors heaven.* A common medieval belief.

Part 9.

Orig. pub., along with parts 8 and 10–12, in *Five Points* 10, nos. 1–2 (2006): 261–7.
L, 18–20
Pattern: (6 × 4) (6) (5 × 3)
Time: January
Place: Charlottesville

The poem begins with a retelling of Franz Kafka's parable *The Hunter Gracchus*. As Wright's note at the end of the volume suggests, his version of Kafka's story is indebted to W.G. Sebald's quasi-autobiographical use of the parable of Gracchus's endless sailing over the world's seas in *Dr. K. Takes the Waters at Riva* (*Vertigo* [New York: New Directions, 1999], 139–67). Wright borrows some of Sebald's language ("a wrong turn of the tiller," "inattention"), as well as some of the details of Kafka's story. For Sebald, Kafka's small boat becomes a "barque with masts of inconceivable height" (163), which Wright transforms into "the ship with its infinitely high masts." The two men who carry Gracchus's bier have "dark coats" in Kafka's story, "dark tunics" in Sebald's narrative, and "black tunics" in Wright's poem. Both Sebald and Wright have the ship emerging as a silhouette from the shadows, a detail not in Kafka's story. Sebald interprets the meaning of the tale as "penitence for a longing for love" (165), which is echoed in Wright's "The great ship and the great body, // like lost love, languish and lip the earth." *The Hunter Gracchus* is an exemplary tale for Wright. The image of Gracchus's endless voyage has appeared five times previously—in *Summer Mornings* (SHS, sect. 4), *Buffalo Yoga* (BY, 17), *Buffalo Yoga Coda II* (BY, 29), *Night Thoughts Under a China Moon* (ST, 21), *In Praise of Franz Kafka* (ST, 60)—and he will reappear in part 22 of the present poem. See the commentary for section 4 of *Summer Mornings* (SHS, 58–60).

Kafka's story—and Sebald's retelling of it—form a thematic undercurrent in what follows, and the correspondences between the poet and the Hunter Gracchus's plight are rather obvious. Gracchus's longing, in Kafka's account, to be carried by his boat "to the other side" parallels Wright's repeated references to that archetypal desire. "Thinking of Dante is thinking about the other side," he wrote in *The Southern Cross*, "And the other side of the other side" (WTTT, 45). The "other side" is a phrase that appears thirty times in Wright's poetry—sometimes literally, sometimes figuratively. In the present poem, the poet's statement that there is "no end to longing" (section 1)—a longing for the "body of light" (section 3)—is reminiscent of Gracchus's longing for his boat to reach its destination and so resolve his death-in-life dilemma. Compostela (p. 18, l. 18) is emblematic of the end of the journey, Santiago de Compostela being the final destination of the legendary medieval pilgrimage. The longing for light appears also in the flashback to the bronze Romanesque reliefs on the doors of San Zeno Maggiore in Verona (p. 19, ll. 17–21). We note as well the accidental coincidence—what we might call poetic etymology—of Riva (Ital., shore), the town on Lake Garda where Gracchus arrives, and Rivanna (River Anna), with its muddy waters and dead leaves flowing through Charlottesville. (This is the only occasion where the Hunter Gracchus emerges from a Charlottesville setting; the other six are all set in Montana.)

In the dialectic of dark versus light, the latter wins: the answer to "who will attain" the body of light is "Not us in our body bags, / Dark over dark, not us," even though "love move the stars," as in the last line of the *Paradiso*. Here the stars are "set to one side." And in the poem's concluding lines the spirit stitches its silver, sun-lit garment "outside the body."

p. 20, l. 1. *The needle ... naked.* "The needle that clothes so many people stays naked itself" (Arabian proverb).

Part 10.

Orig. pub., along with parts 8–9 and 11–12, in *Five Points* 10, nos. 1–2 (2006): 261–7.
L, 21
Pattern: (3 × 2)
Time: Summer
Place: Kingsport

This poem of pure description sets the movement of the Holston River and the countervailing wind against the stasis of "Summer enfrescoed in stop-time." Repetition is the key feature of the poem's music—"white ... white," "jade ... jade," and "wind ... wind" (twice). The sounds produce a kind of sonatina or double binary form, the sixth line returning to the "key" of the third. Above what the poet sees and hears directly before him is the slow movement of the summer constellations.

The poem is dedicated to Wilma Hammond from Kingsport, Tennessee. She and her husband Gardner are Wright's friends.

p. 21, l. 1. *Rotherwood.* A historic home in Kingsport, Tennessee, near the junction of the Holston River and the North Fork of the Holston.

p. 21, l. 6. *wind on the water*. Cf. a line from the chorus of Graham Nash's *Wind on the Water* (1975): "Wind on the water carry me home."

Part 11.

Orig. pub., along with parts 8–10 and 12, in *Five Points* 10, nos. 1–2 (2006): 261–7.
L, 22–4
Pattern: (5 × 4) (5 × 2) (5 × 3)
Place: Kingsport

    This is another of the poet's songs of himself. It begins with an appraisal of the pilgrimage. Caught between the tick and tock of time, he can't go home again, and he is not moving toward some grand finale: one of these days he will simply stop—as will we all. What the world will make of his verse lies somewhere between the self-effacing judgment "That's okay" and the disappointing conclusion that "No one was ever interested enough." Time has slipped through his hands, and the moon, with all of its symbolic import, will also "slip through our fingers // with no ripple, without us in it." (This last image is from Tao-chi. See commentary for section 3, below.) The journey has been directed toward both heaven and earth, but which direction the poet should pursue has never become clear, even though what he brings into the world—his birthmark—may begin "to take shape and shine out." Section 1 concludes with an ironic echo of Whitman: "Look for us in the black spaces, somewhere in the outer dark. / Look for us under the dead grass // in winter, elsewhere, self-satisfied, apart."
    Section 2 is thematically an *ars poetica*. The poet's words are bent to his will, like the yew, "obedient to the bender's will," in *The Faerie Queene* (bk. 1, canto 1, st. 8), and yet the personality of the poet is effaced. "Lament," he says, "is strong in the bare places," meaning that the expression of emotion is contained in the image of "bare places." As Archibald MacLeish put it in his own *Ars Poetica*, "For all the history of grief / An empty doorway and a maple leaf" (ll. 19–20). Wright's version of the lament is the gradual fading of the tufted sunset, captured in the metaphor of the vanishing glow of the charcoal: "sunset cloud tufts briquets / Going ash in the ash-going sky."
    Section 3 begins with another objective correlative, the highway (11W) at Orebank running from east to west through Kingsport like the poet's own pilgrimage, from rising to setting sun. But the focus of this last section is on the poet's empathetic identification with Tao-chi (1641–ca. 1710). The phrases in quotation marks are from a 1698 poem by Tao-chi to Chu Ta, a member of the Ming imperial family, who feigned muteness and insanity in order to escape the attention of the government and therefore devote himself to painting. Tao-chi writes: "I read your [Chu Ta's] meaning, yet how do I cleanse everything? / Your words have rung in my ears through the years of dust and sand; / Because of a single unworthy thought, ten thousand years have slipped through my fingers, / I can now only wash everything away into a great void, and await the final crash of thunder" (*Returning Home: Tao-chi's Album of Landscapes and Flowers*, intro. Wen Fong [New York: Braziller, 1976], 25–6). Wen Fong comments: "We can only guess at the depth of Tao-chi's feelings as old age approached, but he clearly regretted his worldly ambitions" (ibid., 26). In his poem of farewell to his friends in Peking, Tao-chi wrote, "My own life is like that of an ant, / And I have made many journeys" (*Returning Home*, 24). The poem's concluding phrase is from Tao-chi's, *Narcissus*, in *Returning Home* (80): "Oh narcissus and plum blossoms ... On a warm day / by a bright window, / I hold my brush, / How my quiet thoughts wander /—beyond the boundless / shores." This last section is a portrait of the artist as Tao-chi.

p. 22, l. 19. *Look for us ... dead grass*. Cf. "I bequeath myself to the dirt to grow from the grass I love, / If you want me again look for me under your boot-soles" (Walt Whitman, *Song of Myself*, pt. 52, ll. 9–10).

p. 23, l. 7. *sunset cloud tufts briquets*. In this bare syntax, "sunset cloud tufts" is a noun phrase, the "cloud tufts" then identified with or compared to "briquets" by a missing copula.

p. 23, l. 13. *Orebank*. A small town just to the east of Kingsport, Tennessee.

p. 24, l. 4. *narcissus plant*. Tao-Chi's painting of the narcissus is reproduced in *Returning Home*, 84.

Part 12.

Orig. pub., along with parts 8–11, in *Five Points* 10, nos. 1–2 (2006): 261–7.
L, 25–7
Pattern: (10 × 2) (3 × 2) (5) (5 × 4) (3)
Time: February 2
Place: Charlottesville

The poem opens with an account of the child's puzzled reaction to the unimaginable nature of rivers and lakes, which seem to begin and end at indeterminate places and so are immeasurable. This leads to a reflection on the immeasurability of the heart and memory, which "live in an infinite otherness." These abstractions are energized by the extended simile of the herons. Like blue herons, the heart and memory rise and settle. The heart is the hunting bird, while memory is the "lonely observer" perching overhead. Both are always camouflaged: "In waters the color that they are, // and air is."

The connections among the other four sections, if any are intended, are difficult to discern. In section 2 the footprints of the poet are visible, moving into the dark and finally "into the vestibules of the end." In section 3 we move from darkness to light, the first line echoing "the light that shineth in darkness" (John 1:5), and "her begot him" appears to refer to Mary and Jesus. If the poet hints at the Christian story in this section, he is not persuaded to believe it. In the final section, the bright sunlight of Groundhog Day is trying to awaken life from the "sleet and icy dreams" of winter, which is not something the poet is eager to see realized. For him, winter is comforting, as in Eliot's *The Waste Land*: "Winter kept us warm, covering / Earth in forgetful snow" (ll. 5–6). Thus, "the sunlight ... eats away / At our joy," and we remain immobilized by the sunlight, "Hoping the darkness will clear things up." Which it does in the final tercet with the pricked scroll of the midnight sky, a "dark player piano." The stars, peeping through the perforations of the piano's spool, produce a nonstop music of the spheres.

p. 25, l. 8. *French Broad ... Indian Path*. The Little Pigeon River runs through Sevier County in east Tennessee, where the confluence of its two forks flows northward until it joins the French Broad just downstream from Douglas Dam. Cherokee Lake is near Morristown, Tennessee; Pickwick Lake was formed by the damming of the Tennessee River at Pickwick Dam, Wright's birthplace.

p. 27, l. 6. *flowers from Delos* = dried flowers brought back from Delos years before by a neighbor, who knew that Wright had had once visited the Greek island.

Part 13.

Orig. pub. in *Subtropics* 3 (January 2007).
L, 28
Pattern: (3 × 3)

The first tercet depicts, in the foreground, ghost-like and aimless lights wandering through the trees. The second describes the equally aimless stars drifting in the heavens. The poet is anxious about the restless wandering of both the lights and the stars, but at the end we are left with, instead of a resolution, three questions: which bodies will gather them in? which waters will provide them rest? and which tide—the altar of darkness or the altar of light—will receive them? If the former, then the rite is apparently sacrificial; if the latter, celebratory.

Part 14.

Previously unpublished.
L, 29–31
Pattern: (4 × 3) (5 × 2) (3 × 4) (2) (4 × 4) (1)
Time: Winter

  A concern for reputation—referred to as renown (p. 29, l. 4), fame (p. 29, l. 13), and accomplishment (p. 31, l. 12)—is rejected by the poet in favor of what should be, in his view, the proper poetic enterprise—which is to keep his eye fixed on the landscape before him and to rely on the power of "Metaphor, metaphor, metaphor // all down the line" to capture it. This is what displaces "renown" on "the other side of death" (ll. 4, 9). The problem, however, is that to transmit spirit through description, to convey the idea by the image, to give structure to "spiritual values" through poetic *topoi* cannot be done. Language fails to capture the ineffable. While art may have "its own satisfactions," the image itself is "Untouchable, untransmutable, // wholly magic." Still, this does not prevent the poet from appealing, by way of the final line from the work-song, to let the light shine on him. And as is the case of Wright's other confessions of failure, represented here by the dark horse and dark rider of section 2, the actual images of landscape provided in the poem gainsay the poet's denial of his ability to reveal their power. These passages may not reach the divine level, but landscape is transmuted in the metaphoric descriptions of the ominous "great mouth" of the sunset and the predator wind in section 1, the dark horses in section 2, and the lethargic clouds and "unbuttery" light of the winter afternoon in section 3.

p. 30, l. 1. *Midnight, Five Minutes to Midnight*. Tennessee Walking Horses. They competed in championship contests in the mid-1950s. Wright saw them perform in Kingsport, Tennessee. He recycles the imagery here of the black horses, with star-like sparks from their hooves, from an early poem, *The Outriders*: "Horses, black horses ... The sparks from their hooves / Spread out through the night / Like stars, O like stars" (*GRH*, 64).

p. 31, l. 5. *breath-resonance-life-motion*. To the Chinese, the one attribute that distinguished great art was the mysterious quality of "vitality," defined by the fifth-century critic Hsieh Ho as ("Breath-Resonance-Life-Motion").

p. 31, l. 11. The source, if there is one, of the three degrees of accomplishment—competent, marvelous, divine—is uncertain.

p. 31, l. 17. *Midnight Special ... on me.* "Let the Midnight Special shine her ever-loving light on me," a line from the traditional work-song by Leadbelly, who wrote the song while in the penitentiary. The Midnight Special was a train, representing freedom, which shone its light into his cell window.

Part 15.

Orig. pub. as "16, from Littlefoot" in *Appalachian Heritage* 34 (Spring 2006): 120.
L, 32
Pattern: (5 × 3)
Time: Winter
Place: Charlottesville, with a flashback to Kingsport in the 1950s

  As the poet half remembers his affection of the things of his youth ("books, records, and people"), the slamming car doors of the neighbors trigger a nostalgic recollection of the "Appalachian downtown" of Kingsport, Tennessee, during a Christmas holiday in the mid-1950s. The memories are of popular songs at the time, spun by the local disk jockey, and fur-coated girls in cars, the entire holiday being marked by a general aimlessness.

p. 32, l. 12. *See the pyramids ... Nile.* A line from a Pee Wee King pop tune of the 1950s, *You Belong To Me*, sung Jo Stafford and numerous others.
p. 32, l. 13. *WKPT*. A radio station in Kingsport, one of the oldest in East Tennessee, first taking the airwaves in 1940.
p. 32, l. 13. *I'm itching ... fuzzy tree.* A line from Elvis Presley's *All Shook Up*.
p. 32, l. 15. *Martin Karant.* A disk jockey for WKTP–AM–1400, where he worked for more than fifty years.

Part 16.

Orig. pub. as *Spring, I* in *Yale Review* 95, no. 2 (April 2007).
L, 33–5
Pattern: (5 × 4 (7) (5 × 2) (3)
Time: March
Place: Knoxville

During March the poet finds himself in Knoxville, Tennessee—where he lived briefly as a child (1936). March, likened to a dark, overhead river, to which we return in the poem's final tercet, is shifty and squint-eyed ("louche") and thus difficult to get a handle on: whatever it intends to deliver is always awaiting us downstream. Free associations ensue: the statement of an old man—overheard during some earlier March in Knoxville—that "Love of the lack of love is still love"; reflections on the brevity of life; a sense of dislocation (the poet's "home" is neither in the present nor in an immortal afterlife); an awareness of the sacredness of life here as opposed to Life there; the tentative affirmation of Camus's contention that "life is the search for a way back / To the few great simple truths / We knew at the beginning," which is a version of Plato's anamnesis and Kierkegaard's repetition. Camus goes on to say that his writing was nourished by a "single stream" of his early life in Algiers, just as Wright's is nourished by the stream flowing from his life in east Tennessee.

The omnipresent moon (it has appeared in seven of the previous numbered parts) makes an appearance in the final section, this time in its crescent phase, and the grey-haired poet is caught up in the great western movement of the heavens. He includes us as well: we are all leaves floating on Heraclitean flux—the March river of the opening stanza—which carries us home, wherever that is.

The old man who said "Love of the lack of love is still love" was right, according to the poet. In this quip the "lack of love" is not an antonym of love: there is no charity in hatred. The accent, rather, falls on the word "lack," so that the poet is registering his affection for the void—the Buddhist *shunyata*, the emptiness celebrated by the T'ang poets, the *hebel* of Ecclesiastes. In section 3 the transubstantiated poet says that "everything's holy now," and a sense of absence or empty space that lacks love and everything else seems to be required for the holy of holies to establish itself.

p. 33, l. 14. *Kingston Pike.* U.S. highways 11 and 70 and Tennessee highway 1 through Knoxville.
p. 34, l. 15. *Camus said.* The passage is from the last paragraph of the 1958 Preface a new edition of Camus's first book, *L'envers et l'endroit* (*Betwixt and Between*, orig. pub. 1937 in Algiers): "A man's work is nothing but this slow trek to rediscover, through the detours of art, those two or three great and simple images in whose presence his heart first opened."
p. 34, l. 19. *Susan's house* = the house of a neighbor across the street.
p. 34, l. 19. *gobba a ponente.* Waning or crescent moon, from a proverb meaning "hump looking west."

Part 17.

Orig. pub. as *Spring, II* in *Yale Review* 95, no. 2 (April 2007).
L, 36–8
Pattern: (6 × 3) (3) (7) (6 × 2) (5 × 2) (4)
Time: Spring
Place: Charlottesville; New York City

The fact that it is difficult to lean on Jesus when the spring landscape has its hackles raised and is otherwise uninviting leads to a memory of the poet's father, "who leaned on no one" as he inspected his spring rose beds. Spring then becomes the backdrop against which the poet offers several versions of his complaint to the muse. Spring should be the time of new beginnings, as Morandi implied. But the full passage from which the lines from Morandi are taken is this: "I too am not getting enough done, and what I do always seems to require so much time and effort. For the past few days I don't think I've done anything worthwhile. Believe me, to feel this way at my age is quite sad, since each time we begin, we always think we've understood, that we have all the answers, but we're always starting over again from the beginning." These sentiments belong to the poet as well. Even when we cut to New York City, spring is having a difficult time getting itself untracked, yet the poet wants to identify with the new leaves just beginning to butt their heads upward. Perhaps "these little ones" (p. 37, l.9) refers also to the reclusive insects, which have not yet emerged from "their hiding holes." This is Wright's version of "April is the cruelest month."

Thus far we have moved by a series of associations that have their center of gravity in a season that offers little solace or support: spring in Charlottesville, a memory of spring in Tennessee, springtime in Giorgio Morandi's bedroom and studio, and spring in New York City. The image of the insects that "cower inside their hiding holes" in New York leads to the poet's own reclusiveness at the beginning of section 4, and his own spiritual and psychic state becomes the focus of the rest of the poem. He feels as if "the absolute," also known as the "Master of words, Lord of signs" and the "Master of What Is About To Be," has abandoned him. God is, again, a *deus absconditus*, the hidden God who may be hanging out "Down by the muddy waters"—and then again He may not. God's absence creates a rather heightened state of anxiety, and the poet wonders if this absence might not signal the beginning of the end. His imperative for God to reveal Himself—to "Step out of the Out"—receives no reply, and we are left with the bittersweet image of the faithless and aging poet "alone in a small boat," unable to account for either the voices from the past or the whiteness of the "snowfall of blossoms" into which he is released. The coda from the Carter Family's *Maple on the Hill* suggests that the crossing to the other side of the river is imminent.

p. 36, l. 1. *Leaning on Jesus.* A variation of a line from the E.A. Hoffman and A.J. Showalter's hymn *Leaning on the Everlasting Arms.*
p.36, ll. 13–16. *Morandi. Each time we begin ... from the beginning.* The lines quoted are from a letter to Janet Abramowicz from Morandi a few years before he died (Janet Abramowicz, *Giorgio Morandi: The Art of Silence* [New Haven: Yale University Press, 2005], 231).
p. 38, ll. 11–14. *Don't forget me ... on my grave.* Verse 4 of a Carter Family bluegrass tune, *Maple on the Hill.*

Part 18.

Orig. pub. in *Front Porch*, issue 1 (2006).
L, 39–41
Pattern: (5 × 4) (5 × 2) (3) (8+6)
Time: Mid-May
Place: Charlottesville

The poem, which originates after a five-year hiatus from the back yard, structures itself around a dialectic of light and darkness, sameness and difference, the substantial and the ephemeral, presence and absence, east and west, present and past. The poem's *ars poetica* themes center on the poet's forebears ("the people we learned from" whose "names are inscribed in my Book of Light") and the function of poetry. As for his audience, the poet thought he was writing for the angels. This is reminiscent of Rilke's late work, where the angels represent the transmutation of the visible world into a transcendent, invisible, symbolic one. But, as it turned out, no such grand project materialized: "Our lines were written in black ink on the midnight sky, / Messages for the wind, // a flutter of billets-doux / From one dark heart to the next." Opposed to this is the realization that "everything's light," that the source of light is "splendor," and that it culminates in a radiant "brilliance."

Sonny Rollins's forebears were Charlie Parker and others, recorded in the lines of the interview that Wright borrows (p. 39, ll. 11–15). Among Wright's own ancestors are the T'ang poets, who are described in a stunningly suggestive metaphor as "prestidigitators of nothingness." These "cloud poets" are "diviners of what wasn't there." This is a version of the Taoist conception of *wu wei*, translated variously as "nothing's own doing," "creative quietude," "an awareness of the unity of life," and "nonbeing burgeoning forth into being." Wright's desire is to be one of the Chinese poets, under whose nimble fingers (prestidigitators) the landscape does burgeon forth into being. And this is in fact what the poet offers us in the rich description of sun and shadow in the last section. Prestidigitation refers to manual skill but also to sleight of hand, and we get both meanings in the last fourteen lines, where nothingness turns into a segment of the world of the ten thousand things.

p. 39, ll. 11–15. *We don't know much ... Book of Light.* "We never really know too much, not really. We need to be humble about that. But we do get to know certain things, and we have to do the best with them. Right now I know what I got from Coleman Hawkins, from Ben Webster, from Dexter Gordon, from Don Byas, from Charlie Parker, and all the other guys who gave their lives to this music. I know that without a doubt. From childhood I've known this" (Sonny Rollins in an interview with Stanley Crouch, qtd. in Crouch's "The Colossus: Sonny Rollins on the Bandstand," *New Yorker* 81, no. 12 [9 May 2005]: 71).

p. 39, l. 18. *Our lines were written in black ink on a midnight sky.* A variation on a line by one of Wright's students, Ryan Fox.

p. 40, l. 19. *like the Green Knight's head.* That is, blood-red. In *Sir Gawain and the Green Knight* we are told that after Gawain smote the Green Knight's neck "the blood spurted forth, and glistened on the green raiment," a description that the poet more or less repeats, *mutatis mutandis*, in l. 41, where the sunlight forms "Bright drops in the bright green hedge."

Part 19.

Orig. pub. as "22" in *Appalachian Heritage* 34 (Summer 2006): 99.
L, 42
Pattern: (4) (2) (4)
Time: Late May
Place: Charlottesville

This is Wright's parody of the poet-as-nightingale convention. In the gnat-floating, blossom-falling evening of late May, the poet observes the sparrows flitting from one hedge to the next. He then asks, "Is love stronger than unlove?"—picking up on the "lack of love" motif in part 16. The answer is that the unloved know that love is stronger. The unloved belong to the company of the mockingbird whose "heart is cloned and colorless" and can thus only mimic other bird songs. The suggestion is that the poet's songs are not genuine if they only imitate those of others and do not spring from the heart.

In the punch line the poet likens himself and his "brother" to the small, unnamed "chirper," an antitype of Keats's nightingale that soars above the earth on "the viewless wings of poesy." This tiny bird is "lost in the loose leaves of the weeping cherry tree" and his song is "going nowhere"—which is an image of the poet as a minimalist songster.

Part 20.

Orig. pub., along with part 21, in *Laurel Review* 40, no. 2 (Summer 2006): 248–54.
L, 43–5
Pattern: (3 × 3) (2) (6 × 2) (5 × 3) (4) (6 × 3) (3)
Time: June
Place: Montana

At the beginning of summer the change of scenery from Charlottesville to Montana reminds the poet once more of the cycle of the seasons. Without the myth of the eternal return "our lives appear meaningless"; with it, "all ends must meet." Clouds are the poem's central emblem, appearing in all but the first and last of the seven sections and dominating the imagery. They signal the "turn-round" of the evening, the inexplicable, and the feature of the landscape that keeps drawing the poet's attention. He also says that the landscape "is the way of the absolute, // dead grass and waste / Of water, clouds where it all begins, clouds where it ends," where "clouds" can serve as either a noun or a verb—or both. If the self is extinguished, the absolute may emerge from this ouroboros—landscape's cyclical and primordial unity. In *Sitting Alone on a Summer Night* Wang Wei, quoted later in the poem, says "To eliminate decrepitude / Study the absolute."

The problem, however, is that the poet does not feel at home in this "country of deep inclemency," a place that "whets isolation," even as it wets it. He becomes acutely conscious of the difference between the eternal recurrence of the seasons and the brevity of the span of human life. In the landscape "time is constant and circular"; in consciousness, it is something to be measured. This triggers stock-taking: "What is the span of one's life? / How to you measure it?" Is it to be measured in terms of "Cubits or years, missed opportunities, // the minor, self-satisfied / Successes"? If so, then the poet concludes that whatever his achievements and however long it took him to achieve them, it all adds up to nothing. This leads not to despair but to resignation, serenity, and even a sense of "a freshness that we abide." An example of such freshness is the view of the creatures the poem affords: the herons and cliff swallows that "harangue and arabesque / Over the lawn and lilac rim of the late lilacs, / Then dwindle against the dark green of the evergreens." Still, it is difficult to overcome the sense of existential isolation, and the poet declares that when the birds have disappeared and the sun has set, "All that I know goes with it, like a body pulled down by weights // into the depths." This seems to follow from the lines of Wang Wei, which Wright has adopted for himself: the world may know my name and style, but they do not know my heart. The quoted passage is the last four lines of Wang Wei's *Lines*, the concluding poem in *Poems of Wang Wei*, trans. G.W. Robinson (Harmondsworth: Penguin, 1973), p. 140. The first four lines of the poem, which appear not be original with Wang Wei, are a lament on old age: "With age I am growing too lazy to write verses / And now old age is my only company / In a past life I was mistakenly a poet / In a former existence I must have been a painter." Wright is anything but lazy at age seventy, but he does leave us with a poignant sense that he and all that he knows, including his "remnant habits," are descending into the abyss

p 43, ll. 1–3. These customs and taboos are taken from Elizabeth Kolbert's article on the mysterious Eyak people of Alaska, whose language has only one remaining native speaker: "Among the many customs ... attribute[d] to the Eyak are building small wooden houses over the graves of their loved ones, observing a taboo against sewing the skins of land and sea animals into the same garment, and burning children's toys in order to secure good weather" ("Last Words: Letter from Alaska: A Language Dies," *New Yorker* 81, no. 16 [6 June 2005]: 46–50).

Part 21.

Orig. pub., along with part 20, in *Laurel Review* 40, no. 2 (Summer 2006): 248–54.
L, 46–9
Pattern: (7 × 2) (7 × 2) (3) (6 × 2) (3) (7 × 3) (3)
Time: June
Place: Montana

In section 1, as the shadows move across the landscape and the creatures take their leave, "everything moves toward its self-appointed end." This includes the poet, who at seventy begins the inexorable descent of his "dark decade." Time's winged chariot causes the poet to reflect on his vocation. In section 2 this is focused on the hope that if he waits long enough a brilliant line, rising "like some miraculous fish to the surface, / Brilliant and lithe in the late sunlight," will offer itself to him in his solitude. The verbal calligraphy that follows might well qualify as candidates for such a gift: "The sky is cloudless, the meadow seems like a vast plain / Without dust, // the Chinese vocabulary of the grasses / Shining like water wherever I dip my dark brush."

The poet calls the falling June light "the Sundown Special"—the train that is to carry him to the other side (section 5). His seat is presently taken, but one has been reserved for him. This sense of the approaching end of things raises a further question about the poetic vocation: the difficulty of being original (section 4): "What does one do when one finds out one's thoughts // are the thoughts of everyone else?" Coupled with this sense of the burden of the past is the realization that "We're always, apparently, on our way to anywhere else, / And miss what we're here for, // the objects we never realize / Will constitute our desire, / The outtakes and throwaways of the natural world" (section 6).

"This is the entry of evening light," says the poet in the penultimate section, meaning, on the one hand, that the scene before him marks the entrance to the stairwell of the hereafter, and on the other, that this section is another item to be recorded in the Appalachian Book of the Dead. "Where I am, it seems, is always just before sunset"—literally and figuratively. The poet announces that "local color" is "still deep in the heart," including the local color of the Italian landscape forty-seven years earlier. We are reminded of the earlier declaration in *Apologia Pro Vita Sua*: "Affection's the absolute // everything rises to." But the poem concludes on the somber and disheartening note that the objects of the poet's attention, which make for the plenitude of the landscape, are slowly disappearing. The earth abides; we will not.

p. 48, l. 10. *as I said one time, I love to see that evening sun go down*. Wright is referring to the opening line of *Looking across Laguna Canyon at Dusk, North by Northwest*: "I love the way the evening sun goes down" (NB, 64).

p. 48, l. 15. *Desenzano*. Town on the southwestern tip of Lake Garda.

Part 22.

Orig. pub. in *Subtropics* 3 (January 2007).
L, 50
Pattern: (6) (1)
Time: Summer
Place: Montana

This is the seventh and final appearance of the Hunter Gracchus in Wright's poetry. For the previous appearances of Kafka's haunting image, see in *Summer Mornings* (SHS, sect. 4), *Buffalo Yoga* (BY, 17), *Buffalo Yoga Coda II* (BY, 29), *Night Thoughts Under a China Moon* (ST, 21), *In Praise of Franz Kafka* (ST, 60), and *Littlefoot*, part 9, as well as the commentary for section 4 of *Summer Mornings* (SHS, 58–60). In Kafka's death-in-life tale the body of the Hunter Gracchus continues to travel the seas, docking at one port after another in an apparently endless attempt to find its proper resting place. In the present poem, Wright attributes Gracchus's failure to a "lack of love." There is little hope in the poet's aging heart for a solution to Gracchus's plight: having been transported to the upper air, Gracchus will continue to wheel round the empyrean "Like the four seasons."

Part 23.

Orig. pub. as "XXVII" in *Poetry Northwest* (Fall 2006–Winter 2007): 10–11.
L, 51–3
Pattern: (5 × 2) (1) (4 × 3) (6) (7 × 2) (2–3) (4) (2)
Time: Summer
Place: Montana

Wright's note (p. 91) indicates that the poem owes a debt to Wallace Stevens, which is apparently to the first line. In *Sunday Morning* the speaker wonders why she should assent to some ethereal conception of paradise when she experiences within herself "Passions of rain, or moods in falling snow; / Grievings in loneliness, or unsubdued / Elations when the forest blooms; gusty / Emotions on wet roads on autumn nights; / All pleasures and all pains, remembering / The bough of summer and the winter branch" (pt. 2, ll. 9–14). She later asks rhetorically, "But when the birds are gone, and their warm fields / Return no more, where, then, is paradise?" (*Collected Poems* [New York: Knopf, 1967], 68). One needs no Paradise either after the rain subsides, when "a small splendor" shines through in the stillness.

The "image picker" (p. 52, l. 2) catalogues other features of the earthly paradise, but their "inscape" proves to be elusive, even after "Pushing the boughs aside."

Part 24.

Orig. pub. as "XXIX" in *Poetry Northwest* (Fall 2006–Winter 2007): 11–12.
L, 54–6
Pattern: (6 × 3) (4) (6 × 2) (4) (8) (5) (2)
Time: Summer
Place: Montana

The metaphysical question raised by the poem is whether we can live in a metaphysical world. The poet's answer is that it is "nonsense" to think that we can or should, like eremites, cut ourselves off from the "riches of the earth"—to think that "It's not such a poverty ... to live in a metaphysical world." Wright, of course, is forever entering the metaphysical world with his speculations on life and death, time and eternity, memory and forgetfulness, light and darkness and a host of other ontological subjects. What he means, therefore, is that we should never live *solely* in a metaphysical world. The physical and the metaphysical worlds do not offer for him and *either/or* alternative. The physics of nature, as described in sections 1, 4, and 5, are often the spur for his meditations on metaphysics. "The mind's the affliction," he says, but only if it is separated from heart and soul, which are attentive to the "simple things" that surround him. This is a version of Stevens' line "Beauty is momentary in the mind / ... But in the flesh it is immortal" (*Peter Quince at the Clavier*, ll. 51, 53).

Wright's poem affirms the good earth: "We are the generations of the soil," he writes in section 6. The soil is "our destination, / our Compostela." But, as we learn in the poem's concluding line, there is another destination to which "we're transplanted," which rather serves to undercut the earlier metaphysical claim that there is no second world (p. 54, l. 18). The pilgrims, after all, undertook their journey to Compostela not just to feel the dirt under their feet. The second-world motif also haunts the Orpheus legend.

Wright only occasionally draws on Classical mythology, but in the *ars poetica* section 3 he represents himself as Orpheus. In his embellishment of the myth, the oarsman of the Styx thinks that Orpheus's song "won't work." And "it didn't," says the poet, referring apparently to the Bacchic howlings of the Ciconian women who drown out Orpheus' songs and eventually tear him apart. But miraculously Orpheus's severed head was still able to sing as it floated down toward Lesbos, and so far as we know he is still singing, his soul having been united with Eurydice's in Tartarus, where they stroll together side by side. They are like us, "somnambulists" who "lie down in our own hearts."

p. 55, l.5. *Orpheus walked, the poets say, down to the black river*. Wright embroiders the tale of Orpheus as it comes to us from Ovid, Virgil, and Apollonius. The black river of the underworld was the Styx. One of the other poets Wright perhaps has in mind is his teacher Donald Justice, who assumes the persona of Orpheus in several of his poems and whose *New and Selected Poems* was entitled *Orpheus Hesitated beside the Black River* when published in England, the title coming from a line in his *There Is a Gold Light in Certain Old Paintings*.

p. 56, l. 11. *Compostela*. The final destination of one of the legendary medieval pilgrimages.

Part 25.

Not previously published.
L, 57–9
Pattern: (15) (8) (4 × 2) (5 × 2) (2) (12) (2)
Time: Summer
Place: Montana

    This poem begins as a celebration of the landscape, for which the poet declares his affection—his love of the rising mists and the sunlit "chinks in the forest" with their "thrust and retreat." But toward the end the poem turns into a lament. Haunted by the apocalyptic lyrics of *The Great Speckled Bird*, the poet reveals that he has exhausted his supply of short stories—"Unstoppable storyteller with nothing to say." The little narratives of the book of the wind stall, yielding nothing but silence, and so its pages remain blank. But although the poet cannot sing the songs of transcendence—those "on the other side of language"—he is unable to follow the injunction to himself to "stub out your pencil." Witness the final couplet with its description of the bundles of light about to burst into the darkness. This will provide at least one paragraph in Wright's unsystematic theology of immanence. Others will, of course, follow from the Pilgrim's pencil.

p. 57, ll. 16–17. *Auden*. The reference is to the conclusion of W.H. Auden's *Nones*: "Not knowing quite what has happened, but awed / By death like all the creatures / Now watching this spot, like the hawk looking down / Without blinking, the smug hens / Passing close by in their pecking order, / The bug whose view is balked by grass, / Or the deer who shyly from afar / Peer through chinks in the forest" (*Collected Poems*, ed. Edward Mendelson [New York: Random House, 1976], 482).

p. 58, ll. 5–6. *not this enduring verdancy / And chapterless blue*. Cf. Wallace Steven's line: "not this dividing and indifferent blue" (*Sunday Morning*, l. 15).

p. 58, l. 14, 35. *Rock of Ages* = a familiar gospel tune written by Augustus M. Toplady in 1776 and set to music by Thomas Hastings in 1830. *Life Is Like a Mountain Railroad* = a gospel tune from the late nineteenth century: music by Charles D. Tillman and lyrics by Eliza R. Snow and M.E. Abbey.

p. 58, ll. 14, 16–18. *The Great Speckled Bird*. "She is spreading her wings for a journey / She is going to leave by and by, / When the trumpet shall sound in the morning, / She will rise and go up in the sky. / In the presence of all her despisers / With a song never uttered before, / She will rise and be gone in a moment / Till the great tribulation is o'er. // I am glad to have learned of her meekness, / I am glad that my name's on the Book, / And I want to be one never fearing / On the face of my Savior to look. / When He cometh descending from Heaven / On the cloud, as He wrote in the Word, / I'll be joyfully carried up to meet Him / On the wings of the Great Speckled Bird" (*The Great Speckled Bird*, stanzas 3–4). The song is based on Jeremiah 12:9, "Mine heritage is unto me as a speckled bird, the birds round about are against her; come ye, assemble all the beasts of the field, come to devour."

p. 59, l. 16. *fatwood*. Regional expression (chiefly in Georgia and Florida) for kindling.

Part 26.

Orig. pub. in *Subtropics* 3
L, 60–2

Pattern: (11 × 2) (2) (16) (12) (2 × 2) (3)
Time: Summer
Place: Montana

The dialectic at the beginning is between the Horatian *res* and *verba*, and the poet comes down on the side of *res*: wisdom and truth come not from words but from mute things: "give me a thing that says nothing." (Cf. the *res* and *verba* dialectic in *Words Are the Diminution of All Things*, in BY, 45.) Words are never sufficient to represent the things of this world: the book of nature contains only a wordless ignorance, like that of the caretaker's dog Yugo, who sees but "can't say" and has no concern for "what's to come." In section 2 the poet addresses his "witness" to look for him—not that he is lost but that he needs other eyes to help him see. The first thing he sees is metal rooster that had been nailed to the chicken house by a Lincoln County old-timer, Snuffy Bruns. The memory of Snuffy triggers a series of free associations, in the vignette that follows, about him and his wife Beryl.

The central images are avian—the finches of section 2, the ravens and ducks of section 4, and the unidentified birds that fly into the windows in concluding tercet. These last creatures "keep on breaking their necks," sailing into what they think is the sky reflected in the panes, so the poem concludes with a rather foreboding instance of negative blue, anticipated by the ominous picture of the ravens, "looking for blood," under whose shadow we live, as well as the "yellow dust" image from Tu Fu.

p. 61, l. 5. *Snuffy Bruns.* This toothless Lincoln County truck driver made a cameo appearance in Tim McIntire's song "Stockman's Bar Again, Boys," in *Sun-Saddled, Coke-Copping, Bad-Boozing Blues* (BY, 68), where he was seen "feeding the squirrels," as his wife (his sister!) does in the present flashback.

p. 61, l. 17. *air kiss* = a facial expression in which the lips are pursed as if kissing.

p. 62, l. 10. *The past is a yellow dust.* Cf. Tu Fu: "The great heroes and generals of old time / Are yellow dust forever now. / Such are the affairs of men. / Poetry and letters / Persist in silence and solitude" (*Night in the House by the River*, in *One Hundred Poems from the Chinese*, trans. Kenneth Rexroth [New York: New Directions, 1971], 29).

Part 27.

Orig. pub. as part 35 of *Littlefoot* in *Virginia Quarterly Review* 82, no. 1 (Winter 2006): 190–2. L, 63–5

Pattern: (8 × 2) (5 × 2) (6–1) (5 × 2) (8) (5)
Time: Early August
Place: Montana

The poem opens with the common snipe, transformed under the poet's fertile imagination into an angelic creature that appears to walk on water. The snipe next becomes a phoenix-like apparition, transformed by the aura of the sun's reflection on the pond into a mysterious spirit, emerging from the landscape just as the figures in Fra Angelico's frescoes emerged from the plaster of San Marco. In section 3 the bird settles down to become an image of himself in the pond's mirrored surface, where "he drinks from his own mouth." These striking scenes occur just before nightfall, when mother August has summoned home her children, the insects. This, along with the world of the voracious hummingbird (p. 65, l. 12), is the locus of the poet's affection.

In section 5 the poet announces that the "voyage into the interior is all that matters," echoing a common poetic theme. Much of what he reads—"the asininities"—apparently have to do with the exterior life recorded by other writers, perhaps other poets. The poem itself dwells hardly at all on the journey into the self, other than the comfort the poet says he takes from knowing the stars are overhead and the half-wish of the conclusion to abandon the "raucous" life, leaving the world to "settle, like some white bird, // on another mountain."

p. 63, l. 9. *Fra Angelico*. A Dominican monk who was commissioned to decorate the friar's cells at San Marco with frescoes.

Part 28.

Orig. pub as part 37 of *Littlefoot* in *Virginia Quarterly Review* 82, no. 1 (Winter 2006): 193–96.
L, 66–9
Pattern: (10–1) (10) (10) (5) (6) (4–1) (3) (8 × 2) (3)
Time: August
Place: Montana

The question in the first stanza is a poetic version of the faith-and-works question in the Epistle of James: what does it profit us to say that we have faith without works. The poet is concerned here with the "works" side of the matter: what profit follows from what he has devoted his life to? what is the end of all the "Description and metaphor, / The fancy dancing of language"? The poet can't answer the question because he doesn't know, just as he can't specify the benefits of the thunderstorm that has begun to growl to the north and south. Ignorance, however, leads neither to bliss nor to abandoning the poetic project: section 2 resumes the "description and metaphor," this time to record the approaching and somewhat ominous change of the seasons. It also leads to the panegyric of section 3 with its litany of praises for things absent and dispossessed: the left-out, the left-behind, the left-over, the over-looked, and so on.

The thunderstorm passes, displaced by the sun and its "over-heated vocabulary" and then the rain, as autumn shifts into low gear. The horses, which populate quite a few of the Montana poems, are introduced in section 5, and two of them, Monte and Littlefoot, return in section 8, the latter of course now immortalized by the book's title. The poet confesses that he is "Struck by the paucity of [his] imagination / To winnow anything from the meadow," but the metaphor of the rope—the lariat and noose used to describe the cruising and circling of the yellow-tail hawk—quickly comes to the rescue. We are then left with the poet and his two horses, caught in a moment of calm serenity, liking the meadow the way it is and waiting for what comes next, even if it is the end of a lifetime.

p. 67, l. 7. *bling* = glittering accessories (hip-hop diction).
p. 67, l. 20. *scorgle* = Wright's coinage, meaning to tickle and rub.
p. 69, l. 2. *Monte and Littlefoot*. Monte is Holly Wright's horse. Littlefoot was at the time a yearling brought in to keep Monte company.

Part 29.

Orig. pub. as part 38 of *Littlefoot* in *Virginia Quarterly Review* 82, no. 1 (Winter 2006): 196.
L, 70
Pattern: (3)

In this tercet the poet declares that "We all have the same book, // identically inscribed." As the page of this book happens to be dark, we cannot read it, but one day we will be able to. This is another version of the Appalachian Book of the Dead, though there are connections with other mysterious, imaginary books scattered throughout Wright's poems: the book of What I Can Never Know (*1975*) and its companion, the thin book of All I Will Ever Know (*Buffalo Yoga Coda II*); the darker book of revelation (*Thinking of Wallace Stevens at the Beginning of Spring*), the Book of White Hair (*Portrait of the Artist by Li Shang-Yin*), the magic book of the world (*Buffalo Yoga*), the Book of Unknowing (*Homage to Mark Rothko*), and the Book of Poverty (*Littlefoot*, part 5).

Wright's poems often enjoin us to listen (the verb appears several scores of times in his work), and when we are asked to "listen to the book" (the reference in this case is to *The Nag Hammadi Library*), there is a sense in which the book is authoritative: listen and you will hear. But as reading is also a matter of the eye, at the appropriate time we will be able to read because the page is no longer dark. The expectation is for an impending recognition or revelation—or, given the biblical ring of "appointed day," even a Revelation.

Part 30.

Orig. pub. as part 39 of *Littlefoot* in *Virginia Quarterly Review* 82, no. 1 (Winter 2006): 196–9. L, 71–3
Pattern: (1) (6) (4) (3) (5) (10) (5 × 3) (2)
Time: August
Place: Montana

The opening of the poem announces "a kind of depression that empties the soul." In the context of the weather ("drained / And overcast") depression refers to a period of low barometric pressure but refers as well as to the poet's melancholy. Both the atmosphere and the poet's gloom (the "uneasy remove" that "everything falls to") stir but do not disappear. But after the rain a seasonal change sets in and the poet, looking at the reflection of the mountains in the rain-pimpled pond, can announce, on his seventieth birthday, that the weather is "wonderful." With this mood swing, he identifies with the light of things seen and is still searching for the messages of things unseen.

p. 72, l. 1. *you*. A poet friend who was suffering from Lyme disease.
p. 72, l. 5. *My 70th birthday*. 25 August 2005.
p. 72, l. 14. *held the bag*. The reference here is to the "wild goose chase" known as the snipe hunt, a practical joke in which naive young people are told that they are to run through the woods and catch an imaginary bird known as a snipe in a gunnysack.
p. 72, l. 19. *aluminum pennies*. Because copper was needed to make brass shell casings in World War II, in 1943 pennies were minted in zinc-coated steel.

Part 31.

Orig. pub. as part 41 of *Littlefoot* in *Virginia Quarterly Review* 82, no. 1 (Winter 2006): 199–201. L, 74–6
Pattern: (5 × 2) (3) (10) (6) (10) (11) (4)
Time: September
Place: Montana

The poet returns to the theme of emptiness, using the simile of the end of the dead pine-tree branch as an emblem for the void. The mossy-bearded branch "ends in nothing," but it moves ever so slightly, and the poet hopes in due course to be moved like that beyond the present state of life. The meditation continues with a distinction between two kinds of emptiness, the easy to recognize and the difficult. The first is existential *Angst*. The second is the Buddhist sense of *shunyata*, the metaphysical idea that everything in life is impermanent and without an independent reality. Some have experienced the second, which they have used, even though it is distant like love or resurrection, to overcome the first, which "is bespoke" (the archaic intransitive form, meaning that emptiness as anxiety is exclaimed or widely bruited about). Resurrection reminds us of another form of emptiness—the *kenosis* of Philippians 2: 6–7, where we're told that Jesus, who did not regard equality with God as something to be exploited "emptied himself." This is the self-annihilation that comes with Jesus' descent into history, on the other side of which is resurrection. The suggestion is that the poet yearns for *shunyata*, the sense of the interpenetration of all things in a spiritual world.

The dominant subnarrative relates to death, that state in which the "great purity" (p. 74, l. 13) awaits the poet, who will be looking for us "on the other side" of the river (p. 75, l. 10). The theme is picked up in section 3—"an almanac of the afterhour"—with a rare Classical reference—the retelling of the Icarus myth. The poet identifies with Icarus, just as earlier he had identified with Orpheus (part 24). The context is the growing darkness and the poet's inability literally to see the page and figuratively to imagine what Icarus' fall from the sky was like. The poet nevertheless does project a scene of Icarus' being scalded by the melting wax as he plummets seaward and then his being cooled by the wind. His plunge into the sea, the poet speculates, must have been like a descent into nothingness and yet at the same time a welcome relief from the sun's heat and the terror of the fall. Wright alters the myth by imagining the sun still in pursuit of the drowned Icarus, which is why he says at the end of the section, "So many worlds since then, all of them so alike, so welcoming, / Suncatcher, father and son." Death by water and the father's grief are all part of the myth of the eternal return. Wright apparently wants us to see the Suncatcher as both father and son, as in Joyce's *A Portrait of the Artist*, where Stephen flies sunward like Daedalus to escape from the nets that constrain him and yet at the same time falls from the aesthetic paradise he has soared to—at least from Joyce's ironic perspective.

Sections 5 and six are flashbacks to Verona and Lake Garda and its environs forty-seven years earlier, interrupted only by the poet's recording of what he sees in the meadow before him, Monte and Littlefoot—"One horse up and one horse down." Revisiting the past through memory, which can be either superficial or deep, leads to the conclusion, first, that at age twenty-three you think "you'll live forever" and, second, that one cannot go home again: "The past is a dark disaster, and no one returns," an echo of the opening lines of *Littlefoot*. This bleak meditation is reinforced by the image of the hanging bodies, an oblique reference to the hanging of the corpses of Mussolini and his collaborators in Milan after their execution.

The poem closes with the *Rags and Jags* nursery rhyme, signaling the return of Wright from Montana to his Charlottesville home.

p. 75, l. 9. *cousin*. This is one of the several places in *Littlefoot* where Wright, in addressing his readers, lightheartedly names or otherwise identifies them. Cf. "Slick" in parts 5 and 34, "Hernando" in part 17, "hermano" in part 19, and "Horatio" in part 28.

p. 75, l. 15. *Valpolicella*. A red wine created from the Veneto region of Italy, north-northwest of Verona.

p. 75, l. 16. *Salò ... Bardolino*. A town on the western shore of Lake Garda, now associated with the failed fascist regime of Mussolini, who, with Hitler's blessing, set up a power base in Salò in 1943. Bardolino is a town on the eastern shore of Lake Garda, just south of the town of Garda.

p. 76, l. 1. *Punta S. Vigilio*. A promontory jutting into Lake Garda a few miles west of the town of Garda.

p. 76, l. 4. *Riva ... Gardone*. Riva del Garda is a town located at the northernmost tip of Lake Garda; Gardone is a town on the western shore of the lake. Wright refers to it as a "myth-bag" because it and the other towns along the western shore were a repository of stories associated with Mussolina's Repubblica Sociale (1943–45) and Gabriele D'Annunzio's escapades.

p. 76, l. 5. *Sirmione*. Sirmione, a town on Lake Garda, has been famous since ancient times for its health-giving spas. At the tip of Sirmione lie the ruins of a Roman Villa, known for centuries as "Grotte di Catullo," which was built in the early Imperial Era. On numerous occasions Wright has described his first encounter with Pound's poetry on the Sirmione peninsula in the very ruins of what is said to have been Catullus' villa. *Nocturne* (CM, 6) commemorates that experience.

p. 76, l. 6. The people mentioned here were all friends or members of Wright's army unit in Verona: Winfrid Thorpe [Thorp] (a chief warrant officer), Peter Hobart (an art history major from Yale), Harold Schimmel (a Hebrew poet who had majored in English at Cornell; in 1959 he had urged Wright to visit Catullus' villa at Lake Garda and to read Pound's poems), and George Schneeman (a painter).

p. 76, l. 7. *Via Mazzini ... Piazza Erbe*. The Via Mazzini is a well-known Verona street, running from the Piazza Erbe to the Piazza Bra. La Greppia is a restaurant in Verona, on Vicolo Samaritana near the Piazza Erbe.

Part 32.

Orig. pub. *New Yorker* 19 and 26 February 2007: 142–3.
L, 77–9
Pattern: (10) (10) (10) (2) (7) (3) (8) (3–1)
Time: Early October
Place: Charlottesville

The poet has journeyed east, returning to his familiar backyard, but the eight vignettes of the poem have little to connect them except the description of the Charlottesville landscape at the beginning and the end, and the idea of paradise. At the beginning, he is a bit out of joint: his mind in headed north against the backwash of the geese, which are flying south. Then he records the fugitive verse of the Flatt and Scruggs tune in order that, he says, it won't be forgotten. But the implication is that the poet also desires to rest "by the banks of the river," anticipating a "reunion in heaven" with his dead "loved ones." In any event, as he sits in the dark, heaven is on his mind: "Paradise, Pound said, was real to Dante because he saw it." The poet's own intimations of immortality come in the form of the flaming edge of the darkness and the "orange, rectangular breath" of the black dog—emblems of a surreal experience, to be sure, but emblems nevertheless of light coming from darkness.

Death continues to haunt the poet, who sees life as both a "brief stay" and a "long walk on a short pier." Still, the time has not come: Charon's empty boat drifts across the latter-day Acheron, which offends the poet. But death is no more mysterious than the dragonflies of early December, which reawaken his descriptive energy, and the poem concludes with the symbolism of the dogwood trees, the mythology of which points to a momentarily postponed resurrection beyond death.

p. 77, l. 7. *Pipistrello*. A bat.
p. 78, l. 1. *Paradise is real*. If this is from one of Pound's prose works, the reference has not been found. But compare Pound's "Le paradis n'est pas artificial" (*Canto* 76).
p. 78, l. 6. *black dog*. In *Apologia Pro Vita Sua* the black dog was associated with melancholy.

Part 33.

Orig. pub. *Ploughshares* 32, no. 4 (Winter 2006–7): 151–3.
L, 80–2
Pattern: (10) (11) (2–1–2–1) (10) (2) (8) (3) (5) (2)
Time: October
Place: Charlottesville

This poem is about the end of the journey and the ensuing emptiness. In addition to these now familiar motifs, the poem draws on the sister arts—music in section 1, painting in section 3, and photography in section 4. It returns to the Orpheus myth, which we met in part 24. Here Orpheus emerges overhead in the context of an "Attic procession," so ritual, another poetic forebear is introduced. The allusions range from Dante (the antitype of *Nel mezzo del cammin di nostra vita* and the "leaf-littered driveway" being like "the entrance to Hell") and the Bible (the imagery at the end of section 2 is from Revelation; the "left undone" phrase in section 5 is from the Anglican Confession) to Christina Rossetti. The reference to "The Great Speckled Bird" introduces another context, the country music tune of Roy Acuff and with it another Biblical allusion ("Mine heritage is unto me as a speckled bird," from Jeremiah 12:9; see note to p. 58, ll. 14, 16–18 of part 25, above). Memory enters the poem in the two flashbacks—to Italy, and by way of the photograph, to California. In the Italian flashback (section 2) the poet and his friends are in front of the Ducale Palace in Mantova, having taken the Via Mantovana south from Verona. The ensuing vision is a symbolic one: he and his friends are not yet ready to undertake the hike up the terraces of Purgatory with Sordello, the thirteenth-century troubadour from Mantova who volunteered to guide Dante and Virgil up the mountain (*Purgatorio*, 6–8). Finally, we have the *ars poetica* themes: the poet becomes the mouthpiece for the "lost voices" in the natural world (section 1) and what he has left undone he hopes someone will complete (section 5). This, then, is archetypical Wright: he has gathered together a number of the sources and thematic elements that have come before, and these lead up to the meditation on emptiness after the poet has said "Goodbye to the promise of What's Left." What's Left, in fact, turns out to be the "emptiness of nonbeing," one of the many versions of the *via negativa* we have met before.

The concluding couplet is a reference to the poem cited in his notes, Giussepe Ungaretti's *Mattino* (*Morning*), an almost untranslatable two-line gem: "M'illumino / d'immenso." Andrew Frisardi translates the line as "I turn luminous in an immensity of spaces," and Clive Wilmer, "I flood myself with light of the immense." John Frederick Nims remarks that the "real point of Ungaretti's insight is the effect of any vast reality of the physical universe on the human soul" (*The Poem Itself*, ed. Stanley Burnshaw, et al. [New York: Penguin, 1960]). Wright's couplet focuses on a metamorphosis (the self and the morning are identified) through the (Buddhist) process of emptying or nonbeing—a concept found not just in Philippians but among the T'ang poets as well. The mood is one of inner radiance. About Ungaretti's two-line poem, Wright has remarked that it "says about all there is to say on the subject of epiphanic discovery (and it is my favorite example of why translation is ultimately impossible)" (QN, 33).

p. 80, ll. 12–13. *palude* = wetland. *Sabbionetta*. A town about twenty miles southwest of Mantova.
p. 81, l.6. *fine del cammin*. The end of the journey. Cf. the first line of Dante's *Paradiso: Nel mezzo del cammin di nostra vita* = Midway in the journey of our life.
p. 81, l. 19. *Moon riseth not, as some Victorian must have said*. As indeed Christina Rossetti did say: "Where the moon riseth not, / Nor sun seeks the west, / There to sing their glory / Which they sing at rest" (*Paradise: In a Symbol*, in *Lyra Eucharistica* (2nd ed., 1965).
p. 82, ll. 15–16. *I empty myself with light*. Cf. Mark Strand: "I empty myself of my life and my life remains" (*The Remains*, l. 12).

Part 34.

Orig. pub. *New Yorker* 83 (2 April 2007): 54–5
L, 83–5
Pattern: (10) (10) (3 × 2) (2) (3) (6 × 2) (4)
Time: Late October
Place: Charlottesville

This Halloween poem is also archetypical Wright, combining virtuoso description (especially sections 1 and 6) with meditations. The poet's reaction to the sights and sounds before him moves from faint praise ("this isn't all bad") to panegyric ("Within such splendor [of the brilliant October leaves], everything falls away, even our names"). The meditations have largely to do with those who have come before: the saints (what would they say if they returned?), the High Modernists ("I think of the masters of a century ago, / And often wish they'd come and whisper their secrets in my ear"), the angels (who are "still among us"), and the ancient masters ("Who here can inhabit them? / Whose arms among us can fill their sleeves...?")

The poet concludes by wondering, in the face of October's plenitude, whether "there is an emptiness we all share." It is fitting that emptiness sounds the final chord in *Littlefoot*, and it may well be that we do share one form or another of emptiness and its congeners as they have been woven in and out of Wright's poetry: the Nothing of Stevens and Heidegger, the *deus absconditis* of *The Cloud of Unknowing*, the abyss of Boehme's *Urgrund*, the presence of absence, the Negative Capability of Keats, the spirit of darkness in St. John of the Cross, the self-negation of the Incarnation in Philippians 12:7, the ascesis of the spiritual life, the "way down" of Heraclitus, and Eliot's vacancy. In addition, there are the Eastern forms in the *shunyata* of the Mahayana Buddhists, the restraint, patience, and *wu wei* of the *Tao Te Ching* (which takes us back to the opening poem of *Negative Blue*), and the nonbeing of the T'ang poets.

Wright is not referring to the emptiness of death, the undiscovered country about which we can say nothing, but to emptiness as experienced in life—"Before the end." "Heaven and earth," he adds, "depend on this clarity." Emptiness, then, in theological terms is immanent. Again, Philippians proposes that Christ emptied himself of his divine nature in the Incarnation. This is an emptiness of the here and now, represented by the golden maple leaves, not the there and then of the underworld, which is trying to escape from the light. *Shunyata* has become "openness," inseparable from the clarity born of light, and as enlightenment is the goal of the religious quest, it is significant that we end with the word "light" at this way-station.

p. 83, l. 13. *moon looks good.* "Don't the moon look good, mama / Shinin' through the trees?" (Bob Dylan, It Takes a Lot To Laugh, It Takes a Train To Cry (1965), ll. 9–10.

Part 35.

L, 86
Pattern: (4) (3) (4) (3) (4) (4) (3)

In *Littlefoot* Wright frequently integrates lines from country music songs, hymns, and other tunes into his poems: *Wildwood Flower* (part 5); *Precious Memories* (part 7); *Midnight Special* (part 14); *You Belong to Me* and *All Shook Up* (part 15); *Leaning on the Everlasting Arms* and *Maple on the Hill* (part 17); *The Great Speckled Bird* (part 25); and *Reunion in Heaven* (part 32). Such practice is fashionably called intertextuality. In the present poem we have an absolute and categorical instance of the practice: Wright makes the Carter Family tune *Will You Miss Me When I'm Gone* (1928) his own. *Will You Miss Me* is the interrogative version of the Carter lyrics from *Maple on the Hill* quoted in part 17: "Don't forget me little darling when they lay me down to die." It is worth remarking, as we conclude our account of Wright's extraordinary and continuing pilgrimage, that the answer to the two questions asked in the present song will be, *mutatis mutandis*, for many of his readers a resounding "yes."

Appendix: Reviews of Wright's Books from Chickamauga through Littlefoot: A Poem

Note: Giannelli = *High Lonesome: On the Poetry of Charles Wright*, ed. Adam Giannelli. Oberlin, Ohio: Oberlin College, 2006.

1. *Chickamauga.* New York: Farrar, Straus and Giroux, 1995.

Anon. *Virginia Quarterly Review* 71, no. 4 (Autumn 1995): 137.
Alexander, Pamela. "A Measure of Measures." *Boston Book Review*, 1 December 1995: 36. Also available at Bookwire. http://www.bookwire.com/bookwire/perlscript/review.pl?1944
Andrews, Tom. "Via Negativa: A Symposium." *Ohio Review* 56 (1997): 123–37.
Bagby, George F. "Wright Sets Autumn of Life to Verse." *Richmond Times-Dispatch*, 23 July 1995: F4.
Baker, David. "On Restraint." *Poetry* 168, no. 1 (April 1996): 33–47. Rpt. in Baker's *Heresy and the Ideal: On Contemporary Poetry*. Fayetteville: University of Arkansas Press, 2000. 216–19; and in Giannelli, 76–8.
Bastian, Kim. *The Alembic* [Providence College] (Spring 1996).
Bedient, Calvin. "Poetry and Silence at the End of the Century." *Salmagundi* 111 (Summer 1996): 195–207.
_____. "Facing the River." *Southern Review* 33 (Winter 1997): 136–49.
Brainard, Dulcy. *Publishers Weekly* 242, no. 9 (27 February 1995): 97–8.
_____. "Wanted More Complexity." *Southern Review* 33 (Winter 1997): 136–49.
Collins, Floyd. "A Fine Excess." *Gettysburg Review* 9, no. 2 (Spring 1996): 331–9.
Guillory, Daniel L. *Library Journal* 120, no. 6 (1 April 1995): 99.
Hart, Henry. *Verse* 14, no. 1 (1995): 114–18.
Hunter, Lynn Dean. "Three Collections Make Myth from American Memory." *Virginian-Pilot*, 11 June 1995: J12.
Kitchen, Judith. "What Persists." *Georgia Review* 51, no. 2 (Summer 1997): 332–6.
Koeppel, Frederic. "Wright's Poems Search for Cosmic Touch in Daily Life." *Commercial Appeal* [Memphis] 30 April 1995.
LaFemina, Gerry. *Colorado Review* 22, no. 2 (Winter 1996–97): 214–23.
Longenbach, James. "Poetry in Review." *Yale Review* 83, no. 4 (October 1995): 148–51. Rpt. in Giannelli, 79–82.
Mason, David. "Poetry Chronicle." *Hudson Review* 49, no. 1 (Spring 1996): 166–7. Rpt. as "Charles Wright, Josephine Jacobsen and Ellen Bryant Voigt" in Mason's *The Poetry of Life and the Life of Poetry: Essays and Reviews* (Ashland, OR: Story Line Press, 2000), 146–51.
Pratt, William. *World Literature Today* 70, no. 4 (Fall 1996): 967.
Seaman, Donna. *Booklist* 91, no. 15 (1 April 1995): 1374.
Simpson, Megan. "Naked in the Workshop, or, Demystifying the Teaching and Writing of Poetry," *North Carolina Literary Review* 5 (1966): 226–35.
Sullivan, James. *Magill's Literary Annual 1996*. Pasadena, CA: Salem Press, 103–6.
Vendler, Helen. "The Nothing That Is." *New Republic* 213, no. 6 (7 August 1995): 42–5. Rpt. in Giannelli, 68–75.
Walker, Kevin. "A Poetic Contradiction Gives a Clear View of the Mystical." *Detroit Free Press* 23 April 1995.
Ward, David C. "The Mask of Battle." *PN Review* 22, no. 6 (1996): 67–9.

2. *Black Zodiac.* New York: Farrar, Straus and Giroux, 1997.

Aaron, Jonathan. "Inner and Outer Landscapes: New Poems by Charles Wright and Les Murray." *Boston Globe* 17 August 1997: N13, N15.
Anon. *New York Times Book Review* 103 (31 May 1998): 50. Brief review.

_____. *Off the Wall* [newsletter of Books & Co.] February 1997.
_____. *Publisher's Weekly.* 244, no. 8 (24 February 1997): 84.
_____. *Virginia Quarterly Review* 73, no. 4 (Autumn 1997): 136.
Autry, Bruce. "*Black Zodiac* by Charles Wright." *Poetic Voices* (April 1998). Also found at: http://www.poetic voices.com/9804Wright.html
Brainard, Dulcy. *Publisher's Weekly* 244, no. 8 (24 February 1997): 84.
Broaddus, Will. "All the Heart's Threads." *Boston Book Review* (September 1997): 32.
Byrne, Mairéad. *Sycamore Review* 9, no. 2 (1997): 146–50. Also found at http://www.sla.purdue.edu/academic/engl/sycamore/Vol9/v92-b1.html
Collins, Floyd. "A Poetry of Transcendence." *Gettysburg Review* 10, no. 4 (Winter 1997): 683–701.
D'Angelo, Dennis. "Review of Charles Wright's *Black Zodiac.*" Written for Professor Ira Sadoff, 5 March 1999. http://216.239.37.104/search?q=cache:GOkkDzyc9CIJ:www.colby.edu/~isadoff/apw/MODEL_Review-C.Wright.doc+%22Poem+Almost+Wholly+in+My+Own+Manner %22+%22charles+wright%22&hl=en&start=2&ie=UTF-8
de la Fuente, Daniel. "Trae poetica de Wright." *El Norte* (México), 9 December 2002. Rev. of the Spanish translation.
Dilling, Jynne. "'Zodiac' Landscape Shines with Imagery." *Cavalier Daily* 31 March 1998.
Gussow, Mel. "A Good Ear for the Music of His Own Life." *New York Times* 147 (16 April 1998): B1.
Harayda, Janice. "Why the Critics' Awards Usually Surprise." *Plain Dealer* [Cleveland] 29 March 1998.
Hecht, James. "Redactions." *American Book Review* 20, no. 2 (January–February 1999).
Henry, Brian. "Charles Wright Puts Past To Good Use." *Richmond Times Dispatch*, 21 September 1997: K4.
Hoffert, Barbara. *Library Journal* 122, no. 7 (15 April 1997): 85–6.
Hosmer, Robert Ellis, Jr. "Poetry Roundup." *America* 177 (20–27 December 1997): 24–6.
Koeppel, Fredric. "Mystical Poet Futilely Aspires to Wordlessness." *Commercial Appeal* [Memphis], 20 April 1997: G3.
Logan, William. "Hardscrabble Country." *New Criterion.* 15, no. 10 (June 1997): 68–76. Also found at http://www.newcriterion.com/archive/15/jun97/logan.htm
Longenbach, James. "Between Soil and Stars." *Nation* 264, no. 14 (14 April 1997): 27–30.
Marcus, Jacqueline. "The Imperishable Quiet at the Heart of Form." *Literary Review* 41, no. 4 (Summer 1998): 562–6.
Miller, Christopher R. "Poetic Standard Time: The Zones of Charles Wright." *Southern Review* 34, no. 3 (Summer 1998): 566–86. Rpt. in Giannelli, 285–303.
Mobilio, Albert. "The Word's Worth." *Village Voice*, 29 April 1997: 55.
Muske, Carol. "Guided by Black Stars." *New York Times Book Review* 102 (31 August 1997): 11–12. Rpt. in Giannelli, 83–6.
Oser, Lee. *World Literature Today.* 71, no. 4 (Autumn 1997): 794–5.
Pankey, Eric. "The Woman Who Died in Her Sleep." *Partisan Review* 66, no. 2 (Spring 1999): 344–9.
Penn, David. "Wright Stuff: Poet Charles Wright's 'Black Zodiac' Is a Pulitzer Prize-Winning Tour de Force." *Tucson Weekly*, 11 May 1998.
Seaman, Donna. "Poetry on the Wing." *Booklist* 93, no. 16 (15 April 1997): 1377.
Silberg, Richard. *Poetry Flash* September 1998.
Smith, Dave. *Oxford American* 17 (September 1997), 81–2.
Smith, Thomas R. *Star Tribune* [Minneapolis/St. Paul], September 1997: F16.
Spiegelman, Willard. "Poetry in Review." *Yale Review* 85, no. 4 (October 1997): 166–75.
_____. "The Nineties Revisited." *Contemporary Literature* 42, no. 2 (Summer 2001): 206–37.
Sullivan, James. *Magill's Literary Annual 1998.* Pasadena, CA: Salem Press, 117–20.
Veale, Scott. *New York Times Book Review* 147 (31 May 1998): 50.
Walcott, Ellison Austen. *Ace*, 5 November 1997: 26.
Wojahn, David. "Survivalist Selves." *Kenyon Review* 20, nos. 3–4 (Summer–Fall 1998): 180–9.

3. *Appalachia.* New York: Farrar, Straus and Giroux, 1998.

Anon. *Publishers Weekly* 245 (28 September 1998): 95.
_____. *Virginia Quarterly Review* 75, no. 3 (Summer 1999): 100–1.
_____. *Wall Street Journal* 103 (2 April 1999): W6. Brief review.
Beasley, Bruce. *Bellingham Review* 22, no. 1 (Summer 1999): 115–18.
Bagby, George F. "Spiritual Theme Marks Wright's New Verse." *Richmond Times-Dispatch*, 27 June 1999: F4.
Branam, Harold. *Magill's Literary Annual 1999.* Pasadena, Calif.: Salem Press, 1999. 61–3.
Canady, John. *Poetry International* 4 (2000): 165–7.
Chasar, Mike. "'Appalachia' Is Homespun Meditation." *Dayton Daily News*, 11 April 1999: 90.
_____. *Texas Review* 20, nos. 1–2 (1999): 116–18.
Cohea, David. *Florida Review* 24, no. 2 (1999): 106–16.
Daniels, Kate. "Old Masters." *Southern Review* 35, no. 3 (Summer 1999): 621–34

Dilling, Jynne. "Wright's 'Appalachia' Springs with Beauty." *The Cavalier Daily: Online Edition*, 16 November 1998. http://www.cavalierdaily.com:2001/.Archives/1998/November/Book_Reviews/aef.asp
Getty, Matt. "Straw Poetry." *Redland Review*, 1999. Also at http://mattgettynonfiction.blogspot.com/2005/03/straw-poetry.html
Gioia, Dana, and James Wood. "Piddling Around by the Lemon Tree" and "Regularly Scheduled Passionate Intensity." *Slate* 13–14 January 1999. http://slate.msn.com/id/2000022/entry/1002201/
Graber, Michael. "Dour Worldview Diminishes Power of Wright's New Effort in Poetics." *Commercial Appeal* [Memphis], 4 March 1999.
Hamill, Sam. *Seattle Weekly*, 8 April 1999; rpt. in issue of 4 March 1999.
Hass, Robert. "Poet's Choice." *Washington Post*, 4 April 1999: X12.
Hoffert, Barbara. *Library Journal* 124 (1 April 1999): 96.
Hurley, Tom. "A Universe in the Back Yard: Collection Reflects 18 Dark and Light Months of Poet Charles Wright's Soul." *San Francisco Chronicle Book Review*, 24 January 1999: 2.
Kendrick, Leatha. "Poet Ends Trilogy by Examining Place and Its Effect." *Lexington Herald Leader*, 19 April 1999.
Kirsch, Adam. "Between Heaven and Earth." *New York Times Book Review* 104 (28 February 1999): 21. Rpt. in Giannelli, 98–100.
Logan, William. "Poetry." *Washington Post Book World*, 10 January 1999: 11. Rpt. as a part of chapter 24 ("Three Magi") in Logan's *Desperate Measures* (Gainesville: University of Florida Press, 2002), 269–70.
Longenbach, James. *Boston Review* 23, no. 6 (December 1998–January 1999). Rpt. in Giannelli, 94–7.
McClatchy, J.D. "Ars Longa." *Poetry* 175, no. 1 (October–November 1999): 78–89. Rpt. in Giannelli, 101–10.
Miller, Sarah. "Conclusion to Poetry Trilogy Set in Charlottesville." *Roanoke* [Virginia] *Times* 7 February 1999.
Muratori, Fred. *Library Journal* 123, no. 16 (1 October 1998): 94.
Oser, Lee. *World Literature Today* 73, no. 3 (Summer 1999): 535–6.
Pankey, Eric. "What Hast Thou, O My Soul, with Paradise: Charles Wright's *Appalachia*." *Verse* 16, no. 2 (1999): 165–70.
Rauschenbusch, Stephanie. "Serving a Darker Music." *American Book Review* 21, no. 1 (November–December 1999): 27.
Rector, Liam. *Harvard Review* (Spring 1999): 115–17.
Schuldt, Morgan. "*Appalachia* Springs Eternal." *The Angle* [University of Virginia Online Magazine], 27 October 1999. http://www.theangle.com/stgyle/1999_1027/appalachia.shtml
Seaman, Donna. *Booklist* 95, no. 5 (1 November 1998): 466.
Smith, Thomas R. *Star Tribune* [Minneapolis], 28 March 1999.
Taylor, Henry. "Land of the Poets: Charles Wright and Eavan Boland Tell of the Landscapes of Fact and Poetry." *Boston Sunday Globe*, 13 December 1998, M1, M4.
Webster, Loren. "Charles Wright's *Appalachia*." *In Dark Time*, 23 March 2003. http://lorenwebster.net/In_a_Dark_Time/archives/000395.html
White, Edith R. "Award-winning Poets Offer New Volumes of Work." *Virginian-Pilot*, 24 January 1999: J2.
Wood, James. See Gioia, above.

4. Negative Blue: Selected Later Poems. New York: Farrar, Straus and Giroux, 2000.

Anon. *Virginia Quarterly Review* 76, no. 4 (Autumn 2000): 142.
_____. *Publishers Weekly* 247 (24 April 2000): 81.
Brown, Ashley. *World Literature Today* 74, no. 4 (Autumn 2000): 821–2.
Byrne, Edward. "Time and Again: Charles Wright's *Negative Blue: Selected Later Poems*." *Valparaiso Poetry Review*. http://www.valpo.edu/english/vpr/byrnereviewwright.html
Crippen, Jeri Lynn. "Delve into Genius Territory with These Creative Tomes." *Arizona Senior World*, April 2003. Brief notice.
Freeman, John. *City Pages: The Online News & Arts Weekly of the Tri-Cities* 21, no. 1019 (14 June 2002).
Frimmer, Justin. Online review at http://btobsearch.barnesandnoble.com/booksearch/isbnInquiry.asp?sourceid=0039384190&btob=Y&isbn=0374220204&pwb=1
High, Graham. "Charles Wright: *Negative Blue*." *New Hope International Review On-line*, ed. Gerald England. http://www.nhi.clara.net/bs0289.htm
Martinez, Dionisio D. "Ethereal Visions and the Everyday." *Herald of South Florida*, 16 July 2000: 10M.
Oxley, William. What? Again? More Kuppner? Or Just Wright? Right? *Stride Magazine* http://www.stridemag.pwp.blueyonder.co.uk/2001/feb/what.htm
Pankey, Eric. "Charles Wright's Negative Blue" *VA Books* (Virginia Foundation for the Humanities), January 2002. http://www.vabook.org/lit_links/columns/jan02-pankey.pdf
Pugh, Christina. *Harvard Review* 21 (Fall 2001): 177–8.
Redmond, John. "Backyard Poetics." *Thumbscrew* 18 (Spring 2001): 52–5.
Schuldt, M.L. "Search Light: Charles Wright Scans The Landscape of Language." *Tucson Weekly* 16 November 2000: 34–5.

Seaman, Donna. "Spotlight on Poetry." *Booklist* 96, no. 14 (15 March 2000): 1317.
Smith, Ron. "Charles Wright Excels Once More in New Collection of Verse." *Richmond Times-Dispatch*, 12 November 2000, F4. Rpt. as "An Enchanted, Diminished World" in Giannelli, 111–12.
Suarez, Ernest. "The Year in Poetry." *Dictionary of Literary Biography Yearbook: 2000*, ed. Matthew J. Bruccoli. Detroit: Gale, 2001. 90–101.
Wadsworth, Lois. *Eugene Weekly* 13 April 2000.
Webster, Loren. "Charles Wright's *Negative Blue*." *In a Dark Time*, 10 March 2002. http://lorenwebster.net/In_a_Dark_Time/archives/000390.html

5. Night Music. Exeter, Devon, England: Stride Publications, 2001.

Beer, John. *Chicago Review* 47, no. 4/48, no. 1 (Winter 2001–Spring 2002): 263–70.
Caseley, Martin. "The Wheel, Turning." *Stride Magazine*. http://www.stridemag.pwp.blueyonder.co.uk/2001/nov/caseley.htm
Higgins, Kevin. "Charles Wright: *Night Rider*." *New Hope International Review On-line*, ed. Gerald England http://www.nhi.clara.net/bs0289.htm

6. A Short History of the Shadow. New York: Farrar, Straus and Giroux, 2002.

Anon. "Briefly Noted." *New Yorker* 78 (8 July 2002): 77.
Bere, Carol. *Boston Review* (December 2002–January 2003). http://bostonreview.net/BR27.6/poetmic.html
Brier, Peter. *Magill's Literary Annual 2003*. Pasadena, Calif.: Salem Press, 2003. 741–5.
Brosi, George. *Appalachian Heritage* (Summer 2002): 120.
Buchanan, Oni. "Back Yard Blues: Charles Wright's Lawn-chair Poems." *Boston Phoenix*, 19 July 2002.
Citino, David. *Columbus Dispatch*, 16 June 2002: F7.
Crippen, Jeri Lynn. "Delve into Genius Territory with These Creative Tomes." *Arizona Senior World*, April 2003. Brief notice.
Daniels, Kate. "Don't Be Cruel: Appreciating the Year-round Joys of Poetry." *Book Page Online*, April 2002: 11. http://www.bookpage.com/0204bp/nonfiction/poetry_roundup.html
Dargen, Kyle. *Meridian* 9 (Spring–Summer 2002): 180–1.
Doreski, William. *Harvard Review* 24 (Spring 2003): 178–80.
Flaherty, Dolores. "Poems to Read Aloud for All of Us." *Chicago Sun-Times*, 13 April 2003. Brief notice.
Hammer, Langdon. "Ways of Seeing." *Los Angeles Times*, 18 August 2002: R6.
Gonzalez, Garcia. *GOYA* 263 (March–April 1998): 127.
Johnson, Charles H. "Listen to the Rhythm of the Falling Verse." *New Jersey Home Tribune*, 16 March 2003
Kornbluth, Jesse. "Celebrating Poetry Month: Poetry Book Roundup." *Book Reporter.Com* http://www.bookreporter.com/features/020419-poetry.asp. Brief notice.
Lang, John. "Charles Wright's *A Short History of the Shadow*." *Appalachian Heritage* 30, no. 4 (Fall 2002): 79–84.
Lauzon, Lorraine. "In New Books, Authors Offer Poetry to Inspire, Ease the Spirit." *Catholic Observer*, 25 July 2003: 21.
Logan, William. "Falls the Shadow." *New Criterion* 20, no. 10 (June 2002): 75–82.
Loydell, Rupert. "Lucky Dip: Thoughts on Recent American Poetry." *Slope* 17 (Winter–Spring 2003). Online journal at: http://www.slope.org/archive/issue17/criticism17loydell.html. Also at: http://www.stridemag.pwp.blueyonder.co.uk/2002/july/luckydip.htm
McMaster, Arthur. *Tampa Tribune*, 8 June 2003. Brief notice.
Muratori, Fred. *Library Journal* 127, no. 6 (1 April 2002): 112–3.
Oser, Lee. *World Literature Today* 77, no. 1 (April–June 2003): 105–6. Brief review.
Parini, Jay. "A 'Thirst for the Divine.'" *Nation* 274, no. 19 (20 May 2002): 31–2.
Podgurski, David. "'A Short History of the Shadow' Is a Walk on the Dark Side." *Stamford Advocate & Greenwich Time*, 7 April 2002: D5, D8.
Scharf, Michael. *Publishers Weekly* 249, no. 8 (25 February 2002): 56.
Simic, Charles. "You Can't Keep a Good Sonnet Down." *New York Review of Books* 49 (26 September 2002): 40–2.
Smith, Ron. "Wright Continues Lyrical Trips in Nature." *Richmond Times-Dispatch*, 29 September 2002: F4.
Sparks, Amy. "Noted Poet Shares Fleeting Thoughts about Life." *Plain Dealer* [Cleveland], 26 May 2002.
Wilson, James Matthew. "Changing Shadows." *Notre Dame Review* 15 (Winter 2003).

7. Snake Eyes. Exeter, Devon, England: Stride Publications, 2004.

Couth, John. *Shearsman* 62 online: www.shearsman.com/pages/magazine/back_issues/shearsman62/couth_cw.html
Hardy, Alan. *New Hope International Reviews On-line.* http://www.nhi.clara.net/bs0289.htm
Smith, Jules. *Times Literary Supplement* No. 5303 (19 November 2004): 34.

8. Buffalo Yoga. New York: Farrar, Straus and Giroux, 2004.

Anon. *Publisher's Weekly* 251, no. 17 (26 April 2004): 56.
Freeman, John. "Paging Through: Poetry Books." *Milwaukee Journal Sentinel*, 28 March 2004.
Garrett, George. "New Poems by Four Appalachian Masters." *Appalachian Heritage* 32, no. 3 (Summer 2004): 74–82.
Kennedy, S. *Shenandoah* 54, no. 3 (Winter 2004): 184–6
Lewis, Leon. *Magill's Literary Annual 2005*, ed. John D. Wilson and Steven G. Kellman. Pasadena, CA: Salem Press, 2005. 98–103.
Logan, William. "Stouthearted Men." *New Criterion* 22, no. 10 (June 2004): 60–7.
Lucas, Dave. *Meridian* 13 (Spring–Summer 2005): 150–2.
Rand, Richard. *Harvard Review* 27 (2004): 203–5.
Seaman, Donna. *Booklist* 100, no. 14 (15 March 2004): 1259.

9. Scar Tissue. New York: Farrar, Straus and Giroux, 2006.

Anon. *Open Books* August 2006. http://www.openpoetrybooks.com/thegoods/archives/2006_08.html
_____. *Publishers Weekly*, 243, no. 18 (1 May 2006): 37.
Blakely, Diann. *The Nashville Scene*, 7 December 2006. http://www.nashvillescene.com/Stories/Arts/Books/2006/12/07/Proud_Flesh/index.shtml
Brouwer, Joel. "A World in Permanent Flux." *New York Times Book Review*, 17 September 2006.
Courtwright, Nick. *Front Porch* [Texas State University], issue 1.0. http://www.frontporchjournal.com/pdf/Issue10_Review_Wright.pdf
Krajeski, Jenna. "A Poet's Metamorphosis." *San Francisco Chronicle* 6 August 2006: M2.
Muratori, Fred. *Library Journal*, 131, no. 11 (15 June 2006): 74
O'Conner, James. "Looking for Lethe." *The Brooklyn Rail* February 2007. http://www.brooklynrail.org/2007-02/books/looking-for-lethe#bio
Sattar, Sanyat. *Star Weekend Magazine* 5, no. 114 (26 September 2006). http://www.thedailystar.net/magazine/2006/09/05/books.htm
Seamon, *Booklist* 102, no. 21 (1 July 2006): 22.
Spaar, Lisa Russ. *Virginia Quarterly Review* 82, no. 2 (Spring 2007): 301.
Wilson, Melinda. "On Impending Twilight." *Coldfront* 12 (2006). http://reviews.coldfrontmag.com/2006/12/scar_tissue_by_.html

10. Littlefoot. New York: Farrar, Straus and Giroux, 2007.

Curwen, Thomas. "*Littlefoot*: A Poem by Charles Wright." *Los Angles Times* 24 June 2007. http://www.latimes.com/features/printedition/books/la-bk-curwen24jun24,1,1350181.story?coll=la-headlines-bookreview&ctrack=1&cset=true
D'Evelyn, Tom. "Poets Who Celebrate Nature." *Providence Journal* 29 July 2007. http://www.projo.com/books/content/BOOK-POETRY_07-29-07_1B62EOM.549625.html.
Latta, John. "Metaphor, metaphor, metaphor..." *Isola di Rifuti.* 19 June 2007. http://isola-di-rifiuti.blogspot.com/2007/06/metaphor-metaphor-metaphor.html
MacDougall, Ian. "Littlefoot." *C-ville: Charlottesville's Nerws Weekly* 19, no. 26 (26 June–2 July 2007). http://www.c-ville.com/index.php?cat=1990812060534937&ShowArticle_ID=11042506073456165
Martinez, Dionisio. "Growing Old Gracefully, with No Regrets." *Miami Herald* 3 July 2007. http://www.miamiherald.com/215/v-print/story/157763.html

Index

Numbers in **_bold italics_** indicate the primary entries for individual poems.

A Lume Spento (Pound) 161
ABC of Reading (Pound) 65
Abramowicz, Janet 46
Absence Inside and Absence **_45_**
absence, motif of 19, 31, 34, 39, 45, 46, 50, 53, 54, 64, 69, 77, 78, 79, 80, 83, 94, 96, 98, 106, 108, 110, 115, 126, 149, 166, 173, 176, 179, 180–1, 186, 191, 193, 205, 207, 216, 224, 217, 225, 232, 237
Acts, Book of 185
Acuff, Roy (1903–92) 178
Adagia (Stevens) 90
Adrift (Tu Fu) 51
affection, motif of 26, 46, 58, 69, 75, 98, 112, 117, 127, 223, 215, 224, 228, 230, 231
After Liu Ch'ai-Sang's Poem (T'ao Ch'ien) 125
After Reading "Antony and Cleopatra" (Stevenson) 25
After Reading T'ao Ch'ing, I Wander Untethered Through the Short Grass 25, 27, **_124–5_**
After Reading Tu Fu, I Go Outside to the Dwarf Orchard 25, 27, **_29_**, 50
After Reading Wang Wei, I Go Outside to the Full Moon 25, **_26–7_**
After Rereading Robert Graves, I Go Outside to Get My Head Together 25, 75, **_125–6_**
After the Flood (Rimbaud) 169
Against the American Grain **_193–4_**
Akhmatova, Anna (1889–1966) 36
Alberti, Leon Battista (1404–72) 151
Alice in Wonderland (Carroll) 32
All Landscape Is Abstract, and Tends to Repeat Itself **_108_**
All Shook Up (Presley) 223
Allogenes (Nag Hammadi Library) 69
L'Ame de Napoleon (Bloy) 169
American Hot Wax 184
American Twilight **_127_**
Anatomy of Melancholy (Burton) 66
Anderson, Laurie (1947–) 153
Andrea del Castango (1423–57) 132
Andrewes, Lancelot (1555–1626) 147

Andrews, Tom (1962–2001) 168–9, 174
Antonioni, Michelangelo (1912–) 17
The Apocalypse of Adam (Nag Hammadi Library) 68
The Apocryphon of John (Nag Hammadi Library) 148
Apologia Pro Vita Sua 18, 58, **_61–70_**, 113, 127, 129, 214, 228
Appalachia (book) **_97–134_**
Appalachia Dog **_203–4_**
The Appalachian Book of the Dead 71, **_74–6_**, 111
The Appalachian Book of the Dead II **_111_**
The Appalachian Book of the Dead III **_118_**, 123, 153
The Appalachian Book of the Dead IV 56, **_120–1_**
The Appalachian Book of the Dead V **_123_**
The Appalachian Book of the Dead VI **_127–8_**
Appalachian Farewell 57, **_188_**
Appalachian Lullaby **_153_**
April 107
Aquinas, St. Thomas 108, 119
Archaeology 153, **_204–5_**
Ariel (Plath) 29
Aristotle (384–322 B.C.E.) 9, 12, 13, 14, 15, 19, 150, 155
Arkansas Traveler 56
Arrivederci Kingsport **_175–6_**
An Arrowhead from the Ancient Battlefield of Ch'ang-p'ing (Li Ho) 71
Ars Poetica 42–3, 89, 106, 112, 126, 154, 160–1, 162, 168, 199, 221, 229
Ars Poetica II **_106_**
Ars Poetica III **_160–1_**
Ars Poetica (MacLeish) 221
Artemis (Nerval) 84
As Our Bodies Rise, Our Names Turn into Light **_44–5_**
Asclepius (Nag Hammadi Library) 94, 123
Ashbery, John (1927–) 113, 173
Ashton, Dore 65, 101
The Assumption (Titian) 174
Assurbanipal (d. 626?) 129

At Ch'u-Chou on the Western Stream (Wêi Ying-wu) 190
At the End of Spring (Po Chü-I) 49
Auden, W.H. (1907–73) 104, 230
Auguries of Innocence (Blake) 132
Augustine, St. (354–430) 13, 30–1, 77–8, 90, 112, 132–3, 167, 208
Autobiographical Essay (Huai Su) 60
Autumn 107
Autumn Pastoral (Tu Fu) 50
Autumn's Sidereal, November's a Ball and Chain 98, 108, **_112_**
Avery, Milton (1893–1965) 17, 85, 137

Bachelder, Champ 175
Back Home Again Chant (T'ao Ch'ien) 124
Back Yard Boogie Woogie **_117_**
A Bad Memory Makes You a Metaphysician, a Good One Makes You a Saint **_101–2_**
Ballad of a Hundred Worries (Tu Fu) 51
The Baptism of the Selenites (Carpaccio) 104
Bar Giamaica 1959-60 35
Bashō (1644–94) 212
Basic Dialogue 64, **_100–1_**, 113
Basin Creek (Montana) 37, 106, 172, 210
Battle of Chickamauga 37, 38
Bauer, Johann 171
Beall, Karen 175
Beckett, Samuel (1906–89) 77–8, 137
Bedtime Story **_196_**
Begin the Beguin (Porter) 54
The Beheading of St. John (Caravaggio) 17, 163
Belli, Giuseppe Gioacchino (1791–1864) 35
Bells in Winter (Milosz) 185
Bernstein, Richard (1944–) 164
Berry, Chuck (1926–) 103
Berryman, John (1914–72) 174, 175
Bertran de Born (1445–1215) 80
Betwixt and Between (Camus) 224
Bidart, Frank (1939–) 103
Bidding a Friend Farewell at Ching-mên Ferry (Li Po) 31–2

245

Index

Bishop, Elizabeth (1911–79) 42–3
Bistami, Bayezid (803–75) 116
Black and Blue 15, **37**, 38
Black Night (Avery) 137
Black Zodiac (book) **60–96**
Black Zodiac (poem) **89–90**, 91, 107
Blaise Pascal Lip-syncs the Void **38–9**
Blake, William (1757–1827) 17, 25, 42, 49, 111, 119, 121, 132, 146, 156, 163, 169, 171
Bloodlines (book) 11, 20
Bloy, Léon (1847–1917) 169
The Blue Octavo Notebooks (Kafka) 44
Body and Soul 153, **162**
Body and Soul II 17, 27, **163–4**
"Body and Soul" (Hawkins) 162
Body Language **119**
Boehme, Jakob (1575–1624) 40, 78, 93
The Bolivar Letters 55
Book of Divine Works (Hildegard of Bingen) 209
The Book of Thel (Blake) 171
The Book of Thomas the Contender (Nag Hammadi Library) 52, 63, 83, 154
Borges, Jorge Luis (1899–1986) 32, 116, 169
Brecht, Bertolt (1898–1956) 25
"Bremen Address" (Celan) 173
Brewsie and Willie (Stein) 79
Broadway Boogie-Woogie (Mondrian) 89, 117
Broken English **36**, 38
"Brown-Eyed Handsome Man" (Berry) 103
Browning, Robert (1812–89) 76, 111, 181, 209
Brumley, Alfred E. 138
Bruns, Snuffy and Beryl 231
Buber, Martin (1878–1965) 114, 115, 116, 117
Buddhism, Zen 49–50, 92, 163–4
Buffalo Yoga (book) **165–87**
Buffalo Yoga (poem) 81, 153, 158, **166–9**, 220, 228
Buffalo Yoga Coda I 67, **170**
Buffalo Yoga Coda II 158, **170–1**, 220, 228
Buffalo Yoga Coda III 56, **171–2**
Bunyan, John (1628–88) 209–10
Burnt Norton (Eliot) 179
Burton, Robert (1577–1640) 66
Bus Stop (Justice) 80
Buzzi, Aldo (1910–) 103–4, 155
Bye Bye Blackbird (Dixon and Henderson) 193
Bygones 9
"Bytes and Pieces" 36 107

Calasso, Roberto (1941–) 57, 90, 145, 147, 148
Campana, Dino (1885–1932) 150–1
Camus, Albert (1913–60) 224
Canaletto (Giovanni Antonio Canal) (1697–1768) 175
Cancer Rising 107

Candide (Voltaire) 74
Canti (Leopardi) 72
Cantos (Pound) 119, 143, 192, 235
Ca' Paruta (Italy) 29
Caravaggio, Michelangelo Merisi da (ca. 1571–1610) 17, 163
Carpaccio, Vittore (ca. 1460–1526) 17, 104
Carroll, Lewis (1832–98) 32
Carter Family 37, 143, 215, 218, 237
Catullus (84–54 B.C.E.) 138
Cavafy, Constantine P. (1863–1933) 195
Cavalcanti, Guido de (1255–1300) 154
Celan, Paul (1920–70) 28–9, 52, 90, 93, 131, 134, 173
Ceronetti, Guido (1927–) 91–2, 108
Cézanne, Paul (1839–1906) 17, 46, 64, 88, 117, 172, 181
Charles Wright and the 940 Locust Avenue Heraclitean Rhythm Band **178**
Charlottesville Nocturne **142**
Chatterton, Thomas (1752–70) 177–8
Chatwin, Bruce (1940–) 39
Chekov, Anton (1860–1904) 110, 171
Cherokee 107
Chickamauga (book) **23–59**
Chickamauga (poem) 16, **37–8**, 124
China Journal 27
China Mail 50, 62, **90–1**
China Trace (book) 10, 11, 206
China Traces **206–7**
Chinese Journal 64
Chinoiserie 27
Christmas East of the Blue Ridge **80–1**
Chuang Tzu (4th cent. B.C.E.) 186
Churchill, Kay 175
Cicada 27, **30–1**, 50
Cicada Blue **107–8**
Cioran, C.M. (1911–95) 87, 101, 102
Citronella **140–1**
Cleek, Zeke 204
The Cloud of Unknowing 93, 147
Cold Mountain (Han Shan) (8th or 9th cent.) 166, 184, 186–7, 207
Coleridge, Samuel Taylor (1772–1834) 13, 25, 70, 156, 197–8, 200, 205–6
College Days **194–5**
Collins, Billy (1941–) 25
Colossians, Epistle to the 141
Composition in Grey and Red (Mondrian) 17, 54
Composition No. 8 (Mondrian) 89
Compostela 220, 229
The Concept of Our Great Power (Nag Hammadi Library) 67
Confessions (Augustine) 30–1, 133
Confessions of a Song and Dance Man **193**, 210
Conner, Eddie and Nancy 48
Conrad, Joseph (1857–1924) 89, 138

Contingency, Irony, and Solidarity (Rorty) 28
"Conversation about Dante" (Mandelstam) 140
Corinthians, Epistles to the 128, 150
Corvo, Baron (Frederick Rolfe) (1860–1913) 104, 172
Cosimo Tura (ca. 1430–95) 17
Costello, Bonnie 53, 114
Country Music (book) 1, 11
Craig, Francis (1919–94) 191
Crane, Hart (1889–1932) 19–20
The Creation and Expulsion of Adam and Eve from Paradise (Giovanni di Paolo) 23
Criticisms (Li Ho) 71
cycle, seasonal 23, 36–7, 45, 49–50, 70, 84, 90, 92, 93, 113, 122, 137, 138, 149, 150, 188, 190, 197, 202, 216, 227

Dante Alighieri (1265–1321) 13, 32, 35, 61, 62, 65, 79, 126, 134, 138, 152, 181, 192–3
The Dark Night of the Soul (St. John of the Cross) 160
Davidson College 194
Davis, Miles (1926–91) 42–3
Dawn in Stone City (Li Ho) 71
Day's End (Tu Fu) 51
death, motif of 12, 23, 26, 33, 37, 40, 41, 58, 61, 63, 67, 70, 71, 74–6, 79, 80, 82, 89, 93, 94, 99, 100, 102, 104, 106, 108, 109, 110, 111, 119, 123, 124, 126, 129, 133, 134, 138, 141, 142, 146, 153, 156–7, 158, 159, 160, 162, 168–9, 176–7, 183, 192, 195–6, 208, 213, 220, 223, 228, 234, 235, 237
Debris of Life and Mind (Stevens) 154
de Chirico, Giorgio (1888–1978) 17
Deep Measure 64, **84–5**, 210
Defoe, Daniel (ca. 1659–1731) 115
Dejection: An Ode (Coleridge) 13
Depression before the Solstice 55, 154
Description without Place (Stevens) 154
de Stael, Nicholas (1914–55) 17
deus absconditus (hidden God) 27, 28, 93, 98–9, 147, 176, 193, 225
Devotion XVII (Donne) 26
dianoia (thought) 13–14
Diaries (Woolf) 123
DiCenzo, Ed 203
Dickinson, Emily (1830–86) 167, 177, 179
Dillard, Annie (1945–) 149
Dino Campana 107
Dio ed Io **176**
Dionysus 57, 192
The Discourse on the Eighth and Ninth (Nag Hammadi Library) 123
Disjecta Membra 16, 27, **91–6**, 99, 107, 173
Dr. K. Takes the Waters at Riva (Sebald) 219–20

Dr. Syntax (Rowlandson) 95
Dog Creek Mainline 10
Dog Day Vespers 55
La Dolcemara Vita 56, **183**
Domenico di Michelino (1417–91) 132
Donne, John (1572–1631) 26
Don't Go Out the Door (Li Ho) 70
Dostoevsky, Fyodor (1821–81) 162
A Dream, After Reading Dante's Episode of Paolo and Francesca (Keats) 25
Drinking Wine (T'ao Ch'ien) 161
Drone and Ostinato 107, **114–15**
dropped-down line 1–2, 18–19
The Drunken Boat (Rimbaud) 58
Duke, C.B. (Boots) 175
Dürer, Albrecht (1471–1528) 65
Dylan, Bob (1941–) 120

Eakins, Thomas (1844–1916) 79
Early Saturday Afternoon, Early Evening 75, **122**
East of the Blue Ridge, Our Tombs Are in the Dove's Throat **43**
Easter 27–8, 63, 138, 189
Easter 1989 **27–8**
Eating Poetry (Strand) 98
Ecclesiastes, Book of 213, 224
Eckhart, Meister (1260–1328) 114, 115
Ecstatic Confessions (Buber) 114, 115, 116, 117
Effusion, After Reading the Interesting Account of the Young Savage of Aveyron (Coleridge) 25
The Egyptian Book of the Dead 74–4, 111, 118, 120, 123, 206
ekphrasis 17, 105
Elegy (Levis) 103
Eleventh Moon (Li Ho) 71
Eliot, T.S. (1888–1965) 24, 61, 63, 65, 78, 88, 94, 120, 126, 134, 138, 151, 179, 193
Emory (Virginia) 160
emptiness (*shunyata*), motif of 25–6, 30, 32, 37, 45, 50, 53, 80, 92, 95, 123, 160, 163, 179–80, 189, 218, 223, 235, 236–7; *see also* nothingness; *wu wei*
Encountering Sorrow (Qu Yuan) 128
Enoch, Book of 39
Entering Tung-t'ing Lake (Tu Fu) 51
Entertaining Literary Men in My Official Residence on a Rainy Day (Wêi Ying-wu) 198
Envoi **69–70**
Ephesians, Epistle to the 94
Epitaph on Robert Canynge (Rowley) 177
erasure, motif of 78–9, 81, 89, 94, 179
E.T. The Extra-Terrestrial (Spielberg) 29
eternal return, myth of 112, 122, 138, 227, 234
ethos (character) 12–13
Eucharist 63, 75, 78, 82, 170, 172
Eugnostos the Blessed (Nag Hammadi Library) 65

Eurydice 131, 230
The Eve of St. Agnes (Keats) 95
Evening in Lans (Trakl) 157
Ezekiel, Book of 69, 78, 98, 144
Ezra, Book of 87

Fasti (Ovid) 54
Faulkner, William (1897–1962) 73
Felix Randal (Hopkins) 204
Fellini, Federico (1920–93) 183
Ficino, Marsilio (1433–99) 159, 167
A Field Guide to the Birds of the Upper Yaak **191**
Fifth Ennead (Plotinus) 52
'54 Chevy **161**
Finnegans Wake (Joyce) 152, 190
The First Apocalypse of James (Nag Hammadi Library) 68
Five T'ang Poets (Young) 71, 166
Flyer's Fall (Stevens) 84
For the Time Being (Dillard) 149
Ford, Mary (1924–77) 204
form, poetic 13, 72
Form, Shadow, Spirit (T'ao Ch'ien) 124
Foscolo, Ugo (1778–1827) 139
Four Quartets (Eliot) 24, 78
The Fourth Ennead (Plotinus) 118
Fra Angelico (1395–1455) 231
Francesco del Cossa (ca. 1435–77) 17
Freed, Alan (1921–65) 184
Freezing Rain **130**
From My Portfolio (Machado) 139
"From the Tract of 'Sister Katrei'" (Eckhart) 114
Frost, Robert (1874–1963) 85
Frye, Northrop (1912–91) 24
Full of Feeling (Tu Fu) 53
Fulton, William Savin (1795–1844) 183
Futurist movement 47

Gadda, Carlo Emilio (1893–1973) 47
Gallie, W.B. (1912–98) 14, 88
The Game of Chess (Borges) 116
Garcias, Anna (1549–1626) 117
Garda, Lake (Italy) 35, 63, 138, 201, 202, 234
Gargantua and Pantagruel (Rabelais) 32
General Kê-Shu (poet of the Western front) 131–2
Genesis, Book of 53, 75, 119, 122, 149
Gerontion (Eliot) 94
Get a Job **204**
Get a Job (Silhouettes) 204
Ghost Days **211**
Giorgio Morandi (Wilken) 101
Giorgio Morandi and the Talking Eternity Blues 64, 75, **113–14**, 118, 137–8, 180
Giorgio Morandi: The Art of Silence (Abramowicz) 46
Giovanni di Paolo (ca. 1403–83) 23
Gnosticism 63–4, 67, 74, 83, 216
God, idea of 13, 36, 44, 45, 47, 49,

50, 62, 69, 70, 71, 79, 89, 92, 94, 98–9, 102, 105, 106, 111, 114, 116, 118, 123, 125, 128, 134, 139, 141, 162, 165, 166, 167, 176–7, 181, 193, 198, 199, 200, 201, 213, 217, 225, 233–4
Godard, Jean-Luc (1930–) 17
God's Grandeur (Hopkins) 190
Goethe, Johann Wolfgang (1749–1832) 169
Going Home 5
Golden-Rain Rapids (Wang Wei) 185
Goldstein, Arnie 202, 203
Good-bye (Wang Wei) 113
"Good Times Bad Times" (Led Zeppelin) 103
Goodnight Sweetheart (The Spaniels) 175
Gopnik, Adam (1956–) 79
The Gospel According to St. Someone 56, **172**
The Gospel of Philip (Nag Hammadi Library) 69, 84, 152
Gospel of Thomas (Nag Hammadi Library) 50, 148
The Gospel of Truth (Nag Hammadi Library) 213
Graham, A.C. 70
La Grande Guerra (Monicelli) 35
The Grave of the Right Hand (book) 11
Graves, Robert (1895–1985) 80, 83, 125–6
great chain of being 61
The Great Speckled Bird 230, 237
Guardi, Francesco (1712–ca.1793) 175
Guidoriccio da Fogliano (d. 1352) 48
Gyges of Lydia (ca. 680–644 B.C.E.) 17, 84

Hadrian (76–138) 74
Half February **116–17**
Hammond, Wilma 220
Han Shan (8th or 9th cent.) *see* Cold Mountain
Handy, W.C. (1873–1958) 73
Hard Dreams 17, **163**
Hard Freight (book) 11, 81
Hardy, Thomas (1840–1928) 146
Hawkins, Coleman (1904–69) 162, 226
Hawksbane **212**, 213
Hearts of Stone (Jackson and Ray) 194
Heath, Percy 66
Hebrews, Epistle to the 133
Heidegger, Martin (1889–1976) 62, 147, 173, 200
Hennessy, Timothy (1925–) 174
Heraclitean Backwash **205–6**
Heraclitus (535–475 B.C.E.) 51, 103–4, 138, 139, 178, 205–6
Hesiod (8th cent. B.C.E.) 153
hidden God *see deus absconditus*
High Country Canticle **190**
High Country Spring **206**
High Lonesome: On the Poetry of Charles Wright (Giannelli) 1

Hildegard of Bingen (1098–1179) 209
history, motif of 37, 38
Hiwassee Dam (North Carolina) 205, 218
Hobart, Peter 234
The Hollow Men (Eliot) 78, 151
Holston River 66, 188, 216, 220
"The Holy Ghost Asketh for Us with Mourning and Weeping Unspeakable" 122
Homage to Baron Corvo 104
Homage to Giorgio Morandi 64, 81, 113, **180-1**
Homage to Mark Rothko 65, **172-3**
Homage to Paul Cézanne 107
Homage to the Memory of Wallace Stevens (Justice) 36
Home Again Among Gardens and Fields (T'ao Ch'ien) 125
Homer 138
Hopkins, Gerard Manley (1844–89) 13, 23, 33, 83, 86, 105, 109, 190, 193–4, 200, 204, 210
Horace (66–8 B.C.E.) 66, 91, 200, 231
Hsieh Ling-yün (385–433) 185
Hsuan Tsang (7th century) 163, 164
Huai Su (725–785) 60
Hugh Selwyn Mauberley (Pound) 62
The Humped-back Flute Player (Snyder) 121
"The Hunter Gracchus" (Kafka) 158–9, 168, 169, 171, 195–6, 208, 219–20, 228
Hussein al Halladj (d. 309) 116
Hymns to the Night (Novalis) 153

I Promessi Sposi (Manzoni) 203
Iacopone da Todi (1236–1306) 77
The Iberian God (Machado) 139
Icarus (Jensen) 174
Icarus myth 234
iconostasis 20, 191
"If I Had Possession over Judgment Day" (Johnson) 148
If My Glasses Were Better, I Could See Where I'm Headed For **142-3**, 160
If This Is Where God's at, Why Is That Fish Dead? 141
If You Talk the Talk, You Better Walk the Walk 132
I'll Fly Away (Brumley) 138
Images from the Kingdom of Things **192-3**
Impromptu (Meng Chiao) 93
"Improvisations: With Father Hopkins on Lake Como" 86
In a Station of the Metro (Pound) 16
In Answer to Assistant Magistrate Chang (Wang Wei) 113
In Praise of Franz Kafka 159, **208**, 220, 228
In Praise of Han Shan **186-7**
In Praise of Thomas Chatterton **177-8**
In Praise of Thomas Hardy 146
In Reply to Vice-Magistrate Chang (Wang Wei) 185

In the Hills at Nightfall in Autumn (Wang Wei) 27
In the Kingdom of the Past. The Brown-Eyed Man Is King 103
In the Valley of the Elwy (Hopkins) 105
In the Valley of the Magra 105
In the Village (Trakl) 157
Indian Summer **111-12**
Inland Sea 189
inscape 193, 200, 210
Is **148-9**
Isaiah, Book of 52
It Takes a Lot to Laugh, It Takes a Train to Cry (Dylan) 237
Italian Days 152
It's Dry for Sure, Dry Enough to Spit Cotton 142
It's Not the Bullet That Kills You (Anderson) 153
"*It's Turtles All the Way Down*" **115-16** 124

Jacobsen, Jerry 34
James, Epistle of 232
January II 176
Jensen, Axel (1932–2003) 173–4
Jeremiah, Book of 63, 230, 235
Jesuit Graves **85-6**
Job, Book of 40, 65, 68, 83, 110, 201
John, Gospel of 64–4, 157, 207, 222
John of Patmos 154
John the Baptist 142
John the Solitary (d. 586) 45
Johnson, Junior (1931–) 204
Johnson, Robert (1911–38) 73, 146, 148
Johnson, Samuel (1709–84) 66
Jones, George (1931–) 184
Jonga (Stevens) 112
A Journal of English Days 16, 108
A Journal of One Significant Landscape 107, 153
A Journal of the Year of the Ox 17, 56, 81, 108, 134
A Journal of True Confessions 16, 56, 64, 65, 67, 107, 173
Journey to the Land of Flies and Other Travels (Buzzi) 104
Joyce, James (1882–1941) 35, 152, 234
Juliana of Norwich (1342–ca. 1416) 67
Justice, Donald (1925–2004) 80, 230
Just Like Tom Thumb's Blues (Dylan) 120

Ka: Stories of the Mind and Gods of India (Calasso) 145, 148
Kafka, Franz (1883–1924) 43, 44, 158–9, 171, 195–6, 208, 219–20
Kafka and Prague (Bauer) 171
Kahn, Wolf (1927–) 17, 85, 181
Kao Shih (T'ang Dynasty) 23
Karant, Martin (1917–2004) 223
katabasis 85, 146
Keats, John (1795–1821) 25, 82, 87, 95, 101, 177, 226

Kennedy, John F. 34
King Lear (Shakespeare) 168
Kingsport (Tennessee) 33, 35, 61, 66–7, 175, 188, 204, 218, 221, 223
Klein, Yves (1928–62) 176
Koffler, Bob 181
Kolbert, Elizabeth 227
Kubla Khan (Coleridge) 197–8
Kundera, Milan (1929–) 176

Laguna Beach (California) 34, 57, 162
Lake Garda *see* Garda, Lake
Landscape (Morandi) 180
Landscape as Metaphor, Landscape as Fate and a Happy Life 27, **128**
landscape, as poetic subject 10, 13, 15, 37, 59, 60, 62, 106, 108, 128, 156, 158, 160, 163, 167, 172, 173, 179, 213, 216, 217, 224
Landscape with Missing Overtones **165**
language, as poetic subject 13, 15, 25, 28, 32, 38, 45, 59, 62, 63, 68, 69, 71, 73, 80, 83, 87, 93, 95, 104, 106, 108, 109–10, 114, 116, 120, 125, 131, 139, 142, 152, 154, 155, 156, 157, 162, 165, 166, 167, 168, 178, 194, 198, 199, 200, 203, 210, 217–18, 223, 230
Language Journal 27
Lao Tzu (ca. 600–300 B.C.E.) 24, 25–6, 186, 192, 208
Larkin, Philip (1922–1985) 13
Last Supper 188–9
Leadbelly (Huddie William Ledbetter) (1888–1949) 223
Leaning on the Everlasting Arms (Hoffman and Showalter) 225, 223
Led Zeppelin 103
Leda and the Swan (Yeats) 76
Lee, Robert E. (1807–72) 182, 183
The Legend of the True Cross (Piero della Francesca) 48
Leonardo da Vinci (1452–1519) 17, 48
Leopardi, Giacomo (1798–1837) 13, 72, 94
Let's Murder the Moonlight (Marinetti) 47
The Letter of Philip to Peter (Nag Hammadi Library) 68
Letters on Cézanne (Rilke) 95
Levis, Larry (1946–96) 102–3
lexis (diction) 15–17
Li Ho (791–817) 70–1
Li Po (701–62) 31–2, 113, 166, 207
Li Shang-yin (813–58) 132, 166
Li Tüan (T'ang Dynasty) 198–9
Life Is Like a Mountain Railroad (Snow and Abbey) 230
Lines (Wang Wei) 164, 227
Lines After Reading T.S. Eliot **24-5**
Lines on Seeing a Photograph for the First Time in Thirty Years 35
Little Apocalypse 181, 198
Little Apokatastasis 185, 198
Little Gidding (Eliot) 78, 151

Little Landscape 191, **210**
Littlefoot: A Poem (book) 12, 57, **214–37**
Liu' Chang-ch'ing (710–87) 169
Liu Tsung-yüan (773–819) 166
Lives (Plutarch) 37
Lives of the Artists **81–4**
Lives of the Artists (Vasari) 48, 84
Lives of the Saints 62, **78–80**, 81, 107, 155
Llewellyn, Titus 203
Local Journal 108
Lonesome Pine Special 64
Longinus (1st or 3rd cent. C.E.) 98, 112
Looking Across Laguna Canyon at Dusk, West-by-Northwest 56, **57**, 197, 228
Looking again at What I Looked At for Seventeen Years **54–5**
Looking Around 64, 113, 114, **137–8**, 139
Looking Around II 15, **138–9**
Looking Around III **139–40**
Looking at Pictures 65
Looking Outside the Cabin Window, I Remember a Line by Li Po 27, **31–2**, 107
Looking West from Laguna Beach at Night 54
Lorca, Federico Garcia (1898–1936) 43, 107, 152, 153
Lord Jim (Conrad) 89
Lorrain, Claude (ca. 1600–82) 17, 173
Lost Language **143**
Lost Souls 107
The Love Song of J. Alfred Prufrock (Eliot) 178, 193, 211
Lowell, Robert (1917–77) 131
Lucia (Blake) 17
Luke, Gospel of 94

Machado, Antonio (1875–1939) 139
MacLeish, Archibald (1892–1982) 38, 221
Magic Strings (Li Ho) 71
Magnolia Slope (Wang Wei) 113
Malatesta, Sigismondo (1417–68) 48
Mallarmé, Stéphane (1842–98) 158, 167, 169
Man Carrying Things (Stevens) 41
Mancini, George 95, 173
Mandelstam, Osip (1891–1938) 140, 151, 156–7
Mankind (Trakl) 157
Mantegna, Andrea (1431–1506) 17
Mantova 107
Manzoni, Alessandro (1785–1873) 203
Maple on the Hill **36–7**, 38
Maple on the Hill (Carter Family) 37, 225, 223
March Journal 108
Marderstieg, Martino (1941) 161
Marinetti, F.T. (1876–1944) 47
The Marriage of Cadmus and Harmony (Calasso) 57

The Marriage of Heaven and Hell (Blake) 42
The Martyrdom of St. Lawrence (Titian) 17, 105
Marvell, Andrew (1621–78) 133
mathematical metaphors 24, 43, 75, 77–8, 79, 103, 126
Matins **207–8**
Matisse, Henri (1869–1954) 47, 181
Matthew, Gospel of 147, 209
Matthiessen, Peter (1927) 92
Mattino (Ungaretti) 236
McClatchy, J.D. (1945–) 10, 182
McIntire, John (1907–91) 96, 171–2, 184
McIntire, Tim (1944–86) 169, 184
Meandering River (Tu Fu) 51
measure 84–5
Meditation on Form and Measure 14, 64, **86–7**, 108
Meditation on Song and Structure 16
Meditation on Summer and Shapelessness 74
Melancholia (Dürer) 65
melos (song) 14–15
memory 34, 35, 55, 65, 81, 89–90, 126, 151, 173, 174, 191, 194, 196–7, 225, 235
Meng Chiao (751–814) 93, 110, 128
Mêng Hao-jan (689–740) 144, 185
Metamorphoses (Ovid) 54
metaphor 16, 17, 41, 55, 71, 78, 97–9, 179, 186, 196–7, 223
Michelangelo (1475–1654) 82
Midnight Special (Leadbelly) 223, 237
Mid-winter Snowfall in the Piazza Dante **32**
Mildly Depressed, Far from Home, I Go Outside for a While 27, **144**
Miles Davis and Elizabeth Bishop Fake the Break **42–3**
millennium project 140
Milli Vanilli 39
Milosz, Czeslaw (1911–2004) 185
Milton, John (1608–74) 98, 138
The Minor Art of Self-Defense **199–200**
Mitchell, Billy (d. 1968) 184
Mondo Angelico **41**
Mondo Cane (film) 41
Mondo Henbane **41–2**, 43
Mondo Orfeo **144–5**
Mondrian, Piet (1872–1944) 17, 46, 54, 88–9, 181
Monet, Claude (1840–1926) 88
Monicelli, Mario (1915–) 35
Montaigne, Michel de (1533–92) 31, 168
Montale, Eugenio (1896–1981) 13, 14–15, 97
Montana 31, 37, 41, 71, 128, 140, 150, 156, 158, 162, 170, 172, 178, 190, 192, 205, 208, 213, 226
The Moon at the Fortified Pass (Li Po) 154
Morandi 113
Morandi II **46–7**, 64
Morandi, Giorgio (1890–1964) 17, 46–7, 53, 64, 101, 113–14, 118, 137–8, 173, 180–1, 225

Morning Occurrence at Xanadu **197–8**
Mt. Caribou at Night 106
Mountain Home (Hinton) 166, 184, 185
Munch, Edvard (1863–1944) 17
"La Musique et les lettres" (Mallarmé) 169
Mussolini, Benito (1883–1945) 234
My Last Duchess (Browning) 111
My Own Little Civil War **182–3**
mythos (plot) 9–12, 14

Nag Hammadi Library 63, 67–9, 96, 147
"The Narrative of the Image" 19
The Narrow Road to the Distant City **209**
Nash, Graham (1942–) 221
Natura Morta (Morandi) 53
Natural History (Pliny) 30
"Near You" (Craig) 191
Negative Blue: Selected Later Poems 1, 11, 18, **23–134**
negative capability 25–6
negative transcendence 47, 64, 181
Negatives II 81
Neoplatonism 118
Nerval, Gérard de (1808–55) 84
Never Again the Same (Tate) 110
The New Gods (Cioran) 87
The New Poem 106
Newman, John Cardinal Henry 61
Nietzsche, Friedrich (1844–1900) 36
A Night Abroad (Tu Fu) 29
Night at the Tower (Tu Fu) 91
Night in the House by the River (Tu Fu) 30, 231
Night-Mooring on the Chien-tê River (Mêng Hao-jan) 144
Night Music 14, 146, **153–4**
Night Rider 16, **147–8**
Night Thoughts Afloat (Tu Fu) 130
Night Thoughts Under a China Moon 158–9, **195–6**, 220, 228
Nijinsky, Vaslaw (1890–1950) 171
Nine-Panel Yaak River Screen **156–7**
Nocturna 150
A Noiseless Patient Spider (Whitman) 167
Nolan, Jeanette (1911–98) 54, 184
Nones (Auden) 230
Nooteboom, Cees (1933–) 103, 104
North **208**
North American Bear (book) 11, **129–34**
North American Bear (poem) **130–2**
Nostalgia **151**
Nostalgia II **161–2**
Nostalgia III 56, **177**
"Not everyone can see the truth, but he can be it" 44 210
Notes for Oscar Wilde at San Miniato 150
Notes toward a Supreme Fiction (Stevens) 79
nothingness 23, 24, 28, 78, 79–80, 93, 98–9, 100, 106, 107, 125, 134,

179, 186, 194, 206–7, 209, 213, 218–19; *see also* emptiness; *wu wei*
Novalis (1772–1801) 153
Numbers, Book of 189

Oak Ridge (Tennessee) 66
objective correlative 69, 70, 110, 166, 194, 203, 221
October 78
October II 64, **77–8**
Ode on Melancholy (Keats) 82
Ode to a Nightingale (Keats) 87, 226
Odyssey (Homer) 163
Of Modern Poetry (Stevens) 154
On First Looking into Chapman's Homer (Keats) 25
On Hearing Her Play the Harp (Li Tüan) 199
On Heaven Considered as a Tomb (Stevens) 143
On Heaven Considered as What Will Cover Us and Stony Comforter **143–4**
On Painting (Alberti) 152
On Reading a Recent Greek Poet (Brecht) 25
On Thatch-Hut Mountain (Hsieh Ling-yün) 185
On the Mönchsberg (Trakl) 157
On the Moor (Trakl) 157
On the Origin of the World (Nag Hammadi Library) 83–4
One Day's Poem (Machado) 139
opsis (spectacle) 15–20
Opus Posthumous 16, **108–9**, 119, 129, 153
Opus Posthumous II **118–19**
Opus Posthumous III **128–9**
Opus Posthumous (Stevens) 109
An Ordinary Afternoon in Charlottesville **40–1**
An Ordinary Evening in New Haven (Stevens) 40, 41, 80
Orebank (Tennessee) 188, 221, 222
Orpheus 94, 106, 131, 145, 229–30
Orpheus, Eurydice, and Hermes (Lowell) 131
Orphic Songs (Campana) 150
Oscar Wilde at San Miniato (Campana) 150
Ostinato and Drone **115**
The Other Side of the River (book) 12, 214
The Other Side of the River (poem) 55, 56
Ovid (43 B.C.E.–17 C.E.) 54, 145
Ozymandias (Shelley) 129, 176

Paesaggio Notturno 14, **52**
Papini, Giovanni (1881–1956) 47
Paris (France) 66
Pascal, Blaise (1623–62) 38–9
Passing the Morning under the Serenissima **103–4**
Paul, Les (1915–) 204
Pavese, Cesare (1908–50) 173
Peccatology **43**
Pei, I.M. (1917–) 120
Pensées (Pascal) 39
Penzel, Charles F. (1840–1906) 182

Peter Quince at the Clavier (Stevens) 229
Phelan, Big John (d. 1964) 184
Philippians, Epistle to the 233, 236, 237
photographs 17, 29, 34, 35, 37, 53, 76, 80, 81, 103, 113–14, 131, 138, 140, 149–50, 173–4, 174, 176–7, 184, 215, 235
Piazza Belli (Rome) 35
Picasso, Pablo (1881–1973) 88
Picasso's Walk (Prévert) 58, 88
Pico della Mirandola, Giovanni (1463–94) 17
Picture of Little J.A. in a Prospect of Flowers (Ashbery) 173
Pied Beauty (Hopkins) 87
Piero della Francesca (1420–92) 17
pilgrimage, Wright's poetic 9–12, 33, 34, 44, 59, 60, 61, 62, 89, 96, 112, 168, 196, 209–10
Pilgrim's Progress **209–10**
The Pilgrim's Progress (Bunyan) 209–10
Pisan Cantos (Pound) 89
The Plague (Camus) 115
The Plague of Ashdod (Poussin) 82
Plath, Sylvia (1932–63) 29
Plato (ca. 427–ca. 347 B.C.E.) 53, 151, 162, 224
Platonic Theology (Ficino) 159
Pliny the Elder (23–79) 30
Plotinus (ca. 205–270) 52, 118
Plutarch (ca. 46–ca. 120) 37
Po Chü-I (772–846) 48–9
Poe, Edgar Allan (1808–49) 17
Poem Almost Wholly in My Own Manner 70–71, **73**
"The Poem as Journey" 44
Poem Half in the Manner of Li Ho 27, **70–1**, 108
Poem of the Deep Song (Lorca) 43
The Point Where All Things Meet (Andrews) 1, 168–9
Polaroids **149–51**
Ponti, Carlo (ca. 1823–93) 29
A Portrait of the Artist as a Young Man (Joyce) 35, 173, 234
Portrait of the Artist by Li Shang-Yin 27, 165, **166**, 173
Portrait of the Artist in a Prospect of Stone **173–4**
Portrait of the Artist with Hart Crane 173
Portrait of the Artist with Li Po 27, 107, 173
Portrait of the Poet in Abraham von Werdt's Dream 17, 173
Pound, Ezra (1885–1972) 13, 17, 19, 62, 63, 65, 72, 75, 89, 118, 119, 138, 143, 172, 192, 235
Poussin, Nicholas (1594–1665) 17, 82
Prajapati 145
Prampolini, Gaetano 125
Precious Memories (J.F.B. Wright) 219, 237
The Prelude (Wordsworth) 13, 203
Presley, Elvis (1935–77) 223
Prévert, Jacques (1900–77) 85

Prezzolini, Giuseppe (1882–1982) 47
Private Madrigal II 19
Purgatorio (Dante) 62
Psalms, Book of the 32, 100, 161, 189, 211
Pseudo-Dionysus (5th cent.) 27, 28
Punta San Vigilio (Italy) 35

Qu Yuan (340–78) 128
The Queen of the Air (Ruskin), Quotations 97, 110

Raleigh, Sir Walter (1552–1618) 79
Raymond of Toulouse (ca. 1041–1105) 74
Reading an Anthology of Chinese Poems of the Sung Dynasty, I Pause to Admire the Length and Clarity of Their Titles (Collins) 25
Reading Lao Tzu Again in the New Year **25–6**
Reading Rorty and Paul Celan One Morning in Early June 25, **28–9**, 107
Real Presences (Steiner) 35
Reflections in Autumn (Tu Fu) 50, 51, 52
"Reflections on Sin, Pain, Hope, and the True Way" (Kafka) 43, 171
Relics **154–5**
Remembering Spello, Sitting Outside in Prampolini's Garden 16, 18, **125**
Renoir, Pierre-Auguste (1824–1919) 110
Reply to Wang Wei 27, **113**
Resolution and Independence (Wordsworth) 178
The Resurrection (Piero della Francesca) 17
"A Retrospect" (Pound) 75
Returned to the Yaak Cabin, I Overhear an Old Greek Song **106**
Returning Home (Tao-chi) 221
Reunion 166
Reunion in Heaven 237
Revelation, Book of 119, 152, 154, 181, 235
Rexroth, Kenneth (1905–82) 30, 113
Le Ricordanze (Leopardi) 72
Rilke, Rainer Maria (1875–1926) 95, 131, 225
Rimbaud, Arthur (1854–91) 36, 58, 160, 161, 169, 172
Rime (Guido de Cavalcanti) 65
Rivanna River 121, 147, 220
River Jordan (Carter Family) 143
River Run 43, 81
Robinson Crusoe (Defoe) 115
Rock of Ages (Toplady) 230
The Roethkeodore (1908–63) 190, 217
Rollins, Sonny (1930–) 226
Roma II 124
Romano, Giulio (ca. 1499–1546) 17
Romans, Epistle to the 122
Rome (Italy) 33, 34, 211

Rorty, Richard (1931–) 28
Ross, Chuck 66
Rosso Venexiano 56, **174–5**
Rothko, Mark (1903–70) 17, 64–5, 88, 165, 173
Rowlandson, Thomas (1756–1827) 95
Rowley, Thomas 177
Rubenstein, Johnny (1946–) 184
The Ruins of Kasch (Calasso) 90
Ruskin, John (1819–1900) 81
Ryder, Albert Pinkham (1847–1917) 17, 69

Sachs, Nelly (1891–1970) 93
Sailing to Byzantium (Yeats) 51, 76, 169, 211
St. Augustine and the Arctic Bear **132–3**
St. Catherine of Siena (1347–80) 117, 170
St. Cyprian (d. 258) 216
St. John of the Cross (1542–91) 40, 41, 67, 74, 160
St. Lawrence 105
St. Louis Blues (Handy) 57
Salon of the Months (Francesco del Cossa) 17
San Apollinare in Classe, basilica of 211
San Pietro, cathedral of 29
Santa Maria della Salute (Venice) 58
Santa Maria Gloriosa dei Frari (Venice) 58
Sappho (ca. 620–ca. 570 B.C.E.) 13, 59, 82
Satires (Horace) 91
Saturday Afternoon **179**
Saturday Morning Satori **198**
Scar Tissue (book) 12, **188–213**
Scar Tissue (poem) 57, **200–2**
Scar Tissue II **202–3**
Scheiwiller, Vanni 161
Schifanoia Palace 17
Schimmel, Harold (1935–) 161–2, 234
Schneeman, George 234
Sebald, W.G. (1944–2001) 219–20
The Second Apocalypse of James (Nag Hammadi Library) 68
The Second Coming (Yeats) 118
The Secret of Poetry **145**
Seeing Li Po in a Dream (Tu Fu) 29
The Seine at Le Grande Jatte (Seurat) 16
Self-Portrait 17, 81
Self Portrait in 2035 81
Sent to Ch'ao the Palace Reviser (Meng Hao-jan) 185
Sentences 107
Sentences of Sextus (Nag Hammadi Library) 83
Setti Ponti, via di 29
Seurat, Georges (1859–91) 16, 17
Seven Songs at T'ung-ku (Tu Fu) 50
Sforza gardens 141
Shakespeare, William (1564–1616) 32, 155
Shelley, Percy Bysshe (1792–1822) 118, 129, 176

A Short History of My Life **191–2**
A Short History of the Shadow (book) 12, **137–64**
A Short History of the Shadow (poem) 56, **151–2**
shunyata see emptiness
The Silence of the Body (Ceronetti) 91–2, 108
The Silent Generation **40**, 83, 211
The Silent Generation II **189–90**
The Silent Generation III **211**
Simic, Charles (1938–) 19–20, 47
Sims, Mary 174
Singing Lesson **213**
Sinology 27, **184–5**
Sir Gawain and the Green Knight 226
Sitting Alone on an Autumn Night (Wang Wei) 91
Sitting at Dusk in the Back Yard After the Mondrian Retrospective **88–9**
Sitting Outside at the End of Autumn **23–4**
Sixth Moon (Li Ho) 71
Skins 10, 20, 209
Sky Diving 133–4
Sky Valley (North Carolina) 51, 87, 131
Snake Eyes (poem) **181–2**
The Snow Man (Stevens) 145, 209
Snow Storm (Tu Fu) 30
Snyder, Gary (1930–) 121
The Sodbuster's Saloon and Hall of Fame **205**
Soliloquy in a Spanish Cloister (Browning) 209
solitude, motif of 31, 50
Song of Myself (Whitman) 26, 221
A Song of the Yen Country (Kao Shih) 23
Songlines (Chatwin) 39
sottonarrativa (subnarrative) 10, 12, 44
The Southern Cross (book) 12, 214
The Southern Cross (poem) 107, 152
Soutine, Chaim (1893–1943) 17, 55
Spielberg, Steven (1946–) 29
Spring Storm **121**, 153
Springtime of the Soul (Trakl) 157
Sprung Narratives **33–5**, 210
Stabat Mater 61, 76, 77
Stafford, Jo (1917–) 223
Stand by Your Man 184
Star Turn **101**, 124
Star Turn II 101
Star Turn III **186**
Stein, Gertrude (1874–1946) 79
Steiner, George (1929–) 33, 35
Stella, Frank (1936–) 88
Step-children of Paradise **129–30**
Stevens, Wallace (1879–1955) 13, 23, 40, 41, 50, 68, 69, 79, 80, 89, 90, 108, 112, 121, 140, 143, 145, 154, 158, 209, 210, 229, 230
Stevenson, Robert Louis (1850–94) 25
Still Life on a Matchbox Lid **38**
Still Life with Spring and Time to Burn **45–6**, 107

Still Life with Stick and Word 50, 52–3, 64
"Stockman's Bar Again, Boys" (McIntire) 184
Stopping on a Journey at the East Water Pavilion at Lo-ch'eng (Meng Chiao) 110
Strand, Mark (1934–) 41, 97, 98
Stray Paragraphs in April, Year of the Rat 18, **99–100**
Stray Paragraphs in February, Year of the Rat **97–9**
Streamlined Cannonball (Acuff) 178
Su Tung P'o (1036–1101) 30
the sublime (*ekstasis*) 98, 112
Summer Mornings 107, **158–9**, 220, 228
Summer Storm 17, **53–4**
Summers, David 29–30
Sunday Afternoon on the Island of La Grande Jatte (Seurat) 16
Sunday Morning (Stevens) 23, 50, 68, 69, 80, 121, 140, 229, 230
Sunrise to a Settling Cup of Tea (Llewellyn) 203
Sun-Saddled, Coke-Copping, Bad-Boozing Blues 169, **183–4**
Swinburne, Charles Algernon (1837–1909) 17
syllabic measure 72

Taking the Cool of the Evening (Wang Wei) 113
T'ang Notebook 27, 56, 210
T'ang poets 13, 37, 62, 96, 166, 191, 207, 226, 236
Tao-chi (1641–ca. 1710) 221
T'ao Ch'ien (365–427) 124–5, 161
Tao Te Ching (Lao-Tzu) 24, 26, 186, 187, 208
Taoism 24, 25–6, 48, 186–7
Tate, James (1943–) 110
Tattoos 17, 20, 31, 48, 124
The Teachings of Sylvanus (Nag Hammadi Library) 67–8, 83, 217
Tears and Saints (Ciroan) 101
Teilhard de Chardin, Pierre (1881–1955) 86
The Tempest (Shakespeare) 32
The Temptation of St. Augustine: Left Panel (Andrews) 174
Tennessee Line **31**
The Terrace in the Snow (Su Tung P'o) 30
There Is a Balm in Gilead 27, 165–6
There Is No Shelter **49**
Thessalonians I, Epistle to the 89
Thinking about Poet Larry Levis One Afternoon in Late May **102–3**
Thinking about the Night Sky, I Remember a Poem by Tu Fu 50, **130**
Thinking of David Summers at the Beginning of Winter **29–30**,
Thinking of Georg Trakl 107
Thinking of Marsilio Ficino at the First Hint of Autumn **159**
Thinking of Wallace Stevens at the Beginning of Spring **154**
Thinking of Winter at the Beginning of Summer 61, **85**, 163

Thomas, Dylan (1914–53) 194, 195
Thorp, Winfrid 202, 203, 234
Three Poems of Departure 56, 210
Three Travelers Watch a Sunrise (Stevens) 145
Thrones (Pound) 161
"The Thunder, Perfect Mind" (Nag Hammadi Library) 84, 216
Tiberius (42 B.C.E.–37 C.E.).
The Tibetan Book of the Dead 74–6, 111, 121
Tintoretto (Jacobo Comin) (1518–94) 17
Titian (Tiziano Vecelli) (1485–1676) 17, 105, 174
titleism 97
Time Will Tell **212**, 213
Tlön, Uqbar, Orbis Tertius (Borges) 32
To a Skylark (Shelley) 118
To Giacomo Leopardi in the Sky 81, 152–3
To His Coy Mistress (Marvell) 133
To Juan in Winter Solstice (Graves) 83
To the Egyptian Mummy in the Etruscan Museum at Cortona **47–8**
To the Roaring Wind (Stevens) 158
Tom o' Bedlam 168
Tom Strand and the Angel of Death **41**
Tongues 55
Toplady, Augustus M. (1740–78) 230
Trakl, Georg (1887–1914) 151, 156–7, 169
Transfiguration (Trakl) 151
Transparencies **196–7**
Travelling Northward (Tu Fu) 192
The Tripartite Tractate (Nag Hammadi Library) 63, 64, 67, 69
Truffaut, François (1932–84) 17
The Trumpet Part (Celan) 90
Tu Fu (712–77) 29, 50–1, 90–1, 113, 130, 192, 231
T'u Lung (1542–1605) 206
Turning Seasons (T'ao Ch'ien) 125
"Twist and Shout" (Isley Brothers) 54

Uccello, Paolo (1397–1475) 17
The Ultimate Journey (Bernstein) 164
The Ultimate Poem Is Abstract (Stevens) 108
Umbrian Dreams 15, 16, 67, 76–7, 104, 124, 129, 146
The Unbearable Lightness of Being (Kundera) 176
Under a Border Fortress (Wang Ch'ang-ling) 192
Under the Nine Trees in January **26**
Ungaretti, Giussepe (1888–1970) 236

ut pictura poesis 17

Vallejo, César (1892–1938) 139
Vasari, Giorgio (1511–74) 48, 84
Vendler, Helen (1933–) 206
Venetian Dog 17 **104–5**, 121
Venexia I **57–8** 124
Venexia II **58**
Venice (Italy) 58, 104–5, 174
Verona (Italy) 35, 62–3, 81, 138, 161–2, 174, 191, 203, 220, 234
Veronese, Paolo (1528–88) 175
Vertigo (Sebald) 219
Vespers **208–9**
Via Negativa 74, **159–60**
via negativa 45, 78, 79, 85, 98, 160
Victory Garden 107
A View of the Wilderness (Tu Fu) 29
Villa Gusatalla 141
Virgil (70–19 B.C.E.) 62, 138, 236

Waiting for God (Weil) 100, 101, 117
Waiting for the Barbarians (Cavafy) 195
Waiting for Tu Fu 16, 27, **50–1**
Waking Up After the Storm **192**
Wang Ch'ang-ling (8th cent.) 192
Wang Wei (701–61) 26–7, 113, 163, 185, 227
The Waste Land (Eliot) 24, 61, 123, 142, 145, 189
Watching the Equinox Arrive in Charlottesville, September **49–50**
A Weakness for Almost Everything (Buzzi) 155
Wednesday Morning **179**
Wêi Ying-wu (737–92) 179–80, 190, 198
Weil, Simone (1909–43) 100, 117
Welty, Eudora (1909–2001) 73
What Do You Write About, Where Do Your Ideas Come From? 18, **109–10**
"When You're Lost in Juarez, in the Rain, and It's Eastertime Too" 120
While Visiting on the South Stream the Taoist Priest Ch'ang (Liu' Changch'ing) 169
White, E.B. (1899–1985) 88
The White Goddess (Graves) 126
Whitman, Walt (1819–92) 18, 26, 167, 221
Why, It's as Pretty as a Picture **155–6**
Wildwood Flower (Carter Family) 218, 237
Wilken, Karen 101
Will You Miss Me When I'm Gone (Carter Family) 218
Williams, William Carlos (1883–1963) 156
The Wind Is Calm and Comes from Another World **157–8**
Wind on the Water (Nash) 221

The Windhover (Hopkins) 83
Winter-Worship **39**
Wiseman, Mac (1925–) 121
With Eddie and Nancy in Arezzo at the Caffè Grande 27
With Simic and Marinetti at the Giubbe Rosse **47**
The Woodpecker Pecks, but the Hole Does Not Appear **212–13**
Woolf, Virginia (1882–1941) 123
Words Are the Diminution of All Things **175**, 231
Wordsworth, William (1770–1850) 13, 17, 156, 177, 193, 203
Works and Days (Hesiod) 153
The World of the Ten Thousand Things (book) 1, 11, 12, 14, 23, 26
The Wreck of the Deutschland (Hopkins) 86
Wright, Charles (musician) 178
Wright, Charles Penzel (father) (1904–72) 67
Wright, Hildegard (sister) 85
Wright, Holly (wife) (1941) 23, 215
Wright, Isaac (1780–1865) 182, 183
Wright, Luke (son) (1970–) 67, 203, 215
Wright, Mary Winter (mother) (1910–64) 61, 67, 72, 218
Wright, Moorehead (1807–57) 182, 183
Wright, Winter (brother) 33, 37, 85, 205
The Writing Life 16, 75, **112**, **126**
Written on a Monastery Wall (Li Shang-yin) 132
Written on the Wall at Chang's Hermitage (Tu Fu) 30
The Wrong End of the Rainbow **190–1**
Wrong Notes 198–9
wu wei (nondoing) 25, 186, 226; *see also* emptiness; nothingness

Xionia (book) 11, 97, 214

Yard Journal 107
Yard Work **58–9**
Yeats, William Butler (1865–1939) 51, 76, 118, 134, 169, 211
Yellow Dog Blues (Handy) 57, 73
You Belong to Me (Stafford) 223, 237
You Will Hear the Thunder (Akhmatova) 36
Young, David 71

Zen Flesh, Zen Bones (Reps) 50, 164
Zen Journals (Matthiesson) 92
Zocchi, Cesare (1875–1922) 32
Zone Journals (book) 11, 12, 88, 97, 213
Zostrianos (Nag Hammadi Library) 69

www.ingramcontent.com/pod-product-compliance
Lightning Source LLC
Chambersburg PA
CBHW081548300426
44116CB00015B/2800